Lecture Notes in Artificial Intelli

Edited by J. G. Carbonell and J. Siekmann

Subseries of Lecture Notes in Computer Science

Karl Tuyls   Ann Nowe   Zahia Guessoum
Daniel Kudenko (Eds.)

Adaptive Agents and Multi-Agent Systems III

Adaptation and Multi-Agent Learning

5th, 6th, and 7th European Symposium, ALAMAS 2005-2007
on Adaptive and Learning Agents and Multi-Agent Systems
Revised Selected Papers

 Springer

Series Editors

Jaime G. Carbonell, Carnegie Mellon University, Pittsburgh, PA, USA
Jörg Siekmann, University of Saarland, Saarbrücken, Germany

Volume Editors

Karl Tuyls
Maastricht University
The Netherlands
E-mail: k.tuyls@micc.unimaas.nl

Ann Nowe
Vrije Universiteit Brussel
Belgium
E-mail: ann.nowe@vub.ac.be

Zahia Guessoum
University of Pierre and Marie Curie
France
E-mail: zahia.guessoum@lip6.fr

Daniel Kudenko
The University of York
United Kingdom
E-mail: kudenko@cs.york.ac.uk

Library of Congress Control Number: 2008920332

CR Subject Classification (1998): I.2.11, I.2, D.2, C.2.4, F.3.1,D.3.1, H.5.3, K.4.3

LNCS Sublibrary: SL 7 – Artificial Intelligence

ISSN   0302-9743
ISBN-10   3-540-77947-7 Springer Berlin Heidelberg New York
ISBN-13   978-3-540-77947-6 Springer Berlin Heidelberg New York

Springer is a part of Springer Science+Business Media

springer.com

© Springer-Verlag Berlin Heidelberg 2008
Printed in Germany

Typesetting: Camera-ready by author, data conversion by Scientific Publishing Services, Chennai, India
Printed on acid-free paper   SPIN: 12225323   06/3180   5 4 3 2 1 0

Preface

This book contains selected and revised papers of the European Symposium on Adaptive and Learning Agents and Multi-Agent Systems (ALAMAS), editions 2005, 2006 and 2007, held in Paris, Brussels and Maastricht.

The goal of the ALAMAS symposia, and this associated book, is to increase awareness and interest in adaptation and learning for single agents and multi-agent systems, and encourage collaboration between machine learning experts, software engineering experts, mathematicians, biologists and physicists, and give a representative overview of current state of affairs in this area. It is an inclusive forum where researchers can present recent work and discuss their newest ideas for a first time with their peers.

The symposia series focuses on all aspects of adaptive and learning agents and multi-agent systems, with a particular emphasis on how to modify established learning techniques and/or create new learning paradigms to address the many challenges presented by complex real-world problems.

These symposia were a great success and provided a forum for the presentation of new ideas and results bearing on the conception of adaptation and learning for single agents and multi-agent systems. Over these three editions we received 51 submissions, of which 17 were carefully selected, including one invited paper of this year's invited speaker Simon Parsons. This is a very competitive acceptance rate of approximately 31%, which, together with two review cycles, has led to a high-quality LNAI volume.

We hope that our readers will be inspired by the papers included in this volume.

Organizing a scientific event like ALAMAS, and editing an associated book, requires the help of many enthusiastic people. First of all, the organizers would like to thank the members of the Program Committee, who guaranteed a scientifically strong and interesting LNAI volume. Secondly, we would like to express our appreciation to the invited speakers of the the editions 2005, 2006 and 2007: Michael Rovatsos (2005), Tom Lenaerts (2006), Eric Postma (2007), and Simon Parsons (2007), for their distinguished contributions to the symposium program. Finally, we also would like to thank the authors of all contributions for submitting their scientific work to the ALAMAS symposium series.

November 2007

Karl Tuyls
Ann Nowé
Zahia Guessoum
Daniel Kudenko

Organization

Organizing Committee

Co-chairs   Karl Tuyls
Ann Nowé
Zahia Guessoum
Daniel Kudenko

Program Committee (2005, 2006, 2007)

Bram Bakker	Steven de Jong	Enric Plaza
Ana Bazzan	Dimitar Kazakov	Marc Ponsen
Ozalp Babaoglu	Franziska Kluegl	Michael Rovatsos
Frances Brazier	Ville Kononen	Olivier Sigaud
Patrick de Causmaekcker	Daniel Kudenko	Henry Soldano
Philippe De Wilde	Paul Marrow	Malcolm Strens
Marina Devos	Peter McBurney	Kagan Tumer
Kurt Driessens	Ann Nowé	Karl Tuyls
Saso Dzeroski	Luis Nunes	Katja Verbeeck
Marie-Pierre Gleizes	Eugenio Oliveira	Danny Weyns
Zahia Guessoum	Liviu Panait	Marco Wiering
Pieter Jan't Hoen	Simon Parsons	Niek Wijngaards
Tom Holvoet	Paolo Petta	

Table of Contents

To Adapt or Not to Adapt – Consequences of Adapting Driver and Traffic Light Agents

Ana L.C. Bazzan[1], Denise de Oliveira[1], Franziska Klügl[2], and Kai Nagel[3]

[1] Instituto de Informática, UFRGS
Caixa Postal 15064, 91.501-970 Porto Alegre, RS, Brazil
{bazzan,edenise}@inf.ufrgs.br
[2] Dep. of Artificial Intelligence, University of Würzburg
Am Hubland, 97074 Würzburg, Germany
kluegl@informatik.uni-wuerzburg.de
[3] Inst. for Land and Sea Transport Systems, TU Berlin
Salzufer 17–19, 10587 Berlin, Germany
nagel@vsp.tu-berlin.de

Abstract. One way to cope with the increasing traffic demand is to integrate standard solutions with more intelligent control measures. However, the result of possible interferences between intelligent control or information provision tools and other components of the overall traffic system is not easily predictable. This paper discusses the effects of integrating co-adaptive decision-making regarding route choices (by drivers) and control measures (by traffic lights). The motivation behind this is that optimization of traffic light control is starting to be integrated with navigation support for drivers. We use microscopic, agent-based modelling and simulation, in opposition to the classical network analysis, as this work focuses on the effect of local adaptation. In a scenario that exhibits features comparable to real-world networks, we evaluate different types of adaptation by drivers and by traffic lights, based on local perceptions. In order to compare the performance, we have also used a global level optimization method based on genetic algorithms.

1   Introduction

Urban mobility is one of the key topics in modern societies. Especially in medium to big cities, the urban space has to be adapted to cope with the increasing needs of transportation. In transportation engineering, the expression of the transport needs is called *demand*. This demand (in terms volume of vehicles, pedestrians, freight, etc.) is commonly used to evaluate transport *supply*. This is the expression of the capacity of transportation infrastructures and modes. Supply is expressed in terms of infrastructure (capacity), service (frequency), and other characteristics of the network. The increasing demand of transport needs we observe nowadays has to be accommodated either with increasing supply (e.g. road capacity), or with a better use of the existing infrastructure. Since an expansion of the capacity is not always socially or economically attainable or feasible,

K. Tuyls et al. (Eds.): Adaptive Agents and MAS III, LNAI 4865, pp. 1–14, 2008.

transportation and traffic engineering seek to optimize the management of both supply and demand using concepts and techniques from intelligent transportation systems (ITS). These refer to the application of modern technologies in the operation and control of transportation systems [12].

From the side of supply, several measures have been adopted in the last years, such as congestion charging in urban areas (London), restriction of traffic in the historical centre (Rome, Paris, Amsterdam), alternace of vehicles allowed to circulate in a given day (São Paulo, Mexico City).

From the point of view of the demand, several attempts exist not only to divert trips both spatially as well as temporally, but also to distribute the demand within the available infrastructure. In this context, it is now commonly recognized that the human actor has to be brought into the loop. With the amount of information that we have nowadays, it is almost impossible to disregard the influence of real-time information systems over the decision-making process of the individuals.

Hence, within the project "Large Scale Agent-based Traffic Simulation for Predicting Traffic Conditions", our long term goal is to tackle a complex problem like traffic from the point of view of information science. This project seeks to integrate microscopic modelling tools developed by the authors for traffic and transportation control and management. These range from traffic signal optimization [1], binary route choice, and effect of information on commuters [4], to microscopic modelling of physical movement [7].

An important milestone in the project is to propose a methodology to integrate complex behavioral models of human travellers reacting to traffic patterns, and control measures, focusing on distributed and decentralized methods. Classically, this is done via network analysis. Using this technique, it is assumed that individual road users seek to optimize their individual costs regarding the trips they make by selecting the "best" route among the ones they have experienced or have been informed about. This is the basis of the well known traffic network analysis based on Wardrop's equilibrium principle [17]. This method predicts a long term *average* state of the network. However, since it assumes steady state network supply and demand conditions, this equilibrium-based method cannot, in most cases, cope with the dynamics of the modern transportation systems. Moreover, it is definitely not adequate for answering questions related to what happens in the network *within* a given day, as both the variability in the demand and the available capacity of the network tend to be high. Just think about changing weather conditions from day to day and within a single day!

In summary, as equilibrium-based concepts overlook this variability, it seems obvious that they are not adequate for microscopic modelling and simulation. Therefore, the general aim of this paper is to investigate what happens when different actors adapt, each having its own goal. The objective of *local* traffic control is obviously to find a control scheme that minimizes queues in a spatially limited area (e.g. around a traffic light). The objective of drivers is normally to minimize their individual travel time – at least in commuting situations. Finally, from the point of view of the whole system, the goal is to ensure reasonable travel times for *all* users, which can be highly conflicting with some individual utilities (a social dilemma). This is a well-known issue: for instance, Tumer and Wolpert [15] have shown that there is no general approach to deal with this complex question of collectives.

Specifically, this paper investigates which strategy is the best for drivers (e.g. adaptation or greedy actions). Similarly, traffic lights can act greedily or simply carry out a "well-designed" signal plan. At which volume of local traffic does decentralized control of Traffic Lights start to pay off? Does isolated, single-agent reinforcement learning make sense in dynamic traffic scenarios? What happens when many drivers adapt concurrently? These are hot topics not only in traffic research, but also in a more general multi-agent research as they refer to co-adaptation.

In this paper we depart from binary route choice scenarios and use a more realistic one, that shows features such as: heterogeneity of origin-destination pairs, heterogeneous capacity, and agents knowing about a set of routes between their origins and destinations. To the best of our knowledge, the question on what happens when drivers and traffic lights co-adapt in a complex route scenario has not been tackled so far.

In the next section we review these and related issues. In section 3 we describe the approach and the scenario. Section 4 discusses the results, while section 5 presents the concluding remarks.

2 Background: Supply and Demand in Traffic Engineering

Learning and adaptation is an important issue in multiagent systems. Here, we concentrate on pieces of related work which either deal with adaptation in traffic scenarios directly or report on close scenarios.

2.1 Management of Traffic Demand

Given its complexity, the area of traffic simulation and control has been tackled by many branches of applied and pure sciences, such as mathematics, physics, computer science, engineering, geography, and architecture. Therefore, several tools exist that target only a part of the overall problem. For example, simulation tools in particular are quite old (1970s) and stable. On the side of demand forecasting, the arguably most used computational method is the so-called 4-step-process [11]. It consists of: trip generation, destination choice, mode choice, and route assignment. Route assignment includes route choice and a very basic traffic flow simulation that may lead to a Nash Equilibrium. Over the years, the 4-step-process has been improved in many ways, most mainly by (i) combining the first three steps into a single, traveller-oriented framework (*activity-based demand generation (ABDG)*) and by (ii) replacing traditional route assignment by so-called *dynamic traffic assignment (DTA)*. Still, in the actual implementations, all travellers' information gets lost in the connection between ABDG and DTA, making realistic agent-based modelling at the DTA-level difficult.

Another related problem is the estimation of the overall state of the complete traffic network from partial sensor data. Although many schemes exist for incident detection, there are only few applications of large scale traffic state estimation. One exception is www.autobahn.nrw.de. It uses a traffic microsimulation to extrapolate between sensor locations, and it applies intelligent methods combining the current state with historical data in order to make short-term predictions. However, the travellers themselves are very simple: They do not know their destinations, let alone the remainder of their daily plan. This was a necessary simplification to make the approach work for simulating the real infrastructure. However, for evaluating the effects of travellers' flexible decision making, it is necessary to overcome this simplification for integrating additional information about dynamic decision-making context.

A true integration of these and other approaches is still missing. Agent technology offers the appropriate basis for this. However, until now agent-based simulations with a scale required for the simulation of real-world traffic networks have not been developed.

2.2   Real-Time Optimization of Traffic Lights

Signalized intersections are controlled by signal-timing plans (we use signal plan for short) which are implemented at traffic lights. A signal plan is a unique set of timing parameters comprising the cycle length L (the length of time for the complete sequence of the phase changes), and the split (the division of the cycle length among the various movements or phases). The criterion for obtaining the optimum signal timing *at a single intersection* is that it should lead to the minimum overall delay at the intersection. Several plans are normally required for an intersection to deal with changes in traffic volume. Alternatively, in a traffic-responsive system, at least one signal plan must be pre-defined in order to be changed on the fly.

In [1], a MAS based approach is described in which each traffic light is modelled as an agent, each having a set of pre-defined signal plans to coordinate with neighbours. Different signal plans can be selected in order to coordinate in a given traffic direction. This approach uses techniques of evolutionary game theory. However, payoff matrices (or at least the utilities and preferences of the agents) are required. These figures have to be explicitly formalized by the designer of the system.

In [10], groups of traffic lights were considered and a technique from distributed constraint optimization was used, namely cooperative mediation. However, this mediation was not decentralized: group mediators communicate their decisions to the mediated agents in their groups and these agents just carry out the tasks. Also, the mediation process may take long in highly constrained scenarios, having a negative impact in the coordination mechanism.

Also a decentralized, swarm-based model of task allocation was developed in [9], in which the dynamic group formation without mediation combines the advantages of decentralization via swarm intelligence and dynamic group formation.

Regarding the use of reinforcement learning for traffic control, some applications are reported. Camponogara and Kraus [2] have studied a simple scenario with only two intersections, using stochastic game-theory and reinforcement learning. Their results with this approach were better than a *best-effort* (greedy), a random policy, and also better than Q-learning [18]. In [8] a set of techniques were tried in order to improve the learning ability of the agents in a simple scenario. Performance of reinforcement learning approaches such as Q-learning and Prioritized Sweeping in non-stationary environments are compared in [13]. Co-learning is discussed in [19] (detailed here in Section 2.3).

Finally, a reservation-based system [3] is also reported but it is only slightly related to the topics here because it does not include conventional traffic lights.

2.3   The Need for Integration

Up to now, only few attempts exist to integrate supply and demand in a single model. We review three of them here.

Learning Based Approach. A paper by [19] describes the use of reinforcement learning by the traffic light controllers (agents) in order to minimize the overall waiting time of vehicles in a small grid. Additionally, agents learn a value function which estimates the expected waiting times of single vehicles given different settings of traffic lights. One interesting issue tackled in this research is that a kind of co-learning is considered: value functions are learned not only by the traffic lights, but also by the vehicles which thus can compute policies to select optimal routes to the respective destinations. The ideas and results presented in that paper are interesting. However, it makes strong assumptions that may hinder its use in the real world: the kind of communication and knowledge or, more appropriate, communication *for* knowledge formation has high costs. Traffic light controllers are supposed to know vehicles destination in order to compute expected waiting times for each. Given the current technology, this is a quite strong assumption. Secondly, it seems that traffic lights can shift from red to green and opposite at each time step of the simulation. Third, there is no account of experience made by the drivers based on their local experiences only. What about if they just react to (few) past experiences? Finally, drivers being autonomous, it is not completely obvious that they will use the best policy computed by the traffic light and not by themselves. Therefore, in the present paper, we depart from these assumptions regarding communication and knowledge the actors must have about each other.

Game Theoretic Approach. In [16] a two-level, three-player game is discussed that integrates traffic control and traffic assignment, i.e. both, the control of Traffic Lights and the route choices by drivers are considered. Complete information is assumed, which means that all players (including the population of drivers) have to be aware of the movements of others. Although the paper reports interesting conclusions regarding e.g. the utility of cooperation among the players, this is probably valid only in that simple scenario. Besides, the assumption that drivers always follow their shortest routes is difficult to justify in a real-world application. In the present paper, we want to depart from both, the two-route scenario and the assumption that traffic management centres are in charge of the control of Traffic Lights. Rather, we follow a trend of decentralization, in which each traffic light is able to sense its environment and react accordingly and autonomously, without having its actions computed by a central manager as it is the case in [16]. Moreover, it is questionable whether the same mechanism can be used in more complex scenarios, as claimed. The reason for this is the fact that when the network is composed of tens of links, the number of routes increases and so the complexity of the route choice, given that now it is not trivial to compute the network and user equilibria.

Methodologies. Liu and colleagues [6] describe a modelling approach that integrates microsimulation of individual trip-makers' decisions and individual vehicle movements across the network. Moreover their focus is on the description of the methodology that integrates both demand and supply dynamics, so that the applications are only briefly described and not many options for the operation and control of Traffic Lights are reported. One scenario described deals with a simple network with four possible routes and two control policies. One of them can roughly be described as greedy, while the other is fixed signal plan based. In the present paper, we do not explore the methodological issues as in [6] but, rather, investigate in more details particular issues of the integration and interaction between actors from the supply and demand side.

3   Co-adaptation in an ITS Framework

Figure 1 shows a scheme of our approach based on the interaction between supply and demand. This framework was developed using the agent-based simulation environment SeSAm [5] for testing the effects of adaptation of different elements of the supply and demand. The testbed consists of sub-modules for specification and generation of the network and the agents – traffic lights and drivers. Currently the approach generates the network (grid or any other topology), supports the creation of traffic light control algorithms as well as signal plans, the creation of routes (route library), and the algorithms for route choice. The movement of vehicles is queue-based.

The basic scenario we use is a typical commuting scenario where drivers repeatedly select a route to go from an origin to a destination. As mentioned before, we want to go beyond simple two-route or binary choice scenario; we deal with route choice in a network with a variety of possible routes. Thus, it captures desirable properties of real-world scenarios.

We use a grid with 36 nodes connected using one-way links, as depicted in Figure 2. All links are one-way and drivers can turn to two directions in each crossing. Although it is apparently simple, this kind of scenario is realistic and, from the point of view of route choice and equilibrium computation, it is also

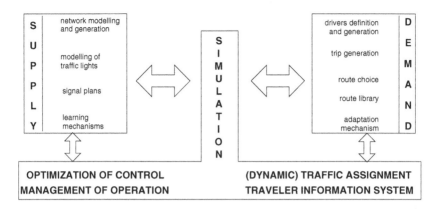

Fig. 1. Elements of Co-Adaptation in an ITS Framework

a very complex one as the number of possible routes between two locations is high.

In contrast to simple two-route scenarios, it is possible to set arbitrary origins (O) and destinations (D) in this grid. For every driver agent, its origin and destination are randomly selected according to probabilities given for the links: To render the scenario more realistic, neither the distribution of O-D combinations, nor the capacity of links is homogeneous. On average, 60% of the road users have the same destination, namely the link labelled as E4E5 which can be thought as something like a main business area. Other links have, each, 1.7% probability of being a destination. Origins are nearly equally distributed in the grid, with three exceptions (three "main residential areas"): links B5B4, E1D1, and C2B2 have, approximately, probabilities 3, 4, and 5% of being an origin respectively. The remaining links have each a probability of 1.5%. Regarding capacity, all links can hold up to 15 vehicles, except those located in the so called "main street". These can hold up to 45 (one can think it has more lanes). This main street is formed by the links between nodes B3 to E3, E4, and E5.

The control is performed via decentralized Traffic Lights. These are located in each node. Each of the Traffic Lights has a signal plan which, by default, divides the overall cycle time – in the experiments 40 time steps – 50-50% between the two phases. One phase corresponds to assigning green to one direction, either north/south or east/west.

The actions of the Traffic Lights consist in running the default plan or to prioritize one phase. The particular strategies are:

  i. fixed: always keep the default signal plan
 ii. greedy: allow more green time for the direction with higher current occupancy
iii. use single agent Q-learning

Regarding the demand, the main actor is the simulated driver. The simulation can generate any number of them; in the experiments we used 400, 500, 600,

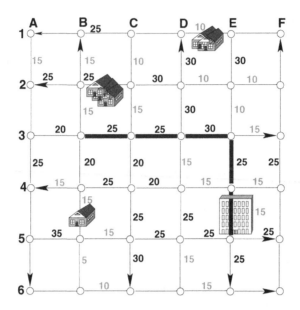

Fig. 2. 6x6 grid showing the main destination (E4E5), the three main origins (B5B4, E1D1, C2B2), and the "main street" (darker line). Numbers at the links represent the green times for the particular direction (determined by global optimization).

and 700 driver agents. Every driver is assigned to a randomly selected origin-destination pair. Initially it is informed about only a given number of routes. The experiments presented next were performed with each agent knowing five routes. These route options are different for each driver and were generated using an algorithm that computes the shortest path (one route) and the shortest path via arbitrary detours (the other four). We notice that, due to topological constraints, it was not always possible to generate five routes for each driver. One example is the following: origin and destination are too close. Thus, in a few cases they know less than this number, but at least one. Drivers can use three strategies to select a route (before departure):

  i. random selection
 ii. greedy: always select the route with best average travel time so far
iii. probabilistically: for each route, the average travel time perceived so far is use to compute a probability to select that route again.

The actual movement of the driver agents through the net is queue-based.

4   Results and Discussion

4.1   Metrics and Parameters

In order to evaluate the experiments, travel time (for drivers) and occupation (for links) were measured. We discuss here only the mean travel time over the last 5 trips (henceforward *attl5t*) and travel time in a single trip. All experiments were repeated 20 times.

The following parameters were used: time out for the simulation of one trip (t_{out}) equal to 300 when the number of drivers is 400 or 500; 400 when there are 600 drivers; and 500 when there are 700 drivers.

The percentage of drivers who adapt is either 0 or 100 (in this case all act greedily) but any value can be used; percentage of Traffic Lights that act greedily is either 0 or 100; a link is considered jammed if its occupancy is over 50%; cycle length for signal plans is 40 seconds.

For the Q-learning, there is an experimentation phase of $10 \times t_{out}$, the learning rate is $\alpha = 0.1$ and the discount rate is $\lambda = 0.9$.

4.2   Global Optimization

For the sake of comparison, we show the results of a centralized approach before we continue with the main focus of the paper on local (co-)adaptation approaches. We use a centralized and heuristic optimization method in order to compute the optimal split of the cycle time between two traffic directions at each intersection.

This centralized optimization was performed using the DAVINCI (Developing Agent-based simulations Via INtelligent Calibration) Calibration Toolkit for SeSAm, that is a general purpose calibration and optimization tool for simulation. Although DAVINCI provides several global search strategies such as genetic algorithm (GA), simulated annealing or gradient based search, here we have used standard GA only, with a fitness proportional selection.

The input parameters for the GA are the default split values for each of the 36 traffic light agents (see next). The optimization objective is to minimize the average travel time over all drivers in a scenario with 400 drivers, where all drivers have only one route (the shortest path).

For a cycle length of 40 seconds, we have set seven possible values for the split at each intersection: 5/35, 10/30, 15/25, 20/20, ..., 35/5. Using four bits to codify each of these splits, for each of the 36 intersection, this leads to 144 bits for each GA string. We have allowed the GA to run for 100 generations.

The resulting optimized splits can be seen in Figure 2: numbers depicted close to the respective links indicate how much green time the link receives in the best solution found by the GA. Using these optimized splits, the average travel time of drivers is 105. This value can be used as a benchmark to assess the utility of adapting drivers and Traffic Lights in a decentralized way.

4.3   Drivers and Traffic-Lights Learning in a Decentralized Way

In this section we discuss the simulations and results collected when drivers and Traffic Lights co-adapt using different strategies, as given in Section 3. As a measure of performance, we use the *attl5t* defined previously (Section 4.1). These are summarized in Table 1. For all scenarios described in this subsection, 400 drivers were used. As said, all experiments were repeated 20 times. Standard deviations are not higher than 4% of the mean value given here.

Table 1. Average Travel Time Last 5 Trips (*attl5t*) for 400 drivers, under different conditions

Type of Simulation	Average Travel Time Last 5 Trips
greedy drivers / fixed traffic lights	100
probabilistic drivers / fixed traffic lights	149
greedy drivers / greedy traffic lights	106
probabilistic drivers / greedy traffic lights	143
greedy drivers / Qlearning traffic lights	233
probabilistic drivers / Qlearning traffic lights	280

Greedy or Probabilistic Drivers; Fixed Traffic Lights. In the case of probabilistic drivers, the *attl5t* is 149 time units, while this is 100 if drivers act greedily. The higher travel time is the price paid for the experimentation that drivers continue doing, even though the optimal policy was achieved long before (remember that the *attl5t* is computed only over the last 5 trips). The greedy action is of course much better after the optimal policy was learned. In the beginning of a simulation run, when experimentation does pay off, the probabilistic driver performs better.

Notice that this travel time is slightly better than the one found by the heuristic optimization tool described before, which was 105. In summary, greedy actions by the drivers work because they tend to select the routes with the shortest path and this normally distributes drivers more evenly than the case where drivers take longer routes.

Greedy or Probabilistic Drivers; Greedy Traffic Lights. When Traffic Lights also act greedily we can see that this does not automatically improve the outcome (in comparison with the case in which Traffic Lights are fixed): the *attl5t* is 106. This happens because the degree of freedom of Traffic Lights' actions is low, as actions are highly constrained. For example, acting greedily can be highly sub-optimal when, for instance, traffic light A serves direction D_1 (thus keeping D_2 with red light) but the downstream flow of D_1 is already jammed. In this case, the light might indeed provide green for vehicles on D_1 but these cannot move due to the downstream jam. Worse, jam may appear on the previously un-jammed D_2 too due to the small share of green time. This explains why acting greedily at Traffic Lights is not necessarily a good policy. The travel time of 106, when compared to the travel time found by the centralized optimization tool (105), is of course similar. This is not surprising because the decentralized strategy does exactly the same as the centralized optimizer, namely drivers use their best route and Traffic Lights optimize greedily.

Q-Learning Traffic Lights. We have expected Q-learning to perform bad because it is already known that it does not have a good performance in noisy and non-stationary traffic scenarios [13]. In order to test this, we have implemented a

Q-learning mechanism in the traffic lights. Available actions are: to open the phase serving either one direction (e.g. D_1), or the other (D_2). The states are the combination of abstract states in both approaching links, i.e. $\{D_1\_jammed, D_1\_not\_jammed\} \times \{D_2\_jammed, D_2\_not\_jammed\}$.

The low performance of Q-learning in traffic scenarios is due basically to the fact that the environment is non-stationary, not due to the poor discretization of states. Convergence is not achieved before the environment changes again, and thus Traffic Lights remain in the experimentation phase.

4.4   Scenarios with More Drivers

For more than 400 drives, we only investigate the cases of greedy drivers / fixed Traffic Lights *versus* the scenario in which both drivers and Traffic Lights act greedily. This was done in order to test whether or not increasing volume of traffic (due to increasing number of drivers in the network) would cause greedy Traffic Lights to perform better. This is expected to be the case since once the number of drivers increases, greedy actions by the drivers alone do not bring much gain; some kind of control in the Traffic Lights is expect to be helpful in case of high occupancy of the network. Notice that 400, 500, 600 and 700 drivers mean an average occupancy of $\approx$ 40%, 47%, 59%, and 72% per link respectively.

In Table 2 the *attl5t* for these numbers of drivers are shown. The case for 400 drivers was discussed above. With more than 600 drivers, the *attl5t* is lower when Traffic Lights also act greedily. In the case of 700 drivers, the improvement in travel time (411 *versus* 380) is about 8%. Thus, the greedy traffic lights are successful in keeping the occupancy of links lower, resulting in a reduction of travel times.

Table 2. Average Travel Time Last 5 Trips for Different Number of Drivers and Different Adaptation Schemes

Average Travel Time Last 5 Trips				
Type of Simulation	Nb. of Drivers			
	400	500	600	700
greedy drivers / fixed traffic lights	100	136	227	411
greedy drivers / greedy traffic lights	106	139	215	380

4.5   Overall Discussion

In the experiments presented, one can see that different strategies concerning the adaptivity of drivers, as well as of Traffic Lights have distinct results in different settings. We summarize here the main conclusions.

For the 6×6 network depicted, increasing the links capacity from 15 to 20 would lead to travel time levels that are the same we have achieved *without* this increase in capacity, i.e. substituting this increase by a better use of the available infrastructure. This is important because increasing network capacity is not always economically feasible, so that other measures must be taken. Diverting people by giving information to them, has only limited performance. Thus the idea is to use the control infrastructure in a more intelligent way. Therefore, we have explored the capability of the Traffic Lights to cope with the increasing demand.

Regarding travel time, it was shown that the strategies implemented in the Traffic Lights pay off in several cases, especially when the demand increases. We have also measured the number of drivers who arrive before time t_{out}. This is not shown here but, to give a general idea of the figures, bad performance (around 75% arrived) was seen only when the drivers adapt probabilistically. The general trend is that when the traffic lights also adapt, the performance increases, for all metrics used.

Regarding the use of Q-learning, as said, single-agent learning, i.e. each agent learns isolated using Q-learning, is far from optimum here due to the non-stationarity nature of the scenario. This is true especially for those links located close to the main destination and the main street as they tend to be part of each driver's trip so that the pattern of volume of vehicles changes dramatically. A possible solution is to use collaborative Traffic Lights. In this case, traffic light A would at least ask/sense traffic light B downstream whether or not it shall act greedily. This however leads to a cascade of dependencies among the Traffic Lights. In the worst case, everybody has to consider everybody's state. Even if this is done in a centralized way (which is far from desirable), the number of state-action pairs prevents the use of multiagent Q-learning in its standard formulation.

5   Conclusion

Several studies and approaches exist for modelling travellers' decision-making. In commuting scenarios in particular, probabilistic adaptation in order to maximize private utilities is one of those approaches. However, there is hardly any attempt to study what happens when *both* the driver and the traffic light use some evolutionary mechanism in the same scenario or environment, especially if *no central control exist*. In this case, co-adaptation happens in a decentralized fashion. This is an important issue because, although ITS have reached a high technical standard, the reaction of drivers to these systems is fairly unknown. In general, the optimization measures carried out in the traffic network both affect and are affected by drivers' reactions to them. This leads to a feedback loop that has received little attention to date. In the present paper we have investigated this loop by means of a prototype tool constructed in an agent-based simulation environment. This tool has modules to cope with the demand and the supply sides, as well as to implement the ITS modules and algorithms for the learning, adaptation etc.

Results show an improvement regarding travel time and occupancy (thus, both the demand and supply side) when all actors co-evolve, especially in large-scale situations e.g. involving hundreds of drivers. This was compared with situations in which either only drivers or only Traffic Lights evolve, in different scenarios, and with a centralized optimization method.

This work can be extended in many directions. First, we are already working to integrate the tools developed by the authors independly for supply and demand, namely ITSUMO [14] and MATSim (`http://www.matsim.org/`) which are simulators with far more capabilities than the prototype described here, and allow the modeling of even more realistic scenarios. For instance, drivers' trips can be described in MATsim in a richer way including activities that compose a trip such as dropping children at school, shopping, etc. The results are not expect to differ in the general trends, though, unless en-route adaptation is added.

Therefore, a second extension relates to the implementation of en-route adaptation of drivers in reaction to the perception of jammed links.

Finally, another extension is the use of heuristics for multiagent reinforcement learning in order to improve its performance. This is not trivial as it is known that reinforcement learning for non-stationary environments is a hard problem, especially when several agents are involved. In this context we also want to test a scenario where drivers and traffic lights learn taking turns.

Acknowledgments

The authors would like to thank CAPES (Brazil) and DAAD (Germany) for their support to the joint, bilateral project "Large Scale Agent-based Traffic Simulation for Predicting Traffic Conditions". Ana Bazzan is partially supported by CNPq and Alexander von Humboldt Stiftung; Denise de Oliveira is supported by CAPES.

References

1. Bazzan, A.L.C.: A distributed approach for coordination of traffic signal agents. Autonomous Agents and Multiagent Systems 10(1), 131–164 (2005)
2. Camponogara, E., Kraus, J.W.: Distributed learning agents in urban traffic control. In: Moura-Pires, F., Abreu, S. (eds.) EPIA 2003. LNCS (LNAI), vol. 2902, pp. 324–335. Springer, Heidelberg (2003)
3. Dresner, K., Stone, P.: Multiagent traffic management: A reservation-based intersection control mechanism. In: Jennings, N., Sierra, C., Sonenberg, L., Tambe, M. (eds.) The Third International Joint Conference on Autonomous Agents and Multiagent Systems, pp. 530–537. IEEE Computer Society, Los Alamitos (2004)
4. Klügl, F., Bazzan, A.L.C.: Route decision behaviour in a commuting scenario. Journal of Artificial Societies and Social Simulation 7(1) (2004)
5. Klügl, F., Herrler, R., Oechslein, C.: From simulated to real environments: How to use SeSAm for software development. In: Schillo, M., Klusch, M., Müller, J., Tianfield, H. (eds.) Multiagent System Technologies. LNCS (LNAI), vol. 2831, pp. 13–24. Springer, Heidelberg (2003)
6. Liu, R., Van Vliet, D., Watling, D.: Microsimulation models incorporating both demand and supply dynamics. Transportation Research Part A: Policy and Practice 40(2), 125–150 (2006)
7. Nagel, K., Schreckenberg, M.: A cellular automaton model for freeway traffic. Journal de Physique I 2, 2221 (1992)

8. Nunes, L., Oliveira, E.C.: Learning from multiple sources. In: Jennings, N., Sierra, C., Sonenberg, L., Tambe, M. (eds.) AAMAS. Proceedings of the 3rd International Joint Conference on Autonomous Agents and Multi Agent Systems, vol. 3, pp. 1106–1113. IEEE Computer Society, Los Alamitos (2004)
9. Oliveira, D., Bazzan, A.L.C.: Traffic lights control with adaptive group formation based on swarm intelligence. In: Dorigo, M., Gambardella, L.M., Birattari, M., Martinoli, A., Poli, R., Stützle, T. (eds.) ANTS 2006. LNCS, vol. 4150, pp. 520–521. Springer, Heidelberg (2006)
10. Oliveira, D., Bazzan, A.L.C., Lesser, V.: Using cooperative mediation to coordinate traffic lights: a case study. In: AAMAS. Proceedings of the 4th International Joint Conference on Autonomous Agents and Multi Agent Systems, pp. 463–470. IEEE Computer Society, Los Alamitos (2005)
11. Ortúzar, J., Willumsen, L.G.: Modelling Transport, 3rd edn. John Wiley & Sons, Chichester (2001)
12. Roess, R.P., Prassas, E.S., McShane, W.R.: Traffic Engineering. Prentice Hall, Englewood Cliffs (2004)
13. Silva, B.C.d., Basso, E.W., Bazzan, A.L.C., Engel, P.M.: Dealing with non-stationary environments using context detection. In: Cohen, W.W., Moore, A. (eds.) ICML. Proceedings of the 23rd International Conference on Machine Learning, pp. 217–224. ACM Press, New York (2006)
14. Silva, B.C.d., Junges, R., Oliveira, D., Bazzan, A.L.C.: ITSUMO: an intelligent transportation system for urban mobility. In: Stone, P., Weiss, G. (eds.) AAMAS 2006 - Demonstration Track. Proceedings of the 5th International Joint Conference on Autonomous Agents and Multiagent Systems, pp. 1471–1472. ACM Press, New York (2006)
15. Tumer, K., Wolpert, D.: A survey of collectives. In: Tumer, K., Wolpert, D. (eds.) Collectives and the Design of Complex Systems, pp. 1–42. Springer, Heidelberg (2004)
16. van Zuylen, H.J., Taale, H.: Urban networks with ring roads: a two-level, three player game. In: TRB. Proc. of the 83rd Annual Meeting of the Transportation Research Board (January 2004)
17. Wardrop, J.G.: Some theoretical aspects of road traffic research. In: Proceedings of the Institute of Civil Engineers, vol. 2, pp. 325–378 (1952)
18. Watkins, C.J.C.H., Dayan, P.: Q-learning. Machine Learning 8(3), 279–292 (1992)
19. Wiering, M.: Multi-agent reinforcement learning for traffic light control. In: ICML 2000. Proceedings of the Seventeenth International Conference on Machine Learning, pp. 1151–1158 (2000)

Optimal Control in Large Stochastic Multi-agent Systems

Bart van den Broek, Wim Wiegerinck, and Bert Kappen

SNN, Radboud University Nijmegen, Geert Grooteplein 21, Nijmegen,
The Netherlands
{b.vandenbroek,w.wiegerinck,b.kappen}@science.ru.nl

Abstract. We study optimal control in large stochastic multi-agent systems in continuous space and time. We consider multi-agent systems where agents have independent dynamics with additive noise and control. The goal is to minimize the joint cost, which consists of a state dependent term and a term quadratic in the control. The system is described by a mathematical model, and an explicit solution is given. We focus on large systems where agents have to distribute themselves over a number of targets with minimal cost. In such a setting the optimal control problem is equivalent to a graphical model inference problem. Exact inference will be intractable, and we use the mean field approximation to compute accurate approximations of the optimal controls. We conclude that near to optimal control in large stochastic multi-agent systems is possible with this approach.

1 Introduction

A collaborative multi-agent system is a group of agents in which each member behaves autonomously to reach the common goal of the group. Some examples are teams of robots or unmanned vehicles, and networks of automated resource allocation. An issue typically appearing in multi-agent systems is decentralized coordination; the communication between agents may be restricted, there may be no time to receive all the demands for a certain resource, or an unmanned vehicle may be unsure about how to anticipate another vehicles movement and avoid a collision.

In this paper we focus on the issue of optimal control in large multi-agent systems where the agents dynamics are continuous in space and time. In particular we look at cases where the agents have to distribute themselves in admissible ways over a number of targets. Due to the noise in the dynamics, a configuration that initially seems attainable with little effort may become harder to reach later on.

Common approaches to derive a coordination rule are based on discretizations of space and time. These often suffer from the curse of dimensionality, as the complexity increases exponentially in the number of agents. Some successfull ideas, however, have recently been put forward, which are based on structures that are assumed to be present [1,2].

K. Tuyls et al. (Eds.): Adaptive Agents and MAS III, LNAI 4865, pp. 15–26, 2008.
© Springer-Verlag Berlin Heidelberg 2008

Here we rather model the system in continuous space and time, following the approach of Wiegerinck et al. [3]. The agents satisfy dynamics with additive control and noise, and the joint behaviour of the agents is valued by a joint cost function that is quadratic in the control. The stochastic optimization problem may then be transformed into a linear partial differential equation, which can be solved using generic path integral methods [4,5]. The dynamics of the agents are assumed to factorize over the agents, such that the agents are coupled by their joint task only.

The optimal control problem is equivalent to a graphical model inference problem [3]. In large and sparsely coupled multi-agent systems the optimal control can be computed using the junction tree algorithm. Exact inference, however, will break down when the system is both large and densely coupled. Here we explore the use of graphical model approximate inference methods in optimal control of large stochastic multi-agent systems. We apply the mean field approximation to show that optimal control is possible with accuracy in systems where exact inference breaks down.

2   Stochastic Optimal Control of a Multi-agent System

We consider n agents in a k-dimensional space $\mathbb{R}^k$, the state of each agent a is given by a vector x_a in this space, satisfying stochastic dynamics

$$dx_a(t) = b_a(x_a(t), t)dt + Bu_a(t)dt + \sigma dw(t), \tag{1}$$

where u_a is the control of agent a, b_a is an arbitrary function representing autonomous dynamics, w is a Wiener process, and B and σ are $k \times k$ matrices.

The agents have to reach a goal at the end time T, they will pay a cost $\phi(x(T))$ at the end time depending on their joint end state $x(T) = (x_1(T), \ldots, x_n(T))$, but to reach this goal they will have to make an effort which depends on the agents controls and states over time. At any time $t < T$, the expected cost-to-go is

$$C(x, t, u(t \to T)) =$$
$$\left\langle \phi(x(T)) + \int_t^T d\theta\, V(x(\theta), \theta) + \sum_{a=1}^n \int_t^T d\theta\, \frac{1}{2} u_a(\theta)^\top R u_a(\theta) \right\rangle, \tag{2}$$

given the agents initial state x, and the joint control over time $u(t \to T)$. R is a symmetric $k \times k$ matrix with positive eigenvalues, such that $u_a(\theta)^\top R u_a(\theta)$ is always a non-negative number, $V(x(\theta), \theta)$ is the cost for the agents to be in a joint state $x(\theta)$ at time θ. The issue is to find the optimal control which minimizes the expected cost-to-go.

The optimal controls are given by the gradient

$$u_a(x, t) = -R^{-1} B^\top \partial_{x_a} J(x, t), \tag{3}$$

where $J(x,t)$ the optimal expected cost-to-go, i.e. the cost (2) minimized over all possible controls; a brief derivation is contained in the appendix. An important implication of equation (3) is that at any moment in time, each agent can compute its own optimal control if it knows its own state and that of the other agents: there is no need to discuss possible strategies! This is because the agents always perform the control that is optimal, and the optimal control is unique.

To compute the optimal controls, however, we first need to find the optimal expected cost-to-go J. The latter may be expressed in terms of a forward diffusion process:

$$J(x,t) = -\lambda \log \int dy\, \rho(y,T|x,t)e^{-\phi(y)/\lambda}, \tag{4}$$

$\rho(y,T|x,t)$ being the transition probability for the system to go from a state x at time t to a state y at the end time T. The constant λ is determined by the relation $\sigma\sigma^\top = \lambda BR^{-1}B^\top$, equation (14) in the appendix. The density $\rho(y,\theta|x,t)$, $t < \theta \leq T$, satisfies the forward Fokker-Planck equation,

$$\partial_\theta \rho = -\frac{V}{\lambda} - \sum_{a=1}^{n} \partial_{y_a}^\top b_a \rho + \sum_{a=1}^{n} \frac{1}{2}\mathrm{Tr}\left(\sigma\sigma^\top \partial_{y_a}^2 \rho\right). \tag{5}$$

The solution to this equation may generally be estimated using path integral methods [4,5], in a few special cases a solution exists in closed form:

Example 1. Consider a multi-agent system in one dimension in which there is noise and control in the velocities of the agents, according to the set of equations

$$\begin{cases} dx_a(t) = \dot{x}_a(t)dt \\ d\dot{x}_a(t) = u_a(t)dt + \sigma dw(t). \end{cases}$$

Note that this set of equations can be merged into a single equation of the form (1) by a concatenation of x_a and $\dot{x}_a$ into a single vector. We choose the potential $V = 0$. Under the task where each agent a has to reach a target with location μ_a at the end time T, and arrive with speed $\dot{\mu}_a$, the end cost function ϕ can be given in terms of a product of delta functions, that is

$$e^{-\phi(x,\dot{x})/\lambda} = \prod_{a=1}^{n} \delta(x_a - \mu_a)\delta(\dot{x}_a - \dot{\mu}_a),$$

and the system decouples into n independent single-agent systems. The dynamics of each agent a is given by a transition probability

$$\rho_a(y_a, \dot{y}_a, T|x_a, \dot{x}_a, t) =$$

$$\frac{1}{\sqrt{\det(2\pi c)}} \exp\left(-\frac{1}{2}\left\| c^{-1/2}\begin{pmatrix} y_a - x_a - (T-t)\dot{x}_a \\ \dot{y}_a - \dot{x}_a \end{pmatrix}\right\|^2\right), \tag{6}$$

where

$$c = \frac{1}{6}\begin{pmatrix} 2(T-t)^3 & 3(T-t)^2 \\ 3(T-t)^2 & 6(T-t) \end{pmatrix}\sigma^2.$$

The optimal control follows from equations (3) and (4) and reads

$$u_a(x_a, \dot{x}_a, t) = \frac{6(\mu_a - x_a - (T-t)\dot{x}_a) - 2(T-t)(\dot{\mu}_a - \dot{x}_a)}{(T-t)^2}. \tag{7}$$

The first term in the control will steer the agent towards the target μ_a in a straight line, but since this may happen with a speed that differs from $\dot{\mu}_a$ with which the agent should arrive, there is a second term that initially 'exaggerates' the speed for going in a straight line, so that in the end there is time to adjust the speed to the end speed $\dot{\mu}_a$.

2.1   A Joint Task: Distribution over Targets

We consider the situation where agents have to distribute themselves over a number of targets $s = 1, \ldots, m$. In general, there will be m^n possible combinations of assigning the n agents to the targets—note, in example 1 we considered only one assignment. We can describe this by letting the end cost function ϕ be given in terms of a positive linear combination of functions

$$\Phi(y_1, \ldots, y_n, s_1, \ldots, s_n) = \prod_{a=1}^{n} \Phi_a(y_a, s_a)$$

that are peaked around the location $(\mu_{s_1}, \ldots, \mu_{s_n})$ of a joint target $(s_1, \ldots, s_n)$, that is

$$e^{-\phi(y)/\lambda} = \sum_{s_1, \ldots, s_n} w(s_1, \ldots, s_n) \prod_{a=1}^{n} \Phi_a(y_a, s_a),$$

where the $w(s_1, \ldots, s_n)$ are positive weights. We will refer to these weights as coupling factors, since they introduce dependencies between the agents. The optimal control of a single agent is obtained using equations (3) and (4), and is a weighted combination of single-target controls,

$$u_a = \sum_{s=1}^{m} p_a(s) u_a(s) \tag{8}$$

(the explicit (x, t) dependence has been dropped in the notation). Here $u_a(s)$ is the control for agent a to go to target s,

$$u_a(s) = -R^{-1} B^{\top} \partial_{x_a} Z_a(s), \tag{9}$$

with $Z_a(s)$ defined by

$$Z_a(s_a) = \int dy_a \rho_a(y_a, T | x_a, t) \Phi_a(y_a, s_a).$$

The weights $p_a(s)$ are marginals of the joint distribution

$$p(s_1, \ldots, s_n) \propto w(s_1, \ldots, s_n) \prod_{a=1}^{n} Z_a(s_a). \tag{10}$$

p thus is a distribution over all possible assignments of agents to targets.

Example 2. Consider the multi-agent system of example 1, but with a different task: each of the agents $a = 1,\ldots,n$ has to reach a target $s = 1,\ldots,n$ with location μ_s at the end time T, and arrive with zero speed, but no two agents are allowed to arrive at the same target. We model this by choosing an end cost function $\phi(x,\dot{x})$ given by

$$e^{-\phi(x,\dot{x})/\lambda} = \sum_{s_1,\ldots,s_n} w(s_1,\ldots,s_n) \prod_{a=1}^{n} \delta(y_a - \mu_a)\delta(\dot{y}_a)$$

with coupling factors

$$w(s_1,\ldots,s_n) = \prod_{a,a'=1}^{n} \exp\left(\frac{c}{\lambda n}\delta_{s_a,s_{a'}}\right).$$

For any agent a, the optimal control under this task is a weighted average of single target controls (7),

$$u_a(x_a,\dot{x}_a,t) = \frac{6(\langle\mu_a\rangle - x_a - (T-t)\dot{x}_a) + 2(T-t)\dot{x}_a}{(T-t)^2}, \tag{11}$$

where $\langle\mu_a\rangle$ the averaged target for agent a,

$$\langle\mu_a\rangle = \sum_{s=1}^{n} p_a(s)\mu_s.$$

The average is taken with respect to the marginal p_a of the joint distribution

$$p(s_1,\ldots,s_n) \propto w(s_1,\ldots,s_n) \prod_{a=1}^{n} \rho_a(\mu_{s_a},0,T|x_a,\dot{x}_a,t),$$

the densities ρ_a given by (6).

In general, and in example 2 in particular, the optimal control of an agent will not only depend on the state of this agent alone, but also on the states of other agents. Since the controls are computed anew at each instant in time, the agents are able to continuously adapt to the behaviour of the other agents, adjusting their control to the new states of all the agents.

2.2 Factored End Costs

The additional computational effort in multi-agent control compared to single-agent control lies in the computation of the marginals of the joint distribution p, which involves a sum of at most m^n terms. For small systems this is feasible, for large systems this will only be feasible if the summation can be performed efficiently. Whether an efficient way of computing the marginals exists, depends on the joint task of the agents. In the most complex case, to fulfil the task each agent will have to take the joint state of the entire system into account. In less complicated cases, an agent will only consider the states of a few agents in the system, in other words, the coupling factors will have a nontrivial factorized form:

$$w(s_1, \ldots, s_n) = \prod_A w_A(s_A),$$

where the A are subsets of agents. In such cases we may represent the couplings, and thus the joint distribution, by a factor graph; see Figure 1 for an example.

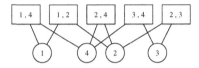

Fig. 1. Example of a factor graph for a multi-agent system of four agents. The couplings are represented by the factors A, with $A = \{1,4\}, \{1,2\}, \{2,4\}, \{3,4\}, \{2,3\}$.

2.3 Graphical Model Inference

In the previous paragraph we observed that the joint distribution may be represented by a factor graph. This implies that the issue of assigning agents to targets is equivalent to a graphical model inference problem. Both exact methods (junction tree algorithm [6]) and approximate methods (mean field approximation [7], belief propagation [8]) can be used to compute the marginals in (8). In this paper we will use the mean field (MF) approximation to tackle optimal control in large multi-agent systems.

In the mean field approximation we minimize the mean field free energy, a function of single agent marginals q_a defined by

$$F_{\mathrm{MF}}(\{q_a\}) = -\langle \lambda \log w \rangle_q - \sum_a \langle \lambda \log Z_a \rangle_{q_a} - \lambda \sum_a H(q_a),$$

where $q(s) = q_1(s_1) \cdots q_n(s_n)$. Here the $H(q_a)$ are the entropies of the distributions q_a,

$$H(q_a) = -\sum_s q_a(s) \log q_a(s).$$

The minimum

$$J_{\mathrm{MF}} = \min_{\{q_a\}} F_{\mathrm{MF}}(\{q_a\})$$

is an upper bound for the optimal cost-to-go J, it equals J in case the agents are uncoupled. F_{MF} has zero gradient in its local minima, that is,

$$0 = \frac{\partial F(q_1(s_1), \ldots, q_n(s_n))}{\partial q_a(s_a)} \qquad a = 1, \ldots, n,$$

with additional constraints for normalization of the probability vectors q_a. Solutions to this set of equations are implicitly given by the *mean field equations*

$$q_a(s_a) = \frac{Z_a(s_a) \exp\left(\langle \log w | s_a \rangle\right)}{\sum_{s'_a=1}^{n} Z_a(s'_a) \exp\left(\langle \log w | s'_a \rangle\right)} \tag{12}$$

where $\langle \log w | s_a \rangle$ the conditional expectation of $\log w$ given s_a,

$$\langle \log w | s_a \rangle = \sum_{s_1,\ldots,s_n \backslash s_a} \left(\prod_{a' \neq a} q_{a'}(s_{a'}) \right) \log w(s_1, \ldots, s_n).$$

The mean field equations are solved by means of iteration, and the solutions are the local minima of the mean field free energy. Thus the mean field free energy minimized over all solutions to the mean field equations equals the minimum J_{MF}.

The mean field approximation of the optimal control is found by taking the gradient of the minimum J_{MF} of the mean field free energy, similar to the exact case where the optimal control is the gradient of the optimal expected cost-to-go, equation (3):

$$u_a(x,t) = -R_a^{-1} B_a^{\top} \partial_{x_a} J_{\mathrm{MF}}(x,t) = \sum_{s_a} q_a(s_a) u_a(x_a,t;s_a).$$

Similar to the exact case, it is an average of single-agent single-target optimal controls $u_a(x_a,t;s_a)$, the controls $u_a(x_a,t;s_a)$ given by equation (9), where the average is taken with respect to the mean field approximate marginal $q_a(s_a)$ of agent a.

3   Control of Large Multi-agent Systems

Exact inference of multi-agent optimal control is intractable in large and densely coupled systems. In this section we present numerical results from approximate inference in optimal control of a large multi-agent system. We focus on the system presented in example 2. A group of n agents have to distribute themselves over an equal number of targets, each target should be reached by precisely one agent. The agents all start in the same location at $t = 0$, and the time they reach the targets lies at $T = 1$, as illustrated in figure 3. The variance of the noise equals 0.1 and the control cost parameter R equals 1, both are the same for each agent. The coupling strength c in the coupling factors equals -10. For implementation, time had to be discretized: each time step Δt equaled 0.05 times the time-to-go $T - t$.

We considered two approximate inference methods for obtaining the marginals in (8), the mean field approximation described in section 2.3, and an approximation which at each moment in time assigns each agent to precisely one target. In the latter method the agent that is nearest to any of the targets is assigned first to its nearest target, then, removing this pair of agent and target, this is repeated for the remaining agents and targets, until there are no more remaining agents and targets. We will refer to this method as the *sort distances* (SD) method.

For several sizes of the system we computed the control cost and the required CPU time to calculate the controls. This we did under both control methods. Figures 2(a) and (b) show the control cost and the required CPU time as a function of the system size n; each value is an average obtained from 100 simulations. To emphasize the necessity of the approximate inference methods, in figure 2(b) we included the required CPU time under exact inference; this quantity increases exponentially with n, as we may have expected, making exact inference intractable in large MASs. In contrast, both under the SD method and the MF method the required CPU time appears to increase polynomially with n, the SD method requiring less computation time than the MF method. Though the SD method is faster than the MF method, it also is more costly: the control cost under the SD method is significantly higher than under the MF method. The MF method thus better approximates the optimal control.

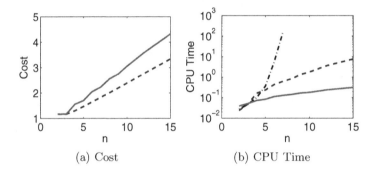

(a) Cost   (b) CPU Time

Fig. 2. The control cost (a) and the required CPU Time in seconds (b) under the exact method $(\cdot - \cdot)$, the MF method $(--)$, and the SD method $(—)$

Figure 3 shows the positions and the velocities of the agents over time, both under the control obtained using the MF approximation and under the control obtained with the SD method. We observe that under MF control, the agents determine their targets early, between $t = 0$ and $t = 0.5$, and the agents velocities gradually increase from zero to a maximum value at $t = 0.5$ to again gradually decrease to zero, as required. This is not very surprising, since the MF approximation is known to show an early symmetry breaking. In contrast, under the SD method the decision making process of the agents choosing their targets takes place over almost the entire time interval, and the velocities of the agents are subject to frequent changes; in particular, as time increases the agents who have not yet chosen a target seem to exchange targets in a frequent manner. This may be understood by realising that under the SD method agents always perform a control to their nearest target only, instead of a weighted combination of controls to different targets which is the situation under MF control.

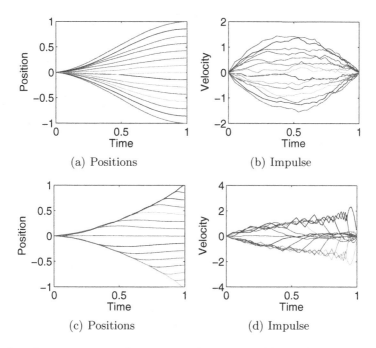

Fig. 3. A multi-agent system of 15 agents. The positions (a) and the velocities (b) over time under MF control, and the positions (c) and the velocities (d) over time under SD control.

Further more, compared with the velocities under the MF method the velocities under the SD method take on higher maximum values. This may account for the relatively high control costs under SD control.

4   Discussion

In this paper we studied optimal control in large stochastic multi-agent systems in continuous space and time, focussing on systems where agents have a task to distribute themselves over a number of targets. We followed the approach of Wiegerinck et al. [3]: we modeled the system in continuous space and time, resulting in an adaptive control policy where agents continuously adjust their controls to the environment. We considered the task of assigning agents to targets as a graphical model inference problem. We showed that in large and densely coupled systems, in which exact inference would break down, the mean field approximation manages to compute accurate approximations of the optimal controls of the agents.

We considered the performances of the mean field approximation and an alternative method, referred to as the sort distances method, on an example system in which a number of agents have to distribute themselves over an equal number of targets, such that each target is reached by precisely one agent. In the sort distances method each agent performs a control to a single nearby target, in such a way that no two agents head to the same target at the same time. This method has an advantage of being fast, but it results in relatively high control costs. Because each agent performs a control to a single target, agents switch targets frequently during the control process. In the mean field approximation each agent performs a control which is a weighted sum of controls to single targets. This requires more computation time than the sort distances method, but involves significantly lower control costs and therefore is a better approximation to the optimal control.

An obvious choice for a graphical model inference method not considered in the present paper would be belief propagation. Results of numeric simulations with this method in the context of multi-agent control, and comparisons with the mean field approximation and the exact junction tree algorithm will be published elsewhere.

There are many possible model extensions worthwhile exploring in future research. Examples are non-zero potentials V in case of a non-empty environment, penalties for collisions in the context of robotics, non-fixed end times, or bounded state spaces in the context of a production process. Typically, such model extensions will not allow for a solution in closed form, and approximate numerical methods will be required. Some suggestions are given by Kappen [4,5]. In the setting that we considered the model which describes the behaviour of the agents was given. It would be worthwhile, however, to consider cases of stochastic optimal control of multi-agent systems in continuous space and time where the model first needs to be learned.

Acknowledgments

We thank Joris Mooij for making available useful software and the reviewers for their useful remarks. This research is part of the Interactive Collaborative Information Systems (ICIS) project, supported by the Dutch Ministry of Economic Affairs, grant BSIK03024.

References

1. Guestrin, C., Koller, D., Parr, R.: Multiagent planning with factored MDPs. In: Proceedings of NIPS, vol. 14, pp. 1523–1530 (2002)
2. Guestrin, C., Venkataraman, S., Koller, D.: Context-specific multiagent coordination and planning with factored MDPs. In: Proceedings of AAAI, vol. 18, pp. 253–259 (2002)
3. Wiegerinck, W., van den Broek, B., Kappen, B.: Stochastic optimal control in continuous space-time multi-agent systems. In: UAI 2006 (2006)
4. Kappen, H.J.: Path integrals and symmetry breaking for optimal control theory. Journal of statistical mechanics: theory and experiment, 11011 (2005)
5. Kappen, H.J.: Linear theory for control of nonlinear stochastic systems. Physical Review Letters 95(20), 200–201 (2005)

6. Lauritzen, S., Spiegelhalter, D.: Local computations with probabilities on graphical structures and their application to expert systems (with discussion). J. Royal Statistical Society Series B 50, 157–224 (1988)
7. Jordan, M., Ghahramani, Z., Jaakkola, T., Saul, L.: An introduction to variational methods for graphical models. In: Jordan, M.I. (ed.) Learning in Graphical Models, MIT Press, Cambridge (1999)
8. Kschischang, F.R., Frey, B.J., Loeliger, H.A.: Factor graphs and the sum-product algorithm. IEEE Trans. Info. Theory 47, 498–519 (2001)

A Stochastic Optimal Control

In this appendix we give a brief derivation of equations (3), (4) and (5), starting from (2). Details can be found in [4,5].

The optimal expected cost-to-go J, by definition the expected cost-to-go (2) minimized over all controls, satisfies the stochastic Hamilton-Jacobi-Bellman (HJB) equation

$$-\partial_t J = \min_u \sum_{a=1}^{n} \left(\frac{1}{2} u_a^\top R u_a + (b_a + B u_a)^\top \partial_{x_a} J + \frac{1}{2} \mathrm{Tr} \left(\sigma \sigma^\top \partial_{x_a}^2 J \right) \right) + V,$$

with boundary condition $J(x,T) = \phi(x)$. The minimization with respect to u yields equation (3), which specifies the optimal control for each agent. Substituting these controls in the HJB equation gives a non-linear equation for J. We can remove the non-linearity by using a log transformation: if we introduce a constant λ, and define $Z(x,t)$ through

$$J(x,t) = -\lambda \log Z(x,t), \tag{13}$$

then

$$\frac{1}{2} u_a^\top R u_a + (B u_a)^\top \partial_{x_a} J = -\frac{1}{2} \lambda^2 Z^{-2} (\partial_{x_a} Z)^\top B R^{-1} B^\top \partial_{x_a} Z,$$

$$\frac{1}{2} \mathrm{Tr} \left(\sigma \sigma^\top \partial_{x_a}^2 J \right) = \frac{1}{2} \lambda Z^{-2} (\partial_{x_a} Z)^\top \sigma \sigma^\top \partial_{x_a} Z - \frac{1}{2} \lambda Z^{-1} \mathrm{Tr} \left(\sigma \sigma^\top \partial_{x_a}^2 Z \right).$$

The terms quadratic in Z vanish when $\sigma^\top \sigma$ and R are related via

$$\sigma \sigma^\top = \lambda B R^{-1} B^\top. \tag{14}$$

In the one dimensional case a constant λ can always be found such that equation (14) is satisfied, in the higher dimensional case the equation puts restrictions on the matrices σ and R, because in general $\sigma \sigma^\top$ and $B R^{-1} B^\top$ will not be proportional.

When equation (14) is satisfied, the HJB equation becomes

$$\partial_t Z = \left(\frac{V}{\lambda} - \sum_{a=1}^{n} b_a^\top \partial_{x_a} - \sum_{a=1}^{n} \frac{1}{2} \mathrm{Tr} \left(\sigma \sigma^\top \partial_{x_a}^2 \right) \right) Z$$
$$= -H Z, \tag{15}$$

where H a linear operator acting on the function Z. Equation (15) is solved backwards in time with $Z(x,T) = e^{-\phi(x)/\lambda}$. However, the linearity allows us to reverse the direction of computation, replacing it by a diffusion process, as we will now explain.

The solution to equation (15) is given by

$$Z(x,t) = \int dy \rho(y,T|x,t) e^{-\phi(y)/\lambda},\tag{16}$$

the density $\rho(y,\vartheta|x,t)$ ($t < \vartheta \leq T$) satisfying the forward Fokker-Planck equation (5). Combining the equations (13) and (16) yields the expression (4) for the optimal expected cost-to-go.

Continuous-State Reinforcement Learning with Fuzzy Approximation

Lucian Buşoniu[1], Damien Ernst[2], Bart De Schutter[1], and Robert Babuška[1]

[1] Delft University of Technology, The Netherlands
[2] Supélec, Rennes, France
i.l.busoniu@tudelft.nl, damien.ernst@supelec.fr,
b@deschutter.info, r.babuska@tudelft.nl

Abstract. Reinforcement learning (RL) is a widely used learning paradigm for adaptive agents. There exist several convergent and consistent RL algorithms which have been intensively studied. In their original form, these algorithms require that the environment states and agent actions take values in a relatively small discrete set. Fuzzy representations for approximate, model-free RL have been proposed in the literature for the more difficult case where the state-action space is continuous. In this work, we propose a fuzzy approximation architecture similar to those previously used for Q-learning, but we combine it with the model-based Q-value iteration algorithm. We prove that the resulting algorithm converges. We also give a modified, asynchronous variant of the algorithm that converges at least as fast as the original version. An illustrative simulation example is provided.

1 Introduction

Learning agents can tackle problems that are difficult to solve with pre-programmed solutions. Reinforcement learning (RL) is a popular learning paradigm for adaptive agents, thanks to its mild assumptions on the environment (which can be a nonlinear, stochastic process), and thanks to its ability to work without an explicit model of the environment [1,2]. At each time step, an RL agent perceives the complete state of the environment and takes an action. This action causes the environment to move into a new state. The agent then receives a scalar reward signal indicating the quality of this transition. The agent's objective is to maximize the cumulative reward over the course of interaction. There exist several convergent and consistent RL algorithms which have been intensively studied [1,2,3]. Unfortunately, these algorithms apply in general only to problems having discrete and not too large state-action spaces since, among others, they require to store estimates of cumulative rewards for every state or state-action pair. For problems with discrete but large state-action spaces, or continuous state-action spaces, approximate algorithms have to be used.

In this paper, we analyze the convergence of some model-based reinforcement learning algorithms exploiting a fuzzy approximation architecture. Our algorithms deal with problems for which the complexity comes from the state space,

K. Tuyls et al. (Eds.): Adaptive Agents and MAS III, LNAI 4865, pp. 27–43, 2008.

but not the action space, i.e., where the state space contains an infinite or extremely large number of elements and the action space is discrete and moderate in size. Most of our results also hold in the case where the action space is large or continuous, but in that case require a discretization procedure that selects a moderate number of representative actions. A significant number of related fuzzy approximators have been proposed, e.g., for Q-learning [4, 5, 6] or actor-critic algorithms [6, 7, 8, 9, 10]. However, most of these approaches are heuristic in nature, and their theoretical properties have not been investigated. Notable exceptions are the actor-critic algorithms in [8, 9].

On the other hand, a rich body of literature concerns the theoretical analysis of approximate RL algorithms, both in a model-based setting [11, 12, 13, 14] and when an a priori model is not available [15, 16, 17, 18, 19].[1] While convergence is not ensured for an arbitrary approximator (see [11, 14] for examples of divergence), there exist approximation schemes that do provide convergence guarantees. These mainly belong to the family of linear basis functions, and are encountered under several other names: kernel functions [15, 16], averagers [13], interpolative representations [17]. Some authors also investigate approximators that alter their structure during learning in order to better represent the solution [16, 20, 21]. While some of these algorithms exhibit impressing learning capabilities, they may face convergence problems [16].

Here, we consider an approximator that represents the Q-function using a fuzzy partition of the state space. While similar representations have previously been used in fuzzy Q-learning, in this paper the fuzzy approximator is combined with the model-based Q-value iteration algorithm. The resulting algorithm is shown to converge. Afterwards, we propose a variant of this algorithm, which we name asynchronous fuzzy Q-iteration, and which we show converges at least as fast as the original version. Asynchronous Q-iteration has been widely used in exact RL, but its approximate counterpart has not been studied before.

The remainder of this paper is structured as follows. Section 2 describes briefly the RL problem and reviews some relevant results from the dynamic programming theory. Section 3 introduces the approximate Q-iteration algorithm, which is an extension of the classical Q-iteration algorithm to cases where function approximators are used. Section 4 presents the proposed fuzzy approximator. The properties of synchronous and asynchronous approximate Q-iteration using this approximator are analyzed in Section 5. Section 6 applies the algorithms introduced to a nonlinear control problem with four continuous state variables, and compares the performance of the algorithms with that of Q-iteration with radial basis function approximation. Section 7 describes possible extensions of the algorithm for stochastic tasks and online learning. Section 8 outlines ideas for future work and concludes the paper.

---

[1] Some authors use 'model-based RL' when referring to algorithms that build a model of the environment from interaction. We use the term 'model-learning' for such techniques, and reserve the name 'model-based' for algorithms that rely on an a priori model of the environment.

2   Reinforcement Learning

In this section, the RL task is briefly introduced and its optimal solution is characterized. The presentation is based on [1, 2].

Consider a deterministic *Markov decision process (MDP)* with the state space X, the action space U, the transition function $f : X \times U \to X$, and the reward function $\rho : X \times U \to \mathbb{R}$.[2] As a result of the agent's action u_k in state x_k at the discrete time step k, the state changes to $x_{k+1} = f(x_k, u_k)$. At the same time, the agent receives the scalar reward signal $r_{k+1} = \rho(x_k, u_k)$, which evaluates the immediate effect of action u_k, but says nothing about its long-term effects.[3]

The agent chooses actions according to its policy $h : X \to U$, using $u_k = h(x_k)$. The goal of the agent is to learn a policy that maximizes, starting from the current moment in time ($k = 0$) and from any state x_0, the discounted return:

$$R = \sum_{k=0}^{\infty} \gamma^k r_{k+1} = \sum_{k=0}^{\infty} \gamma^k \rho(x_k, u_k) \tag{1}$$

where $\gamma \in [0, 1)$ and $x_{k+1} = f(x_k, u_k)$ for $k \geq 0$. The discounted return compactly represents the reward accumulated by the agent in the long run. The learning task is therefore to maximize the long-term performance, while only receiving feedback about the immediate, one-step performance. This can be achieved by computing the optimal action-value function.

An action-value function (Q-function), $Q^h : X \times U \to \mathbb{R}$, gives the return of each state-action pair under a given policy h:

$$Q^h(x, u) = \rho(x, u) + \sum_{k=1}^{\infty} \gamma^k \rho(x_k, h(x_k)) \tag{2}$$

where $x_1 = f(x, u)$ and $x_{k+1} = f(x_k, h(x_k))$ for $k \geq 1$. The optimal action-value function is defined as $Q^*(x, u) = \max_h Q^h(x, u)$. Any policy that picks for every state the action with the highest optimal Q-value:

$$h^*(x) = \arg\max_u Q^*(x, u) \tag{3}$$

is optimal, i.e., it maximizes the return (1).

A central result in RL, upon which many algorithms rely, is the *Bellman optimality equation*:

$$Q^*(x, u) = \rho(x, u) + \gamma \max_{u' \in U} Q^*(f(x, u), u') \quad \forall x, u \tag{4}$$

---

[2] Throughout the paper, the standard control-theoretic notation is used: x for state, X for state space, u for control action, U for action space, f for environment dynamics. We denote reward functions by ρ, to distinguish them from the instantaneous rewards r and the return R. We denote policies by h.

[3] A stochastic formulation is possible. In that case, expected returns under the probabilistic transitions must be considered.

This equation can be solved using the Q-value iteration algorithm. Let the set of all Q-functions be denoted by $\mathcal{Q}$. Define the Q-iteration mapping $T : \mathcal{Q} \to \mathcal{Q}$, which computes the right-hand side of the Bellman equation for any Q-function:

$$[T(Q)](x, u) = \rho(x, u) + \gamma \max_{u' \in U} Q(f(x, u), u') \tag{5}$$

Using this notation, the Bellman equation (4) states that Q^* is a fixed point of T, i.e., $Q^* = T(Q^*)$. The following result is also well-known.

Theorem 1. *T is a contraction with factor $\gamma < 1$ in the infinity norm, i.e., for any pair of functions Q and Q', it is true that $\|T(Q) - T(Q')\|_\infty \le \gamma \|Q - Q'\|_\infty$.*

The Q-value iteration (Q-iteration, for short) algorithm starts from an arbitrary Q-function Q_0 and in each iteration κ updates the Q-function using the formula $Q_{\kappa+1} = T(Q_\kappa)$. From Theorem 1, it follows that T has a unique fixed point, and since from (4) this point is Q^*, the iterative scheme converges to Q^* as $\kappa \to \infty$.

Q-iteration uses an *a priori* model of the task, in the form of the transition and reward functions f, ρ. There also exist algorithms that do not require an *a priori* model. Model-free algorithms like Q-learning work without an explicit model, by learning directly the optimal Q-function from real or simulated experience in the environment. Model-learning algorithms like Dyna estimate a model from experience and use it to derive Q^* [1].

3   Q-iteration with Function Approximation

In general, the implementation of Q-iteration (5) requires that Q-values are stored and updated explicitly for each state-action pair. If some of the state or action variables are continuous, the number of state-action pairs is infinite, and an exact implementation is impossible. Instead, approximate solutions must be used. Even if the number of state-action pairs is finite but very large, exact Q-iteration might be impractical, and it is useful to approximate the Q-function.

The following mappings are defined in order to formalize approximate Q-iteration (the notation follows [17]).

1. The *Q-iteration* mapping T, defined by equation (5).
2. The *approximation* mapping $F : \mathbb{R}^n \to \mathcal{Q}$, which for a given value of the parameter vector $\theta \in \mathbb{R}^n$ produces an approximate Q-function $\widehat{Q} = F(\theta)$. In other words, the parameter vector θ is a finite representation of $\widehat{Q}$.
3. The *projection* mapping $P : \mathcal{Q} \to \mathbb{R}^n$, which given a target Q-function Q computes the parameter vector θ such that $F(\theta)$ is as close as possible to Q (e.g., in a least-squares sense).

The notation $[F(\theta)](x, u)$ refers to the value of the Q-function $F(\theta)$ for the state-action pair (x, u). The notation $[P(Q)]_l$ refers to the l-th component in the parameter vector $P(Q)$.

Approximate Q-iteration starts with an arbitrary (e.g., identically 0) parameter vector θ_0 and at each iteration κ updates it using the composition of the
mappings P, T, and F:

$$\theta_{\kappa+1} = PTF(\theta_\kappa) \tag{6}$$

Unfortunately, the approximate Q-iteration is not guaranteed to converge for
an arbitrary approximator. Counter-examples can be found for the related value-
iteration algorithm (e.g., [11]), but they apply directly to the Q-iteration algorithm, as well. One particular case in which approximate Q-iteration converges
is when the composite mapping PTF is a contraction [11,13]. This property will
be used below to show that fuzzy Q-iteration converges.

4 Fuzzy Q-iteration

In this section, we propose a fuzzy approximation architecture similar to those
previously used in combination with Q-learning [4,6], and apply it to the model-
based Q-iteration algorithm. The theoretical properties of the resulting fuzzy
Q-iteration algorithm are investigated in Section 5.

In the sequel, it is assumed that the action space is discrete. We denote it by
$U_0 = \{u_j | j = 1, \ldots, M\}$. For instance, this discrete set can be obtained from the
discretization of an originally continuous action space. The state space can be
either continuous or discrete. In the latter case, fuzzy approximation is useful
when the number of discrete states is large.

The proposed approximation scheme relies on a fuzzy partition of the state
space into N sets $\mathcal{X}_i$, each described by a membership function $\mu_i : X \to [0, 1]$.
A state x belongs to each set i with a degree of membership $\mu_i(x)$. In the sequel
the following assumptions are made:

1. The fuzzy partition has been normalized, i.e., $\sum_{i=1}^{N} \mu_i(x) = 1$, $\forall x \in X$.
2. All the fuzzy sets in the partition are normal and have singleton cores, i.e.,
   for every i there exists a unique x_i for which $\mu_i(x_i) = 1$ (consequently,
   $\mu_{\underline{i}}(x_i) = 0$ for all $\underline{i} \neq i$ by Assumption 1). The state x_i is called the core
   (center value) of the set $\mathcal{X}_i$. This second assumption is required here for
   brevity in the description and analysis of the algorithms; it can be relaxed
   using results of [11].

For two examples of fuzzy partitions that satisfy the above conditions, see
Figure 1, from Section 6.

The fuzzy approximator stores an $N \times M$ matrix of parameters, with one component $\theta_{i,j}$ corresponding to each core-action pair (x_i, u_j).[4] The approximator
takes as input a state-action pair (x, u_j) and outputs the Q-value:

$$\hat{Q}(x, u_j) = [F(\theta)](x, u_j) = \sum_{i=1}^{N} \mu_i(x)\theta_{i,j} \tag{7}$$

---

[4] The matrix arrangement is adopted for convenience of notation only. For the theoretical study of the algorithms, the collection of parameters is still regarded as a
vector, leading e.g., to $\|\theta\|_\infty = \max_{i,j} |\theta_{i,j}|$.

Algorithm 1. Synchronous fuzzy Q-iteration

1: $\theta_0 \leftarrow 0$; $\kappa \leftarrow 0$
2: **repeat**
3:      **for** $i = 1, \ldots, N, j = 1, \ldots, M$ **do**
4:          $\theta_{\kappa+1,i,j} \leftarrow \rho(x_i, u_j) + \gamma \max_j \sum_{\underline{i}=1}^{N} \mu_{\underline{i}}(f(x_i, u_j))\theta_{\kappa,\underline{i},\underline{j}}$
5:      **end for**
6:      $\kappa \leftarrow \kappa + 1$
7: **until** $\|\theta_\kappa - \theta_{\kappa-1}\|_\infty \leq \delta$

This is a linear basis-functions form, with the basis functions only depending on the state. The approximator (7) can be regarded as M distinct approximators, one for each of the M discrete actions.

The projection mapping infers from a Q-function the values of the approximator parameters according to the relation:

$$\theta_{i,j} = [P(Q)]_{i,j} = Q(x_i, u_j) \tag{8}$$

Note this is the solution θ to the problem:

$$\sum_{i=1,\ldots,N,j=1,\ldots,M} |[F(\theta)](x_i, u_j) - Q(x_i, u_j)|^2 = 0$$

The approximator (7), (8) shares some strong similarities with several classes of approximators that have already been used in RL: interpolative representations [11], averagers [13], and representative-state techniques [19].

The Q-iteration algorithm using the approximation mapping (7) and projection mapping (8) can be written as Algorithm 1. To establish the equivalence between Algorithm 1 and the approximate Q-iteration in the form (6), observe that the right-hand side in line 4 of Algorithm 1 corresponds to $[T(\widehat{Q}_\kappa)](x_i, u_j)$, where $\widehat{Q}_\kappa = F(\theta_\kappa)$. Hence, line 4 can be written $\theta_{\kappa+1,i,j} \leftarrow [PTF(\theta_\kappa)]_{i,j}$ and the entire **for** loop described by lines 3–5 is equivalent to (6).

Algorithm 2 is a different version of fuzzy Q-iteration, that makes more efficient use of the updates by using the latest updated values of the parameters θ in each step of the computation. Since the parameters are updated in an asynchronous fashion, this version is called *asynchronous Q-iteration* (in Algorithm 2 parameters are updated in sequence, but they can actually be updated in any order and our results still hold). Although the exact version of asynchronous Q-iteration is widely used [1, 2], the asynchronous variant has received little attention in the context of approximate RL. To differentiate between the two versions, Algorithm 1 is hereafter called *synchronous fuzzy Q-iteration*.

5   Convergence of Fuzzy Q-iteration

In this section, the convergence of synchronous and asynchronous fuzzy Q-iteration is established, i.e., it is shown that there exists a parameter vector θ^* such that for both algorithms, $\theta_\kappa \to \theta^*$ as $\kappa \to \infty$. In addition, asynchronous

---

Algorithm 2. Asynchronous fuzzy Q-iteration

1: $\theta_0 \leftarrow 0$; $\kappa \leftarrow 0$
2: **repeat**
3:     $\theta \leftarrow \theta_\kappa$
4:     **for** $i = 1, \ldots, N, j = 1, \ldots, M$ **do**
5:         $\theta_{i,j} \leftarrow \rho(x_i, u_j) + \gamma \max_{\underline{j}} \sum_{\underline{i}=1}^{N} \mu_{\underline{i}}(f(x_i, u_j))\theta_{\underline{i},\underline{j}}$
6:     **end for**
7:     $\theta_{\kappa+1} \leftarrow \theta$
8:     $\kappa \leftarrow \kappa + 1$
9: **until** $\|\theta_\kappa - \theta_{\kappa-1}\|_\infty \leq \delta$

---

fuzzy Q-iteration is shown to converge at least as fast as the synchronous version. The distance between $F(\theta^*)$ and the true optimum Q^*, as well as the suboptimality of the greedy policy in $F(\theta^*)$, are also shown to be bounded [11,13]. The consistency of fuzzy Q-iteration, i.e., the convergence to the optimal Q-function Q^* as the maximum distance between the cores of adjacent fuzzy sets goes to 0, is not studied here, and is a topic for future research.

Proposition 1. *Synchronous fuzzy Q-iteration (Algorithm 1) converges.*

Proof. The proof follows from the proof of convergence of (synchronous) value iteration with averagers [13], or with interpolative representations [11]. This is because fuzzy approximation is an averager by the definition in [13], and an interpolative representation by the definition in [11]. The main idea of the proof is that PTF is a contraction with factor $\gamma < 1$, i.e., $\|PTF(\theta) - PTF(\theta')\|_\infty \leq \gamma \|\theta - \theta'\|_\infty$, for any θ, θ'. This is true thanks to the non-expansive nature of P and F, and because T is a contraction.   □

It is shown next that asynchronous fuzzy Q-iteration (Algorithm 2) converges. The convergence proof is similar to that for *exact* asynchronous value iteration [2].

Proposition 2. *Asynchronous fuzzy Q-iteration (Algorithm 2) converges.*

Proof. Denote $n = N \cdot M$, and rearrange the matrix θ into a vector in $\mathbb{R}^n$, placing first the elements of the first row, then the second etc. The element at row i and column j of the matrix is now the l-th element of the vector, with $l = (i-1) \cdot M + j$.
    Define for all $l = 0, \ldots, n$ recursively the mappings $S_l : \mathbb{R}^n \rightarrow \mathbb{R}^n$ as:

$$S_0(\theta) = \theta, \quad [S_l(\theta)]_{\underline{l}} = \begin{cases} [PTF(S_{l-1}(\theta))]_{\underline{l}} & \text{if } \underline{l} = l \\ [S_{l-1}(\theta)]_{\underline{l}} & \text{if } \underline{l} \in \{1, \ldots, n\} \setminus l \end{cases}$$

In words, S_l corresponds to updating the first l parameters using approximate asynchronous Q-iteration, and S_n is a complete iteration of the approximate asynchronous algorithm. Now we show that S_n is a contraction, i.e.,

$\|S_n(\theta) - S_n(\theta')\|_\infty \leq \gamma \|\theta - \theta'\|_\infty$, for any θ, θ'. This can be done element-by-element. By the definition of S_l, the first element is only updated by S_1:

$$\begin{aligned}
|[S_n(\theta)]_1 - [S_n(\theta')]_1| &= |[S_1(\theta)]_1 - [S_1(\theta')]_1| \\
&= |[PTF(\theta)]_1 - [PTF(\theta')]_1| \\
&\leq \gamma \|\theta - \theta'\|_\infty
\end{aligned}$$

The last step follows from the contraction mapping property of PTF.

Similarly, the second element is only updated by S_2:

$$\begin{aligned}
|[S_n(\theta)]_2 - [S_n(\theta')]_2| &= |[S_2(\theta)]_2 - [S_2(\theta')]_2| \\
&= |[PTF(S_1(\theta))]_2 - [PTF(S_1(\theta'))]_2| \\
&\leq \gamma \|S_1(\theta) - S_1(\theta')\|_\infty \\
&= \gamma \max\{|[PTF(\theta)]_1 - [PTF(\theta')]_1|, \\
&\qquad\quad |\theta_2 - \theta'_2|, \ldots, |\theta_n - \theta'_n|\} \\
&\leq \gamma \|\theta - \theta'\|_\infty
\end{aligned}$$

where $\|S_1(\theta) - S_1(\theta')\|_\infty$ is expressed by direct maximization over its elements, and the contraction mapping property of PTF is used twice. Continuing in this fashion, we obtain $|[S_n(\theta)]_l - [S_n(\theta')]_l| \leq \gamma \|\theta - \theta'\|_\infty$ for all l, and thus S_n is a contraction. Therefore, asynchronous fuzzy Q-iteration converges. $\qquad\square$

This proof is actually more general, showing that approximate asynchronous Q-iteration converges for any approximation mapping F and projection mapping P for which PTF is a contraction. It can also be easily shown that synchronous and fuzzy Q-iteration converge to the same parameter vector; indeed, the repeated application of any contraction mapping will converge to its unique fixed point regardless of whether it is applied in a synchronous or asynchronous (element-by-element) fashion.

We now show that asynchronous fuzzy Q-iteration converges at least as fast as the synchronous version. For that, we first need the following monotonicity lemma. In this lemma, as well as in the sequel, vector and function inequalities are understood to be satisfied element-wise.

Lemma 1 (Monotonicity of PTF). If $\theta \leq \theta'$, then $PTF(\theta) \leq PTF(\theta')$.

Proof. It will be shown in turn that F, T, and P are monotonous. To show that F is monotonous we show that, given $\theta \leq \theta'$, it follows that for all x, u_j:

$$[F(\theta)](x, u_j) \leq [F(\theta')](x, u_j) \quad \Leftrightarrow \quad \sum_{i=1}^N \mu_i(x)\theta_{i,j} \leq \sum_{i=1}^N \mu_i(x)\theta'_{i,j}$$

The last inequality is true by the assumption $\theta \leq \theta'$.

To show that T is monotonous we show that, given $Q \leq Q'$, it follows that:

$$\begin{aligned}
&[T(Q)](x, u) \leq [T(Q')](x, u) \\
&\Leftrightarrow \rho(x, u) + \gamma \max_{u' \in U} Q(f(x, u), u') \leq \rho(x, u) + \gamma \max_{u' \in U} Q'(f(x, u), u') \\
&\Leftrightarrow \max_{u' \in U} Q(f(x, u), u') \leq \max_{u' \in U} Q'(f(x, u), u')
\end{aligned}$$

The last inequality is true because $Q(f(x,u), u') \leq Q'(f(x,u), u')$ for all u', which follows from the assumption $Q \leq Q'$.

To show that P is monotonous we show that, given $Q \leq Q'$, it follows that for all i, j:

$$[P(Q)]_{i,j} \leq [P(Q')]_{i,j} \quad \Leftrightarrow \quad Q(x_i, u_j) \leq Q'(x_i, u_j)$$

The last inequality is true by assumption. Therefore, the composite mapping PTF is monotonous. □

Proposition 3. *If a parameter vector θ satisfies $\theta \leq PTF(\theta) \leq \theta^*$, then:*

$$(PTF)^k(\theta) \leq S^k(\theta) \leq \theta^* \quad \forall k \geq 1$$

Proof. This follows from the monotonicity of PTF, and can be shown element-wise, in a similar fashion to the proof of Proposition 2. Note that this result is an extension of Bertsekas' result on exact value iteration [2]. □

In words, Proposition 3 states that k iterations of asynchronous fuzzy Q-iteration move the parameter vector at least as close to the convergence point as k iterations of the synchronous algorithm.

The following bounds on the sub-optimality of the convergence point, and of the policy corresponding to this point, follow from [11, 13].

Proposition 4. *If the action space of the original problem is discrete and all the discrete actions are used for fuzzy Q-iteration, then the convergence point θ^* of asynchronous and synchronous fuzzy Q-iteration satisfies:*

$$\|Q^* - F(\theta^*)\|_\infty \leq \frac{2\varepsilon}{1 - \gamma} \tag{9}$$

$$\|Q^* - Q^{\widehat{h}^*}\|_\infty \leq \frac{4\gamma\varepsilon}{(1 - \gamma)^2} \tag{10}$$

where $\varepsilon = \min_{\underline{Q}} \|Q^* - \underline{Q}\|_\infty$ is the minimum distance between Q^* and any fixed point $\underline{Q}$ of the composite mapping FP, and $Q^{\widehat{h}^*}$ is the Q-function of the approximately optimal policy $\widehat{h}^*(x) = \arg\max_u [F(\theta^*)](x, u)$.

For example, any Q-function that satisfies $Q(x, u_j) = \sum_{i=1}^N \mu_i(x) Q(x_i, u_j)$ for all x, j is a fixed point of FP. In particular, if the optimal Q-function has this form, i.e., is exactly representable by the chosen fuzzy approximator, the algorithm will converge to it, and the corresponding policy will be optimal (since in this case $\varepsilon = 0$).

In this section, we have established fuzzy Q-value iteration as a theoretically sound technique to perform approximate RL in continuous-variable tasks. In addition to the convergence of both synchronous and asynchronous fuzzy Q-iteration, it was shown that the asynchronous version converges at least as fast as the synchronous one, and therefore might be more desirable in practice. When the action space is discrete, the approximation error of the resulting Q-function is bounded (9) and the sub-optimality of the resulting policy is also bounded (10) (the latter may be more relevant in practice). These bounds provide confidence in the results of fuzzy Q-iteration.

6   Example: 2-D Navigation

In this section, fuzzy Q-iteration is applied to a two-dimensional (2-D) simulated navigation problem with continuous state and action variables. A point-mass with a unit mass value (1kg) has to be steered on a rectangular surface such that it gets close to the origin in minimum time, and stays there. The state x contains the 2-D coordinates of the point mass, c_x and c_y, and its 2-D velocity: $x = [c_x, c_y, \dot{c}_x, \dot{c}_y]^T$. The motion of the point-mass is affected by friction, which can vary with the position, making the dynamics non-linear. Formally, the continuous-time dynamics of this system are:

$$\begin{bmatrix} \ddot{c}_x \\ \ddot{c}_y \end{bmatrix} = \begin{bmatrix} u_x \\ u_y \end{bmatrix} - b(c_x, c_y) \begin{bmatrix} \dot{c}_x \\ \dot{c}_y \end{bmatrix} \tag{11}$$

where the control input $u = [u_x, u_y]^T$ is a 2-D force (acceleration), and the scalar function $b(c_x, c_y)$ is the position-dependent damping coefficient (friction). All the state and action variables are bounded. The bounds are listed in Table 1, along with the meaning and units of all the variables.

Table 1. Variables for the navigation problem

Symbol	Parameter	Domain; Unit
c_x, c_y	horizontal, vertical coordinate	$[-5, 5]$ m
$\dot{c}_x, \dot{c}_y$	horizontal, vertical velocity	$[-2, 2]$ m/s
u_x, u_y	horizontal, vertical control force	$[-1, 1]$ N
b	damping coefficient	$\mathbb{R}^+$ kg/s

To obtain the transition function f for RL, time is discretized with a step of $T_s = 0.2$ s, and the dynamics (11) are numerically integrated between the sampling instants.[5] The goal of reaching the origin in minimum time is expressed by the following reward function:

$$\rho(x, u) = \begin{cases} 10 & \text{if } \|x\|_\infty \le 0.2 \\ 0 & \text{otherwise} \end{cases} \tag{12}$$

This means that the coordinates and the velocities along each axis have to be smaller than 0.2 in magnitude for the agent to get a non-zero reward.

The control force is discretized into 9 discrete values: $U_0 = \{-1, 0, 1\} \times \{-1, 0, 1\}$. These correspond to full acceleration into the 4 cardinal directions, diagonally, and no acceleration at all. Each of the individual velocity domains is partitioned into a triangular fuzzy partition with three fuzzy sets centered at $\{-2, 0, 2\}$, as in Figure 1, left. Since the triangular partition satisfies Assumptions 1, 2, the set of cores completely determines the shape of the membership functions. Triangular partitions are also used for the position coordinates. Different partitions of the position variables are used for each of the two damping landscapes considered in the sequel.

---

[5] The numerical integration algorithm is the Dormand-Prince variant of Runge-Kutta, as implemented in the MATLAB 7.2 function `ode45`.

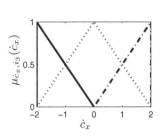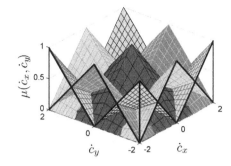

Fig. 1. *Left:* triangular fuzzy partition for $\dot{c}_x \in [-2,2]$. Each membership function is plotted in a different line style. The partition for $\dot{c}_y$ is identical. *Right:* composition of the fuzzy partitions for $\dot{c}_x, \dot{c}_y$, yielding the two-dimensional fuzzy partition for $[\dot{c}_x, \dot{c}_y]^{\mathrm{T}}$. Each membership surface is plotted in a different style. The original single-dimensional fuzzy partitions are highlighted in full black lines.

The fuzzy partition of the state space $X = [-5,5]^2 \times [-2,2]^2$ is then defined as follows. One fuzzy set is computed for each combination (i_1, i_2, i_3, i_4) of individual sets for the four state components: μ_{c_x, i_1}; μ_{c_y, i_2}; $\mu_{\dot{c}_x, i_3}$; and $\mu_{\dot{c}_y, i_4}$. The membership function of each composite set is defined as the product of the individual membership functions, applied to their individual variables:

$$\mu(x) = \mu_{c_x, i_1}(c_x) \cdot \mu_{c_y, i_2}(c_y) \cdot \mu_{\dot{c}_x, i_3}(\dot{c}_x) \cdot \mu_{\dot{c}_y, i_4}(\dot{c}_y) \qquad (13)$$

where $x = [c_x, c_y, \dot{c}_x, \dot{c}_y]^{\mathrm{T}}$. It is easy to verify that the fuzzy partition computed in this way still satisfies Assumptions 1, 2. This way of building the state space partition can be thought of as a conjunction of one-dimensional concepts corresponding to the fuzzy partitions of the individual state variables. An example of such a composition for the two velocity variables is given in Figure 1, right.

6.1   Uniform Damping Landscape

In a first, simple scenario, the damping was kept constant: $b(c_x, c_y) = b_0 = 0.5\,\mathrm{kg/s}$. Identical triangular fuzzy partitions were defined for c_x and c_y, with the cores in $\{-5, -2, -0.3, -0.1, 0, 0.1, 0.3, 2, 5\}$. Asynchronous and synchronous fuzzy Q-iteration were run with the discount factor $\gamma = 0.98$ and the threshold $\delta = 0.01$ (see Algorithms 1 and 2). The parameters γ and δ are set somewhat arbitrarily, but their variation around the given values does not significantly affect the computed policy. The asynchronous algorithm converged in 339 iterations; the synchronous one in 343. Therefore, in this particular problem, the speed of convergence for the asynchronous algorithm is close to the speed for the synchronous one (i.e., the worst-case bound). The policies computed by the two algorithms are similar.

A continuous policy was obtained by interpolating between the best local actions, using the membership degrees as weights: $\widehat{h}^*(x) = \sum_{i=1}^{N} \mu_i(x) u_{j_i^*}$, where j_i^* is the index of the best local action for the core state x_i, $j_i^* = \arg\max_j [F(\theta^*)]$ $(x_i, u_j) = \arg\max_j \theta_{i,j}^*$.

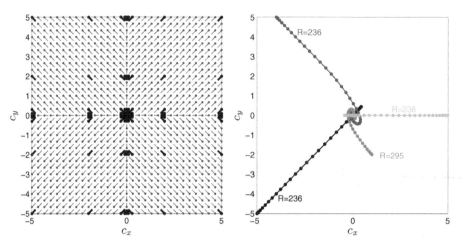

Fig. 2. *Left:* The policy for constant damping, when $\dot{c}_x = \dot{c}_y = 0$. The direction and magnitude of the control force in a grid of sample points (marked by dots) is indicated by lines. Thick, black lines indicate exact policy values in the cores of the fuzzy sets (marked by thick, black dots). *Right:* A set of representative trajectories, each given in a different shade of gray. The initial velocity is always zero. The position of the point-mass at each sample is indicated by dots. The closer the dots, the smaller the velocity is. The accumulated discounted return is displayed alongside each trajectory, rounded off toward zero.

Figure 2 presents a slice through the computed policy for zero velocity, $\widehat{h}^*(c_x, c_y, 0, 0)$, and plots some representative trajectories. The zero-velocity slice is clearly different from the optimal continuous-action policy, which would steer the agent directly towards the goal zone from any position. Also, since the actions are originally continuous, the bound (10) does not apply. Nevertheless, the zero-velocity slice presented in the figure is close to the best that can be achieved with the given action quantization.

6.2 Varying Damping Landscape

In the second scenario, to increase the difficulty of the problem, the damping (friction with the surface) varies as an affine sum of L Gaussian functions:

$$b(c_x, c_y) = b_0 + \sum_{i=1}^{L} b_i \exp\left[-\frac{(c_x - g_{x,i})^2}{\sigma_{x,i}^2} - \frac{(c_y - g_{y,i})^2}{\sigma_{y,i}^2} \right] \tag{14}$$

The chosen values were: $b_0 = 0.5$, $L = 2$, $b_1 = b_2 = 8$, $g_{x,1} = 0$, $g_{y,1} = -2.3$, $\sigma_{x,1} = 2.5$, $\sigma_{x,2} = 1.5$, and for the second Gaussian function: $g_{x,2} = 4.7$, $g_{y,2} = 1$, $\sigma_{x,2} = 1.5$, $\sigma_{y,2} = 2$. So, the damping is largest (around $8.5\,\text{kg/s}$) at positions $(0, -2.3)$ and $(4.7, 1)$. The damping variation can be observed in Figure 3, where the surface is colored darker when the damping is larger.

The fuzzy set cores for the position partition are marked by thick black dots in Figure 3, left. They were chosen based on prior knowledge about the

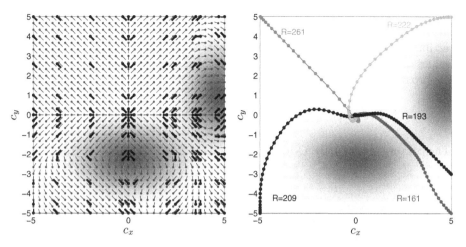

Fig. 3. *Left:* The policy for varying damping (14), when $\dot{c}_x = \dot{c}_y = 0$. Darker areas indicate larger damping. The direction and magnitude of the control force in a grid of sample points is indicated. The thick, black lines indicate exact policy values in the cores of the fuzzy partition. *Right:* A set of representative controlled trajectories with the associated returns.

position of the high-friction areas. The cores include representative points around these areas, and some points near the goal. Asynchronous and synchronous fuzzy Q-iteration were run with the same settings as before, and converged in the same number of iterations. Figure 2 presents a slice through the resulting policy for zero velocity, $\widehat{h}^*(c_x, c_y, 0, 0)$, together with several sample trajectories. It can be clearly seen how the policy steers around the high-friction areas, and how the interpolation helps in providing meaningful commands between the fuzzy cores.

6.3   Comparison with RBF Q-iteration

There exist other approximators than fuzzy partitions that could be combined with Q-iteration to yield convergent algorithms. These approximators are usually restricted classes of linear basis functions, satisfying conditions related to (but different from) Assumption 2 of Section 4. As space limitations do not allow for an extensive comparison of fuzzy Q-iteration with such algorithms, this section compares it with one of them, namely Q-iteration with normalized radial basis function (RBF) approximation.

Define a set of N normalized RBFs $\varphi_i : X \to \mathbb{R}$, $i = 1, \ldots, N$, as follows:

$$\varphi_i(x) = \frac{\underline{\varphi}_i(x)}{\sum_{i'=1}^{N} \underline{\varphi}_{i'}(x)} \ , \qquad \underline{\varphi}_i(x) = \exp\left(-\sum_{d'=1}^{d} \frac{(x_{d'} - x_{i,d'})^2}{\sigma_{i,d'}^2} \right) \qquad (15)$$

where $\underline{\varphi}_i$ are (unnormalized) Gaussian axis-oriented RBFs, x_i is the d-dimensional center of the i-th RBF, and σ_i is its d-dimensional radius. Axis-oriented RBFs were selected for a fair comparison, because the triangular fuzzy partitions are also defined separately for each variable and then combined.

Denote $\varphi(x) = [\varphi_1(x), \ldots, \varphi_N(x)]^{\mathrm{T}}$. Assume that $x_1, \ldots, x_N$ are all distinct from each other. Form the matrix $\varphi = [\varphi(x_1), \ldots, \varphi(x_N)] \in \mathbb{R}^{N \times N}$, which is invertible by construction. Define also a matrix $Q \in \mathbb{R}^{N \times M}$ that collects the Q-values of the RBF centers: $Q_{i,j} = Q(x_i, u_j)$. RBF Q-iteration uses the following approximation and projection mappings:

$$[F(\theta)](x, u_j) = \sum_{i=1}^{N} \varphi_i(x)\theta_{i,j} , \qquad P(Q) = (\varphi^{-1})^{\mathrm{T}} Q \qquad (16)$$

The convergence of RBF Q-iteration to a fixed point θ^* can be guaranteed if:

$$\sum_{i'=1, i' \neq i}^{N} \varphi_{i'}(x_i) < \frac{1 - \gamma/\gamma'}{2} \qquad (17)$$

for all i and some $\gamma' \in (\gamma, 1)$. Equation (17) restricts the sum of the values that the other RBFs take at the center of the i-th RBF. This is an extension of the result in [11] for normalized RBFs (the original result is given for un-normalized basis functions).

For a fair comparison with fuzzy Q-iteration, the number of RBFs is set equal to the number of fuzzy membership functions, and their centers are identical to the cores of the fuzzy membership functions. In order to have a set of radii ensuring convergence, that is a set of radii satisfying the inequalities (17), a problem involving linear constraints has been solved. The details of this procedure are left out due to space constraints.

When used with the same reward function and action quantization as fuzzy Q-iteration, RBF Q-iteration was unable to learn an appropriate solution. To help the algorithm, a finer quantization of the action space was provided: $U = \{-1, -0.2, 0, 0.2, 1\} \times \{-1, -0.2, 0, 0.2, 1\}$, and the reward function was changed to include a quadratic term in the state:

$$\rho(x, u) = -x'^{\mathrm{T}} \operatorname{diag}(0.2, 0.2, 0.1, 0.1) \, x' + \begin{cases} 10 & \text{if } \|x\|_\infty \leq 0.2 \\ 0 & \text{otherwise} \end{cases} \qquad (18)$$

where $x' = f(x, u)$ and $\operatorname{diag}(\cdot)$ denotes a square matrix with the elements given as arguments on the diagonal, and zeros elsewhere.

The results for varying damping are presented in Figure 4 (compare with Figure 3). A discrete policy was used, because it gave better results than the interpolated policy. To make the comparison with fuzzy Q-iteration easier, the original reward function (12) was used to compute the returns. Comparing the returns of the respective trajectories, the performance of the policy computed with RBF Q-iteration is worse than for fuzzy Q-iteration. From some of the initial states considered the RBF policy is not able to reach the goal region at all. In the left part of Figure 4, it can be seen that the RBF policy is incorrect on an entire vertical band around $c_x = 1$. Also, there is no sign that the high-damping regions are considered in the policy.[6]

---

[6] In the uniform damping case, the goal region is reached by the RBF policy from all the considered initial states, but in a longer time than using the fuzzy policy.

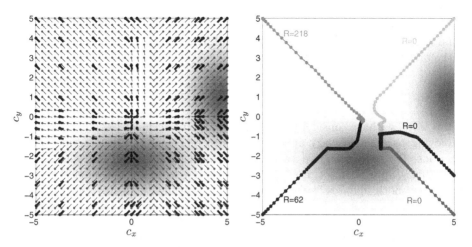

Fig. 4. *Left:* The discrete policy for RBF Q-iteration and varying damping. *Right:* A set of representative system trajectories when controlled with the RBF policy, with the associated returns.

A possible reason for the worse results of RBF approximation is that the Q-functions obtained by RBF interpolation are less smooth than those obtained with triangular fuzzy partitions (which lead essentially to multi-linear interpolation). This effect becomes more pronounced due to the convergence constraints (17) imposed on the RBF radii.

7   Possible Extensions

Although the results above were given for deterministic MDPs, fuzzy Q-iteration can be extended to stochastic problems. For instance, the asynchronous update in line 5 of Algorithm 2 becomes in the stochastic case $\theta_{i,j} \leftarrow \mathrm{E}\{\rho(x_i, u_j, x') + \gamma \max_{\underline{j}} \sum_{\underline{i}=1}^{N} \mu_{\underline{i}}(x')\theta_{\underline{i},\underline{j}}\}$. Here, x' is sampled from the density function $f(x_i, u_j, \cdot)$ of the next state given x_i and u_j. If this expectation can be computed exactly (e.g., there is a finite number of possible successor states), our results apply. In general, Monte-Carlo estimation can be used to compute the expectation. Asymptotically, as the number of samples grows to infinity, the estimate converges to the true expectation and our results can again be applied. When the number of samples is finite, [12] provides error bounds for the value iteration algorithm. These bounds could be extended to the Q-value iteration algorithm.

Fuzzy approximation can also be used online and without a model, with an arbitrary (but fixed) exploration policy, by applying the results of [17]. The same paper provides an adaptive multi-stage algorithm that converges to the true optimum as the basis functions (fuzzy membership functions, in this case) become infinitely dense in the state space.

An intermediate step is to use an offline algorithm, but with arbitrary state samples that might be different from the fuzzy cores. For this case, the dynamics and reward function of a discrete MDP with the state space equal to the set of fuzzy cores can be computed as in [19]. A solution to this discrete MDP can be computed with a model-based algorithm, and from this an approximate solution to the original problem can be derived.

8   Conclusion and Future Work

In this work, we have considered a model-based reinforcement learning approach employing parametric fuzzy approximators to represent the state-action value functions. We have proposed two different ways for updating the parameters of the fuzzy approximator, a synchronous and an asynchronous one. We have shown that both updates lead to convergent algorithms, with the asynchronous version converging at least as fast as the synchronous one. The algorithms performed well in a nonlinear control problem with four continuous state variables. Fuzzy Q-iteration also performed better than Q-iteration with normalized RBF approximation.

There exist other approximators than fuzzy partitions and RBF that could be combined with Q-iteration to yield convergent algorithms. These approximators are usually restricted classes of linear basis functions, satisfying conditions related to (but different from) Assumption 2 of Section 4. It would certainly be interesting to investigate which convergent approximator provides the best performance when combined with approximate Q-iteration.

The fuzzy approximator plays a crucial role in our approach. It determines the computational complexity of fuzzy Q-iteration, as well as the accuracy of the solution. While we considered in this paper that the membership functions were given a priori, we suggest as a future research direction to develop techniques to determine for a given accuracy an approximator with a small number of membership functions. The computational cost of these techniques should not be larger than using a more complex, pre-designed approximator that ensures the same accuracy. Another interesting direction would be to study the consistency properties of fuzzy Q-iteration: whether the algorithm converges to the optimal solution as the distance between fuzzy cores decreases to 0.

Acknowledgement. This research is financially supported by the BSIK-ICIS project "Interactive Collaborative Information Systems" (grant no. BSIK03024), by the NWO Van Gogh grant VGP 79-99, and by the STW-VIDI project "Multi-Agent Control of Large-Scale Hybrid Systems" (DWV.6188).

References

1. Sutton, R.S., Barto, A.G.: Reinforcement Learning: An Introduction. MIT Press, Cambridge (1998)
2. Bertsekas, D.P.: Dynamic Programming and Optimal Control, 2nd edn., vol. 2. Athena Scientific (2001)
3. Watkins, C.J.C.H., Dayan, P.: Q-learning. Machine Learning 8, 279–292 (1992)

4. Glorennec, P.Y.: Reinforcement learning: An overview. In: ESIT 2000. Proceedings European Symposium on Intelligent Techniques, Aachen, Germany, September 14–15, 2000, pp. 17–35 (2000)
5. Horiuchi, T., Fujino, A., Katai, O., Sawaragi, T.: Fuzzy interpolation-based Q-learning with continuous states and actions. In: FUZZ-IEEE 1996. Proceedings 5th IEEE International Conference on Fuzzy Systems, New Orleans, US, September 8–11, 1996, pp. 594–600 (1996)
6. Jouffe, L.: Fuzzy inference system learning by reinforcement methods. IEEE Transactions on Systems, Man, and Cybernetics—Part C: Applications and Reviews 28(3), 338–355 (1998)
7. Berenji, H.R., Khedkar, P.: Learning and tuning fuzzy logic controllers through reinforcements. IEEE Transactions on Neural Networks 3(5), 724–740 (1992)
8. Berenji, H.R., Vengerov, D.: A convergent actor-critic-based FRL algorithm with application to power management of wireless transmitters. IEEE Transactions on Fuzzy Systems 11(4), 478–485 (2003)
9. Vengerov, D., Bambos, N., Berenji, H.R.: A fuzzy reinforcement learning approach to power control in wireless transmitters. IEEE Transactions on Systems, Man, and Cybernetics—Part B: Cybernetics 35(4), 768–778 (2005)
10. Lin, C.K.: A reinforcement learning adaptive fuzzy controller for robots. Fuzzy Sets and Systems 137, 339–352 (2003)
11. Tsitsiklis, J.N., Van Roy, B.: Feature-based methods for large scale dynamic programming. Machine Learning 22(1–3), 59–94 (1996)
12. Szepesvári, C., Munos, R.: Finite time bounds for sampling based fitted value iteration. In: ICML 2005. Proceedings Twenty-Second International Conference on Machine Learning, Bonn, Germany, August 7–11, 2005, pp. 880–887 (2005)
13. Gordon, G.: Stable function approximation in dynamic programming. In: ICML 1995. Proceedings Twelfth International Conference on Machine Learning, Tahoe City, US, July 9–12, 1995, pp. 261–268 (1995)
14. Wiering, M.: Convergence and divergence in standard and averaging reinforcement learning. In: Boulicaut, J.-F., Esposito, F., Giannotti, F., Pedreschi, D. (eds.) ECML 2004. LNCS (LNAI), vol. 3201, pp. 477–488. Springer, Heidelberg (2004)
15. Ormoneit, D., Sen, S.: Kernel-based reinforcement learning. Machine Learning 49(2–3), 161–178 (2002)
16. Ernst, D., Geurts, P., Wehenkel, L.: Tree-based batch mode reinforcement learning. Journal of Machine Learning Research 6, 503–556 (2005)
17. Szepesvári, C., Smart, W.D.: Interpolation-based Q-learning. In: ICML 2004. Proceedings Twenty-First International Conference on Machine Learning, Bannf, Canada, July 4–8, 2004 (2004)
18. Singh, S.P., Jaakkola, T., Jordan, M.I.: Reinforcement learning with soft state aggregation. In: NIPS 1994. Advances in Neural Information Processing Systems 7, Denver, US, pp. 361–368 (1994)
19. Ernst, D.: Near Optimal Closed-loop Control. Application to Electric Power Systems. PhD thesis, University of Liège, Belgium (March 2003)
20. Munos, R., Moore, A.: Variable-resolution discretization in optimal control. Machine Learning 49(2–3), 291–323 (2002)
21. Sherstov, A., Stone, P.: Function approximation via tile coding: Automating parameter choice. In: Zucker, J.-D., Saitta, L. (eds.) SARA 2005. LNCS (LNAI), vol. 3607, pp. 194–205. Springer, Heidelberg (2005)

Using Evolutionary Game-Theory to Analyse the Performance of Trading Strategies in a Continuous Double Auction Market

Kai Cai[1], Jinzhong Niu[1], and Simon Parsons[1,2]

[1] Department of Computer Science, Graduate Center, City University of New York,
365 5th Avenue, New York, NY 10016, USA
{kcai,jniu}@gc.cuny.edu
[2] Department of Computer and Information Science, Brooklyn College,
City University of New York, 2900 Bedford Avenue, Brooklyn, NY 11210, USA
parsons@sci.brooklyn.cuny.edu

Abstract. In agent-based computational economics, many different trading strategies have been proposed. Given the kinds of market that such trading strategies are employed in, it is clear that the performance of the strategies depends heavily on the behavior of other traders. However, most trading strategies are studied in homogeneous populations, and those tests that have been carried out on heterogeneous populations are limited to a small number of strategies. In this paper we extend the range of strategies that have been exposed to a more extensive analysis, measuring the performance of eight trading strategies using an approach based on evolutionary game theory.

1 Introduction

An *auction*, according to [2], is a market mechanism in which messages from traders include some price information — this information may be an offer to buy at a given price, a *bid*, or an offer to sell at a given price, an *ask* — and which gives priority to higher bids and lower asks. The rules of the auction determine, on the basis of the offers that have been made, the allocation of goods and money between traders. Auctions have been widely used in solving real-world resource allocation problems [9], and in structuring stock or futures exchanges [2]. Auctions are used for three reasons: (i) to increase the speed of sale by providing a public forum where buyers and sellers can look for trading partners (ii) to reveal information about traders' valuations allowing efficient transactions to take place, and (iii) to prevent dishonest dealing between the representatives of the seller and the buyer.

There are many different kinds of auction. One of the most widely used is the *double auction* (DA), in which both buyers and sellers are allowed to exchange offers simultaneously. The flexibility of double auctions means that their study is of great importance, both to theoretical economists and those seeking to implement real-world market places. The *continuous double auction* (CDA) is a DA in which traders make deals continuously throughout the auction (rather than, for example, at the end of the auction). The CDA is one of the most common exchange institutions, and is in fact the primary institution

K. Tuyls et al. (Eds.): Adaptive Agents and MAS III, LNAI 4865, pp. 44–59, 2008.
© Springer-Verlag Berlin Heidelberg 2008

for trading of equities, commodities and derivatives in markets such as New York Stock Exchange (NYSE) and Chicago Mercantile Exchange.

Models of CDAs have been extensively studied using both human traders and computerized agents. Starting in 1955, Smith carried out numerous experiments investigating the behavior of such markets, documented in papers such as [22,23]. The experiments in [22], for example, involved human traders and showed that even with limited information available, and only a few participants, the CDA can achieve very high efficiency, comes close to the theoretical equilibrium, and responds rapidly to changing market conditions. This result was in contrast to classical theory, which suggested that high efficiency would require a very large number of traders. Smith's results led to the suggestion that double auction markets are bound to lead to efficiency irrespective of the way that traders behave. Gode and Sunder [6] tested this hypothesis, introducing two automated trading strategies which they dubbed "zero-intelligence". The two strategies Gode and Sunder studied were *zero intelligence without constraint* (ZI-U) and *zero intelligence with constraint* (ZI-C). ZI-U traders make offers at random, while ZI-C traders make offers at random, but are constrained so as to ensure that traders do not make a loss (it is clear that ZI-U traders can make a loss, and so can easily lead to low efficiency markets). In the experiments reported in [6], the ZI-C traders gained high efficiency and came close enough to the performance of human traders that Gode and Sunder claimed that trader intelligence is not necessary for the market to achieve high efficiency and that only the constraint on not making a loss is important[1].

This position was attacked by Cliff and Bruten [1], who showed that if supply and demand are asymmetric, the average transaction prices of ZI-C traders can vary significantly from the theoretical equilibrium[2]. They then introduced the *zero intelligence plus* (ZIP) trader, which uses a simple machine learning technique to decide what offers to make based on previous offers and the trades that have taken place. ZIP traders outperform ZI-C traders, achieving both higher efficiency and approaching equilibrium more closely across a wider range of market conditions (though [1][page 60] suggests conditions under which ZIP will fail to attain equilibrium), prompting Cliff and Bruten to suggest that ZIP traders embodied the minimal intelligence required.

A range of other trading algorithms have been proposed — including those that took part in the Santa Fe double auction tournament [18,19], the reinforcement learning *Roth-Erev* approach (RE) [17] and the expected-profit maximizing *Gjerstad-Dickhaut* approach (GD) [5] — and the performance of these algorithms have been evaluated under various market conditions. However, many of the studies of trader behavior leave something to be desired. In particular, those described above, with the honorable exception of the Santa Fe tournament [18], concentrated on the efficiency of markets as a whole and on markets in which the population of traders was homogeneous (in other words they all used the same strategy for deciding what to bid).

---

[1] In fact, for the markets tested in [6], even the ZI-U traders achieved pretty high efficiency, they were just outperformed by ZI-C traders in this regard.

[2] The experiments in [6], while reflecting typical market conditions, might be considered to represent easy conditions from which to attain equilibrium. In contrast, the experiments in [22] show convergence to equilibrium from a much wider range of initial conditions.

Both of these aspects are unsatisfactory from the perspective of someone who is interested in deciding whether to use a specific automated trader in a given market. If you want to adopt a trading agent to bid on your behalf, you don't much care about the efficiency of the market. What you care about is the profit you will make, and you'll quite happily use a ZI-C trader if it makes you more profit than a ZIP trader. Furthermore, even if we look at profit, it is not enough to know what a given type of trader will do in a homogeneous population. You're only going to want to use that ZI-C trader if you know that it will get you a good profit across all possible combinations of traders that you will encounter (in a game-theoretic sense you'd like adopting the ZI-C trader to be a dominant strategy). Tesauro and Das addressed both these problems [24]. In their paper, they examined the profit generated by a modified version of GD (MGD), ZI-C, ZIP, and the Kaplan strategy [19] from the Santa Fe double auction tournament in both homogeneous populations and mixed populations. The mixed populations studied in [24] were made up of two different kinds of trader, with one trader of one type, and the remainder of the traders being of the second type[3].

One way to consider the results of the kind of study carried out in in [24] is as an analysis of the stability of a homogeneous population. If the analysis shows that a single trader using strategy A in a population of B traders gets a higher profit than a homogeneous population of traders using strategy B, then there is an incentive to introduce a single A trader into a homogeneous B population, and that population is not stable. However, this kind of analysis does not say whether introducing a second A trader, or a third, or a fourth will necessarily be appropriate. As a result, these "one-to-many" experiments, while they will tell us something about the relative merits of A and B, will not give us any idea of the optimal mixture of traders (or, alternatively, what is the best strategy to adopt given the existing mix). To get closer to identifying the optimal mix, Walsh *et al.* [26] adopted techniques from evolutionary game theory, and applied them to more complex mixtures of trading strategies than were used in [24], an approach that has become known as *heuristic strategy analysis*. In particular, one can compute plausible equilibria for heterogeneous populations, and thus identify combinations of trading strategies that are likely to be adopted (assuming that traders are picked from a limited pool of possible strategies).

This paper extends the work of [24] and [26] exploring a larger set of trading strategies, thus expanding our understanding of the interaction between trading strategies, and giving us a more complete understanding of the possible equilibria that may arise in a continuous double auction. Such an analysis can also provide the groundwork for learning new kinds of trading strategy, as illustrated in [13], as well as for evaluating new varieties of auction such as those in [11].

2 Preliminaries

In this section we describe the precise scenario that we analyse in the rest of the paper.

---

[3] The same kind of analysis was later carried used by Vytelingum *et al.* to evaluate their risk-based bidding strategy [25].

2.1   The Market

We are concerned with a specific kind of continuous double auction market (CDA). We have a population of traders, each of which is either a buyer or seller. Buyers have a supply of money which they seek to exchange for a certain kind of good, and sellers have a supply of that good which they seek to exchange for money. Each trader has a *private value* that specifies the value that they place on each unit of the good. Once the market opens, buyers place *bids*, specifying to all other traders in the market the amount of money that they are willing to exchange for a unit of the good (though we deal with traders that wish to trade multiple units of the good, they do this sequentially). Sellers make *asks*, specifying the amount of money they require in exchange for a unit of the good. We use the terms *offer* and *shout* to mean either a bid or an ask.

The market is controlled by an auctioneer, who notes all the offers, and, as each offer is made (offers are made sequentially in the implementation we use) compares the highest bid with the lowest ask. If the highest bid is higher, or equal to, the lowest ask, the offers are *matched*, and the auctioneer establishes a *trade price* or *sale price*. The trade price is constrained to be no greater than the bid price and no less than the ask price — the auctioneer chooses the trade price to fall in this bid/ask spread[4]. A trader with an offer that is matched is obligated to make the exchange at the trade price. (The existence of the auctioneer, and the obligation to trade once offers have matched distinguish our setup from, for example, that in the Santa Fe tournament where traders identified matches for themselves, and could choose whether or not to exchange when matches occurred [18].) If a bid is higher than two or more asks, the auctioneer gives priority to the lower ask, and if an ask is made that is lower than two or more bids, the auctioneer gives priority to the higher bid.

2.2   The Traders

The traders we consider in this paper are all automated — what economists would call *program traders*. Each trader uses a specific strategy to choose what offers to make. The trading strategies we study in this paper are a mixture of established strategies from the literature, and some that we came up with ourselves. Those from the literature are:

- Zero Intelligence with Constraint (ZI-C), as introduced by Gode and Sunder [6]. Traders employing this strategy submit offers that are generated randomly subject to a simple constraint. This constraint states that bids are drawn from a uniform distribution between the buyer's private value and a specified lower bound (typically 0) while asks are restricted to the range between seller's private value and a specified higher bound (a value higher than any trader thinks the good in question is worth).
- Zero Intelligence Plus (ZIP), as introduced in [1]. ZIP traders use a simple heuristic to adjust their offers. Broadly speaking, traders increase their profit margin[5] if recent market activity suggests that doing so will still allow them to trade, and reduce

---

[4] Typical rules for choosing where to set the trade price are to set it in the middle of the bid/ask spread, or to set it to the value of the earlier of the two offers to be made.

[5] The profit margin for a trader is the difference between their private value and their offer price.

their profit margin if recent market activity suggests they are making offers too far from where the market is trading. The traders employ a simple form of machine learning to adjust their offers, smoothing out fluctuations in the market.

- Truth-Telling (TT). Traders using this strategy submit shouts equal to their private value for the resource being traded. TT is an interesting strategy to experiment with since in strategy-proof markets[6] TT will be a dominant strategy. The failure of TT to dominate is thus an indication of the degree to which traders in a particular market can benefit by clever strategic behavior.
- Pure Simple (PS), is an inadvertent copy of the strategy "Gamer" which was an entrant in the Santa Fe tournament [19][page 90][7], and traders using PS bid a constant 10% below their private value. This is not a strategy that one would expect to perform well — Gamer placed 24th out of 30 entries in the Santa Fe tournament — but, like TT is a useful control, and one that comfortably out-performs TT. Indeed, as shown in [27], with the right choice of margin, PS can be very efficient.
- Roth-Erev (RE), introduced in [17], is a strategy that considers the problem of what offer to make as being a reinforcement learning problem. RE experiments, making offers and recording how many times they are successful, and makes choices based on the expected value of each possible offer, computed using the past probability of success. We set the free parameters of RE as described in [10].
- Gjerstad-Dickhaut (GD) as introduced in [5]. A GD trader makes its decision on what to offer based on previous offers, but unlike RE, GD uses offers made by all other traders. A GD trader uses this list of past offers to estimate the likelihood of any sensible bid (that is one in the gap between the highest bid and the lowest ask at the time the offer is made) being accepted, and uses this probability distribution to compute the offer with the highest expected profit.

Those we came up with are:

- Linear Gjerstad-Dickhaut (GDL). GD runs more slowly than other trading strategies that we have been using, and it spends most of its time computing the probability of offers being accepted — it computes this by fitting recent offers to a cubic equation, and then uses the cubic to define the cumulative probability of a given offer being accepted. Frustrated by the running time of experiments that used GD, we replaced the cubic with a piecewise linear approximation to create GDL, which runs considerably faster, hoping that the performance drop would not be too great.
- Estimated Equilibrium Price (EEP). If all traders are rational (in other words make profitable offers) and make offers around the theoretical equilibrium, then the market will be efficient. Thus bidding at the theoretical equilibrium is good for the market as a whole. We were interested to test whether bidding at the theoretical equilibrium is also good for individual agents and EEP is an attempt to evaluate this. EEP seeks to make offers at the theoretical equilibrium, estimating this as the mid-point of the highest accepted ask and the lowest accepted bid so far, and so our estimate of the equilibrium is similar to of [25].

---

[6] A strategy proof market, such as that discussed in [8], is one in which traders cannot manipulate results in their favor by misrepresenting the extent to which they value resources.

[7] The copy was inadvertent since we devised PS in ignorance of the existence of Gamer.

This is, clearly, not an exhaustive selection — we could, for instance, have included the RB strategy from [25] — but is a large enough set of strategies to be going on with.

Note that though the many of the strategies we use are *adaptive*, in the sense that the offers they make change over time in response to other offers, a given trader uses the same strategy throughout a given auction. This contrasts with the work of Posada [15,16] which studies agents that are allowed to switch bidding strategy during an auction.

2.3 The Simulation Environment

All of the experiments reported here are based on the open-source JASA auction simulator [12], devised by Steve Phelps of the University of Liverpool. The current version of JASA implements a CDA marketplace much as described in [24] as well as all the trading strategies described above. In JASA the auction runs for a number of *days*, and each day is broken up into discrete *rounds*. In each round, every trader is selected to make an offer, and this selection takes place in a random order. At the end of every day, every trader has its initial allocation of goods and money replenished, so that trading on every day in a given experiment takes place under the same conditions, but trading strategies that record information will remember what took place in previous days.

We ran every experiment described here for five trading days, and each day consisted of 300 rounds. The private values of traders are drawn at the start of the first trading day of each experiment from a uniform distribution between 100 and 200. Every experiment was repeated 100 times.

3 Heterogeneous Trading Populations

In this section we describe the first series of experiments we carried out with mixed populations of traders. The methodology used for this series of experiments is that of [24], outlined above. For the first group of experiments we used 20 traders, 10 buyers and 10 sellers. For each of the eight trading strategies, we ran an experiment in which all but one agent used that strategy and the remaining agent used another strategy, carrying out one such "one-in-many" experiment for each of the other strategies. In other words, we tested every "one-in-many" combination. For all these experiments, we measured the average profit of traders using both the trading strategies under test.

Tables 1 and 2 show the results of "one-in-many" tests for the first group of experiments, those involving 20 agents. Note that the standard deviations of the payoffs are usually high, as a result of the fact that we are picking the private value of the "one" agent at random. As a result it is inevitable that there will be times when the "one" agent is an extra-marginal trader[8] because it has a low private value (the "one" agent is always a buyer) and in a market of savvy traders will not make any profit. Such occurrences will increase the standard deviation. Since the high standard deviations make direct comparisons of the profits difficult, we carried out hypothesis tests (in particular t-tests) to find out the confidence level for the "one" to "many" pairs of payoffs.

---

[8] An extra-marginal trader is one with a private value to the right of the intersection of the supply and demand curves for the market, and so should not trade if the market operates at its theoretical equilibrium.

Table 1. Profits for agents using different trading strategies in a 20 agent CDA market. The top line of each cell gives the average value of the profits — the value to the left of colon is the average profit of the one agent, the value to the right is the average profit of the majority populations. The second line gives the standard deviation of the profit. The third line indicates whether the "one" performs better (>) or worse (<) than the "many" on average. The fourth line gives the confidence in this relationship.

	Many EEP	Many GD	Many GDL	Many PS	Many RE	Many TT	Many ZIC	Many ZIP
1-EEP	8.027	8.529: 10.038	8.33: 10.036	10.348: 9.121	11.837: 9.302	12.431: 7.584	12.383: 9.483	10.216: 9.695
stdev	(1.958)	(12.943): (0.696)	(12.514): (0.679)	(11.661): (0.852)	(13.955): (0.776)	(12.695): (0.78)	(13.957): (0.722)	(11.75): (0.636)
rel	-	<	<	>	>	>	>	<
conf	-	85.00%	90.00%	85.00%	95.00%	99.95%	97.50%	< 75%
1-GD	9.29: 8.198	9.972	8.89: 10.018	12.249: 9.194	13.271: 9.308	13.492: 7.632	13.487: 9.475	11.6: 9.637
stdev	(13.189): (1.93)	(0.024)	(13.229): (0.699)	(15.651): (0.845)	(15.749): (0.806)	(15.864): (0.861)	(14.33): (0.755)	(13.313): (0.685)
rel	>	-	<	>	>	>	>	>
conf	75.00%	-	80.00%	95.00%	99.00%	99.95%	90.00%	90.00%
1-GDL	9.598: 8.289	9.028: 10.02	9.96	12.501: 9.177	13.449: 9.285	13.87: 7.605	13.806: 9.459	11.693: 9.646
stdev	(13.773): (1.801)	(13.316): (0.704)	(0.038)	(15.571): (0.837)	(15.824): (0.829)	(15.805): (0.859)	(14.753): (0.775)	(15.1): (0.768)
rel	>	<	-	>	>	>	>	>
conf	80.00%	75.00%	-	97.50%	99.50%	99.75%	99.50%	90.00%
1-PS	4.956: 8.108	5.405: 10.189	5.313: 10.191	9.281	8.926: 9.5	10.566: 7.719	9.281: 9.708	7.129: 9.838
stdev	(7.262): (2.005)	(7.821): (0.437)	(7.617): (0.421)	(0.349)	(9.333): (0.587)	(9.039): (0.7)	(8.884): (0.522)	(8.088): (0.509)
rel	<	<	<	-	>	>	<	<
conf	99.95%	99.95%	99.95%	-	99.50%	99.75%	< 75%	99.90%

Table 2. Profits for agents using different trading strategies in a 20 agent CDA market. The top line of each cell gives the average value of the profits — the value to the left of colon is the average profit of the one agent, the value to the right is the average profit of the majority populations. The second line gives the standard deviation of the profit. The third line indicates whether the "one" performs better (>) or worse (<) than the "many" on average. The fourth line gives the confidence in this relationship.

	Many EEP	Many GD	Many GDL	Many PS	Many RE	Many TT	Many ZIC	Many ZIP
1-RE	6.88: 8.32	7.046: 10.119	6.956: 10.118	9.814: 9.319	9.422	11.339: 7.69	10.236: 9.664	10.454: 9.652
stdev	(9.081): (1.542)	(9.555): (0.519)	(9.462): (0.508)	(10.278): (0.552)	(0.237)	(9.879): (0.758)	(10.914): (0.585)	(11.549): (0.651)
rel	<	<	<	>	-	>	>	>
conf	90.00%	99.90%	99.90%	<75%	-	99.95%	<75%	75.00%
1-TT	2.951: 8.291	3.514: 10.29	3.322: 10.294	6.175: 9.364	6.011: 9.565	7.755	5.95: 9.802	4.737: 9.928
stdev	(4.353): (1.929)	(5.189): (0.307)	(4.909): (0.29)	(5.827): (0.513)	(6.072): (0.463)	(0.595)	(5.373): (0.376)	(6.301): (0.398)
rel	<	<	<	<	<	-	<	<
conf	99.95%	99.95%	99.95%	99.95%	99.95%	-	99.95%	99.95%
1-ZIC	6.864: 8.485	7.657: 10.059	7.585: 10.065	9.282: 9.386	9.795: 9.437	10.503: 7.727	9.715	8.021: 9.743
stdev	(10.387): (1.451)	(11.024): (0.593)	(10.893): (0.583)	(11.969): (0.584)	(12.907): (0.711)	(12.04): (0.84)	(0.125)	(9.485): (0.563)
rel	<	<	<	<	>	>	-	<
conf	90.00%	97.50%	97.50%	<75%	<75%	97.50%	-	95.00%
1-ZIP	8.592: 8.325	9.397: 9.984	9.704: 9.977	10.091: 9.327	11.128: 9.385	12.736: 7.678	12.098: 9.554	9.712
stdev	(12.087): (1.558)	(14.36): (0.753)	(14.507): (0.771)	(11.059): (0.637)	(11.449): (0.624)	(12.204): (0.758)	(10.166): (0.524)	(0.132)
rel	>	<	<	>	>	>	>	-
conf	<75%	<75%	<75%	75.00%	90.00%	99.95%	99.00%	-

These results give some suggestion of the complexities of bidding in continuous double auctions. If we think of Tables 1 and 2 as payoff matrices for the game where one player picks the strategy for the "one", and the other picks the strategy for the "many", we can immediately rule out TT as a choice — it is dominated. This is the same kind of analysis that is used in [25] to argue for the success of RB traders. However, we also found more complex relationships than in [24,25]. Thus, once we have eliminated TT from consideration, PS can be eliminated as a strategy for the "one", as it performs worse than any of the "many" against which it might be played, but it works as a "many" strategy against ZIC. In a similar way, ZIC is not a great performer, but as a "many" strategy will outperform PS, and as "one" strategy will outperform RE. RE performs poorly as a majority strategy, but can generate higher profits than ZIP, a strong performer, when it is the "one" (though the low confidence we have for this results suggests that this performance is not consistent).

Looking at the high performing strategies, if an agent with a strategy other than GD or GDL is in an otherwise homogeneous GD or GDL populations, that agent will do better by switching to GD or GDL. In other words, GD and GDL come close to being dominant strategies for the "one". However each prevents the other from dominating. The performance of GDL is rather impressive — it even performs slightly better than GD does when it's the lone strategy amongst a population of PS, RE, TT, EEP or ZIC strategies (in most cases both in terms of the raw average payoff and confidence that it outperforms the general population). Thus, it seems that the switch from cubic to linear approximation might not only not hurt the strategy, but might even improve it.

When we look at slightly less well-performing strategies than GD and GDL, the situation is less clear. Indeed from Tables 1 and 2 it is hard to get a good feel for the relative merits of RE, ZIP and EEP. A lone RE trader will outperform a set of ZIP traders, a lone ZIP trader will outperform sets of EEP traders and RE traders, while a lone EEP trader will outperform sets of RE and ZIP traders.

4   Evolutionary Game-Theoretic Analysis

Since we can't easily see how some combinations of strategies stack up against one another using the analysis in the previous section, we turn to a more sophisticated approach, *heuristic strategy analysis*. Heuristic strategy analysis was first proposed by Walsh et al. [26] precisely for the analysis of double auctions, and we have used it for this purpose in several papers [13,14] though on a rather smaller scale than here.

4.1   Heuristic Strategy Analysis

The idea behind the heuristic strategy analysis is as follows. If we wanted to obtain a game theoretic solution to the continuous double auction, we would need to compute a payoff matrix that gives the expected outcome for an agent that bids in a particular way. Indeed, since there is no dominant strategy[9] we would need to compute such a payoff matrix for *all* possible offers or combinations thereof (since the CDA offers multiple

---

[9] Unlike, for example, the case of the buyer's bid double auction [7].

opportunities for making offers we would need to consider all possible offers that might be made at all opportunities). Clearly such a matrix would be extremely large, and that is why there is no analytical solution to the auction [21]. However, we can get around the need to consider all possible combinations of offers. Since there are a number of powerful strategies for computing the best offer to make — exactly the ones we have been studying so far — we can reasonably assume that each trader in the auction picks one of these *heuristic strategies* and lets that strategy pick offers. Under such an assumption, not only does the game we are trying to analyse become a single step game, but the number of possible strategies reduces to those that we know work well.

Now, for small numbers of players and heuristic strategies, we can construct a relatively small normal-form payoff matrix which we can analyse using game theory. This *heuristic payoff matrix* is calibrated by running many simulations of the auction. If we restrict the analysis to symmetric games in which each agent has the same set of strategies and the same distribution of private values (or *types* in the usual terminology of game theory), we can reduce the size of the payoff matrix, since we simply need to specify the number of agents playing each strategy to determine the expected payoff to each agent. Thus for a game with k strategies, we present entries in the heuristic payoff matrix as vectors of the form:

$$p = (p_1, ...p_k) \tag{1}$$

where p_i specifies the number of agents who are playing the ith strategy. Each entry $p \in P$ is mapped onto an outcome vector $q \in Q$ of the form:

$$q = (q_1, ...q_k) \tag{2}$$

where q_i specifies the expected payoff to the ith strategy. For a game with n agents, the number of entries in the payoff matrix is given by

$$s = \frac{(n + k - 1)!}{n!(k - 1)!} \tag{3}$$

For small n and small k this results in payoff matrices of manageable size. For $n = 20$, $k = 3$, as in the experiments we consider here, the symmetric payoff matrix contains just 231 entries.

Given the payoff matrix, we have a full description of a game in which traders pick between the heuristic strategies, and we can carry out an equilibrium analysis on that game. Any equilibria that we find are only equilibria for the game of choosing between heuristic strategies, not for the game of choosing a sequence of bids in a double auction — it is possible, for example, for traders to use different heuristic strategies than the ones we have analysed, in which case the equilibrium analysis will not help. However, as argued in [13], the equilibria of the heuristic strategy game are useful precisely because they only consider strategies that are commonly known and widely used. If we consider an exhaustive set of widely used strategies, we can be confident that no commonly known strategy will generate different equilibria from the ones we find, and thus the equilibria stand some chance of persisting until new trading strategies become established.

4.2 Evolutionary Game Theory

Now, even given the heuristic payoff matrix, standard game theory does not tell us which of the many possible Nash equilibrium strategies will result. *Evolutionary game theory* [3,20] and its variants attack this problem by positing that, rather than computing the Nash strategies for a game using brute-force and then selecting one of these to play, traders are more likely to gradually adjust their strategy over time in response to to repeated observations of their own and others' payoffs. One approach to evolutionary game-theory uses the *replicator dynamics* equation to specify the frequency with which different pure strategies should be played depending on the payoffs of different strategies:

$$\dot{m}_j = [u(e_j, \boldsymbol{m}) - u(\boldsymbol{m}, \boldsymbol{m})] \, m_j \qquad (4)$$

where $\boldsymbol{m}$ is a mixed-strategy vector, $u(\boldsymbol{m}, \boldsymbol{m})$ is the mean payoff when all players play $\boldsymbol{m}$, and $u(e_j, \boldsymbol{m})$ is the average payoff to pure strategy j when all players play $\boldsymbol{m}$, and $\dot{m}_j$ is the first derivative of m_j with respect to time. Strategies that gain above-average payoff become more likely to be played, and this equation models a simple process of learning by copying, in which agents switch to strategies that appear to be more successful[10]. For any initial mix of strategies we can find the eventual outcome from this *co-evolutionary* process by solving $\dot{m}_j = 0$ for all j to find the final mixed-strategy of the converged population. This model has the attractive properties that: (i) all Nash equilibria of the game are stationary points under the replicator dynamics; and (ii) all focal points of the replicator dynamics are Nash equilibria of the evolutionary game.

What this means is that the Nash equilibrium solutions are a subset of the stationary points of the direction field of the dynamics specified by equation 4. Although not all stationary points are Nash equilibria, we can use the direction field to see which solutions are more likely to be discovered by *boundedly-rational* agents. The Nash equilibria at which a larger number of initial states will end up, are equilibria that are more likely to be reached (assuming an initial distribution that is uniform, and that the replicator dynamics is an accurate reflection of the way that traders adjust their strategy[11]).

4.3 Results

We applied the analysis as described so far to sets of strategies we used in the "one-to-many" experiments, concentrating on the strategies which we felt had the most interesting interactions. Since the computational complexity of establishing the payoff matrix depends on not only the number of traders, but also on the number of strategies, we restricted our analysis to sets of three strategies (which also makes the results easier to visualize), and for every strategy vector p, allocated the given set of strategies randomly between all traders (so that a given strategy has equal probability of being used by a buyer or a seller). Some of the results we obtained may be found in Figures 1 and 2.

---

[10] Though they switch *between* auctions rather than in the middle as in [15,16].

[11] Though the Nash equilibria cannot be disputed, the route by which they are reached is dependent upon the precise assumptions encoded in the replicator dynamics, and those, like all assumptions, are open to argument.

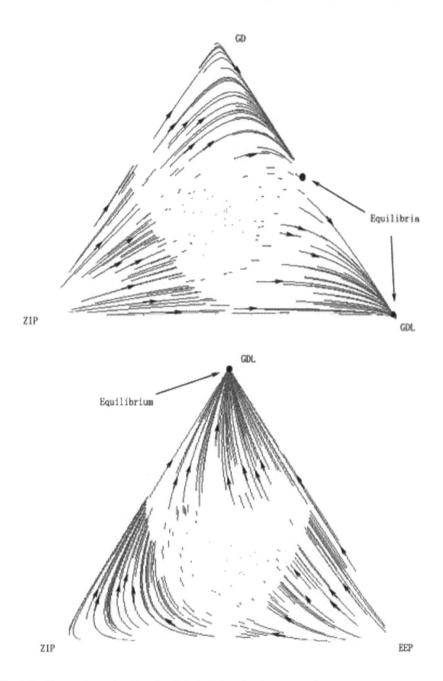

Fig. 1. Replicator dynamics direction field for 20 traders in a CDA where (top) the traders choose between the ZIP, GD and GDL strategies, and (bottom) the traders choose between the ZIP, GDL and EEP strategies

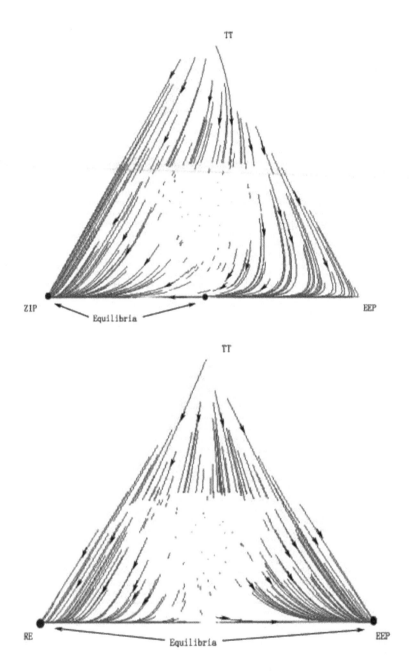

Fig. 2. Replicator dynamics direction field for 20 traders in a CDA where (top) the traders choose between the ZIP, GD and GDL strategies, and (bottom) the traders choose between the ZIP, GDL and EEP strategies

Figure 1 analyses the performance of GDL and GD. While the "one-to-many" experiments suggested that neither of these strategies dominates the other, the upper replicator dynamics plot in Figure 1 suggests that, at least in the presence of ZIP — which as [1] and our own analysis suggest is a pretty good strategy and thus a likely choice in trading scenarios — there is one equilibrium in which all traders adopt GDL, and there is another in which about half of the traders use GDL, the rest adopting GD. If we switch GD for a lesser strategy, such as EEP, as in the lower part of Figure 1, then the only equilibrium is when all traders adopt GDL.

The results in Tables 1 and 2 suggest that the relationship between ZIP and EEP deserves a little more attention since one EEP trader out performs the average ZIP trader when the latter are in a majority, while one ZIP trader will outperform the majority EEP traders. In other words, neither dominates the other. The upper part of Figure 2 shows us how this relationship plays out when the other possible strategy is TT. Here ZIP is powerful enough that it is a pure strategy equilibrium, but there is a second equilibrium in which roughly half of the traders use EEP and half use ZIP. The lower part of Figure 2 shows us that switching ZIP for RE allows EEP to become a pure strategy equilibrium and that RE is also a pure strategy equilibrium. Overall this suggests that, when faced with EEP, RE is a less powerful strategy than ZIP.

5   Conclusions

The main point of this paper is to report on work that has extended the analysis of the continuous double auction, and, in particular, the relative performance of trading strategies for making offers in the continuous double auction. As things stand, it is not clear whether there is a dominant strategy for the auction. However, if there is, then we will only discover it empirically, and the best way that we currently have for making this discovery is to continue to analyse the performance of different strategies against one another. The approach taken in this paper is one, we believe promising, way to do this. The "one-to-many" experiments that we started with allow us to identify pairs of strategies where one strategy does not dominate the other (that is when "one" of both strategies outperforms the "many" of the other). The heuristic strategy analysis experiments then home in on the relative merits of these strategies, giving us a way to compute equilibrium solutions for the continuous double auction under the assumption that traders are restricted to pick from a fixed set of trading strategies. The results we get are, as one would expect from a heuristic analysis, approximate, and not as exhaustive as the analysis of the double auction in [27]. However, unlike those of [27], our results are not restricted to a single trading strategy.

From this perspective, we can conclude three things. First, we can conclude that our analysis has shown, once again, the value of evolutionary game theory in analysing complex games. Second, we can conclude that the analysis has highlighted the powerful performance of our GDL variant of GD. Third, we can conclude that EEP, while not a winning strategy is also not a losing strategy in every situation. All of these results, though, should be taken with a pinch of salt — all performances in the CDA, as we have stressed above, are conditional on the mix of strategies present, and as [13] shows, it is perfectly possible to find (indeed, automatically generate) a strategy that beats GD.

However, given the dependence of results on the mix, the only course open to us is to keep expanding the set of strategies that are analysed in competition to each other, and with that aim our work is a straightforward extension of that of [24] and [26]. Of course, we can go further in this direction, and a natural way to do this is to extend the set of strategies with RB from [25] and the meta-strategy studied in [15,16].

Finally, we should note that the research described here, like that of [24] and [26], only views matters from the perspective of the traders. The analysis is all couched in terms of the profits generated by different strategies — as described above, this is an analysis that is appropriate from the perspective of selecting a trader to operate on one's behalf. This research will not, in contrast, tell one much about the effect of the different trading strategies on the market as a whole. For that, one must turn to work like that of [4].

Acknowledgments

This work was supported by the National Science Foundation under grant IIS-0329037. We are grateful to Steve Phelps and Peter McBurney for generously sharing code and ideas with us, to Marek Marcinkiewicz for his work on JASA, to Jeff Mackie-Mason and Michael Wellman for helpful comments, and to the anonymous reviewers for helping us to improve the paper.

References

1. Cliff, D., Bruten, J.: Minimal-intelligence agents for bargaining behaviours in market-based environments. Technical report, Hewlett-Packard Research Laboratories (1997)
2. Friedman, D.: The double auction institution: A survey. In: Friedman, D., Rust, J. (eds.) The Double Auction Market: Institutions, Theories and Evidence, pp. 3–25. Perseus Publishing, Cambridge (1993)
3. Friedman, D.: Evolutionary economics goes mainstream: A review of The Theory of Learning in Games. Journal of Evolutionary Economics 8(4), 423–432 (1998)
4. Gil-Bazo, J., Moreno, D., Tapia, M.: Price dynamics, informational efficiency and wealth distribution in continuous double auction markets. Computational Intelligence 23(2), 176–196 (2007)
5. Gjerstad, S., Dickhaut, J.: Price formation in double auctions. Games and Economic Behavior 22, 1–29 (1998)
6. Gode, D.K., Sunder, S.: Allocative efficiency of markets with zero-intelligence traders: Market as a partial substitute for individual rationality. Journal of Political Economy 101(1), 119–137 (1993)
7. Kagel, J.H., Vogt, W.: Buyer's bid double auctions: Preliminary experimental results. In: Friedman, D., Rust, J. (eds.) The Double Auction Market: Institutions, Theories and Evidence, Santa Fe Institute Studies in the Sciences of Complexity, ch. 10, pp. 285–305. Perseus Publishing, Cambridge (1993)
8. McAfee, R.P.: A dominant strategy double auction. Journal of Economic Theory 56, 343–450 (1992)
9. McMillan, J.: Reinventing the Bazaar: A Natural History of Markets. W. W. Norton & Company (2003)

10. Nicolaisen, J., Petrov, V., Tesfatsion, L.: Market power and efficiency in a computational electricity market with discriminatory double-auction pricing. IEEE Transactions on Evolutionary Computation 5(5), 504–523 (2001)

11. Niu, J., Cai, K., Parsons, S., Sklar, E.: Reducing price fluctuation in continuous double auctions through pricing policy and shout improvement. In: Proceedings of the 5th International Conference on Autonomous Agents and Multi-Agent Systems, Hakodate, Japan (2006)

12. Phelps, S.: Java auction simulator API.,
    http://sourceforge.net/projects/jasa/

13. Phelps, S., Marcinkiewicz, M., Parsons, S., McBurney, P.: A novel method for automated strategy acquisition in n-player non-zero-sum games. In: Proceedings of the 5th International Conference on Autonomous Agents and Multi-Agent Systems, Hakodate, Japan (2006)

14. Phelps, S., Parsons, S., McBurney, P.: An evolutionary game-theoretic comparision of two double auction market designs. In: Agent-Mediated Electronic Commerce VI. Springer, Heidelberg (2004)

15. Posada, M.: Srategic software agents in a continuous double auction under dynamic environments. In: Corchado, E., Yin, H., Botti, V., Fyfe, C. (eds.) IDEAL 2006. LNCS, vol. 4224, pp. 1223–1233. Springer, Heidelberg (2006)

16. Posada, M., Hernández, C., López-Paredes, A.: Strategic behaviour in continuous double auction. In: Bruun, C. (ed.) Advances in Artificial Economies: The Economy as a Complex Dynamic System. Lecture Notes in Economics and Mathematical Systems, vol. 584, pp. 31–43. Springer, Berlin (2006)

17. Roth, A.E., Erev, I.: Learning in extensive-form games: Experimental data and simple dynamic models in the intermediate term. Games and Economic Behavior 8, 164–212 (1995)

18. Rust, J., Miller, J.H., Palmer, R.: Behaviour of trading automata in a computerized double auction market. In: Friedman, D., Rust, J. (eds.) The Double Auction Market: Institutions, Theories and Evidence, pp. 155–199. Perseus Publishing, Cambridge (1993)

19. Rust, J., Miller, J.H., Palmer, R.: Characterizing effective trading strategies. Journal of Economic Dynamics and Control 18, 61–96 (1994)

20. Samuelson, L.: Evolutionary Games and Equilibrium Selection. MIT Press, Cambridge (1997)

21. Satterthwaite, M.A., Williams, S.R.: The Bayesian theory of the k-double auction. In: Friedman, D., Rust, J. (eds.) The Double Auction Market: Institutions, Theories and Evidence, pp. 99–123. Perseus Publishing, Cambridge (1993)

22. Smith, V.L.: An experimental study of competitive market behaviour. Journal of Political Economy 70(2), 111–137 (1962)

23. Smith, V.L.: Experimental auction markets and the Walrasian hypothesis. The Journal of Political Economy 73(4), 387–393 (1965)

24. Tesauro, G., Das, R.: High-performance bidding agents for the continuous double auction. In: Proceedings of the 3rd ACM Conference on Electronic Commerce (2001)

25. Vytelingum, P., Dash, R.K., David, E., Jennings, N.R.: A risk-based bidding strategy for continuous double auctions. In: Proceedings of the 16th European Conference on Artificial Intelligence, Valencia, Spain, pp. 79–83 (2004)

26. Walsh, W., Das, R., Tesauro, G., Kephart, J.O.: Analyzing complex strategic interactions in multi-agent systems. In: Proceedings of Workshop on Game-Theoretic and Decision-Theoretic Agents (2002)

27. Zhan, W., Friedman, D.: Markups in double auction markets. Technical report, LEEPS, Department of Economics, University of Santa Cruz (2005)

Parallel Reinforcement Learning with Linear Function Approximation

Matthew Grounds and Daniel Kudenko

Department of Computer Science, University of York
York, YO10 5DD, UK
{mattg,kudenko}@cs.york.ac.uk

Abstract. In this paper, we investigate the use of parallelization in reinforcement learning (RL), with the goal of learning optimal policies for *single-agent* RL problems more quickly by using parallel hardware. Our approach is based on agents using the SARSA(λ) algorithm, with value functions represented using linear function approximators. In our proposed method, each agent learns independently in a *separate* simulation of the single-agent problem. The agents periodically exchange information extracted from the weights of their approximators, accelerating convergence towards the optimal policy. We develop three increasingly efficient versions of this approach to parallel RL, and present empirical results for an implementation of the methods on a Beowulf cluster.

1 Introduction

Reinforcement learning (RL) is by far the most popular machine learning method employed in agent applications, due to its suitability to the paradigm of situated agents. However, real-world applications of RL have been hampered by the fact that the standard algorithms do not scale up well in complex feature-rich environments. Therefore, scaling up RL is of crucial importance for these techniques to make their way into practical real-world solutions.

The approach we take in this paper is to parallelize the RL process in order to speed up convergence. The primary goal of such an approach would be to find good solutions to *single-agent* learning problems more quickly than is possible using non-parallel hardware. This focus differs from most previous work on Multi-Agent Learning [1,2], which is primarily concerned with agents that share an environment and learn to coordinate or compete. While there have been preliminary analyses [3,4] demonstrating the promise of a parallel approach to RL, the cost of inter-agent communication has tended to be excluded from the analysis. There are currently no parallel algorithms for RL that are practical for solving large-scale problems using real parallel hardware.

In this paper, we present an approach where the parallel agents learn using identical simulations of a given single-agent RL domain. Each parallel agent uses SARSA, a popular RL algorithm, and represents its value function using a *linear function approximator*. The features of the approximator are generated using tile-coding [5]. Agents extract information from their value functions which

K. Tuyls et al. (Eds.): Adaptive Agents and MAS III, LNAI 4865, pp. 60–74, 2008.

is then exchanged by passing messages over a limited bandwidth network. By aggregating the information each agent has learned from the environment, the agents converge more quickly towards an optimal policy. We first present an algorithm where agents periodically *merge* their approximators, then refine the method to reduce its communication overhead. Finally, we define a similar asynchronous algorithm which eliminates the synchronization penalty suffered by the other algorithms. A Beowulf cluster of networked Linux computers provides the basis for a true parallel implementation of the method.

2   Reinforcement Learning Background

A reinforcement learning problem can be described formally as a *Markov Decision Process* (MDP). An MDP is a tuple $< S, A, T, R >$, where S is a set of problem states, A is a set of actions, $T(s, a, s') \rightarrow [0, 1]$ is a function which defines the probability that taking action a in state s will result in a transition to state s', and $R(s, a, s') \rightarrow \mathcal{R}$ defines the reward received when such a transition is made.

If all the parameters of the MDP are known, an optimal policy can be found by *dynamic programming*. If T and R are initially unknown, however, then RL methods can learn an optimal policy from *direct interaction with the environment*.

2.1   SARSA

The SARSA algorithm [6] is a well-established reinforcement learning method, perhaps not as popular as Q-learning [5], but with properties that often make it more stable than Q-learning when combined with a function approximator [7]. The SARSA algorithm is used to learn the function $Q^\pi(s, a)$, defined as the *expected total discounted return* when starting in state s, executing action a and thereafter using the policy π to choose actions:

$$Q^\pi(s, a) = \sum_{s'} T(s, a, s') \left[R(s, a, s') + \gamma Q^\pi(s', \pi(s')) \right]$$

The discount factor $\gamma \in [0, 1]$ determines the relative importance of short term and long term rewards. For each s and a we store a floating point number $Q(s, a)$ for the current estimate of $Q^\pi(s, a)$. As experience tuples $< s, a, r, s', a' >$ are generated through interaction with the environment, a table of state-action values is updated using the following rule:

$$Q(s, a) \leftarrow (1 - \alpha)Q(s, a) + \alpha(r + \gamma Q(s', a'))$$

The learning rate $\alpha \in [0, 1]$ determines how much the existing estimate of $Q^\pi(s, a)$ contributes to the new estimate. If the agent's policy tends towards greedy choices as time passes, then under certain conditions the $Q(s, a)$ estimates are guaranteed to converge to the *optimal* value function $Q^*(s, a)$, as was proved in [8]. To achieve this, we use an ϵ-*greedy* [5] exploration strategy, where $\epsilon \in [0, 1]$ determines the probability of a random (non-greedy) action. The value of ϵ

decays towards zero over the course of the learner's lifetime. We also use a *replacing eligibility trace* [9] in combination with the SARSA algorithm.

2.2 Value Function Approximation

In more complex learning domains, the number of states $|S|$ can be infeasibly large, or even infinite. To use RL methods in these domains, an enumeration of states can be avoided by describing each state using a finite set of *state features*. It is often the case that states with similar state features have similar value and/or require a similar action to be taken. If this is the case, *function approximation* can be used to represent the state-action value function $Q(s, a)$ during learning.

A *linear* value function approximation uses a set of n basis functions $\{\phi_i(s, a)\}$ and a set of n weights $\{\theta_i\}$ to express an approximate value function $\widetilde{Q}$:

$$\widetilde{Q}(s, a) = \sum_{i=1}^{n} \theta_i \phi_i(s, a)$$

Each basis function ϕ_i can be interpreted as a single learning feature. We use *tile-coding* [5] to generate the set of features $\{\phi_i\}$. The features are grouped into a number of *tilings*, which are sets of binary features which *partition* the state space. In any state, only one of the features from each tiling is active (value=1.0), and the remainder are inactive (value=0.0). Each tiling is offset in the state space by a different amount, improving the generalization which can be achieved. The weights of the approximator are trained using a *gradient descent* rule. For details of an efficient implementation of the SARSA algorithm with linear function approximation and eligibility traces, we refer the reader to [10].

3   Parallelization

In related research, parallel methods which *partition* the state space have been proposed [11]. These may be appropriate for MDP planning, but are inappropriate for learning in an MDP where the transition and reward parameters are not known, for the following reasons:

- The transition function is initially unknown, so a partition minimizing inter-partition transitions can only be derived from external prior knowledge of the problem.
- One advantage of RL is that value function updates are focused on states with a high probability of visitation under the current policy. Restricting updates to an agent's partition changes the overall distribution of updates.
- If value function approximation is being used, this change in the distribution of updates may break the conditions required for converging to a near-optimal policy.

In this paper we have pursued an alternative approach, one where each parallel agent learns an approximate value function for *the whole state space*. This means that agents do not have exclusive specializations, so there may be some duplication of effort. The advantage of this approach is that all the agents can focus on the states with a high probability of visitation, and can generalize based on identical criteria.

We assume that an *identical* simulation of a single-agent learning problem is available to each agent. While this restricts our approach to learning in simulation only, almost all practical applications of RL involve some degree of environment simulation, so this assumption is reasonable. The basic parallel architecture which is used in this paper is thus illustrated in Figure 1. During learning each parallel agent interacts with a local simulation and updates its own private value function. There also exists a channel for *inter-process communication* (IPC).

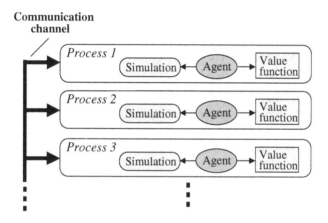

Fig. 1. The basic parallel architecture underlying the parallel RL methods described in this paper

To accelerate learning, the agents must periodically *exchange information* over the communication channel, allowing one agent to exploit information learned by another. The environmental knowledge acquired by each agent is expressed in the weights $\{\theta_i\}$ of the linear value function approximation. Therefore we need to define a communication and update mechanism which allows one agent's weights to be affected by another agent.

We also assume that all the agents use the same set of learning features $\{\phi_i\}$. This has some important advantages:

- No mechanism is required for projecting from one set of basis functions to another.
- The only weights from other agents that are relevant for modifying one agent's value of θ_i are the other agents' values for θ_i.
- A weight θ_i has the same meaning for every agent, a set of weights is efficiently communicated as either the full vector $\boldsymbol{\theta}$, or a sparse set of index-value tuples $\{(i, \theta_i)\}$.

Communicating the weights $\{\theta_i\}$ forms the basis of all the methods described in this paper. However, we have found that if the *only* parameters updated and communicated by the agents are the weights, parallelism is difficult to exploit. This is because the weights only provide an estimate of the value of a feature. They provide no information about *how often* a feature has been updated, or *how much a weight has changed* since an agent last communicated. A comparison of the *relative experience* of agents in each area of the state space seems to be vital for good parallelization.

4   Algorithms

We now describe our basic algorithm, and two refinements which reduce communication overhead.

4.1   Merging Value Functions

Our basic method (algorithm M) is based on a synchronous merging operation, which takes place after every p steps in the simulation. Parameter p is known here as the *merge period*. Note that p defines the number of *discrete simulation time steps* which take place between consecutive merges, it does not define a period of real time. Parameter p requires careful selection to trade off the cost of communication delays against the reduced number of simulation steps required for convergence.

To favour the weight estimates of agents with more experience in each area of the state space, each of the agents maintains an additional set of parameters $\{c_i\}$. Parameter c_i counts the number of times binary feature ϕ_i has been active since the last merge. We call this parameter a *visit count*.

We can use visit counts to define a weighted average of the agents' feature value estimates (lines 7–13 of Listing 1), favouring agents with more experience of a particular feature.

Initially we implemented the merging process using a central manager agent, which received weights and visit counts from all the agents, calculated the merged weights and broadcast the result. This naive implementation performed poorly for larger numbers of agents, since for n_a agents the growth of the merging time was $O(n_a)$. Our second implementation used the MPI parallel programming interface [12] to calculate the merged weights using two distributed computations, one for each of the summations required. With this implementation, the growth of the merging time was reduced to $O(\log n_a)$. The merging time is also directly proportional to the number of features $\{\phi_i\}$.

We use the term *experiment* to mean a single run of our parallel method, with n_a agents starting with the same initial weights, performing learning episodes in parallel and communicating every p time steps. Each experiment finishes after a fixed time t_{end}. We produce results averaged over a set of experiments to smooth out noise from random exploration.

Listing 1. Pseudocode for algorithm M

Require: $\theta_{n,i}$ is the ith weight of agent n
Require: $c_{n,i}$ is the ith visit count of agent n
 1: Initialize all $\theta_{n,i}$ and $c_{n,i}$ to 0
 2: **while** time elapsed $< t_{end}$ **do**
 3:    **for** each agent n **in parallel do**
 4:       **for** $step = 1$ to p **do**
 5:          Increment $c_{n,i}$ for each active feature ϕ_i
 6:          Execute a simulation step. Update weights $\{\theta_{n,i}\}$
 7:    **for all** i **do**
 8:       $n \leftarrow \sum_n c_{n,i} \theta_{n,i}$ *(parallel summation)*
 9:       $d \leftarrow \sum_n c_{n,i}$ *(parallel summation)*
10:       **if** $d \neq 0$ **then**
11:          **for** each agent n **in parallel do**
12:             $\theta_{n,i} \leftarrow n/d$
13:             $c_{n,i} \leftarrow 0$

4.2   Selecting the Most Significant Information

Algorithm M potentially exchanges a great deal of redundant information between the agents. This is because every weight and visit count of every agent is used in the distributed calculation of the merged weights.

If the change in a particular agent's weight θ_i since the last merge ($\Delta\theta_i$) is close to zero, it could mean one of two things: (a) feature ϕ_i has not been active since the last merge, or (b) feature ϕ_i has been active, but weight θ_i is already a good prediction of the value of the feature. In either case, all the agents will already have a value for θ_i that is close to the best current estimate, so there is little benefit in communicating such a small change.

Conversely, the largest values of $\Delta\theta_i$ occur when an area of the state space is encountered that hasn't yet been seen by any of the agents. In these cases, some weights change rapidly to approximate the value function structure in the new area. This is valuable information to transmit to the other agents.

This leads us to define algorithm SM, which is more *selective* about the information communicated between the agents. It remains synchronous, with each of the agents communicating with the others every p simulation steps.

Variable θ_i^{ref} is used to store the value of weight θ_i at various stages. The weights $\{\theta_i\}$ are modified during learning, but the variables $\{\theta_i^{ref}\}$ are not affected, allowing $\Delta\theta_i = \theta_i - \theta_i^{ref}$ to be tracked for each feature. The weights can now be ranked in significance according to $|\Delta\theta_i|$. When $\Delta\theta_i$ is communicated to other agents, θ_i^{ref} is reset to the value of θ_i.

We choose a number (n_{com}) of weights to communicate out of the total number of weights (n_{tot}). Again, choosing parameter n_{com} is part of a trade-off between communication costs and learning efficiency. Even if n_{com} is much smaller than n_{tot} we can achieve significant convergence speed-ups.

Listing 2. Pseudocode for algorithm SM

1: Initialize all θ_i and θ_i^{ref} to 0
2: **while** time elapsed $< t_{end}$ **do**
3:      Execute p simulation steps, updating weights $\{\theta_i\}$
4:      Calculate $\Delta\theta_i = \theta_i - \theta_i^{ref}$ for all i
5:      $best \leftarrow$ indices of n_{com} largest values of $|\Delta\theta_i|$
6:      $m \leftarrow \{(i, \Delta\theta_i) \mid i \in best\}$
7:      Send message m to all agents (including self)
8:      $mset \leftarrow$ receive 1 message from each agent
9:      **for all** i **do**
10:        $cset \leftarrow \{\Delta\theta_i \mid m \in mset, (i, \Delta\theta_i) \in m\}$
11:        **if** $cset \neq \emptyset$ **then**
12:            $n \leftarrow \sum\limits_{\Delta\theta_i \in cset} |\Delta\theta_i|.\Delta\theta_i$
13:            $d \leftarrow \sum\limits_{\Delta\theta_i \in cset} |\Delta\theta_i|$
14:            $\theta_i^{ref} \leftarrow \theta_i^{ref} + n/d$
15:            $\theta_i \leftarrow \theta_i^{ref}$

To combine several agents' changes, another weighted average is used (see lines 12–15 of Listing 2). We had tried taking the mean of the changes, but performance was poor, because a large change discovered by one agent would be drowned out by the other agents making small changes.

4.3   Using Asynchronous Communication

In algorithm SM the learning and communicating phases of the agents are tightly synchronized. After every interval of p learning steps, an agent must broadcast its changes and wait to receive a message from every other agent before learning can continue. This results in several inefficiencies:

- At the end of each learning interval, the agents all broadcast their messages at the same time, causing their shared network to become congested.
- If the network used by the agents is slow, an agent may be idle for some time waiting for messages. This time could potentially be used for further learning.
- If the agents all discover very similar changes near the start of the learning period, there is no way to find this out until the communications start at the end of the learning period. This means that many of the limited number of changes in each broadcast message could be wasted.

We address these issues with Algorithm ASM, using asynchronous message passing to implement merging. We use the same mechanism of ranking the weights using $|\Delta\theta_i|$, but avoid the need for the agents to synchronize every p steps.

Listing 3. Pseudocode for algorithm ASM

1: Initialize all θ_i and θ_i^{ref} to 0
2: **while** time elapsed $< t_{end}$ **do**
3:     Execute one simulation step and update weights $\{\theta_i\}$
4:     **if** p steps have been taken since last broadcast **then**
5:         Calculate $\Delta\theta_i = \theta_i - \theta_i^{ref}$ for all i
6:         $best \leftarrow$ indices of n_{com} largest values of $|\Delta\theta_i|$
7:         $m \leftarrow \{(i, \Delta\theta_i) \mid i \in best\}$
8:         Send message m to the other agents
9:         **for all** $i \in best$ **do**
10:             $\theta_i^{ref} \leftarrow \theta_i$
11:     **for all** messages m received since last check **do**
12:         **for all** $(i, \Delta\theta_i') \in m$ **do**
13:             $\Delta\theta_i \leftarrow \theta_i - \theta_i^{ref}$
14:             $\theta_i^{ref} \leftarrow \theta_i^{ref} + \Delta\theta_i'$
15:             **if** $sign(\Delta\theta_i') \neq sign(\Delta\theta_i)$ **then**
16:                 $\theta_i \leftarrow \theta_i + \Delta\theta_i'$
17:             **else if** $|\Delta\theta_i'| > |\Delta\theta_i|$ **then**
18:                 $\theta_i \leftarrow \theta_i^{ref}$

We use a *staggered* approach to spread out the messages over time. Given n_a agents, the first agent broadcasts p/n_a steps after the start of the experiment, the second agent after $2p/n_a$ steps, the third agent after $3p/n_a$ steps and so on. Each agent then broadcasts after every p steps counting from its first broadcast. In the absence of synchronization, small variations in the dynamic load of processors will disrupt this uniform pattern. As long as random variations keep the broadcasts fairly well spread out this is not a problem. An alternative approach is to schedule broadcasts randomly with a Poisson process of period p.

Algorithm ASM ranks the weights and constructs messages in the same way as Algorithm SM (see Section 4.2). It differs in that learning can resume immediately after a message has been sent, and that messages from other agents can be processed separately as and when they arrive. $\Delta\theta_i$ here represents *a local change in θ yet to be communicated.*

When an agent receives a message, each change $\Delta\theta_i'$ received from the remote agent is compared with the local change $\Delta\theta_i$. If $\Delta\theta_i'$ and $\Delta\theta_i$ have *equal signs* it is important that part of the local change is *cancelled out* in response to the remote change (see lines 15–18 of Listing 3). Otherwise it is likely the agents will *overshoot* the true value for this weight, interfering with convergence.

4.4   Is Communication Really Necessary?

At this point, it is reasonable to ask whether communication is a necessary component of our approach. To demonstrate that it is, we designed a baseline (algorithm B) where the agents learn in parallel, but in isolation (they do not communicate). The agents record the length of each episode during learning.

After learning, each agent calculates its mean performance[1] over the final 10% of the duration of the experiment. This is used as a measure of the quality of the policy learned by each agent. The policy with the highest quality is output as the result from the set of agents.

5   Evaluation

Our evaluation was based on a *distributed-memory* parallel system: a Beowulf cluster of Linux machines. Each node of the cluster had a 1GHz Pentium III processor and 768MB of memory. The nodes were connected with a switched 100Mbs Ethernet network. The method was implemented in C++ using the MPICH implementation of the MPI parallel programming interface [12].

Two of our evaluation domains are established RL benchmark problems: the *Mountain-Car task* and the *Acrobot task*. These problem domains were implemented according to the descriptions given in [10].

In addition, we required a domain where problems of increasing difficulty could be defined in order to investigate our method's performance in large-scale problems. For this purpose, we used a stochastic grid world domain which is similar to the *Puddle-world* [7].

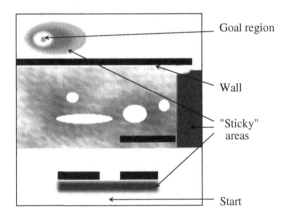

Fig. 2. An instance of the stochastic grid world used as one of the evaluation domains

In this domain, an agent learns to move along a near-optimal path from a starting position to a goal position in a 2D environment. An instance of the grid world is defined by a bitmap image file, such as the one shown in Figure 2. Black pixels in the image denote *walls*, which are impassable. A red pixel indicates the agent's starting point and a group of green pixels indicates a goal region to which the agent must travel. Blue pixels represent *sticky areas* where movement actions have stochastic outcomes. In a sticky area, there is some probability that

---

[1] In our evaluation domains, mean episode length is used as a performance measure.

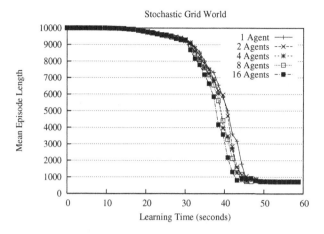

Fig. 3. Algorithm B in the Grid World task

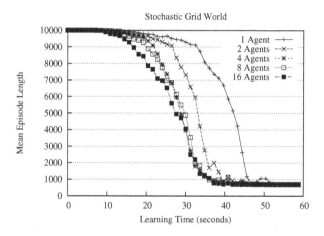

Fig. 4. Algorithm M in the Grid World task

the agent's action may fail, the agent remaining stuck for an extra time step. The more saturated the blue color of the pixel, the greater the probability that the agent's movement actions will fail.

Note that in contrast to the way grid world domains are usually defined, the distance the agent moves after each action need not be equal to one pixel. The move distance s can be an arbitrary value, ranging from multiple pixels down to a fraction of a pixel. What this means is that a domain instance defined by *a single image* can be made progressively more difficult in *quantitative* steps by reducing the size of s. Note also that the resolution of the approximator tiles can vary independently of *both* the image resolution *and* the move distance s.

6   Results

If each agent is given a fixed number of simulation steps to learn from, the performance achievable during the experiment depends on how often the agents communicate. If communication had no cost, we could get arbitrarily close to perfect parallelization by reducing the period between communications towards zero. In practice, messages take some time to travel between the agents. Therefore, the period between communications is chosen to trade off learning efficiency against the cost of communicating.

In the graphs presented here, the performance achieved (i.e. the mean episode length) is plotted against the real time which has elapsed since the start of the

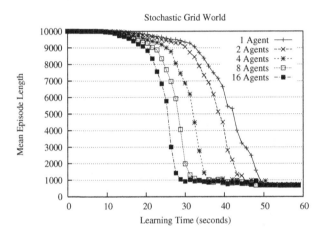

Fig. 5. Algorithm SM in the Grid World task

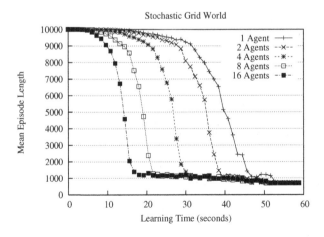

Fig. 6. Algorithm ASM in the Grid World task

experiment. This allows the success of the trade-off to be assessed, with the downside that results will vary depending on the network latency/bandwidth of a particular system.

First, we present results for the stochastic grid world domain. A problem instance of size 256x256 was solved using 16,384 weights for each value function. Initial values of $\epsilon = 0.1$ and $\alpha = 0.2$ were decayed linearly to zero over the experiment time. Additionally, $\lambda = 0.95$, $\gamma = 1.0$, and a reward of -1.0 was given on every time step. The results in Figures 3–6 are averaged over 10 runs. For all the results we chose the number of runs to firmly establish statistical significance (clearly separating the confidence intervals), but did not include the error ranges in the graphs to keep them readable.

The results for baseline algorithm B are shown in Figure 3. The addition of more agents only produces a very small speed-up, constrained by the variance of a single agent's performance. For experiments with high variance in performance, such as the standard Mountain-Car task, adding the first few agents does produce a reasonable speed-up. Adding further agents results in diminishing returns.

Figure 4 shows the results for algorithm M with merge period $p = 50000$. Because the agents send all the weight values over the network during every merge, the communication costs grow rapidly. Using 2 or 4 agents results in a speed-up significantly better than algorithm B. Going beyond 4 agents means that any learning speedup is cancelled out by an increase in merging time.

The results for algorithm SM (see Figure 5) used parameters $p = 100000$ and $n_{com} = 1024$. Communication costs grow much more slowly, so we are able to achieve much better parallel speed-ups for both 8 and 16 agents.

The results for algorithm ASM (see Figure 6) use the same values of p and n_{com}. An extra boost in performance (especially for larger numbers of agents) is achieved by moving to an asynchronous communication model.

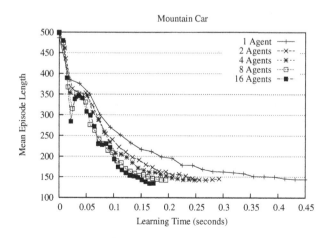

Fig. 7. Algorithm ASM in the Mountain Car task (results averaged over 100 runs)

Table 1. Time (in seconds) required for different numbers of agents to achieve a mean episode length under 145 steps in the Mountain Car task (averaged over 100 runs)

Algorithm	Number of agents				
	1	2	4	8	16
B	0.45	0.29	0.23	0.21	0.20
M	0.45	1.54	1.55	1.47	1.71
SM	0.45	0.36	0.26	0.22	0.17
ASM	0.45	0.33	0.25	0.21	0.17

Table 2. Time (in seconds) required for different numbers of agents to achieve a mean episode length under 140 steps in the Acrobot task (averaged over 100 runs)

Algorithm	Number of agents				
	1	2	4	8	16
B	0.77	0.67	0.56	0.53	0.46
M	0.77	1.82	2.49	N/A	N/A
SM	0.77	0.72	0.65	0.56	0.53
ASM	0.77	0.72	0.60	0.45	0.33

Tables 1 and 2 summarize the performance of the four algorithms in the Mountain-Car and Acrobot tasks. In addition, the graph in Figure 7 provides a more detailed view of the performance of algorithm ASM in the Mountain-Car task. Algorithm M is clearly too inefficient under these bandwidth constraints. Algorithm ASM produces the best performance as the number of agents is increased, although it is also interesting to note that for small numbers of agents Algorithm B performs very well in these two domains. For a complete set of results and detailed experimental settings the reader is referred to [13].

7   Related Work

The novelty of this work compared to previous research lies in the implementation of a parallel RL system based on real hardware with real resource constraints. By evaluating this system in comparison to a simulation of parallel agents, the limiting nature of communication costs has become clear, and future work in this area must consider the *quantity* of information exchanged between agents in addition to the potential speed-up achievable with this information. Previous studies of parallel RL [3,4] have not modeled communication costs.

While the focus of this work has been on how to use parallelization to find solutions to single-agent RL problems more quickly, research in this area has the potential to influence work on *cooperative multi-agent learning* [1,2]. In this area there is the additional challenge of finding an abstraction that hides the differences between two agents, allowing them to share information during learning.

In other related work, Ahmadabadi & Asadpour [14] investigate a number of different measures of an agent's "expertness" at a particular task, allowing knowledge from a number of agents to be combined in proportion to their relative competence. Wingate & Seppi [15] presented a parallel approach to MDP planning which is based on *partitioning* the state space. Each parallel agent in their method exploits the locality of the state space by communicating only the values of states at the *boundaries* of its partition, sending them exclusively to agents with adjoining partitions.

8 Conclusions

We have presented three increasingly efficient versions of a method for parallel RL. In several different domains our method has been shown to learn good policies more quickly with parallel hardware. Our empirical analysis has shown that the *quantity* of information exchanged between agents is the main factor limiting performance on a distributed memory parallel system. To our knowledge, this is the first method proposed for parallel RL that is appropriate for speeding up learning using real parallel hardware.

While we have not presented any theoretical proof of convergence, our empirical study of these methods showed that they work well in a wide range of domains, providing strong evidence that the methods will be very useful in practice. Many of the RL methods currently in use, such as SARSA(λ) with linear approximation and a GLIE[2] exploration strategy (used by individual agents in our approach), have not yet been proven to converge but perform well in practice.

In future work, we plan to conduct similar experiments on parallel systems with different network characteristics. We will also examine whether performance can be improved further using alternative criteria for ranking the weights.

References

1. Tan, M.: Multi-agent reinforcement learning: Independent vs. cooperative agents. In: ICML 1993. Proceedings of the Tenth International Conference on Machine Learning, pp. 330–337 (1993)
2. Nunes, L., Oliveira, E.: Cooperative learning using advice exchange. In: Alonso, E., Kudenko, D., Kazakov, D. (eds.) Adaptive Agents and Multi-Agent Systems. LNCS (LNAI), vol. 2636. Springer, Heidelberg (2003)
3. Whitehead, S.D.: A complexity analysis of cooperative mechanisms in reinforcement learning. In: AAAI 1991. Proceedings of the 9th National Conference on Artificial Intelligence, pp. 607–613 (1991)
4. Kretchmar, R.M.: Parallel reinforcement learning. In: SCI 2002. Proceedings of the 6th World Conference on Systemics, Cybernetics, and Informatics (2002)
5. Watkins, C.J.C.H.: Learning from Delayed Rewards. PhD thesis, Cambridge University, U.K. (1989)
6. Rummery, G.A., Niranjan, M.: On-line Q-learning using connectionist systems. Technical Report TR166, Cambridge University Engineering Dept. (1994)

---

[2] *GLIE* stands for *greedy* in the *limit* with *infinite exploration*. See [8] for details.

7. Sutton, R.S.: Generalization in reinforcement learning: Successful examples using sparse coarse coding. In: Neural Information Processing Systems, vol. 8 (1996)
8. Singh, S., Jaakkola, T., Littman, M.L., Szepesvari, C.: Convergence results for single-step on-policy reinforcement learning algorithms. Machine Learning 38(3), 287–308 (2000)
9. Sutton, R.S.: Learning to predict by the methods of temporal differences. Machine Learning 3, 9–44 (1988)
10. Sutton, R.S., Barto, A.G.: Reinforcement Learning: An Introduction. MIT Press, Cambridge (1998)
11. Archibald, T.: Parallel dynamic programming. In: Kronsjö, L., Shumsheruddin, D. (eds.) Advances in Parallel Algorithms. Blackwell Scientific, Malden (1992)
12. Pacheco, P.S.: Parallel Programming with MPI. Morgan Kaufmann, San Francisco (1997)
13. Grounds, M.J.: Scaling Up Reinforcement Learning using Parallelization and Symbolic Planning. PhD thesis, The University of York, UK (2007)
14. Ahmadabadi, M.N., Asadpour, M.: Expertness based cooperative Q-learning. IEEE Transactions on Systems, Man and Cybernetics 32(1), 66–76 (2002)
15. Wingate, D., Seppi, K.: P3VI: A partitioned, prioritized, parallel value iterator. In: Proceedings of the 21st International Conference on Machine Learning (2004)

Combining Reinforcement Learning with Symbolic Planning

Matthew Grounds and Daniel Kudenko

Department of Computer Science
University of York
York, YO10 5DD, UK
{mattg,kudenko}@cs.york.ac.uk

Abstract. One of the major difficulties in applying Q-learning to real-world domains is the sharp increase in the number of learning steps required to converge towards an optimal policy as the size of the state space is increased. In this paper we propose a method, *PLANQ-learning*, that couples a Q-learner with a STRIPS planner. The planner shapes the reward function, and thus guides the Q-learner quickly to the optimal policy. We demonstrate empirically that this combination of high-level reasoning and low-level learning displays significant improvements in scaling-up behaviour as the state-space grows larger, compared to both standard Q-learning and hierarchical Q-learning methods.

1 Introduction

Even though Q-learning is the most popular reinforcement learning algorithm to date, it scales poorly to problems with many state variables, where the state space becomes so large that the time taken for Q-learning to converge becomes infeasible. While hierarchical reinforcement learning [1] has shown some promise in this area, there remain similar scaling issues.

In this paper, we propose a method, *PLANQ-learning*, that combines STRIPS planning with Q-learning. A high-level STRIPS plan that achieves the goal of the Q-learner is computed, and is then used to guide the learning process. This is achieved by shaping the reward function based on the pre- and post-conditions of the individual plan operators. This enables it to converge to the optimal policy more quickly.

We begin this paper with background information on Q-learning and STRIPS planning, and proceed to describe their combination in the PLANQ-learning algorithm. We then introduce the evaluation domain, and present empirical results that compare the PLANQ-learner's performance to that of a standard Q-learner. While these first results are encouraging, a much greater improvement in performance is achieved by incorporating a state-abstraction mechanism. The performance of this extended PLANQ-learner is compared with a MAX-Q learner [2], a hierarchical algorithm that is also able to exploit the state abstraction. The results show that PLANQ is superior in its scaling-up properties both in terms of time steps and CPU time, but exhibits a large variance in the CPU time expended per time step.

K. Tuyls et al. (Eds.): Adaptive Agents and MAS III, LNAI 4865, pp. 75–86, 2008.
© Springer-Verlag Berlin Heidelberg 2008

2   Q-Learning

A reinforcement learning problem can be described formally as a *Markov Decision Process* (MDP). We can describe an MDP as a 4-tuple $< S, A, T, R >$, where S is a set of problem states, A is the set of available actions, $T(s, a, s') \rightarrow [0, 1]$ is a function which defines the probability that taking action a in state s will result in a transition to state s', and $R(s, a, s') \rightarrow \mathcal{R}$ defines the reward received when such a transition is made.

If all the parameters of the MDP are known then an optimal policy can be calculated using dynamic programming. However, if T and R are initially unknown then reinforcement learning methods can learn an optimal policy by *interacting with the environment* and observing what transitions and rewards result from these interactions.

The Q-learning algorithm [3] is a popular reinforcement learning method with strong theoretical convergence guarantees. It also performs well in practice if the number of states $|S|$ is not too large. The goal of Q-learning is to learn the function $Q^*(s, a)$, defined as the *expected total discounted return* when starting in state s, executing action a and thereafter using the optimal policy π^* to choose actions:

$$Q^*(s, a) = \sum_{s'} T(s, a, s') \left[R(s, a, s') + \gamma \max_{a'} Q^*(s', a') \right]$$

The discount factor $\gamma \in [0, 1)$ defines to what degree rewards in the short term outweigh rewards in the long term. Intuitively, $Q^*(s, a)$ describes the *utility* of taking action a in state s. For each s and a we store a floating point number $Q(s, a)$ as our current estimate of $Q^*(s, a)$. As experience tuples $< s, a, r, s' >$ are generated, the table of Q-values is updated using the following rule:

$$Q(s, a) \leftarrow (1 - \alpha)Q(s, a) + \alpha(r + \gamma \max_{a'} Q(s', a'))$$

The learning rate $\alpha \in [0, 1]$ determines the extent to which the existing estimate of $Q^*(s, a)$ contributes to the new estimate. An *exploration strategy* is also required to make the trade-off between exploration and exploitation. In these experiments, a simple ϵ-*greedy* strategy is used [3].

3   AI Planning

A classical AI planning problem consists of an *initial state*, a set of *actions* or *operators* which can be used to move between states, and a set of *goal states* to be reached. To solve the planning problem, a sequence of operators must be found which transforms the initial state to one of the goal states. States (and sets of states) are typically described using statements in *first-order predicate logic*.

The STRIPS representation [4] and its descendants form the basis of most AI planning systems. This representation can be used for planning in first order domains without requiring the complexity of a full theorem proving system. A STRIPS state is represented by a *list* of the *literals* which are true in that state. A STRIPS goal is a *conjunction* of positive literals. Each STRIPS operator is represented by three components:

Preconditions. The literals which must be true in a state for the operator to be applicable in that state.

Add List The literals which become true in the state which results after applying the operator.

Delete List. The literals which become false in the state which results after applying the operator.

The latest generation of STRIPS planning software based on the influential *Graphplan* algorithm [5] has achieved orders of magnitude gains in speed over previous algorithms. Graphplan itself is based on a data structure called a *planning graph*, which encodes which literals can be made true after n time steps, and which are *mutually exclusive* at that time step.

Our initial experiments used the *FastForward* or FF planner [6], which uses the Graphplan algorithm on a relaxed version of the planning problem. The planning graph then forms the basis of a heuristic for forward search. In our current system we use our own implementation of the Graphplan algorithm, which eliminates parsing and file operations to minimise the CPU time used by the planner.

4   The State Space Explosion

The key problem which arises when reinforcement learning is applied to large real-life problems is referred to as the *state-space explosion*, or the *curse of dimensionality*. The "flat" state space S used by a traditional reinforcement learner can generally be expressed as the Cartesian product of n simpler state variables, $X_1 \times X_2 \times \ldots \times X_n$. As we scale-up to larger problems by increasing the number of state variables involved, the size of the state space S grows exponentially with n. Since the learning time grows at least as fast as the size of the state space, the learning time will also grow exponentially. Even if these were only binary state variables, $|S|$ would be equal to 2^n, and learning would soon become infeasible if n became much larger than about 20.

It is clear that for the fully general case of an MDP with 2^n states, there is an inescapable limit on how large we can allow n to grow and still find the optimal policy in a reasonable amount of time. Thankfully, real-life learning problems do not always exhibit the generality of an unconstrained MDP model. In a particular region of the state space, there may be only a few state variables which are relevant to the action choice. Alternatively, there may be a large group of states with similar state features which can be considered interchangeable in terms of state value and optimal action choice.

Traditionally researchers have used techniques such as *function approximation* [7] and *hierarchical reinforcement learning* [1] to exploit the internal structure of an MDP to make reinforcement learning feasible.

5   The PLANQ-Learning Algorithm

In this paper we introduce a new approach to reinforcement learning in large-scale problems, using symbolic AI plans to explicitly represent prior knowledge of the internal structure of a MDP, and exploiting this knowledge to constrain the number of action steps required before an adequate policy is obtained. We have named this approach *PLANQ-learning*.

The definition of an *adequate* policy will vary according to the application domain, but we use this wording to emphasize that our goal is not to find the optimal policy, but to find an acceptable policy in a reasonable amount of time.

The approach explored in this paper uses a STRIPS knowledge base and planner to define the desired high-level behaviour of an agent, and reinforcement learning to learn the unspecified low-level behaviour. One low-level behaviour must be learned for each STRIPS operator in the knowledge base. There is no need to specify separately a reward function for each of these operators - instead a reward function is derived *directly* from the logical *preconditions and effects* of the STRIPS operator.

As well as a knowledge base describing the high-level operators to be learned, the agent has access to an interface which, given a low-level reinforcement learning state (representing low-level low level percepts), can construct a high-level set of STRIPS literals which describe the state. This includes the *current goal* of the agent. This limits our learning agent to domains where the only reward received is associated with reaching one of a set of goal states.

Initially the agent has no plan, so it uses the above interface to turn the initial state into a STRIPS problem description. The STRIPS planner takes this problem description and returns a sequence of operators which solves the problem. The agent has a subordinate Q-learning agent to learn each operator, so the Q-learner corresponding to the first operator in the plan is activated.

The activated Q-learner takes responsibility for choosing actions, while the primary agent monitors the high-level descriptions of subsequent states. When the high level description changes, the primary agent performs one or more of the following operations:

Goal Changed. If the overall goal of the agent is detected to have changed, a new plan is needed, so the agent must run the STRIPS planner again.

Effects Satisfied. If the changes specified by the Add and Delete Lists of the operator have taken place, the Q-learner has been successful, and receives a reward of +1. The Q-learner for the next operator in the plan is activated.

Preconditions Violated. If the effects are unsatisfied but a precondition has become false, the operator is assumed to have failed.[1] The Q-learner receives a reward of -1, and the STRIPS planner is activated for re-planning.

Operator In Progress. If the effects are unsatisfied and the preconditions inviolate, either the effects are partially complete, or a irrelevant literal has changed truth value. The current Q-learner receives reward 0 and continues.

---

[1] This implies that all post-conditions are achieved in the same time step. To relax this restriction, we could specify an *invariant* for each operator to detect failure events.

6   Evaluation Domain

The evaluation domain used here is a grid world which consists of both smaller *grid squares* and the larger *region squares* which contain groups of grid squares. The region squares represent target areas to which the mobile robot must navigate. Using region squares for the agent's goal rather than individual grid squares is preferable for our purposes, since the regions are intended to provide the basis for *qualitative spatial reasoning* in our system at a later date. There is only one *active* (i.e. goal) region square at any time, and whenever the robot enters the active region, it receives a reward, and a new goal region is chosen at random. The robot is situated in one of the grid squares, and faces in one of the four compass directions, *north*, *east*, *south* and *west*.

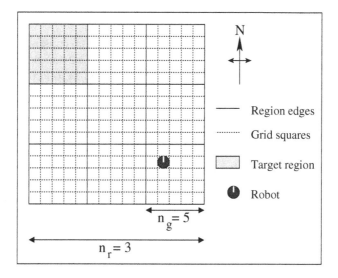

Fig. 1. An instance of the evaluation domain

The simplicity of this domain makes it an ideal choice for illustration purposes. In addition, the size of the state space can be easily altered by changing the grid size, and planning knowledge can be incorporated in the form of high level movement operations.

To evaluate performance as the state space is scaled-up, we define a class of these problems, where the regions are arranged in a square of side n_r (see Figure 1). Each region contains a square set of grid squares, of side n_g. Hence the size of the state space S, which encodes the position and direction of the robot, as well as the current destination region, is:

$$|S| = 4n_g^2 n_r^4$$

There are only three actions available to the robot: *turn left*, *turn right* and *forward*. *Turn left* turns the robot 90° anticlockwise to face a new compass direction. *Turn right* makes a 90° clockwise turn. *Forward* will move the robot one square forward in the current face direction, unless the robot is at the edge of the entire map of grid squares, in which case it has no effect.

The robot receives a reward of 0 on every step, except on a step where the robot moves into the active region. When this happens, the robot receives a reward of 1 and a new active region is picked at random from the remaining regions. This introduces a small element of stochasticity to the domain, but this is not significant for the PLANQ-learner, since it will re-plan each time the goal (the active region) changes.

The high level STRIPS representation of the evaluation domain abstracts away the state variables corresponding to the face direction of the robot and the position of the grid square it occupies in the current region. The representation is limited to reasoning at the region level, to plan a path between the current and target regions using a knowledge base which encodes an adjacency relation over the set of regions.

Each region at a position (x, y) is represented as a constant r_x_y. The adj(r1,r2,dir) predicate encodes the fact that region r2 can be reached from region r1 by travelling in the direction dir, which can be one of the compass points N,S,E or W. The at(r) predicate is used to encode the current location of the robot, and to define the goal region to be reached.

The operators available are NORTH, SOUTH, EAST and WEST, which correspond to low-level behaviours to be learned for moving in each of the four compass directions.

The *Planning Domain Definition Language* [8] was used to pass data to the FF planner. An example of a planning problem in PDDL format is shown in Figure 2.

```
(:objects   r_0_0 r_0_1
            r_1_0 r_1_1)

(:init   (adj r_0_0 r_1_0 E)
         (adj r_0_0 r_0_1 S)
         (adj r_0_1 r_1_1 E)
         (adj r_0_1 r_0_0 N)
         (adj r_1_0 r_0_0 W)
         (adj r_1_0 r_1_1 S)
         (adj r_1_1 r_0_1 W)
         (adj r_1_1 r_1_0 N)
         (at r_0_1))

(:goal   (at r_0_0)))
```

Fig. 2. Part of the PDDL problem encoding for $n_r = 2$

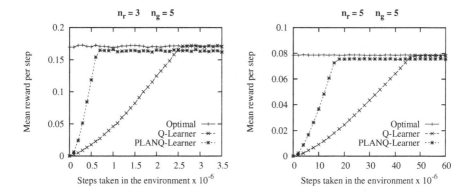

Fig. 3. Results of Experiment 1: these graphs demonstrate that as larger values of n_r are considered, the performance advantage of PLANQ-learning over Q-learning becomes progressively smaller

7 Experiment 1: Results

In our first experiment, the PLANQ-learner was evaluated using a variety of values for n_r and n_g. For purposes of comparison, a standard Q-learning agent and an agent using a hand-coded version of the optimal policy were also evaluated in the domain.

The standard Q-learner uses the full state space S as defined above, and chooses between the three low-level actions, *turn left*, *turn right* and *forward*. Like the PLANQ-learner, it receives a reward of 1 on a step where it enters a goal region, and a reward of 0 everywhere else. In all these experiments, the learning rate α is 0.1, the discount factor γ is 0.9, and the ϵ-greedy parameter ϵ is decayed linearly from 1.0 to 0.0 over the course of the experiment. We choose a decay rate for ϵ such that any slower decay rate will not improve the quality of the solution.

Examples of the performance of the agents over time are shown in Figure 3. The Q-learning agent consistently learns the true optimal policy. The PLANQ-learner learns a good policy, but not quite the optimal one. This is because the planning model of the grid world does not model the cost of making turns - the plans {NORTH, EAST, NORTH, EAST} and {NORTH, NORTH, EAST, EAST} are considered equally suitable by the planner, but in reality the latter plan has a better reward rate. This results in slightly sub-optimal performance.

In both of the experiments, the PLANQ-learner finds a good policy several times more quickly than the Q-learner. This is to be expected: the Q-learner must learn both high and low-level behaviours, whereas the PLANQ-learner need only learn the low-level behaviour. However it can be observed that the advantage of the PLANQ-learner over the Q-learner is less in the $n_r = 5$ experiment than in the $n_r = 3$ experiment. The general trend for the PLANQ-learner to lose advantage as n_r increases is discussed in the next section.

8   Problems with Experiment 1

The learning speed-up achieved by the PLANQ-learner over the Q-learner can be attributed to the *temporal abstraction* inherent in the STRIPS formulation of the problem domain. The temporal abstraction allows us to express the overall problem as a number of *sequential sub-problems*, each of which is easier to learn than the overall task. Because the PLANQ-learner can learn the sub-tasks separately, it can finish learning more quickly than the Q-learner, which must tackle the problem as a whole.

However, the advantage offered by temporal abstraction grows smaller as we scale up to larger domains because we have not supplied a *state-abstraction* to the PLANQ-learner. A state abstraction allows state variables to be excluded from the learner's state space if they are not relevant to learning a particular task (or subtask). For instance, to learn the behaviour for the NORTH operator, only the direction and the position of the agent *within* the current region is relevant - the identities of the current and destination regions are irrelevant.

Without the state abstraction, the PLANQ-learner has no way of knowing that the experience learned for moving NORTH from $r_{0,1}$ to $r_{0,0}$ can be exploited when moving from $r_{2,1}$ to $r_{2,0}$ (writing $r_{x,y}$ to represent the region at position (x,y) in the region grid). This means that the quality of a partially-learned operator can vary considerably in different regions of the grid world.

The PLANQ-learner needs to perform enough exploration in the state space to learn the operator separately in *all* the regions in which it is applicable. As n_r increases, the time taken to perform this exploration approaches the time taken by the Q-learner to learn the entire problem from scratch.

9   Adding State Abstraction

To exploit the STRIPS representation of PLANQ effectively, we incorporated a state abstraction mechanism into our system. Each of the STRIPS operators was annotated with the names of the state variables which were relevant for learning that operator (see bottom right of Figure 4). The Q-learner for that operator learns with a state space consisting only of these relevant variables. This speeds up learning by *generalising* the experience from one region to improve performance in another region.

However, supplying this extra information to the PLANQ-learner gives it a significant advantage over the Q-learner, and comparing their learning times is unlikely to be useful. A more revealing comparison would be with a *hierarchical* Q-learner [1] which can take advantage of the temporal and state abstractions already exploited by PLANQ. We selected a hierarchical Q-learner based on the MAX-Q reward function decomposition [2].

The hierarchy used by the MAX-Q learner (see Figure 4) is based on four abstract actions corresponding to the STRIPS operators of PLANQ. The desired behaviour of each abstract action is determined by an *internal* reward function supplied as part of the hierarchy. The high-level task in the hierarchy is to find a

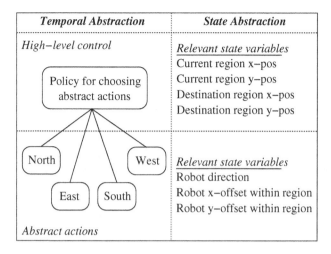

Fig. 4. Temporal and state abstractions used by MAX-Q

policy for executing the abstract actions to maximise the reward obtained from the environment. The hierarchy also encodes which state variables are relevant for learning each operator, and which state variables are relevant for learning the high-level policy for choosing abstract actions.

10 Experiment 2: Results

Figure 5 shows the results obtained by the augmented PLANQ-learner and the MAX-Q learner for two instances of the evaluation domain. The PLANQ-learner consistently achieves a policy close to the optimal within a constant number of steps (around 100,000). Once it has learned a good policy for achieving each of the operators in an arbitrary 5x5 region (thanks to the state abstraction), the PLANQ-learner has enough information to achieve a good rate of return in a region square of arbitrary size. In other words, the number of steps needed for the PLANQ-learner to achieve a good rate of return is dependent only on n_g, not on n_r.

The MAX-Q learner on the other hand needs to learn both the low-level abstract actions *and* the high-level policy for choosing abstract actions. By exploiting both this temporal abstraction and the state abstraction information supplied with the hierarchy, the MAX-Q learner can achieve a *hierarchically-optimal* policy [2] in orders of magnitude less time than the original Q-learner takes to achieve a good rate of return. However, the number of steps the MAX-Q learner needs to achieve this policy does increase with n_r, since the high-level policy becomes more difficult to learn. So as the value of n_r is increased, the PLANQ-learner outperforms MAX-Q to a greater degree.

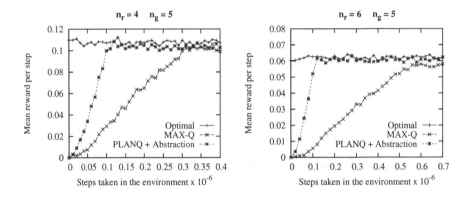

Fig. 5. Results of Experiment 2: The PLANQ learner using state abstraction consistently learns a near-optimal policy in around 10^5 time steps as we increase the value of n_r. In contrast, the MAX-Q learner takes an increasing number of time steps to learn a policy of similar quality as n_r is increased.

11 Computational Requirements

Although PLANQ achieved a good policy after fewer actions in the environment than the other agents, it is important to consider the CPU time required to calculate each action choice. Our original implementation used the FF planner and the STRIPS encoding shown in Figure 2. This scaled very poorly in terms of CPU time - we could only obtain results for $n_r \leq 6$.

To improve the scaling properties of PLANQ, we implemented our own version of a Graphplan planner, eliminating costly operations such as parsing and file-access, but still providing a fully functional domain-independent planner.

We also adopted an alternative STRIPS encoding of the evaluation domain, shown in Figure 6. This involves encoding a subset of the natural numbers with the successor relation s(a,b), and representing the x and y coordinates independently as x(n) and y(n). Replacing the adjacency relation with a successor

```
(:objects   n0 n1 n2)

(:init   (s n0 n1)
         (s n1 n2)
         (x n0)
         {y n0))

(:goal   (x n1) (y n2)))
```

Fig. 6. Alternative PDDL problem encoding for $n_r = 3$

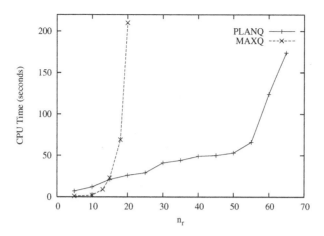

Fig. 7. CPU time required to achieve 95% optimal performance when $n_g = 5$

relation means that the number of formulae in the initial conditions is $O(n_r)$ instead of $O(n_r^2)$, which makes a great improvement to the performance of PLANQ.

Figure 7 shows the amount of CPU time taken for PLANQ to learn a policy with 95% optimal performance. While the MAXQ learning method is infeasible for $n_r > 20$, PLANQ can learn to make near-optimal action choices in under a minute while $n_r < 50$. However, as n_r approaches 70, PLANQ also starts to become infeasible.

A key limitation of the PLANQ algorithm in its current form is the large variance in CPU time required per time step. On most steps an action choice can be made in a few microseconds, but if the planner needs to be invoked the choice may be delayed for 50 or 100 *milliseconds*. For systems with real-time constraints this is clearly unacceptable, and we plan to address this problem in future research.

12   Conclusions and Related Work

In this series of experiments, we have shown that an AI planning algorithm based on the STRIPS representation can be combined successfully with reinforcement learning techniques, resulting in an agent which uses an explicit symbolic description of its prior knowledge of a learning problem to constrain the number of action steps required to learn a policy with a good (but not necessarily optimal) rate of return.

The STRIPS representation used in this work is limited to describing problems which are *deterministic*, *fully observable*, and *goal oriented*. To overcome some of these limitations, the PLANQ method could be adapted to use a more complex planner which can reason about stochastic action effects and plan quality. However, we believe that prior knowledge encoded in the limited STRIPS representation will still be useful for speeding up the learning of many problems, even if some aspects of those problems are inexpressible in the representation.

Our technique for deriving a reward function from the pre-conditions and effects of a STRIPS operator is similar to that used by Ryan [9], although his work is primarily concerned with *teleo-reactive planning* in contrast to the classical STRIPS plans used in our work.

Boutilier *et al.* [10] employ symbolic plans to solve *factored* MDPs with reward functions expressible as an *additive* combination of sub-goals. *Partially-ordered plans* are used as an intermediate representation for constructing a high quality solution which makes a trade-off between the sub-goals.

References

1. Barto, A., Mahadevan, S.: Recent advances in hierarchical reinforcement learning. Discrete Event Dynamic Systems 13(4), 341–379 (2003)
2. Dietterich, T.G.: Hierarchical reinforcement learning with the MAXQ value function decomposition. Journal of Artificial Intelligence Research 13, 227–303 (2000)
3. Watkins, C.J.C.H.: Learning from Delayed Rewards. PhD thesis, Cambridge University, U.K. (1989)
4. Fikes, R., Nilsson, N.: STRIPS: A new approach to the application of theorem proving to problem solving. Artificial Intelligence 2, 189–208 (1971)
5. Blum, A.L., Furst, M.L.: Fast planning through planning graph analysis. Artificial Intelligence 90, 281–300 (1997)
6. Hoffmann, J.: A heuristic for domain independent planning and its use in an enforced hill-climbing algorithm. In: Proceedings of the 12th International Symposium on Methodologies for Intelligent Systems, pp. 216–227 (2000)
7. Bertsekas, D.P., Tsitsiklis, J.N.: Neuro-Dynamic Programming. Athena Scientific (1996)
8. Ghallab, M., Howe, A., Knoblock, C., McDermott, D., Ram, A., Veloso, M., Weld, D., Wilkins, D.: PDDL—the planning domain definition language. Technical Report CVC TR-98-003/DCS TR-1165, Yale Center for Computational Vision and Control (1998)
9. Ryan, M.: Using abstract models of behaviours to automatically generate reinforcement learning hierarchies. In: Proceedings of the 19th International Conference on Machine Learning (2002)
10. Boutilier, C., Brafman, R.I., Geib, C.: Prioritized goal decomposition of Markov decision processes: Towards a synthesis of classical and decision theoretic planning. In: International Joint Conference on Artificial Intelligence (1997)

Agent Interactions and Implicit Trust in IPD Environments

Enda Howley and Colm O'Riordan

Department of Information Technology
National University Of Ireland, Galway
enda.howley@nuigalway.ie,
colm.oriordan@nuigalway.ie

Abstract. The goal of multi-agent systems is to build robust intelligent systems capable of existing in complex environments. Agents must decide with whom to interact. In this paper we investigate how agents may bias their interactions in environments where alternative game payoffs are available. We present a number of game theoretic simulations involving a range of agent interaction models. Through a series of experiments we show the effects of modelling agent interactions when games representing alternative levels of benefit and risk are offered. Individual agents may have a preference for games of a certain risk. We also present analysis of population dynamics, examining how agents bias their peer interactions throughout each generation. We also address the topic of implicit trust, where agents reflect levels of trust through the payoffs presented in a game offer. In this interaction model agents may use levels of trust to choose opponents and to determine levels of risk associated with a game.

1 Introduction

In this paper we examine how agents bias their interactions within a game theoretic environment. Traditionally, interaction models such as spatial [1], tagging [13], kin selection [4] or trust [11] have been used. Each of these interaction models involve players biasing their interactions based on individual preferences for particular peers. These preferences have been based on relatedness, similarity, proximity or trustworthiness. However, to date, research has not examined the effects of agents having individual preferences for desired goals, preferred levels of risk or the necessity to obtain particular services. In this paper we use game theoretic simulations to examine individual agent's preferences for certain game utilities. Therefore, agents must decide with which of their peers to interact, and also for what payoffs they should interact. We examine the important extension of implicit trust which allows players agree game payoffs based on levels of trust. We conduct these simulations using the well known Iterated Prisoner's Dilemma (IPD). We have extended this game to allow players offer and accept games of differing payoffs. In this paper we address the following research questions:

1. What are the effects of biasing peer interactions based on individual game preferences?

K. Tuyls et al. (Eds.): Adaptive Agents and MAS III, LNAI 4865, pp. 87–101, 2008.
© Springer-Verlag Berlin Heidelberg 2008

2. What are the effects of biasing peer interactions and choosing games of risk when game values can be agreed and influenced by trust?

In the following section we will present some background research describing previous work involving tagging, trust and choice and refusal environments. Subsequent sections will outline our simulator design, strategy set and experimental setup. Finally in our results section we will present a series of experiments and provide analysis and commentary of the data. Stemming from these experimental results we will outline our conclusions.

2   Background Research

In this paper we are primarily concerned with how agents bias their interactions. An agent's ability to structure its interactions can fundamentally effect its individual performance and as a result the overall performance of the population. Previous research involving this topic includes techniques such as spatial, tagging, kin selection and trust. In this section we will discuss some of this existing research.

2.1   Spatial, Tagging and Kin Selection

The emergence of cooperation is influenced by the ability of agents to bias their interactions towards their cooperative peers and away from their non-cooperative peers. Numerous interaction models have been examined which have facilitated this process. Kin selection is one mechanism which involves groups of related individuals [4,16]. In this model related individuals are more likely to interact than those who are not related. Another well known interaction model involves agents being located on a spatial topology such as a grid [1]. Agents are more likely to interact with those peers located on adjacent cells of the grid.

Other alternative interaction models have also been proposed in recent times such as tag-mediated interactions models [5,13]. These models allow agents bias their peer interactions based on abstract topologies. Agents of a similar tag value are more likely to interact than others. Tags are similar to visible markings or labels which can be used by agents to bias their interactions. Interactions that are initially random can become highly structured through these visible markings. Tags have been shown to benefit the emergence of cooperation in agent societies through partitioning the agent population and limiting interactions. This involves clustering around certain gene values which resemble groups [7]. The success of these interaction models depends on cooperative groups not being invaded by less cooperative strategies [6]. In this paper we will present a number of tag-mediated interaction models which allow players to bias their interactions based on preferences for certain games.

These interaction models succeed through allowing populations of agents to limit their peer interactions, thereby resembling subgroups. This prevents cooperative clusters from being exploited by non-cooperative peers. In reality this population partitioning is not always possible. Therefore, more realistic agent interaction models such as choice and refusal (CandR) have been proposed.

2.2   Choice and Refusal

Choice and refusal (CandR) models are more expressive agent interaction models which allow agents interact freely within their environment. Choice and refusal environments have been studied initially by Stanley, Ashlock and Smucker [14] and more recently by Howley and O'Riordan [9]. These environments are fundamentally different with those previously described interaction models. No population partitioning is enforced, as all agents are free to interact with each other. Agents usually bias their interactions through indicators of trust based on previous interactions.

2.3   Trust

Trust is fundamental to engendering cooperation in real world agent environments. Many agent interaction models rely heavily on rigorous population partitioning in order to maintain cooperation as in spatial, tagging and kin selection models. These techniques are not suited to environments where agents require the freedom to individually choose peer interactions. Real world multi-agent systems, like trading environments, use more elaborate interaction metrics such as trust. There are not many formal definitions of trust, but one has been proposed describing trust as a form of risk [3]. They state the relationship between trust T and risk R as the following:

$$R = \frac{1}{T} \tag{1}$$

This equation is partly based on the observations of Marsh. He states that 'entering into a trusting relationship is choosing to take an ambiguous path that can lead to either benefit or cost depending on the behaviours of others' [10,15]. A peer's reliability can be determined through their track record which is represented by a metric called trust. Many variants of trust have been proposed including extensions which are classified as reputation models.

An important dimension of trust involves the concept of implicit trust [8]. This concept has been proposed in order to extend our interpretation of trust beyond its more traditional parameters. These traditional concepts of trust have almost exclusively used agent-level metrics to assist agent decision making. They predominantly use static games which do not reflect the changing relationships between agents. In reality game interaction values should reflect the previous actions of players in the same way as market dynamics involving pricing always reflect the actions of competitors. An example of these dynamics would be a duopoly between two producers in a market, or more commonly an oligopoly, which is a market dominated by a small number of producers. In these markets producers can collude through limiting supply to the market and therefore maximise payoffs.

These non-static payoff dynamics have not previously been examined in relation to trust and multi-agent systems where much attention has been paid to static games such as the IPD. Implicit trust allows agents reflect trust levels through two distinct mechanisms. Firstly, through determining peer interactions, and secondly, through agreeing the payoffs or utilities for peer interactions. Traditional trust models have only considered agents' decisions to interact or not, while in reality this decision is often heavily influenced by the utilities involved.

A closely related topic to trust is that of reputation. Reputation is usually modelled through the use of a centralised blackboard system or through message passing. Reputation models are based on aggregating trust metrics and allowing this information to be made available to other agents [2]. Agents who are trusted by many agents are usually said to have a good reputation while conversely agents who are not trusted are considered to have a bad reputation.

2.4   The Iterated Prisoner's Dilemma

The Prisoner's Dilemma (PD) is a simple two-player game where each player must make a decision to either cooperate (C) or defect (D). Both players decide simultaneously and therefore have no prior knowledge of what the other has decided. If both players cooperate they receive a specific payoff. If both defect they receive a lower payoff. If one cooperates and the other defects then the defector receives the maximum payoff and the cooperator receives the minimum. The payoff matrix outlined in Table 1 demonstrates the potential payoffs for each player.

Table 1. Prisoner's Dilemma Payoff Matrix

Players Choice	Cooperate	Defect
Cooperate	$(\lambda 1, \lambda 1)$	$(\lambda 2, \lambda 3)$
Defect	$(\lambda 3, \lambda 2)$	$(\lambda 4, \lambda 4)$

The dilemma is a non-zero-sum, non-cooperative and simultaneous game. For the dilemma to hold in all cases, certain constraints must be adhered to. The following is the first constraint:

$$\lambda 2 < \lambda 4 < \lambda 1 < \lambda 3 \tag{2}$$

These conditions result in $\lambda 2$ being the sucker's payoff, $\lambda 1$ is the reward for mutual cooperation, $\lambda 4$ is the punishment for mutual defection, and $\lambda 3$ provides the incentive or temptation to defect. The second constraint is the following:

$$2\lambda 1 > \lambda 2 + \lambda 3 \tag{3}$$

This constraint prevents players taking alternating turns receiving the sucker's payoff ($\lambda 2$) and the temptation to defect ($\lambda 3$), therefore maximising their score.

The following λ values are commonly used in the Prisoner's Dilemma: $\lambda 1 = 3, \lambda 2 = 0, \lambda 3 = 5, \lambda 4 = 1$.

In the non-iterated game, the rational choice is to defect, while in the finitely repeated game, it is rational to defect on the last move and by induction to defect all the time.

3 Simulator Design

In this section we outline our overall simulator design. We begin with an introduction to the game cycle. We describe how we extended the Iterated Prisoner's Dilemma (IPD) to allow agents express preferences for certain types of games. We also outline our strategy set.

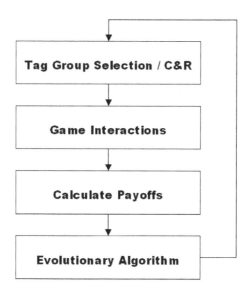

Fig. 1. Game Cycle

In Fig. 1. we show the general structure of the game cycle. Initially, agents determine their peer interactions depending on the interaction model being simulated. Agents then play their selected opponents. Subsequently, payoffs are calculated and used as a measure of fitness for our evolutionary algorithm. This evolutionary algorithm uses replicator dynamics based on fitness to determine agent representation in successive generations.

3.1 The Extended IPD

The extended IPD remains predominantly the same as the traditional game described previously. It remains a simple two player dilemma which is non-zero-sum, non-cooperative and played simultaneously. For this game to remain a

Table 2. Adapted IPD Payoff Matrix

Players Choice	Cooperate	Defect
Cooperate	$(\lambda 1, \lambda 1)$	$(\lambda 2, TD)$
Defect	$(TD, \lambda 2)$	$(\lambda 4, \lambda 4)$

Prisoner's Dilemma it must still remain within the constraints of the original game as outlined above. The extended game uses the following adapted payoff matrix.

In this game $\lambda 1$, $\lambda 2$, $\lambda 4$ remain constant while the value of TD is determined by the players involved in each game interaction. For the game to remain a dilemma the value of TD must remain within the following range of values:

$$\lambda 1 < TD < 2 \times \lambda 1 \tag{4}$$

The IPD payoff values used throughout this research are as follows: $\lambda 1 = 5000$, $\lambda 2 = 0$, $\lambda 3 = TD$, $\lambda 4 = 1$. The TD value must always remain within the following range: $\lambda 1 < TD < 2 \times \lambda 1$. These λ values provide an expressive range of possible TD values.

3.2   Strategy Set

In order to define a strategy set we draw upon existing research involving IPD strategies which use three bit strategy sets [12]. In our model each strategy genome includes four primary strategy genes representing probabilities of cooperation in an initial move p_i and in response to a cooperation p_c or defection p_d. The final strategy gene p_t represents their game preference for TD values. This strategy value, in the range of zero to one, represents their preference for higher or lower TD values. Zero represents the minimum TD value while one represents the maximum. Some strategies will prove more conservative than others in preferring games with low TD values while others will be less conservative. The resulting strategy genome looks like the following:

$$Genome = p_i, p_c, p_d, p_t \tag{5}$$

4   Interaction Models

In this paper we present simulations involving four distinct agent interaction models. In our simulator we use populations of 1000 agents. We present experiments showing the average of 50 experiments which were simulated over 100 generations. Each of these interaction models are closely related and extend each other until finally we present an interaction model which can be considered an implicit trust model. We will now present a number of distinct but related agent interaction models which we will use throughout our experiments.

4.1   Tagging Model Fixed Payoffs

This first agent interaction model is a simple tag-mediated interaction model. Agents bias their interactions probabilistically based on the similarity of their p_t genes. We use this as a experimental base case, and therefore all four λ payoffs remain fixed. The probabilities of two agents interacting is based on their p_t gene similarity. Agents make game offers to selected peers based on players' p_t gene similarity. Agents are less likely to interact with those peers who have a dissimilar p_t gene. We use a formula originally proposed in research involving tag-mediated interactions [13]. The dissimilarity of two individuals (A and C) is defined as follows:

$$d_{A,C} = |p_t^A - p_t^C| \tag{6}$$

Through using this equation agents can use the resulting probabilities to determine their peer interactions.

4.2   Tagging Model with Variable Payoffs

This interaction model extends the previous model by allowing players agree a desired TD payoff in each of their game interactions. As explained in Section 3.1 the value of TD in the extended game is limited to a particular range of values. The value of TD is determined by the agents and reflects their individual preferences. An agent i makes game offers with a TD reflecting its p_t gene. A low p_t gene will result in a low TD value and vice-versa for high p_t genes. An agent j interacts probabilistically based on the similarity of its p_t gene and the TD offered.

4.3   Trust Model with Variable Payoffs

The third interaction model differs from the previous models by introducing choice and refusal (CandR) to players. This allows players to interact freely and independent of any tag bias. In this model an agent i will make game offers based on levels of cooperation over previous rounds. This is considered a good indicator of trust. This differs significantly from the previous two models as players are free to make game offers independent of their p_t gene. The decision of agents to accept or reject game offers is based on their p_t gene preference for the TD offered. A player who prefers games with a low TD is less likely to accept a game with a high TD.

4.4   Implicit Trust Model

The final interaction model extends the previous interaction model sufficiently to be classified as an implicit trust model. The CandR environment remains, and agents continue to make game offers to selected peers based on average cooperation. One important extension allows players make game offers which reflect their level of trust in their chosen opponent. We allow agents revise their

game preference to reflect levels of trust in their opponent. In this model an agent
i adjusts its game preference to reflect trust in an opponent j. Agent i may offer
a game with a TD value which reflects its trust in j. Agent j chooses game offers
based on its trust for agent i. Since game preferences are determined through
trust the game preferences throughout the population will closely track levels of
trust in the population. If trust falls then preferences for high risk games will
fall and vice-versa. We classify this interaction model as an implicit trust model
since individual game offers reflect levels of trust [8]. In these environments, if
there are high levels of trust, there will be significant rewards to agents who
are prepared to defect. One of our primary concerns in this paper is the effect
of extending well known interaction models to reflect implicit trust. We discuss
this in the following section of this paper.

5   Experimental Results

In this section we will present a series of experimental results involving each of
our interaction models. Each experiment represents an average of 50 runs over
100 generations.

5.1   Agent Game Preferences

In the experiment shown in Fig. 2. we examine the average game preferences
throughout the agent population. These levels are determined by measuring the
average p_t gene values used throughout the population.

In the experiment shown in Fig. 2. we identify the game preferences of agents
in three interaction models. The base case interaction model (tagging with fixed
payoffs) shows no change in preferences for games of higher or lower risk. This is

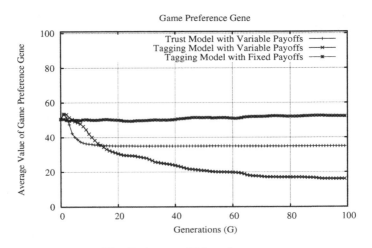

Fig. 2. Average Value of p_t gene

as a result of this base case using fixed payoffs throughout all game interactions. In this environment the game preference p_t gene has no effect on agents performance therefore experiences no evolutionary pressure. Over repeated simulations its average value remains around 0.5.

In the tag-mediated interaction model which permits agents to use their p_t gene to determine game payoffs, we identify an overall decrease in the average value of this p_t gene throughout the population. This is subsequent to an initial increase in this value. Initially exploitation is rewarded in games where the players use higher p_t genes. These agents immediately gain an advantage although this is quickly undermined through their mutual defection which undermines their fitness. All exploiters are quickly outperformed by any mutually cooperative pairings and these emerge to dominate the population. These strategies all have low p_t genes as there is no benefit for cooperative strategies to have high p_t genes.

In the third interaction model, agents make game offers to peers based on payoffs received throughout their previous interactions. This extension results in a more stable average p_t gene level throughout the population. This average p_t gene is as a result of agents initially being rewarded for exploitation and subsequently over exploiting each other. This only effects strategies who enter high TD payoff games. As a result of this mainly cooperative strategies emerge to dominate the population, and these strategies are not rewarded for having high p_t genes. Because of the trust scheme agent interaction are not a rigidly structured based on p_t genes. Therefore there is a greater tolerance of higher p_t gene values. We also noticed a heightened degree of tolerance throughout these populations where intermittent exploitation was acceptable. This was easier to achieve in a CandR environment as the population is not partitioned by tag groups. Furthermore, CandR environments facilitate repeated interactions more easily between agents for these relationships of convenience.

The data in Table 3. presents some statistical analysis of the results shown in the above graph. In a two tailed t-test, the results were found to be statistically significant with a 95% confidence interval.

Table 3. p_t Statistics

Agent Interaction Model	μ_{P_t}	σ
Tagging Fixed Payoffs	0.510	0.00101
Tagging Variable Payoffs	0.251	0.10231
CandR Trust Model Variable	0.359	0.10419

In the final experiment involving game preferences we examine the average game preference using the implicit trust model. This experiment uses a different measurement scale as preferences are different for each agent relationship. We calculate levels of game preferences throughout all games in each generation. We use a separate graph (Fig. 3.) and table (Table 4.) to represent these results.

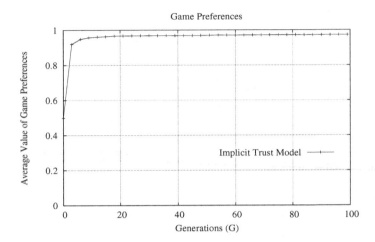

Fig. 3. Average Game Preferences

Table 4. presents some statistical analysis of of the data presented in these simulations.

Table 4. Game Preference Statistics

Agent Interaction Model	$\mu_{GamePreference}$	σ
Implicit Trust Model	0.960	0.05069

In the shown experiment (Fig. 3.) we identify a significant increase in the average game preference throughout the population. In contrast to the previous interaction models, these agents prefer games of higher risk throughout their interactions. We measure average game preferences throughout the population. Agents benefit from participating in a CandR environment by repeatedly playing their most trusted peers.

5.2   Average Fitness

In Fig. 4. we observe levels of average fitness in our simulations across 100 generations. From the results shown we identify the levels of fitness achieved throughout each of our interaction models. Each interaction model achieved high levels of fitness, which indicates that they were effective in allowing agents bias their interactions.

5.3   Pairwise Interactions

In the experiment shown in Fig. 5. we present data examining levels of interactions between agents throughout the population. Agents can be considered

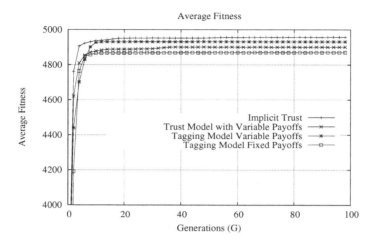

Fig. 4. Average Fitness

nodes in a graph where edges represent interactions between specific nodes in the population. By calculating the average degree of each vertex we can gain an indication of levels of connectivity throughout the population. If $G = (V, E)$ is a simple graph, and $deg(v)$ is the degree of a vertex $v \in V$ in G. The average degree in P is defined as follows:

$$D = \sum_{v \in V} \frac{deg(v)}{|V|} \tag{7}$$

The experiment shown in Fig. 5. presents levels of node connectivity through-out each of the interaction models.

In Fig. 5. we observe levels of pairwise interactions between agents throughout the population. We notice the low levels of pairwise interactions in each of our CandR interaction models. This is as a result of agents being able to reduce their pairwise interactions to their most trusted peers. Game offers are based solely on payoffs received. Tagging models are not as discerning regarding their peer interactions and therefore maintain high levels of interactions. We also note that groups in CandR environments are slower to adopt new members and this significantly effects levels of interactions throughout the population. This phenomenon does not occur in the tag interaction models.

5.4 Repeated Interactions

In the following experiment we consider levels of dependencies between agents throughout the population. Through measuring the levels of repeated interactions between nodes in the population we can evaluate the strength of these dependencies between agents. Let w_{ij} denote the weight of the edge e_{ij} connecting vertex i and j ($w_{ij} = 0$ if there is no edge connecting vertex i and j, and

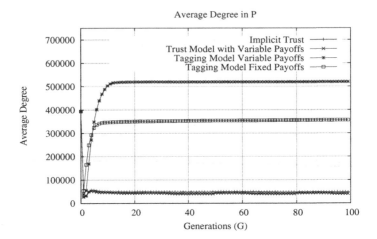

Fig. 5. Pairwise Interactions

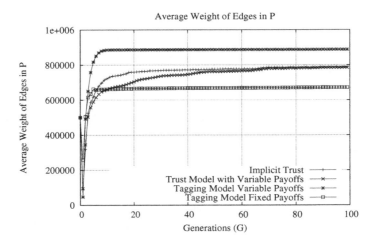

Fig. 6. Repeated Interactions

$w_{ij} = n$ if player i and j have had n game interactions). Repeated interactions are calculated using the following equation:

$$W = \sum_{e_{ij} \in E} \frac{w_{ij}}{D} \tag{8}$$

In the experiment shown in Fig. 6. we present a series of results for each of our interaction models. These metrics of repeated interactions between agents indicate how dependencies between agents develop in each interaction model. From the results presented we note that each of our tagging models converge rapidly. The significant difference in repeated interactions between these two interaction models stems from the distribution of agents across tag groups. In the fixed payoff tag model the population converges to a small number of tag value groups whereas in the variable payoff tag model there remains a larger number of tag value groups throughout the population. This significantly effects levels of repeated interactions as agents in small isolated groups will interact very heavily with each other and thereby contribute to increased levels of repeated interactions throughout the population.

In our CandR models we identify the slower convergence of the population on levels of repeated interactions. This stems from groups being slower to interact heavily with their fellow group members. This characteristic does not occur in the tag interaction models.

6 Conclusions

In this paper we have presented a series of experiments showing the fundamental differences between a number of agent interaction models. We have shown that through simple extensions to each interaction model, significant individual characteristics can emerge. We have provided a detailed examination of how agents can have a preference for games of a certain payoff risk. We have also examined how these agent preferences effect the overall behaviour of the population.

Earlier in this paper we posed two research questions regarding individual agent preferences for types of games, and also preferences based on trust. Firstly, we can conclude that tags which bias agent interactions based on game preference engender cooperation throughout the population. This is similar to tag models discussed in previous research [13,7]. From the results presented we can conclude that through allowing agents agree game payoffs there is merely an initial benefit to agents who choose games of higher risk. These strategies are quickly undermined by their own greed and replaced by much more cooperative strategies who prefer games of lower risk. Throughout out simulations involving variable payoffs we identified a significant amount of intermittent exploitation. This involves strategies maintaining their fitness through intermittently exploiting opponents while still maintaining quite cooperative relationships.

The second question posed earlier in this paper concerns the final two interaction models. These interaction models allow unhindered selection of peers and therefore allow agents exclude any non-cooperative peers. This results in the emergence of groups of heavily interacting agents. Membership of these groups is difficult to achieve for non group members once the group has emerged. Group members are very hesitant to interact with new agents and prefer to interact repeatedly with their fellow group members. From our implicit trust simulations we can clearly identify the preference of players to choose games of higher risk once they are in groups where this cannot be heavily exploited. This reinforces and extends previous research involving implicit trust [8].

7 Summary

In this paper we have shown through a series of simple extensions to an IPD environment that significant behavioural characteristics can emerge through adapting the IPD to include games of varying payoff. We have identified the emergence of strategies who's game preference fundamentally effects their success over time. In both tag and trust environments we identified the dominance of cooperative strategies who prefer games of low risk. Implicit trust differs from this as game preferences are in effect, a function of cooperation, and will always remain high in a cooperative environment like the one simulated.

Acknowledgement

The primary author would like to acknowledge the Irish Research Council for Science, Engineering and Technology (IRCSET) for their assistance through the Embark initiative.

References

1. Axelrod, R.: The Evolution of Cooperation. Basic Books, New York (1984)
2. Dellarocas, C.: The digitization of word of mouth: Promise and challenges of online feedback mechanisms. Manage. Sci. 49(10), 1407–1424 (2003)
3. Griffiths, N., Luck, M.: Cooperative plan selection through trust. In: Garijo, F.J., Boman, M. (eds.) MAAMAW 1999. LNCS, vol. 1647, pp. 162–174. Springer, Heidelberg (1999)
4. Hamilton, W.D: The evolution of altruistic behaviour. The American Naturalist 97, 354–356 (1963)
5. Holland, J.: The effects of labels (tags) on social interactions. Working Paper, Santa Fe Institute 93-10-064 (1993)
6. Howley, E., O'Riordan, C.: Agent cooperation using simple fixed bias tags and multiple tags. In: AICS 2005. The 16th Irish Conference On Artificial Intelligence and Cognative Science (2005)
7. Howley, E., O'Riordan, C.: The emergence of cooperation among agents using simple fixed bias tagging. In: Proceedings of the 2005 Congress on Evolutionary Computation (IEEE CEC 2005), vol. 2, pp. 1011–1016 (2005)
8. Howley, E., O'Riordan, C.: The effects and evolution of implicit trust in populations playing the iterated prisoner's dilemma. In: IEEE CEC 2006. Proceedings of the 2006 Congress on Evolutionary Computation. Held as part of the IEEE World Congress On Computational Intelligence IEEE WCCI 2006. IEEE Press, Los Alamitos (2006)
9. Howley, E., O'Riordan, C.: The effects of viscosity in choice and refusal ipd environments. In: Bell, D.A., Milligan, P., Sage, P.P. (eds.) Procs. of the Seventeenth Irish Conference on Artificial Intelligence and Cognitive Science, Queen's University Belfast, pp. 213–222 (2006)
10. Marsh, S.: Trust in distributed artificial intelligence. In: Castelfranchi, C., Werner, E. (eds.) MAAMAW 1992. LNCS, vol. 830, pp. 94–112. Springer, Heidelberg (1994)

11. Marsh, S.: Formalising trust as a computational concept. Ph.D. Thesis, University of Stirling (1994), `http:citeseer.ist.psu.edu/marsh94formalising.html`
12. Nowak, M., Sigmund, K.: The evolution of stochastic strategies in the prisoner's dilemma. Acta Applicandae Mathematicae 20, 247–265 (1990)
13. Riolo, R.: The effects and evolution of tag-mediated selection of partners in populations playing the iterated prisoner's dilemma. In: ICGA, pp. 378–385 (1997)
14. Stanley, E.A., Ashlock, D., Smucker, M.D.: Iterated prisoner's dilemma with choice and refusal of partners: Evolutionary results. In: Moran, F., Merelo, J.J., Moreno, A., Chacon, P. (eds.) Advances in Artificial Life. LNCS, vol. 929, pp. 490–502. Springer, Heidelberg (1995)
15. Swinth, R.L.: The establishment of the trust relationship. The Journal of Conflict Resolution 11(3), 335–344 (1967)
16. Turner, H., Kazakov, D.: Stochastic simulation of inherited kinship-driven altruism. Journal of Artificial Intelligence and Simulation of Behaviour 1(2) (2002)

Collaborative Learning with Logic-Based Models

Michal Jakob, Jan Tožička, and Michal Pěchouček

Gerstner Laboratory, Department of Cybernetics, Czech Technical University
Technická 2, Prague, 166 27, Czech Republic
{jakob,tozicka,pechouc}@labe.felk.cvut.cz

Abstract. Adaptability is a fundamental property of any intelligent system. In this paper, we present how adaptability in multi-agent systems can be implemented by means of collaborative logic-based learning. The proposed method is based on two building blocks: (1) a set of operations centred around inductive logic programming for generalizing agents' observations into sets of rules, and (2) a set of communication strategies for sharing acquired knowledge among agents in order to improve the collaborative learning process. Using these modular building blocks, several learning algorithms can be constructed with different trade-offs between the quality of learning, computation and communication requirements, and the disclosure of the agent's private information. The method has been implemented as a modular software component that can be integrated into the control loop of an intelligent agent. The method has been evaluated on a simulated logistic scenario, in which teams of trading agents learn the properties of the environment in order to optimize their operation.

1 Introduction

Adaptability is generally accepted as a fundamental property of any intelligent system. It underpins system's ability to operate effectively in open, changing environments, in which control mechanisms cannot be specified in advance.

Various approaches towards engineering adaptability have been proposed. Our framework uses *inductive logic programming* (ILP), a logic-based relational learning technique. We have chosen ILP because it has a number of properties attractive for multi-agent applications, including high expressivity and transferability of learned models, and the ability to incorporate background knowledge.

Inter-agent *communication* is the second pillar of our approach. Different types of communication are possible in multi-agent learning, ranging from indirect signalling through raw observation exchange up to high-level sharing of generalized knowledge in the form of rules and patterns. Although essential for efficient learning in the multi-agent setting, the communication can – if designed incorrectly – actually impair the learning process, and expose agents to privacy and/or security risks. A key research question in this context is how the communication (or the lack of) influences the quality and speed of the adaptation process.

K. Tuyls et al. (Eds.): Adaptive Agents and MAS III, LNAI 4865, pp. 102–116, 2008.

Taking the above into account, we have developed a multi-agent extension of ILP, which supports different levels of inter-agent communication. The method has been implemented as a Java-based component that can be integrated with existing control mechanisms. Specifically, we have incorporated the module into the reflective-cognitive agent architecture [1] used in the agent platform $\mathcal{A}$-**globe**[2]. We have carried out a number of experiments on a complex logistic scenario and evaluated the impact of each information sharing strategy on key evaluation criteria: the quality of adaptation, computation resources and communication resources required.

The paper proceeds as follows. In Section 2 we provide a brief introduction to logic-based learning methods, with particular emphasis on inductive logic programming, and their application to multi-agent learning. Section 3 introduces the $\mathcal{A}$-**globe** multi-agent learning framework and describes the different learning methods implemented. In Section 4, we empirically test all the methods on a realistic multi-agent logistic scenario and discuss each method's strengths and weaknesses. Section 5 discusses in detail assumptions and limitations of our approach. Finally, Section 6 provides concluding remarks and outlines several directions for future research.

1.1 Related Work

The majority of research on learning in multi-agent systems focuses on reactive reward-based approaches and their application to inter-agent coordination [3]. Considerably less work exists on higher-level concept learning and the role explicit inter-agent communication in multi-agent learning. Provost and Hennessy [4] present learning agents learning from disjoint subsets of a training set and show that rules *good* for the whole dataset are good for at least one of the learning agents. Colton et al. [5] use cooperative agents to create a theory in the domains of pure mathematics. Their agents share created concepts and decide which of the received concepts will be re-assessed. Panait and Luke [6] present an exhaustive review of cooperative methods for multi-agent learning. They discuss the role of communication in learning, distinguishing between direct and indirect communication.

When narrowed down to logic-based techniques, the body of research on multi-agent learning turns out surprisingly limited. Kazakov [7] discusses the application of ILP for single-agent learning in the multi-agent setting. Agents individually learn the properties of environment using the Progol ILP system. In contrast to our approach, no communication between agents takes place. Hernandez [8] discusses the application of first-order decision tree induction system ACE to learn about applicability of plans in a BDI architecture. There is no inter-agent communication beyond plain observation exchange and the learning system is not integrated into agent's reasoning architecture. Bartlett and Kazakov [9] describe agents exchanging rules describing routes to resource in their environment. Finally, Alonso [10] advocates the application of ILP and other logic-based techniques to learning in complex multi-agent domains such as conflict simulations.

2   Logic-Based Machine Learning

Learning methods based on formal logic offer a very flexible, extensible representation language, in which observation data, background knowledge and learned models can be expressed. The prominent logic-based learning method is Inductive Logic Programming (ILP)[11]. ILP is built on three pillars: first-order logic[1] as the representation formalism for both training examples (the object language) and theories learned (the concept language), background knowledge in the form of predicates, which extend the concept language, and, finally, induction as a method of learning. ILP is normally used for supervised learning. In addition to the set of labelled training examples, ILP also takes background knowledge as the input to the learning process. The output of learning is a theory, essentially a set of Horn-logic rules which, combined with the background knowledge, can be used to derive classification of unlabelled examples.

ILP has several unique properties which makes it particularly suitable for the application in the multi-agent domain:

- **Expressivity:** Relates both to the description of training examples and the models produced. The application of methods that can work with expressive models is particularly important in complex domains where knowledge-based planning and/or complex coordination is necessary [6].
- **Background Knowledge:** ILP methods can incorporate prior knowledge capturing important concepts and rules known to hold in the domain, which can significantly improve the efficiency of learning.
- **Transparency and Communicability:** Theories produced by ILP methods are expressed in a transparent format. This allows to communicate data and learned models between cooperating learning agents.
- **Semantic Interoperability:** ILP expresses knowledge in a way that is compatible with Semantic Web technologies centred around relational representation formats and description logics [12,13].

ILP methods obviously also have some disadvantages. Perhaps the biggest is their very high computational requirements, although this might be viewed as the necessary price for the flexibility offered.

3 $\mathcal{A}$-globe Multi-agent Learning

Following the description of used logic-based learning, we now describe the design and implementation of our multi-agent learning framework. First, we introduce key concepts used in the framework. We then describe three model adaptation operations, and show how they can be arranged into different learning algorithms with different performance characteristics and different level of inter-agent communication.

---

[1] More precisely the *Horn logic*, a subset of first-order logic also used as a basis for logic programming (Prolog).

3.1   Conceptual Framework

Let us first describe several important concepts of the $\mathcal{A}$-**globe** learning framework:

observation is an event considered for learning, i.e., essentially a training example; an agent can obtain observations either directly by monitoring its own actions, or by communicating with other agents.

observation set is a set of observations the agent has aggregated; each agent has it own observation set, which is used as the training set for the ILP method and/or shared with other agents.

model[2] is the theory obtained by generalizing the observation set; each agent has its own model, which it uses to control its behaviour (or, more precisely, those aspects of the behaviour influenced by learning).

The elements of the learning framework are depicted in Figure 1 including the way they are shared.

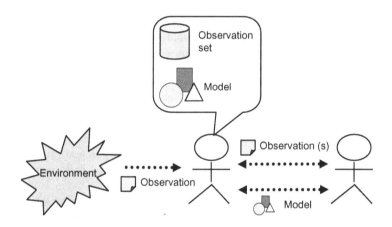

Fig. 1. Conceptual schema of $\mathcal{A}$-**globe** learning framework

3.2   Model Adaptation Operations

$\mathcal{A}$-**globe** learning framework uses three model-adaptation operations – *induce*, *merge* and *filter* – which are applied on the agent's observation set and model in order to adapt agent behaviour:

– **Induce** $(E \rightarrow M)$ is the induction operation provided by the ILP algorithm. Using the induce operation, agents generate a model generalizing its set of recorded observations.

---

[2] Note that we use the term model in its machine learning interpretation as a construct derived through the inductive learning process; its meaning is unrelated to the terminology used in formal logic. We decided to use the term model over theory as the latter is specific to ILP.

- **Merge** $(M_1, M_2 \rightarrow M)$ operation unifies two models into a single model which approximates the behaviour of the original models.
- **Filter** $(M, E \rightarrow E')$ operation reduces the observation set by removing those positive observations that are already covered by the given model. In the context of collaborative learning, observation filtering saves agents from having to generalize observations that have been already generalized and allows it to specialize on the area of the problem space that has not been yet covered.

The adaptation operations can be viewed as modular algorithmic blocks which can be arranged into different *learning workflows* (see Section 3.4). The realization of model adaptation operations can be domain-specific. Their implementation for our experimental setting is described in Section 4.2.

3.3   Inter-agent Communication

As already mentioned, communication has a fundamental impact on the efficiency of any multi-agent learning algorithm. $\mathcal{A}$-**globe** learning framework was therefore designed to support different levels of inter-agent communication. This allows to experiment with the role of communication in multi-agent learning, but, from the practical perspective, also allows customizing the learning method to fit the desired application scenario.

We currently distinguish three different types of communication:

1. **No communication:** This is a trivial case; there is no communication between agents, and, consequently, agents adapt in isolation.
2. **Low-level communication (Observation sharing):** Agents exchange raw observations they acquired. This type of communication establishes *shared information* among agents and allows them to learn from more complete trainig sets.
3. **High-level communication (Model sharing):** Agents exchange models they created by generalizing their observation sets. This type of communication aims at establishing *shared understanding* among agents.

In the context of this communication hierarchy, we are interested in the interplay between low-level and high-level communication, and particularly in the role of *compression* provided by the inductive learning process. On one hand, the compression leads to a reduction in the amount of communication, on the other, though, it might decrease the quality of resulting models. The compression is interesting also from the perspective of protecting the agent's private knowledge as it allows collaborative learning without the need to disclose specific details about agents past operation. This might be of great importance for certain application domains.

3.4   Learning Workflows

The three model adaptation operations described in Section 3.2 can be arranged into a range of different *learning workflows*, which then comprise the basis of

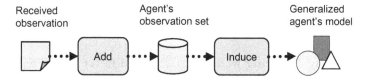

Fig. 2. Observe and Generalize workflow

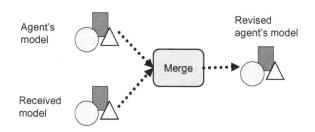

Fig. 3. Integrate by Merge workflow

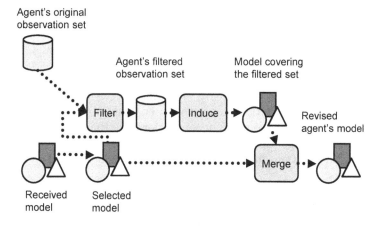

Fig. 4. Integrate by Filtering workflow

different learning methods (see Section 4.2). So far, we have implemented three such workflows, the first employing low-level while the remaining two high-level inter-agent communication.

– **Observe and Generalize** workflow (Figure 2) is the basis of the low-level collaboration learning method. It is used after the agent receives a new observation. The observation is recorded in the agent's observation set and the *induce* operation is applied to update the agent's model.

- **Integrate by Merge** workflow (Figure 3) is used in the high-level collaboration method after receiving a model from another agent. The received model is integrated with the recipient agent's existing model using the *merge* operation.
- **Integrate by Filtering** workflow is also used in the high-level collaboration method (Figure 4). The aim of the workflow to promote specialization between agents. First, a subset of the received model is selected, which is not in contradiction with recipient's observations. The selected model is used to reduce the agent's observation set through the *filter* operation. The reduced observation set is subsequently generalized to a new, more specialized model, and this model is merged with the model that triggered the integration.

4   Experiments

We have conducted a range of experiments on a realistic multi-agent logistics scenario ACROSS . The scenario serves as Gerstner lab's integrated testbed for a wide range of agent-based techniques, not limited to multi-agent learning.

The goal of the experiments was to evaluate the performance of the proposed collaborative methods in enabling the adaptability of individual agents and their teams. By comparing methods using different levels of inter-agent communication, we also wanted to gain insight in the trade-offs that exist between the key performance characteristics: the quality of adaptation, computational resources and communication resources required.

4.1   Scenario

ACROSS is a logistic scenario extended with adversarial behaviour and implemented on top of the $\mathcal{A}$-**globe** [3][2] agent platform. In the scenario, truck transporter agents deliver goods between producers and consumers. The transporter agents can form coalitions in order to improve their chances when competing for transport tasks.

In addition to the transporter agents, adversarial *bandit agents* operate in the domain. Bandit agents attack and rob transporter agents, preventing them from completing their transport tasks, and consequently reducing their profit. Transporter agents are therefore strongly motivated to try and avoid the attacks. The activity of bandit agents is, however, not uniform. Each bandit agent has a set of preferences specifying in which areas and under which conditions it attacks. The preferences are described by a relational Horn logic theory taking into account factors such as location, cargo transported, or delivery destination.

For the purpose of learning, the operation of transporter agents is segmented into a series of discrete observations. In the scenario, each observation corresponds to the act of passing a particular road segment. A transporter agent can either successfully traverse the road segment, or be robbed while attempting to

---

[3] http://agents.felk.cvut.cz/aglobe

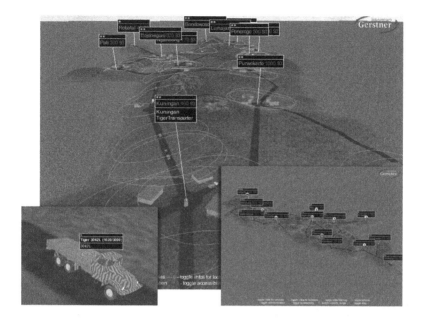

Fig. 5. ACROSS multi-agent logistic scenario

do so. Note that while from the fact that the transporter has been robbed we can conclude that the segment is dangerous, we cannot conclude the contrary from the fact that the segment has been traversed safely – this is because robberies happen when the transporter meets a bandit, i.e. only with a certain probability.

In this scenario, we therefore only have *positive examples*. Each robbery produces a positive example [4] but there are no negative examples (in a logical sense). We therefore use an ILP algorithm that is able to learn from positive-only examples. Information about safe traversals is, however, not completely discarded and it is used to prioritize candidate models during learning (see also Section 4.2).

In order to operate more safely, agents try to learn bandits' preferences and restrictions, and utilize this knowledge in their planning. Individual agents need not create a theory for all possible circumstances, but only for those that are relevant to their properties and the regions they operate in. By sharing the information and models of bandits' behaviour with partners in the coalition, using techniques described in Section 3, agents improve their adaptation process, and consequently their performance in the scenario.

Example. Let us illustrate learning in ACROSS with an example. In this case, a bandit agent uses the following rule do decide whether or not to attack:

---

[4] The observation is positive from the perspective of ILP which learns the concept of "dangerous roads" here.

```
attack(Transporter):-
    endCity(Transporter, C1),
    cityRegion(C1, 'central'),
    startCity(Transporter, C2),
    cityRegion(C2, 'central'),
    notEqual(C1, C2).
```

This bandit agent attacks only transporter agents carrying goods between two different cities in the central region.

Operating in this domain, a transporter agent could learn the following rule[5] representing its view of the bandit the agent's behavior:

```
attack(Transporter):-
    endCity(Transporter, C1),
    cityTribe(C1, 'midlanders'),
    startCity(Transporter, C2),
    cityPopulation(C2, 'village').
```

On the first sight, the rule learned by the transporter agent looks quite different to the actual rule guiding the bandit the agent's behaviour. However, because of the fact that most locations in the central region belong to the midlanders tribe (and vice versa), and some locations next to the border of the central region are villages, this rule in fact closely approximates the actual behaviour of the bandit agent.

Note that the rule learned by the agent uses variables and conjunctions of different predicates to concisely express a condition that covers a large number of specific situations. The same condition would have to be represented as a long enumeration of specific cases if relational, logic-based learning were not used.

4.2 Experiment Setup

Altogether, we have experimented with four types of methods, each utilizing a different level of inter-agent communication (see also Section 3.3).

- **No learning** – this is a trivial case implemented mainly for comparison; here agents do not adapt their behaviour.
- **Isolated learning** – in this case, agents learn individually based solely on the observations they gather on their own; there is no communication between agents.
- **Low-level collaborative learning** – this is the collaborative learning utilizing low-level inter-agent communication involving raw observation exchange.
- **High-level collaborative learning** – this is the most sophisticated method whereby the agents share the rules they have learned from their observations (which are *not* shared).

---

[5] This is just an example, the learned model usually consists of several rules of this kind.

We have used a specific implementation of model adaptation operations and workflows described in Section 3. The *induce* operation has been implemented using a *relational subgroup discovery* ILP algorithm. The algorithm uses propositionalization of the underlying relational problem and is described e.g. in [14]. The *merge* operation (see Section 3.2) is implemented as the concatenation of the two models, i.e. of the two sets of rules. In the *integrate by filtering* workflow (see Section 3.4), the full received model is selected as the input to the workflow. Because, as mentioned in Section 4.1, the scenario uses positive-only learning and there are no negative examples (in a logical sense), no contradictions can arise and the above implementation of merge and integrate by filtering leads to internally consistent models.

In the experiment, we have used five transporter agents, three bandit agents randomly passing the map and robbing transported goods, and twelve location agents providing and consuming resources, and therefore acting as departure and destination points for transporter agents. In each run, all transporter agent use the same learning method.

4.3   Evaluation Criteria

For each method, we were evaluating the following criteria:

Number of attacks per transporter agent. This number should decrease as agents learn to avoid dangerous roads. It is therefore inverse to the *performance* (also termed *quality*) of the adaptation mechanism.

Communication load measures the amount of information exchanged between agents. The measure is defined as the number of observations in the case of low-level communication, and the number or rules in the case of high-level communication.

Computational load amounts to the total CPU time consumed by the learning algorithm (with the ILP induction taking by far the largest part).

4.4   Results

We finally present the results of our experiments. Figure 6 shows the daily number of attacks (days correspond to simulation cycles). Although the long-term average (over many simulation days) of the daily number of attacks is, in the case of non-adapting agents, constant, there exist short term fluctuations when evaluated on per day basis. This is the case in our scenario where there is an increase in daily numbers of attacks in the first half of the simulation.

In order to get a better understanding of the improvement gained by the application of learning, we evaluate the adaptation performance of each method. The performance is computed as the ratio between the numbers of attacks on adaptive agents utilizing the respective method versus non-adaptive agents. For example, the value of 3 on a particular day means that adaptive agents were attacked three times *less* than non-adaptive agents. The resulting graph in Figure 7 therefore gives an account of the quality of adaptation provided by each

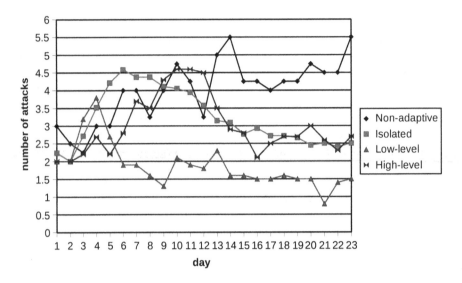

Fig. 6. Number of attacks per day. The values are average per-agent values over the whole team (5 agents).

method. The low-level collaborative method gives the best performance, with the high-level collaborative method and the non-collaborative method achieving similar, lower performance.

Adaptation quality is, however, only one of the criteria we are interested in. For computation and communication requirements, the daily axis has limited significance, and we therefore present these variables in the following table as averages over the entire simulation.

Method	isolated	low-level	high-level
average computation per day (s)	99	221	55
average communication per day (messages)	0	4103	437

From this table, it is immediately apparent that the high adaptation quality of the low-level collaborative method is negatively offset by its very high resource requirements. The method needs four times more computational resources and nearly ten times more communication than the high-level collaborative method.

Thus, in order to provide more comprehensive comparison, taking into account all three evaluation criteria, we have created Figure 8. For each criterion, the graph shows the relative score[6] of each method with respect to the best score

---

[6] The score is equal to the actual value in the case of the adaptation quality metric and is *inverse* of the actual value in the case of computational and communication requirements (in order to have "the higher, the better" semantics).

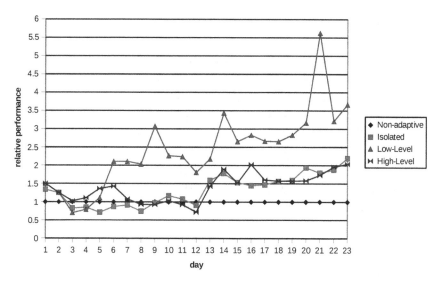

Fig. 7. Adaptation performance measured as the improvement (i.e. the decrease) in the number of attacks in comparison with the non-adaptive agent

achieved for the criterion. Thus, the best method for each criterion has the score of 100%.

4.5   Discussion

When examined closely, Figure 8 presents an interesting picture. It shows that none of the methods is uniformly better than the others. In fact, for each evaluation criterion a different method is the winner. When taking the isolated learning as the basis for comparison, we see that the addition of low-level communication improves the adaptation quality at the expense of very high communication requirements and significant increase in the computation load. High-level communication, on the other hand, decreases the computation requirements while having only modest communication needs.

Overall, the adaptation quality of the high-level collaborative method is slightly disappointing. We believe that this is mainly due to simplistic implementation of the *merge* operation in our method. With the current implementation, a large fraction of potentially important information about merged models is not taken into account (such as the number of examples from which the models were derived, the area covered by these examples etc.). With an implementation that takes such additional information into account, the performance could potentially be significantly improved.

Given the complexity of the experimental scenario, it is however difficult to draw more general conclusions at this stage. More experimentation on carefully designed benchmark problems is necessary, and it is therefore the next task we want to focus on in our research.

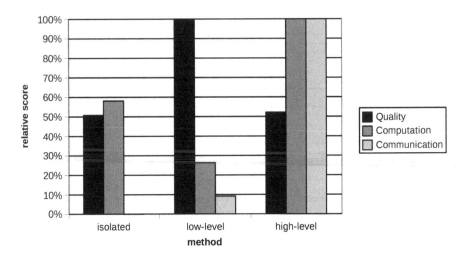

Fig. 8. Overall comparison using all three evaluation criteria. The values depicted are relative scores with respect to the best method in each category (=100%).

5   Assumptions and Limitations

In this section, we comment on several assumptions that were exploited in the design of the presented learning framework. These assumptions place certain limitations on the method and need to be understood properly for the method to be applied successfully.

A fundamental assumption (referred to as the *model independence assumption*) is that models and their quality are independent from agents that have constructed them and/or that are using them, i.e., that a model created by a specific agent can be transferred to and utilized by another agent without significant loss of quality.

One case in which the independence assumption can be violated is a *biased distribution of observations*, either by the observations (and thus also training examples) being limited only to a small subspace of the space of all possible observations, or by the observations having highly non-uniform class distribution (e.g. most observations belonging to a single class). In our simulation, such a situation can arise when agent operation, and consequently also observations it receives, is restricted to a particular subarea of the island. The model generated from such a biased training set can bear very little relevance to other areas of the island. When acquired by agents working in those areas, such a model can actually worsen their performance. Similar situation can arise when class distribution is heavily skewed and agents do have examples from all classes.

Another case in which the model independence assumption can be violated is when agents differ in their ability to acquire observations, in particular with respect to the attributes they can observe. In our simulation, e.g., one transporter may not be able to evaluate city population while the others may not know regions.

The performance of our current approach may degrade in situations where the model independence assumption does not hold. The exact quantification of such degradation and possible extensions of the approach for the case of context-dependent models presents an important area for the future research.

6 Conclusions

We have presented a novel logic-based method for collaborative multi-agent learning. The method uses Horn logic as the underlying representation. This gives it several significant advantages over propositional learning techniques, as well as makes it interoperable with existing and emerging semantic web standards. Semantic interoperability, the ability to represent complex structured concepts and to incorporate background knowledge makes the method attractive also for applications in autonomic computing. The method supports different levels of inter-agent communication. Low-level communication involving raw data exchange results in better adaptation on the expense of very high communication and computational requirements. High-level communication, on the other hand, does not achieve the same adaptation performance but needs only a small fraction of resources required by the method relying on low-level communication. It has an additional advantage of protecting agent's private information by only sharing generalized models and not specific training data, which might disclose details about the agent's past behaviour. In practice, the existence of different performance trade-offs allows to choose the method best suited for the specific application scenario.

In the future, we plan to perform more systematic, in-depth evaluation of the method, both on realistic scenarios and on more abstract benchmark problems designed specifically to test the performance of the method. An important longer-term research direction is the development of manipulation methods for logic-based models (esp. merging and generalization of theories). This should significantly improve the performance of high-level collaborative learning, and could have wider applicability in the field of distributed logic-based learning.

Acknowledgement

We gratefully acknowledge the support of the presented research by US Army Research Laboratory project N62558-03-0819 and US Office for Naval Research project N00014-06-1-0232.

References

1. Foltýn, L., Tožička, J., Rollo, M., Pěchouček, M., Jisl, P.: Reflective-cognitive architecture: From abstract concept to self-adapting agent. In: DIS 2006. Proceedings of the Workshop on Distributed Intelligent Systems. IEEE Comp. Soc., Los Alamitos (2006)

2. Šišlák, D., Rehák, M., Pěchouček, M., Rollo, M., Pavlíček, D.: A-globed: Agent development platform with inaccessibility and mobility support. In: Unland, R., Klusch, M., Calisti, M. (eds.) Software Agent-Based Applications, Platforms and Development Kits, pp. 21–46. Birkhauser Verlag, Berlin (2005)
3. Kudenko, D., Kazakov, D., Alonso, E. (eds.): AAMAS 2004. LNCS (LNAI), vol. 3394. Springer, Heidelberg (2005)
4. Provost, F.J., Hennessy, D.N.: Scaling up: Distributed machine learning with cooperation. In: Proceedings of the Thirteenth National Conference on Artificial Intelligence and the Eighth Innovative Applications of Artificial Intelligence Conference, pp. 74–79. AAAI Press / MIT Press, (1996)
5. Colton, S., Bundy, A., Walsh, T.: Agent based cooperative theory formation in pure mathematics. In: Wiggins, G. (ed.) Proceedings of AISB 2000 Symposium on Creative and Cultural Aspects and Applications of AI and Cognitive Science, pp. 11–18 (2000)
6. Panait, L., Luke, S.: Cooperative multi-agent learning: The state of the art. Autonomous Agents and Multi-Agent Systems 11, 387–434 (2005)
7. Kazakov, D., Kudenko, D.: Machine learning and inductive logic programming for multi-agent systems. In: Luck, M., Mařík, V., Štěpánková, O., Trappl, R. (eds.) ACAI 2001 and EASSS 2001. LNCS (LNAI), vol. 2086, pp. 246–270. Springer, Heidelberg (2001)
8. Guerra-Hernandez, A., Fallah-Seghrouchni, A., Soldano, H.: Learning in BDI multi-agent systems. In: Proceedings of CLIMA 2003, pp. 185–200 (2004)
9. Bartlett, M., Kazakov, D.: Comparing resource sharing with information exchange in co-operative agents, and the role of environment structure. In: Kudenko, D., Kazakov, D., Alonso, E. (eds.) Adaptive Agents and Multi-Agent Systems II. LNCS (LNAI), vol. 3394, pp. 41–54. Springer, Heidelberg (2005)
10. Alonso, E., d'Inverno, M., Kudenko, D., Luck, M., Noble, J.: Learning in multi-agent systems. Knowledge Engineering Review 16, 277–284 (2001)
11. Muggleton, S., Raedt, L.D.: Inductive logic programming: Theory and methods. Journal of Logic Programming 19/20, 629–679 (1994)
12. Beckett, D.: RDF/XML syntax specification. Technical report, W3C (2004)
13. Lee, J.K., Sohn, M.M.: The extensible rule markup language. Communications of the ACM 46, 59–64 (2003)
14. Lavrač, N., Železný, F.: Propositionalization-based relational subgroup discovery with rsd. Machine Learning 62(1-2), 33–63 (2006)

Priority Awareness: Towards a Computational Model of Human Fairness for Multi-agent Systems

Steven de Jong, Karl Tuyls, Katja Verbeeck, and Nico Roos

MICC/IKAT, Maastricht University, The Netherlands
{steven.dejong,k.tuyls,k.verbeeck,roos}@micc.unimaas.nl

Abstract. Many multi-agent systems are intended to operate together with or as a service to humans. Typically, multi-agent systems are designed assuming perfectly rational, self-interested agents, according to the principles of classical game theory. However, research in the field of behavioral economics shows that humans are not purely self-interested; they strongly care about whether their rewards are *fair*. Therefore, multi-agent systems that fail to take fairness into account, may not be sufficiently aligned with human expectations and may not reach intended goals. Two important motivations for fairness have already been identified and modelled, being (i) inequity aversion and (ii) reciprocity. We identify a third motivation that has not yet been captured: priority awareness. We show how priorities may be modelled and discuss their relevance for multi-agent research.

1 Introduction

Modelling agents for a multi-agent system requires a thorough understanding of the type and form of interactions with the environment and other agents in the system, including any humans. Since many multi-agent systems are designed to interact with humans or to operate on behalf of them, for instance in bargaining [1,2], agents' behavior should often be aligned with human expectations; otherwise, agents may fail to reach their goals.

Usually, multi-agent systems are designed according to the principles of a standard game-theoretical model. More specifically, the agents are perfectly rational and optimize their individual payoff disregarding what this means for the utility of the entire population. Experiments in behavioral economics have taught us that humans often do *not* behave in such a self-interested manner [3,4,5]. Instead, they take into account the effects of their actions on others; i.e., they strive for *fair* solutions and expect others to do the same. Therefore, multi-agent systems using only standard game-theoretical principles risk being insufficiently aligned with human expectations. A prime example is the ultimatum game [4], in which purely rational players will not be able to obtain a satisfactory payoff. More generally speaking, the importance of fairness should be studied in any problem domain in which the allocation of limited resources plays an important role [6]. Examples from our own experience include decentralized resource distribution in large storage facilities [7], aircraft deicing [8], and representing humans in bargaining (e.g., [1,9]).

Thus, designers of many multi-agent systems should take the human conception of fairness into account. If the motivations behind human fairness are sufficiently understood and modelled, the same motivations can be transferred to multi-agent systems.

K. Tuyls et al. (Eds.): Adaptive Agents and MAS III, LNAI 4865, pp. 117–128, 2008.

More precisely, *descriptive* models of human fairness may be used as a basis for *prescriptive* models, used to control agents in multi-agent systems in a way that guarantees alignment with human expectations. This interesting track of research ties in with the descriptive agenda formulated by Shoham [10] and the objectives of evolutionary game theory [5,11].

In the remainder of this paper, we first briefly discuss related work in the area of fairness models. Then, we look at problems in which priorities play a role. We show that current descriptive models do not predict human behavior in such problems. Next, we provide our descriptive model, priority awareness, and perform experiments to show that the model performs a much better prediction of human behavior. We conclude with some directions for future work.

2   Related Work

Already in the 1950's people started looking at fairness, for instance in the Nash bargaining game [12]. Recently, research in behavioral economics and evolutionary game theory has examined human behavior in the ultimatum game and the public goods game [3,4,5,13,14]. In all cases, it was observed that standard game theoretical models predict a very selfish outcome in comparison to the fair outcomes reached by human players. In other cases, e.g. the Traveler's Dilemma [15], it was shown that humans can actually obtain a higher payoff by failing to find the rational solution, i.e., the Nash equilibrium. Using neuroscientific research, such as MRI scanning [16] and disrupting certain areas if the brain using magnetic stimulation [17], it has been assessed which brain areas are likely to be responsible for fair behavior. The current state of the art provides two important descriptive models of human fairness.

Inequity aversion. The first descriptive model for human fairness is *inequity aversion*. In [4], this is defined as follows: *"Inequity aversion means that people resist inequitable outcomes; i.e., they are willing to give up some material payoff to move in the direction of more equitable outcomes"*. To model inequity aversion, an extension of the classical game theoretic actor is introduced, named homo egualis [4,5]. Homo egualis agents are driven by the following utility function:

$$u_i = x_i - \frac{\alpha_i}{n-1} \sum_{x_j > x_i} (x_j - x_i) - \frac{\beta_i}{n-1} \sum_{x_i > x_j} (x_i - x_j) \qquad (1)$$

Here, u_i is the utility of agent $i \in \{1, 2, \ldots, n\}$, which is based on its own reward, x_i, minus a term for other agents doing better (weighed by α_i), and minus a term for other agents doing worse (weighed by β_i). Agents using the homo egualis utility function care more about inequity if it is to their disadvantage than if it is to their advantage; i.e., $\alpha_i > \beta_i$. Research with human subjects provides strong evidence that this is a valid assumption [4]. The β parameter must be in the interval $[0, 1]$ to keep behavior realistic; with a higher value for β, agents would be willing to throw away money in order to reduce inequity.

Results obtained in the ultimatum game can be explained by this model as follows [4], assuming that the total sum of money to be shared is 1.[1] First, the proposal chosen by player 1 depends on his β parameter; if $\beta \geq 0.5$, player 1 will offer 0.5 to player 2. If $\beta < 0.5$, player 1's utility function is always increasing. This means that the player would like to keep the whole sum for himself. However, if he knows player 2's α parameter, he knows how much player 2 is willing to accept at least, i.e., $f(\alpha_i) = \frac{\alpha_i}{1+2\alpha_i}$; for a lower proposal, player 2's utility will be negative, making it more attractive to reject the proposal. Note that $\lim_{\alpha_i \to \infty} f(\alpha_i) = 0.5$; thus, player 2 can demand up to half of the sum to be shared. Knowing or estimating this demand, player 1 will propose just enough. It is interesting to note that the initiative thus seems to shift to the second player; the first player can only choose whether 0.5 is a good proposal or not, and if not, he needs to decide purely on the basis of what the second player wants.

Reciprocal fairness. Second, various researchers argue that fairness arises most notably in the presence of *reciprocity* [3,4,5,18,19], i.e., agents can reward and punish others. The notion of reciprocity is already implicitly present in the homo egualis actor; as has been explained above, agents that observe a negative utility with a certain reward distribution, are better off rejecting this distribution. To further model this motivation for fairness, a second actor is developed, named homo reciprocans [3,5]. This actor responds friendly to cooperation of others by maintaining this level of cooperation, and responds to defection by retaliating against the offender(s), even if this reduces her own payoff. In iterated games, this usually leads to an equilibrium in which all players behave in a fair way.

The inequity-averse and reciprocal models are predominantly descriptive: they describe and model human behavior. Another line of research is devoted to developing prescriptive or computational models. More precisely, computational models provide agents in adaptive multi-agent systems with mechanisms to obtain valid solutions, i.e., reward distributions $(x_1, \ldots, x_n)$ for which certain conditions are met. Various research initiatives formulate conditions that relate to fairness and develop mechanisms such as bargaining protocols and utility functions to obtain valid solutions under these conditions. Most notably, in the area of Computational Social Choice, fairness conditions and mechanisms relate to the well-being of society as a whole. This well-being can be measured in various ways, such as utilitarian social welfare (i.e., maximized average reward), egalitarian social welfare (i.e., maximized minimal reward), or Pareto-optimality (see [6,20] for a comprehensive overview). In this work, we present a novel measure for the fairness of an agent society; more precisely, we develop a new descriptive model with which reward distributions $(x_1, \ldots, x_n)$ can be evaluated. Future work will focus on the mechanisms to obtain valid solutions under these conditions.

---

[1] For readers unfamiliar with the ultimatum game: in this game, the first player proposes how to divide a sum of money with the second player. If the second player rejects this division, neither gets anything. If the second accepts, the first gets his demand and the second gets the rest. The individually rational solution to this game is for the first player to propose the lowest possible amount, and for the second player to accept. Human players however consistently offer more, and reject low offers.

3   Fairness in Priority Problems

3.1   Priority Problems

In many situations, humans actually consider it fair that each of them gets a (slightly) different reward, because they take into account additional information. For instance, everybody can agree that priority mail should be delivered faster than regular mail. Such situations are present in many common applications of multi-agent systems and should therefore be addressed when looking at fairness. The nature of the additional information can vary; examples include wealth, probabilities of people belonging to a certain group or priorities involved in the task at hand. We will denote this additional information with one value per agent, i.e., the *priority*. Currently, we assume that the priority values are true and are known by all agents.

3.2   Example and Human Response

In a certain furniture store, customers wait at a service desk while employees fetch the items ordered. Obviously, a customer will not be happy if he observes that five other customers are helped while he is still waiting at the service desk. Neither will customers requesting the most popular item be pleased when they discover that they all have to wait for five minutes because another customer has ordered an extremely rare item. In other words, customers are willing to accept that someone who orders a common item (i.e., an item with high probability of being ordered) is helped slightly more quickly than someone who orders a rare item (with low probability of being ordered).

To investigate how humans deal with such a problem, in [7], we discuss a test of human fairness in a small shop environment, inspired by this example. The store at hand sells two types of fruit (see Figure 1), located at A and B respectively. The human respondents are given the probabilities that customers wish to order the fruit at A (say, p) or the fruit at B $(1 - p)$ and are then asked to place the robot somewhere on the line AB, such that all customers will be satisfied. We found that human behavior in this test is not appropriately predicted by analytical measures. More precisely, if $p > 0.5$, analytical measures would place the robot at A (in order to minimize expected waiting time) or in the middle (in order to minimize the variance in waiting time). Humans on the other hand tend to place the robot somewhere between A and the middle. Thus, they perform a trade-off between the expected waiting time and the variance (i.e., they choose a more fair solution). The larger p becomes, the closer to A the robot is placed. We then tried to apply the two known motivations for fairness (inequity aversion and reciprocity) and found that these did not predict human behavior either.

3.3   Why Current Descriptive Models Do Not Work

More generally speaking, both inequity-averse and reciprocal models cannot be used to sufficiently describe the human conception of fairness in problems where priorities play a role. As a result, they are also not immediately suitable as a starting point for prescriptive models, as needed for multi-agent systems.

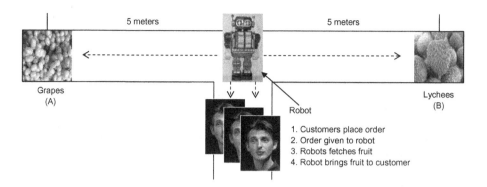

Fig. 1. A human fairness test in a small shop environment

Inequity aversion. In [4,5], the homo egualis model, which is inequity-averse, is applied to the ultimatum game and the public goods game. Obtained results are in line with human behavior, as long as the model's parameters are chosen carefully. Moreover, the homo egualis utility function may lead to different payoffs for different agents. However, there are two problems when trying to use the egualis model for more complicated settings, including those where priorities play a role.

First, as clearly indicated in [4], in many situations, people actually like to be better than other people, and the homo egualis actor does not model this behavior. In priority problems, people do not only tolerate, but even encourage inequity; agents with a high priority should actually like (and be allowed) to be better than agents with a low priority. Priorities would have to be encoded in an indirect way using the model's parameters (most notably α_i); moreover, an agent demanding more than half of the reward at hand would not be possible with this model. Second, if we wish to use homo egualis in order to find solutions in which a maximal, fairly distributed reward is obtained, we can only do this when (i) the total reward is constant and independent from the agents' actions, (ii) agents take 'their piece of the pie' one after the other and (iii) there exists a dependency between the (private) parameters of the agents participating. In practice, this entails that the agents should actually bargain about the model's parameters. In this case, it would be easier to simply bargain about the actual reward.

Reciprocal fairness. Asking our players to place the robot "such that all customers are satisfied" implicitly introduces a threat of punishment to this player; if customers are dissatisfied, they might not return to the shop in question. The outcomes of the test might therefore be explainable in terms of reciprocity. However, there are (once again) two problems when trying to apply a reciprocal model to the customer game.

First, reciprocal models assume a setting in which players receive explicit punishments (or rewards) after performing a certain action. In case of our test, no explicit feedback was given to the respondents. Second, even if explicit punishments are available, the reciprocal model itself does not allow agents to compute when to punish; it just states that there is an option to do so if an 'unfair' action has been observed. As has been mentioned earlier, the homo egualis model can be used to calculate the minimal amount a player should offer in the ultimatum game; below this amount, the other player experiences a negative utility and is thus better off rejecting the offer (i.e., he applies punishment). However, as has been shown above, in more complicated situations, such as problems where the total reward is not constant, or problems in which priorities play a role, the homo egualis model is not easily, if at all, usable. In other words, reciprocal fairness itself is actually more a conceptual model than a descriptive model.

4 Our Proposed Descriptive Model: Priority Awareness

4.1 Fairness Boundaries

In order to describe a fair distribution of rewards over (potentially many) agents with priorities, we introduce a new, descriptive notion of fairness: priority awareness. We define two boundaries in our model. To keep reward distributions within the boundaries, we introduce a parameter $\alpha \in [0, 1]$, called the *greediness* parameter.[2] With $\alpha = 0$, all agents are satisfied when the total reward is shared evenly (i.e., everybody gets the same reward). With $\alpha = 1$, agents want a reward that is proportional to their priority value. Note that situations where $\alpha < 0$ (someone gets less than equal share even though his priority is not lower) as well as situations where $\alpha > 1$ (someone gets more than a priority-based share) are common in the world around us. However, these situations are generally considered to be unfair. Reward distributions obtained by setting the α parameter to valid values can therefore be best described as being 'not definitely unfair'; i.e., we do not allow reward distributions that can immediately be marked as unfair.

4.2 Formal Model

More formally, in our model, we distinguish n different agents i, each with a priority value p_i and a given reward R_i. The priority values are defined such that $\sum_{i=1}^{n} p_i = 1$ and $\forall i : 0 < p_i \leq 1$. We introduce the greediness parameter $\alpha \in [0, 1]$ and define the following class of fairness functions $f_\alpha(i)$, applied to agents i:

$$f_\alpha(i) = \frac{1}{n} + \alpha \left(p_i - \frac{1}{n} \right) \tag{2}$$

Now, we say that agents i and j have a fair share with respect to each other and the parameter α if and only if their rewards R_i and R_j satisfy the following equation:

$$\frac{R_i}{f_\alpha(i)} = \frac{R_j}{f_\alpha(j)} \tag{3}$$

To simulate the flexibility of human fairness, our model needs to tolerate a (small) range of α-values. Therefore, we need to decide on upper and lower bounds for α, i.e. $\alpha \in [\alpha_{\min}, \alpha_{\max}]$. These upper and lower bounds then specify how tolerant we are with

---

[2] In the remainder of this text, we assume that every agent uses the same α-value. The model can easily be equipped with 'personal' values for α, similar to the homo egualis model.

respect to differences in reward. Using these bounds, we define a *score function* for any pair of agents i and j as follows:

$$s\,(i,j) = \begin{cases} 1 & \exists \alpha \in [\alpha_{\min}, \alpha_{\max}] : \frac{R_i}{f_\alpha(i)} = \frac{R_j}{f_\alpha(j)} \\ 0 & \text{otherwise} \end{cases} \tag{4}$$

Thus, two agents i and j yield a $s(i,j)$ of 1 if the reward of agent i is within an interval around the reward of individual j, as specified by the minimum and maximum allowed α-values. The utility for each agent $i \in \{0, 1, \ldots, n\}$ is now determined as:

$$u_i = \frac{1}{n-1} \sum_{j=1, i \neq j}^{n} s(i,j) \tag{5}$$

Thus, each agent scores 1 for every other agent that has a fair reward compared to this agent's reward. In the worst case, an agent obtains a utility of 0. In the best case, an agent has a fair reward compared to all other agents and therefore 'scores' $n - 1$ times; we divide the result, $n - 1$, by $n - 1$, yielding a utility of 1. Thus, $u_i \in [0, 1]$ for all i.

5   Initial Model Validation

To validate our model conceptually, we have performed a number of experiments with human subjects. We will provide an overview of the results here, showing that priorities indeed matter to people, and that our ideas about tolerated intervals might correspond to human behavior.

5.1   Two Simple Tasks

Initially, we performed two small experiments, each using a group of 50 subjects, with different subjects for each experiment. Respondents were asked to mark which of the given answers they considered to be fair. We categorized each possible answer as either within or outside our model's boundaries. The first experiment concerned the fruit store test described in Section 3.2. The second experiment contained two questions, both examples of problems in which priorities play a role (Table 1).

In the first experiment, with a setting of $p = 0.6$, 42 people place the robot somewhat closer to the grapes than to the lychees. Five people place the robot at the grapes; three people place the robot in the middle. Thus, 45 out of 50 positions selected are within our model's boundaries. When the probability that grapes are requested is increased to 0.9, the robot is placed closer to the grapes by everyone who has not placed it at the grapes already. Once again, 45 out of 50 answers given were within our model's boundaries – the five 'misses' are obviously correlated to the first five. Thus, in the first experiment, our model described 90% of the answers.

In the second experiment, 180 answers were given (respondents could select multiple answers, see Table 2). Of these 180 answers, 164 were within our model's boundaries. Thus, in the second experiment, our model described 91% of the human answers.

Table 1. Some small experiments in human fairness

1. A mail company offers priority stamps and regular stamps. Priority stamps are twice as expensive. How should the delivery time of priority mail compare to that of regular mail? a. First deliver each priority mail and after that, if there is time, deliver regular mail. b. Deliver priority mail twice as fast as regular mail. c. Deliver priority mail faster than regular mail if possible. d. Deliver all mail just as fast. e. Deliver regular mail faster than priority mail.
2. You just had dinner with a large group of people. You all ate and drank different things, so everybody's bill is different. The waiter now brings one bill. How should the bill be distributed? a. The person that has used the most expensive food and drinks pays everything. b. Everybody pays his/her own bill. c. Everybody pays so that the amount paid is somewhat proportional to the expenses done. d. Everybody pays the same. e. People that have eaten less expensive food pay more.

Table 2. The results for the experiments presented above

Question	Answ. a $\alpha > 1$	Answ. b $\alpha = 1$	Answ. c $\alpha \in \langle 0, 1 \rangle$	Answ. d $\alpha = 0$	Answ. e $\alpha < 0$	Sum
1	20%	48%	30%	1%	0%	79
2	0%	39%	34%	28%	0%	101
					Total	180
					Correct	164
					Cover	**91%**

5.2   A Prioritized Ultimatum Game

After these initial experiments, we created a larger, more structured experiment, after the example of many experiments with human fairness in ultimatum games (for an overview of such experiments, see [4]). In almost every existing experiment, it is observed that an offer of 50% is very common, and is almost always accepted. Offers below 20% are hardly ever offered, and when they are, they are often rejected.

We asked students and staff members of three faculties of the University of Maastricht to participate in our ultimatum-game survey, which was developed in cooperation with an experimental psychologist. [3] We asked respondents various control questions, and a rather large number of ultimatum game dilemmas were presented. Respondents were then asked how much they would offer (as a first player) or accept at least (as a second player). In the end, 170 surveys were submitted, of which 160 were usable for analysis. Of these 160 respondents, 38 were familiar with the ultimatum game; the remaining 122 were not.

To introduce the notion of priorities more explicitly in the ultimatum game, we varied two quantities. First, after playing some standard ultimatum games, participants were told that the other player was ten times poorer or ten times wealthier than they were. We expected that people would either be fair to poorer people (i.e., give them more) or exploit poorer people (i.e., give them less, because they will accept anyway). Second, the amount of money that had to be divided was varied between EUR.10, EUR.1.000 and EUR.100.000, to determine whether this had any effect on people's attitude with respect to poorer, equal or richer people. We will now present the most important results,

---

[3] The survey can still be viewed at http://www.cs.unimaas.nl/steven.dejong/survey

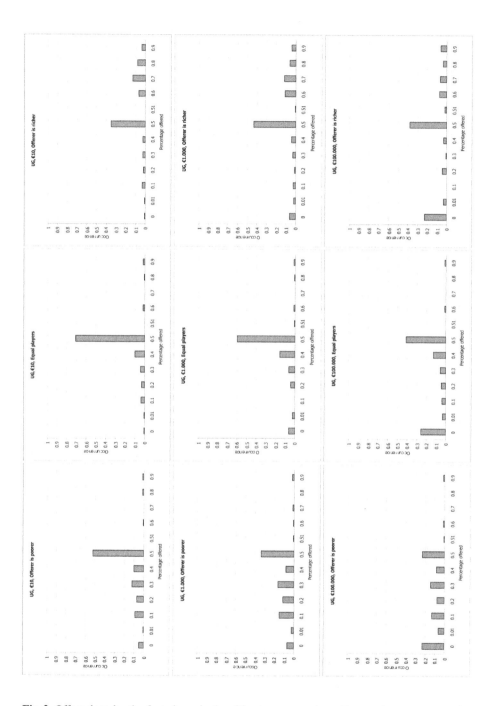

Fig. 2. Offers done by the first player in the ultimatum game, depending on the amount at stake and the relative wealth of the other player. Offers are binned in 12 bins, of which the *lower bound* is displayed in every chart.

which are graphically represented in Figure 2. Note that the answers concerning the second player have not been included; in all cases, respondents answered consistently for the first and second player, meaning that they always offered at least the amount they personally would accept.

Equal players. Note that priority awareness only allows differences in reward if the agents actually have a different priority. Thus, in the ultimatum game, the fact that the first player may keep more than 50% to himself, can only be explained by our model if we assume that this player has a higher priority. This is actually not a strange thing to assume; after all, the first player was chosen as the one who should perform the offer. He can thus make a strategic choice. The second player, on the other hand, can only decide whether or not to accept, which is a distinctively less strategic choice, especially in one-shot games. Since human players usually indicate that they would accept less than 50%, we can conclude that both players are in agreement about the fact that the first player has a higher priority.

Since we were asking people to imagine they had to divide money, instead of giving them actual money to divide, we needed to assess whether this difference had an important impact on the results. This, fortunately, was not the case; the behavior we found was in line with behavior found earlier [4]. For instance, most people were willing to give away 50%, and some people offered less. With an increasing amount, we see that the first player keeps more to himself; this behavior is not punished by the second player. Clearly, *the first player's priority increases with an increasing amount at stake*. This is rather obvious; after all, it is a lot more difficult to say no to 10% of EUR.100.000 than to 10% of EUR.10. Interestingly, most literature on this subject states that the amount at stake does *not* influence the offered (and accepted) proportion (e.g., see [4]). However, experiments with high amounts at stake were mostly performed in relatively poor countries, simply because research institutes cannot afford to let people play games worth EUR.100.000 in Europe; perhaps, this explains why such 'high-stake' games have such a fair outcome in general.

Richer or poorer players. Players' behavior in the normal ultimatum game can already be successfully explained using the homo egualis utility function [4]. However, the results of our survey show that priorities explicitly matter to human players of the ultimatum game. Before confronting participants with ultimatum games in which players had unequal wealth, we asked them whether they had thus far assumed that the other player was poorer, wealthier or equally wealthy. 92% of the participants assumed that the other player was equally wealthy; the remaining 8% was almost equally divided between the other two options. Subsequently, the participants were confronted with games in which the other player was ten times more or less wealthy. Results indicate that people are actually fair to poorer people, and expect the same in return from richer people; poorer opponents were given substantially more money than equal people, richer opponents were given substantially less. Once again, all participants were willing to accept their own offers. This indicates that *the second player's priority decreases with increasing relative wealth*.

Implications. Given the two observations above, we see that priorities indeed matter to human players; thus, the first player is able to keep more for himself when the amount at stake increases. Moreover, depending on the relative wealth of the second player, more or less is given. This behavior clearly is not sufficiently described by the homo egualis function; most notably, (1) the relation between the amount at stake and the relative wealth of participants is not sufficiently described, and (2) the significant number of participants who offer more than half of the amount at stake to a poor second player, is not described by homo egualis at all. The priority awareness model is able to capture this behavior in a straightforward way, using the notion of priorities. For a precise alignment of the priorities with human behavior, more experiments may be necessary.

6   Conclusion and Future Work

In this paper, we have argued why fairness is an important issue for designers of many multi-agent systems. We discussed two existing descriptive models of human fairness and introduced a third model, called *priority awareness*. In contrast to the two existing models, this model is able to describe human behavior in problems where priorities play an important role. We demonstrated this in various experimental settings.

It is important to realize that this model, like the other two models, does not say anything about the optimality of a reward distribution. For instance, a situation in which everyone gets a reward of 0 may very well be fair, but is obviously sub-optimal. In practical situations, people would like to obtain an *optimally fair* reward distribution, meaning that (a) the reward is distributed in a fair way and (b) the total reward is maximized, i.e., the distribution is Pareto-optimal [21]. In our model, this may entail selecting the most optimal α-value. However, more research is needed to assess how fairness may be reached, given optimality requirements.

In the near future, we will conduct more experiments with human subjects in order to support and refine our priority-aware fairness model. One important issue in the ultimatum game, for example, is that some people consider the first player to have the highest priority, regardless of the problem settings at hand, whereas other people are more sensitive to relative wealth. This indicates that priorities might not always lead to a situation in which 'half or more' is tolerated.

As an important current line of research, we are investigating how fairness can actually be engineered into a multi-agent system; our current, descriptive model already allows us to determine utility values for agents, which can for instance be used to learn a fair policy – in the future, we would like to develop a prescriptive model, with which agents can determine which action would be best.

Acknowledgments. The research reported here is partially funded by the 'Breedtestrategie' programme of the Universiteit Maastricht. We thank our colleagues for their constructive criticism, and the anonymous reviewers for useful comments. Finally, we wish to express our gratitude to our respondents for their cooperation and to Lumière Maastricht for supporting our survey.

References

1. Erev, I., Roth, A.E.: Predicting how people play games with unique, mixed strategy equilibria. American Economic Review 88(2/3), 848–881 (1998)
2. Russell, S., Norvig, P.: Artificial Intelligence, A Modern Approach, 2nd edn. Prentice Hall, Englewood Cliffs (1995)
3. Bowles, S., Boyd, R., Fehr, E., Gintis, H.: Homo reciprocans: A Research Initiative on the Origins, Dimensions, and Policy Implications of Reciprocal Fairness. Advances in Complex Systems 4(2/3), 1–30 (1997)
4. Fehr, E., Schmidt, K.: A Theory of Fairness, Competition and Cooperation. Quarterly Journal of Economics 114, 817–868 (1999)
5. Gintis, H.: Game Theory Evolving: A Problem-Centered Introduction to Modeling Strategic Interaction. Princeton University Press, Princeton (2001)
6. Chevaleyre, Y., Dunne, P.E., Endriss, U., Lang, J., tre, M.L., Maudet, N., Padget, J., Phelps, S., guez Aguilar, J.A.R., Sousa, P.: Issues in Multiagent Resource Allocation. Informatica 30, 3–31 (2006)
7. de Jong, S., Tuyls, K., Sprinkhuizen-Kuyper, I.: Robust and Scalable Coordination of Potential-Field Driven Agents. In: Proceedings of IAWTIC/CIMCA 2006, Sydney (2006)
8. Mao, X., ter Mors, A., Roos, N., Witteveen, C.: Agent-based scheduling for aircraft deicing. In: Schobbens, P.Y., Vanhoof, W., Schwanen, G. (eds.) Proceedings of the 18th Belgium - Netherlands Conference on Artificial Intelligence, BNVKI, pp. 229–236 (October 2006)
9. Preist, C., van Tol, M.: Adaptive agents in a persistent shout double auction. In: ICE 1998. Proceedings of the first international conference on Information and computation economies, pp. 11–18. ACM Press, New York, NY, USA (1998)
10. Shoham, Y., Powers, R., Grenager, T.: If Multi-Agent Learning is the Answer, What is the Question? Journal of Artificial Intelligence (to appear)
11. Tuyls, K., Nowe, A.: Evolutionary Game Theory and Multi-Agent Reinforcement Learning. The Knowledge Engineering Review 20, 63–90 (2005)
12. Nash, J.: The Bargaining Problem. Econometrica 18, 155–162 (1950)
13. Gale, J., Binmore, K.G., Samuelson, L.: Learning to be Imperfect: The Ultimatum Game. Games and Economic Behavior 8, 56–90 (1995)
14. Binmore, K.: Natural Justice. Oxford University Press, Oxford (2005)
15. Basu, K.: The Traveler's Dilemma. Scientific American 296(6), 68–73 (2007)
16. Sanfey, A.G., Rilling, J.K., Aronson, J.A., Nystrom, L.E., Cohen, J.D.: The Neural Basis of Economic Decision-Making in the Ultimatum Game. Science 300, 1755–1758 (2003)
17. Knoch, D., Pascual-Leone, A., Meyer, K., Treyer, V., Fehr, E.: Diminishing Reciprocal Fairness by Disrupting the Right Prefrontal Cortex. Science (October 2006)
18. Rabin, M.: Incorporating Fairness into Game Theory and Economics. American Economic Review 83, 1281–1302 (1993)
19. Fehr, E., Fischbacher, U.: The Nature of Human Altruism. Nature 425, 785–791 (2003)
20. Chevaleyre, Y., Endriss, U., Lang, J., Maudet, N.: A Short Introduction to Computational Social Choice. In: van Leeuwen, J., Italiano, G.F., van der Hoek, W., Meinel, C., Sack, H., Plášil, F. (eds.) SOFSEM 2007. LNCS, vol. 4362, pp. 51–69. Springer, Heidelberg (2007)
21. Verbeeck, K.: Coordinated Exploration in Multi-Agent Reinforcement Learning. PhD thesis, Vrije Universiteit Brussel (2004)

Bifurcation Analysis of Reinforcement Learning Agents in the Selten's Horse Game

Alessandro Lazaric, Enrique Munoz de Cote, Fabio Dercole,
and Marcello Restelli

Politecnico di Milano, Department of Electronics and Information,
piazza Leonardo da Vinci 32, I-20133 Milan, Italy
{lazaric,munoz,dercole,restelli}@elet.polimi.it

Abstract. The application of reinforcement learning algorithms to multiagent domains may cause complex non-convergent dynamics. The replicator dynamics, commonly used in evolutionary game theory, proved to be effective for modeling the learning dynamics in normal form games. Nonetheless, it is often interesting to study the robustness of the learning dynamics when either learning or structural parameters are perturbed. This is equivalent to unfolding the catalog of learning dynamical scenarios that arise for all possible parameter settings which, unfortunately, cannot be obtained through "brute force" simulation of the replicator dynamics. The analysis of bifurcations, i.e., critical parameter combinations at which the learning behavior undergoes radical changes, is mandatory. In this work, we introduce a one-parameter bifurcation analysis of the Selten's Horse game in which the learning process exhibits a set of complex dynamical scenarios even for relatively small perturbations on payoffs.

1 Introduction

Game Theory (GT) [9] provides formal models (i.e., games) for the study of the interaction between self-interested rational agents, whose goal is the maximization of the return (i.e., payoff). In particular, GT identifies the conditions for the existence of equilibria (e.g., Nash equilibria), i.e., strategic configurations in which no agent can change her strategy without worsening her payoff. Nonetheless, the computation of equilibria requires each agent to have a complete knowledge of the game (actions available to other agents and their payoffs).

On the other hand, Reinforcement Learning (RL) [11] enables autonomous agents to learn the optimal strategy that maximizes the return through a direct interaction with an unknown environment. Multiagent Reinforcement Learning [8] extends the traditional single-agent RL approach to game theoretic problems in which several agents interact. Although RL algorithms are guaranteed to find the optimal (Nash) strategy in problems with stationary environments, they may fail to converge in environments where other learning agents are involved. As a result, the learning process may exhibit very complex non-convergent (periodic or aperiodic) dynamics [6,10] that are often difficult to study by stochastically simulating single runs of execution.

K. Tuyls et al. (Eds.): Adaptive Agents and MAS III, LNAI 4865, pp. 129–144, 2008.

Evolutionary Game Theory (EGT) [4] studies the evolution of populations of agents as dynamical systems, notably with the replicator dynamics equation. The translation of Q-learning [13], one of the main RL algorithms, into suitable replicator dynamics [1,12] makes possible the study of the dynamics of the learning processes as the study of nonlinear dynamical systems. The simulation (numerical integration) of the replicator dynamics therefore provides an alternative approach to study the behavior of learning agents, which is however effective only when all parameter values are assigned. In fact, as better explained in Sec. 4.2, how robust the observed learning dynamics are, when either learning parameters or parameters defining the structure of the game change because of noise or system perturbations, cannot be assessed by simply organizing extensive simulations.

Bifurcation analysis [7] provides strong theoretical foundations and effective numerical techniques to study the robustness of a dynamical system to parameter perturbations. In particular, robustness, called *structural stability* in the dynamical system jargon, is lost at the critical parameter combinations, called *bifurcations*, at which arbitrarily small parameter perturbations induce radical qualitative, other than quantitative, changes in the system dynamics.

In this paper, we introduce bifurcation theory and we apply it to the analysis of the dynamics of the learning process in a three agents representative extensive form game: the Selten's Horse. We investigate the problem characteristics and the learning solutions through a bifurcation analysis with respect to one of the payoffs of the game. In particular, we show that the dynamical system can repeatedly loose structural stability even in relatively small payoff intervals, that multiple stationary and non-stationary (periodic) attractors can be present, and that several bifurcations regulate their appearance, disappearance, and the catastrophic transitions between them.

The rest of the paper is organized as follows. In Section 2 we introduce definitions of normal and extensive form games. In Section 3 we briefly review Q-learning and how its dynamics can be translated into replicator-like dynamics. An introduction to bifurcation analysis is provided in Section 4 and, finally, in Section 5 we analyze the Selten's Horse game as a case study for bifurcation analysis of multiagent reinforcement learning systems.

2   Game Theory Background

2.1   Normal Form Games

In Game Theory, games are defined as conflict situations between agents. In a normal form game, agents execute actions simultaneously according to their strategies and the outcome of the game is a payoff for each agent. Formally:

Definition 1. *A normal form game Γ is defined by the tuple $\langle \mathcal{N}, \mathcal{A}, \mathcal{R} \rangle$, where:*

- $\mathcal{N} = \{1, \ldots, n\}$ is the set of agents in the game
- $\mathcal{A} = A_1 \times \ldots \times A_i \times \ldots \times A_n$ is the set of joint actions $\mathbf{a} = (a_1, \ldots, a_i, \ldots, a_n)$, where a_i is an element of the set $A_i = \{a_{i1}, \ldots, a_{ij}, \ldots, a_{im_i}\}$ of the m_i actions available to agent i ($m_i = m$ in the following)
- $\mathcal{R} = \{R_1, \ldots, R_n\}$ is the set of payoff functions, where $R_i : \mathcal{A} \to \Re$ is the payoff function for agent i that maps each joint action to a numerical payoff

Furthermore, we define:

- $\mathcal{X} = X_1 \times \ldots \times X_i \times \ldots \times X_n$ as the set of joint strategies $\mathbf{x} = (\mathbf{x}_1, \ldots, \mathbf{x}_i, \ldots, \mathbf{x}_n)$, where strategy $\mathbf{x}_i = (x_{i1}, \ldots, x_{ij}, \ldots, x_{im})$ is a probability distribution over the action set A_i, so that $\mathbf{x}_i \in \Sigma_m = \{\mathbf{x}_i : 0 \leq x_{ij} \leq 1, \sum_{j=1}^m x_{ij} = 1\}$, where Σ_m is the m-dimensional simplex
- $\rho = \{\rho_1, \ldots, \rho_n\}$ as the set of expected payoff functions, where $\rho_i : \mathcal{X} \to \Re$ is the expected payoff function for agent i that maps each joint strategy to a numerical payoff, that is the sum of the payoffs for all the possible joint actions weighted by their probabilities according to the joint strategy

At each round of the game, each agent chooses an action a_i, a joint action $\mathbf{a}$ is executed, and a payoff $R_i(\mathbf{a})$ is returned. When an agent plays deterministically one action (say a_{ij} with $x_{ij} = 1$), then the strategy is *pure*, otherwise is a *mixed* strategy. The joint action of all agents but agent i is usually denoted as $\mathbf{a}_{-i} = (a_1, \ldots, a_{i-1}, a_{i+1}, \ldots, a_n) \in \mathcal{A}_{-i} = A_1 \times \cdots \times A_{i-1} \times A_{i+1} \times \cdots \times A_n$. Similarly, the joint strategy of all the agents but i is defined as $\mathbf{x}_{-i} = (\mathbf{x}_1, \ldots, \mathbf{x}_{i-1}, \mathbf{x}_{i+1}, \ldots, \mathbf{x}_n)$. In the following, we refer to *matrix* games, in which the payoff functions R_i are matrices P_i with dimensions $|A_i| \times |\mathcal{A}_{-i}|$, i.e. $\rho_i(\mathbf{x}) = \mathbf{x}_i P_i \mathbf{x}_{-i}$.

The main solution concept in a normal form game is the *Nash equilibrium*.

Definition 2. *Given a normal form game* $\Gamma = \langle \mathcal{N}, \mathcal{A}, \mathcal{R} \rangle$, *the joint strategy* $\mathbf{x}^* = (\mathbf{x}_1^*, \ldots, \mathbf{x}_n^*)$ *is a Nash equilibrium when:*

$$\rho_i(\mathbf{x}_1^*, \ldots, \mathbf{x}_i^*, \ldots, \mathbf{x}_n^*) \geq \rho_i(\mathbf{x}_1^*, \ldots, \mathbf{x}_i, \ldots, \mathbf{x}_n^*), \quad \forall i \in \mathcal{N}, \forall \mathbf{x}_i \in \Sigma_m. \quad (1)$$

In a Nash equilibrium none of the agent can improve her expected payoff by changing her strategy while all other agents keep playing the same strategies. In other words, each strategy $\mathbf{x}_i^*$ is the best response to $\mathbf{x}_{-i}^*$.

2.2   Extensive Form Games

In contrast with normal form games, extensive form games describe the sequential structure of decision making explicitly, and therefore allow the study of situations in which agents play one after the other and possibly several times at different stages of the game round [9]. An extensive form game is represented by a tree (Fig. 1). Each node represents a *state* of play of the game. The game begins at a unique initial node, and flows through the tree along a path determined by the actions taken by the agents until a terminal node is reached, where the game ends and payoffs are assigned to agents. At each non-terminal node only

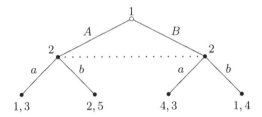

Fig. 1. A two agents, two actions, extensive form game with imperfect information. Dotted lines represent information sets. Labels at decision nodes identify the agent that plays, labels on edges agents' actions, and values at leaves agents' payoffs.

one agent plays by choosing among a set of available actions, each action being represented by an edge leading from a node to another. Games in which each agent knows exactly the node in the tree where she plays are games with *perfect* information, otherwise information is *imperfect*. The agents' uncertainty about the state is represented by *information sets* that group the states that cannot be distinguished by the agents. Formally:

Definition 3. *An extensive form game is a tuple* $\Gamma = \langle \mathcal{N}, \mathcal{G}, \{R_i\}, \iota, \{\mathcal{H}_i\}, \{\mathcal{A}_i\}\rangle$, *where:*

- $\mathcal{N}$ *is the set of the agents*
- $\mathcal{G} = \langle \mathcal{S}, s^0, \mathcal{T} \rangle$ *is a finite tree with a set of decision nodes* $\mathcal{S}$, *a unique initial node* $s^0 \in \mathcal{S}$ *and, a set of terminal nodes* $\mathcal{T}$
- $R_i : \mathcal{T} \to \Re$ *is the payoff function for agent* i *that maps each terminal node to a numerical payoff*
- $\iota : \mathcal{S} \to \mathcal{N}$ *is the agent function that maps decision nodes to the agent that plays at that node*
- *let* $\mathcal{H}$ *be the set of information sets* $h \subset \mathcal{S}$ *that partitions the set of decision nodes:* $\mathcal{S} = \bigcup_{h \in \mathcal{H}} h$ *and* $\forall h, h' \in \mathcal{H}, h \cap h' = \emptyset$; $\mathcal{H}$ *is partitioned into sets of information sets which belong to the same agent:* $\mathcal{H}_i = \{h \in \mathcal{H}, \forall s \in h, \iota(s) = i\}$
- $\mathcal{A}_i(h)$ *is the set of actions available to agent* $i = \iota(s)$ *in each information set* $h \in \mathcal{H}_i$, *such that* $s \in h$

Unlike normal form games, in the extensive form the strategies are defined as functions of the information set perceived by the agent, i.e., $\mathbf{x}_i(h) = (x_{i1}(h), \ldots, x_{im}(h)), h \in \mathcal{H}_i$. This is due to the fact that agent i may play more than once at different stages of the game. Thus, in the following, we denote by $\mathbf{x}_i$ the functional strategy over the information sets, while the joint strategy $\mathbf{x}$ is called *strategy profile* of the game.

In extensive form games some refinements of the Nash equilibrium are usually adopted as solution concepts. In the following, we focus only on the *sequential equilibrium* of Kreps and Wilson [5], which is the most suitable equilibrium for extensive form games with imperfect information. In fact, the sequential equilibrium takes into account not only the strategies, but also the agents' *beliefs* about the state of the game. A belief for agent i is defined as a probability distribution $\boldsymbol{\mu}_i(h) = (\mu_{i1}, \ldots, \mu_{ij}, \ldots, \mu_{i|h|})$ over the states in the perceived information set $h \in \mathcal{H}_i$, where μ_{ij} is the probability for agent i to be in the j-th state of h. The set of beliefs $\boldsymbol{\mu} = (\boldsymbol{\mu}_1, \ldots \boldsymbol{\mu}_i, \ldots, \boldsymbol{\mu}_n)$ is called *system of beliefs*. The expected payoff $\rho_i(\mathbf{x}|\boldsymbol{\mu}_i)$ for agent i, given her belief $\boldsymbol{\mu}_i$ and a joint strategy $\mathbf{x}$, is defined as the expected payoff when the probability to be in the states of her information sets is exactly given by her belief. The system of beliefs together with the strategy profile define an *assessment* $\sigma = \langle \boldsymbol{\mu}, \mathbf{x} \rangle$. A sequential equilibrium is an assessment $\sigma^* = \langle \boldsymbol{\mu}^*, \mathbf{x}^* \rangle$ such that the strategies in $\mathbf{x}^*$ are mutual best responses (*sequential rationality*) and the beliefs in $\boldsymbol{\mu}^*$ are consistent with the probability distribution induced by $\mathbf{x}^*$ on the states of the game (*Bayesian consistency*). Finally, the notion of consistency in the sense of Kreps and Wilson also requires the existence of a sequence of assessments $\sigma_k = \langle \boldsymbol{\mu}_k, \mathbf{x}_k \rangle$, each with fully mixed $\mathbf{x}_k$ and Bayesian consistent $\boldsymbol{\mu}_k$, that converges to σ^*. Technically, this latter condition avoids that beliefs on information sets never visited at the sequential equilibrium remain undetermined. More formally:

Definition 4. *An assessment* $\sigma^* = \langle \boldsymbol{\mu}^*, \mathbf{x}^* \rangle$ *is a sequential equilibrium of an extensive form game* Γ *if:*

- (sequential rationality):

$$\rho_i(\mathbf{x}_1^*, \ldots, \mathbf{x}_i^*, \ldots, \mathbf{x}_n^*|\boldsymbol{\mu}_i^*) \geq \rho_i(\mathbf{x}_1^*, \ldots, \mathbf{x}_i, \ldots, \mathbf{x}_n^*|\boldsymbol{\mu}_i^*), \quad \forall i \in \mathcal{N}. \quad (2)$$

- (Bayesian consistency): *the joint strategy* $\mathbf{x}^*$ *induces a probability distribution on states equal to the system of beliefs* $\boldsymbol{\mu}^*$
- (Kreps and Wilson consistency): *there is a sequence* $\sigma_k = \langle \boldsymbol{\mu}_k, \mathbf{x}_k \rangle$, *such that*

$$\mathbf{x}_k \rightarrow \mathbf{x}^*, k \rightarrow \infty \quad (3)$$

being $\mathbf{x}_k$ *fully mixed and* $\boldsymbol{\mu}_k$ *consistent with* $\mathbf{x}_k$

2.3   From Extensive Form to Normal Form Games

Sometimes it is convenient to transform a game from its extensive form to a normal form, so as to benefit from the results coming from the normal form representations. The transformation from extensive to normal form can be done as follows. The set of agents $\mathcal{N}$ remains the same. For any agent i, the set of actions A_i in the normal form game contains one action for each possible sequence of choices that the agent takes at decision nodes s such that $\iota(s) = i$. Finally, payoff functions are such that for each joint action the payoff is defined as that obtained at the termination node reached in the extensive form game.

It can be shown [9] that sequential equilibria of the extensive form game are always preserved as Nash equilibria of the normal form game. Nonetheless, other Nash equilibria could be generated, and this may prevent learning algorithms designed for normal form games, that are generically aimed at converging to Nash equilibria, from successfully solving extensive form games.

3   Reinforcement Learning and Q-Learning Dynamics

RL is a learning paradigm that enables an agent to learn the optimal strategy to solve a given task through a trial-and-error process of direct interaction
with an unknown environment. At each time instant, the state of the environment evolves in response to the action taken by the agent and a reward
is returned. The goal of a reinforcement learning agent is to learn the strategy $\mathbf{x}^*$ that maximizes the rewards through time. More formally, a strategy
$\mathbf{x}(s) = (x_1(s), \ldots, x_i(s), \ldots, x_m(s))$ is defined as a mapping from a state s to a
probability distribution over actions, where $x_i(s)$ is the probability of taking action i in state s. The quality of a strategy $\mathbf{x}$ can be measured by the action value
function $Q^{\mathbf{x}}(s, a)$, defined as the expected sum of discounted rewards obtained
by taking action a in state s and following $\mathbf{x}$ thereafter:

$$Q^{\mathbf{x}}(s, a) = E\left[\sum_{k=0}^{\infty} \delta^k r_k | a(0) = a\right]$$

where $\delta \in [0, 1)$ is the discount factor, and r_k is the reward returned at time
k. The optimal action value function $Q^*(s, a)$ is defined as the function whose
value is maximum in each state-action pair. Learning the optimal strategy $\mathbf{x}^*$
is equivalent to learning the optimal action value function $Q^*(s, a)$. In order to
learn $Q^*(s, a)$, the agent needs to explore all possible actions in all the states of
the environment. On the other hand, as the learning progresses, in order to assess
the performance of her strategy, the agent should exploit the estimation of the
action value function by taking in each state the greedy action, i.e., the action
whose action value is highest. A common exploration policy is the Boltzmann
strategy:

$$x_i(s) = \frac{e^{\tau Q(s, a_i)}}{\sum_{j=1}^{m} e^{\tau Q(s, a_j)}} \tag{4}$$

where τ is the exploitation factor (the lower [higher] τ, the higher [lower] the
exploration).

While the agent explores the environment according to Eq. 4, the estimation of
the action value function should be updated on the basis of the rewards received
by the agent. In Q-learning [13], one of the most used RL update rules, when
the agent takes an action a and receives a reward r, the action value function is
updated as:

$$Q(s, a) = (1 - \alpha)Q(s, a) + \alpha \left(r_i + \delta \max_{a'} Q(s', a')\right) \tag{5}$$

where $\alpha \in [0, 1]$ is the learning rate and s' is the state after the execution of a.

In a multiagent context, the environment is populated by n agents, at each
time instant k the state evolves according to the joint action $\mathbf{a}(k)$, and the reward for each agent depends on the joint action as well. In the simple case in
which the interaction between the agents is described by a normal form game,
the environment is characterized by a single state, and the reward r_i is defined by
the payoff function $R_i(\mathbf{a})$ (Sec. 2.1). Although Q-learning is guaranteed to find

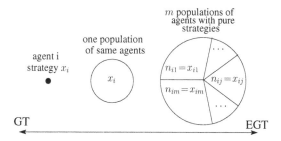

Fig. 2. In the replicator dynamics equations, a learning agent is represented by a set of m populations of identical agents that play pure strategies with proportions such that their densities correspond to the probability to play that strategy

the optimal strategy (that in normal form games corresponds to a Nash equilibrium) in stationary environments under very loose hypotheses [13], in multiagent problems payoffs depend on the joint action and, since agents do not know the other strategies, each agent perceives a non-stationary environment. Thus, the learning process is not guaranteed to converge and may exhibit complex dynamics that are often difficult to study by stochastically simulating single runs of execution.

Evolutionary Game Theory (EGT) is the application of population genetics-inspired models to game theory. With respect to classical game theory, it is more focused on the dynamics of proportions (i.e., the relative abundance or density, also called frequency) of homogeneous populations of agents all playing the same action. As depicted in Fig. 2, agent i can be imagined as a large population of $\mathbf{x}_i$ identical strategists, or, equivalently, as m homogeneous sub-populations of pure strategists, one for each action $a_{ij} \in A_i$ with proportions $n_{ij} = x_{ij}, j = 1, \ldots, m$. Thus, a pure strategist playing action a_{ij} is randomly extracted from the population with the same probability x_{ij} according to which agent i plays that action. Then, assuming that the game is repeatedly played many times in any small time interval dt and that from time to time (but still many times in dt) a pure strategist is randomly extracted from the population and offered the option of switching to the pure strategy of another randomly selected strategist, the continuous-time dynamics of the sub-population proportions or, equivalently, the strategy dynamics, are ruled by the replicator dynamics:

$$\dot{x}_{ij} = x_{ij} \left[(P_i \mathbf{x}_{-i})_i - \mathbf{x}_i P_i \mathbf{x}_{-i} \right] \tag{6}$$

where P_i is the payoff matrix of agent i. In [12], the Q-learning dynamics in normal form games is proved to converge to the following replicator-like dynamics:

$$\dot{x}_{ij} = x_{ij} \alpha \tau \left[(P_i \mathbf{x}_{-i})_i - \mathbf{x}_i \cdot P_i \mathbf{x}_{-i} \right] + x_{ij} \alpha \tau \sum_{k=1}^{m} x_{ik} \ln \left(\frac{x_{ik}}{x_{ij}} \right) \tag{7}$$

where the number of ordinary differential equations (ODEs) for agent i can be reduced to $|A_i| - 1$, since the probabilities $x_{ij}, j = 1 \ldots, n$ sum to 1.

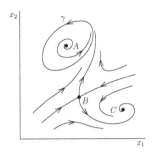

Fig. 3. A skeleton of 13 trajectories for a second-order dynamical system

4   Bifurcation Analysis of Dynamical Systems

In this section we recall the main notions on non-linear dynamical systems, with particular emphasis on structural stability and bifurcations. The following sections are adapted from [2] (Appendix A). We refer the reader to [7] for a more complete treatment of bifurcation theory.

4.1   Dynamical Systems Background

A continuous-time finite-dimensional dynamical system is defined by a system of ordinary differential equations (ODEs):

$$\dot{\mathbf{x}}(t) = f(\mathbf{x}(t)) \tag{8}$$

where the state vector $\mathbf{x}$ is n-dimensional and $\dot{\mathbf{x}}$ is its time derivative. Given the initial state $\mathbf{x}(0)$, the ODEs uniquely define a *trajectory* of the system, i.e., the state vector $\mathbf{x}(t)$ for all $t \geq 0$. Trajectories can be easily obtained through simulation (i.e., numerical integration). The set of all trajectories is the *state portrait* of the system. In Fig. 3 a representative example of 13 trajectories from a two-dimensional (i.e., $n = 2$) system is reported. Three trajectories (A, B, C) are points (corresponding to constant solutions of the system) called *equilibria*, while one (γ) is a closed trajectory (corresponding to a periodic solution of the system) called *limit cycle*. The behavior of the trajectories allow one to conclude that A is a *repellor* (no trajectory starting closing to A tends or remains close to A), B is a *saddle* (almost all trajectories starting close to B go away from B but two trajectories tend to B and compose the so-called *stable manifold*; the two trajectories emanating from B compose the *unstable manifold*) while C and γ are *attractors* (all trajectories starting close to C [γ] tend to C [γ]). Attracting equilibria and cycles are said to be (*asymptotically*) *stable* (*globally stable* if they attract all initial conditions, technically with the exclusion of sets with no measure in state space), while saddles and repellors are *unstable*. The trajectories in Figure 3 also identify the *basin of attraction* of each attractor: in fact all trajectories starting above [below] the stable manifold of the saddle tend toward the limit cycle γ [the equilibrium C].

The study of the stability of equilibria can be done through linearization of the dynamical system at equilibrium points, that is, by approximating the behavior of the system in the vicinity of an equilibrium $\bar{x}$ through the linear system $d/dt(\mathbf{x} - \bar{\mathbf{x}}) = \partial f/\partial \mathbf{x}|_{\mathbf{x}=\bar{\mathbf{x}}}(\mathbf{x} - \bar{\mathbf{x}})$. This way, it is possible to study the stability of $\bar{x}$ by looking at the eigenvalues $\lambda_i, i = 1, \ldots, n$ of the Jacobian matrix $\partial f/\partial \mathbf{x}|_{\mathbf{x}=\bar{\mathbf{x}}}$. If all the eigenvalues have negative real part then the equilibrium is stable, while if at least one eigenvalue has positive real part the equilibrium is unstable. Similarly, the stability of limit cycles can be analyzed through linearization of the $(n-1)$-dimensional discrete-time dynamical system whose state is defined by the intersections of the system trajectories close to the limit cycle with a given transversal manifold (the so-called Poincaré section). Whenever these intersections converge to the equilibrium at which the cycle intersects the manifolds the limit cycle is stable, otherwise is unstable.

4.2   Structural Stability and Bifurcation Analysis

The goal of the structural stability analysis is the study of the asymptotic behavior of parametrized families of dynamical systems of the form:

$$\dot{\mathbf{x}} = f(\mathbf{x}(t), \mathbf{p}) \tag{9}$$

where $\mathbf{p}$ is a vector of *parameters*.

If a parameter is slightly perturbed, by continuity the position and form of the asymptotic behaviors of trajectories, namely attractors, saddles, and repellors, are smoothly affected (e.g., an equilibrium might slightly move or a limit cycle might become slightly bigger or faster), but all trajectories remain topologically the same (e.g., stable equilibria and cycles remain attractive). In regions of the domain of $\mathbf{p}$ in which this continuity holds, the system is *structurally stable*. The above continuity argument fails at particular parameter values called *bifurcation points* [7], which correspond in state space to collisions of attractors, saddles, and repellors. Thus, the robustness of the dynamical characteristics of the system, as summarized by the state portrait, depends on how far the parameters are from bifurcation points. A thorough robustness investigation therefore requires to produce the catalog of all possible modes of behavior of the system family, i.e., its complete bifurcation analysis. An exhaustive review of bifurcation theory is certainly beyond the scope of this paper. In the following, we focus on three types of bifurcations involving a single parameter p that are relevant for the case study in Sec. 4: *saddle-node, Hopf*, and *homoclinic* bifurcations.

The saddle-node bifurcation corresponds to the collision, at a critical value p^*, of two equilibria: a stable node N (i.e., a stable equilibrium characterized by real eigenvalues of the linearized system) and, in its simplest two-dimensional formulation, a saddle S (Fig- 4-top). For $p < p^*$, N has two negative eigenvalues, while the eigenvalues of S are one positive and one negative. For $p > p^*$ no equilibrium is present, so that at the bifurcation point $p = p^*$ the largest eigenvalue of N and the smallest eigenvalue of S both vanish. In short, a saddle-node bifurcation can be identified by the change of sign of one of the eigenvalues of an

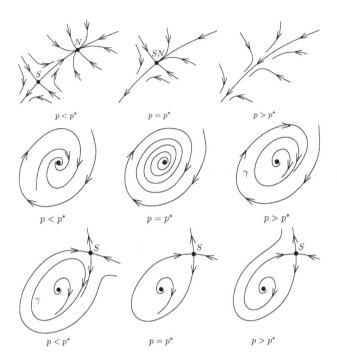

Fig. 4. Example of saddle-node (top), Hopf (mid) and homoclinic (bottom) bifurcations in a two-dimensional dynamical system

equilibrium when a parameter p is varied. Geometrically, two equilibria, which are non necessarily a node and a saddle in higher-dimensional systems, collide and disappear as p crosses the bifurcation.

The second type of bifurcation, the Hopf bifurcation, involves the appearance of limit cycles. With reference to two-dimensional systems, if a *focus*, that is an equilibrium with two complex conjugate eigenvalues, is stable for $p < p^*$ and becomes unstable at $p = p^*$, then a stable limit cycle γ may appear for $p > p^*$ (the so-called supercritical case, see Figure 4-mid). But the cycle may also be unstable and surround the stable focus for $p < p^*$ (subcritical case) and the distinction between the two cases depends upon the nonlinear terms in the expansion of the function f in Eq. 8 and is typically implemented in software packages for numerical bifurcation analysis [3,7]. In both cases, however, the cycle is small for p close to p^*, so that the Hopf bifurcation can be seen geometrically as the collision of a vanishing cycle with a focus. Moreover, the pair of complex conjugate eigenvalues cross the imaginary axis of the complex plane at the bifurcation, thus changing the stability of the equilibrium.

Finally, the homoclinic bifurcation is characterized by the collision of a limit cycle and a saddle (Figure 4-bottom). When p approaches p^*, the cycle γ gets closer to saddle S, so that the period of the cycle diverges, since the state of the system moves very slowly when close to S. At the bifurcation ($p = p^*$) the cycle touches the saddle and collides with its stable and unstable manifolds which coincide at the bifurcation. The identification of a homoclinic bifurcation cannot rely on the analysis of eigenvalues but involve the global behavior of the system. For this reason, the homoclinic bifurcation is classified as a *global* bifurcation, in contrast with *local* bifurcations that can be detected through eigenvalue analysis.

Whenever a perturbation of the parameter from p to $p + \Delta$ ($p < p^* < p + \Delta$) triggers a transient toward a macroscopically different asymptotic regime (i.e., a different attractor), the bifurcation at p^* is called *catastrophic*. By contrast, if the catastrophic transition is not possible, the bifurcation is called *noncatastrophic*.

Although one might hope to detect bifurcations by simulating the system for various parameter settings and initial conditions, saddles, which have a fundamental role in bifurcation analysis, cannot be studied just through simulation. In fact, any small approximation introduced by the numerical scheme of integration would lead to trajectories that miss the saddle and go away from it along its unstable manifold. Moreover, the "brute force" simulation approach is never effective and accurate in practice, since bifurcations are often related to a loss of stability of equilibria and cycles, so that the length of simulations need to be dramatically increased while approaching the bifurcation. This is why the proper tools for numerical bifurcation analysis are based on continuation (see [7], Chap.10 and [3]), a simulation-free numerical method which locates bifurcations by continuing equilibria and cycles in parameter space, that is by studying their position in the state space when the parameter is changed.

5   Bifurcation Analysis on the Selten's Horse Game

In the following, we illustrate the results of the bifurcation analysis on the Selten's horse game [4] (named from its inventor and from the shape of its tree). This game, commonly adopted in GT for the study of sequential equilibria, is particularly suitable for our analysis because *(i)* it involves more than two agents, *(ii)* it is an extensive form game and *(iii)* one agent has imperfect information about the state of the game. All these factors of complexity lead to the definition of a complex learning system exhibiting interesting dynamics. At the same time, the game is simple enough to allow an intuitive analysis of its dynamics and a detailed bifurcation analysis on one of the payoffs.

5.1   Learning Dynamics in the Selten's Horse Game

The Selten's horse game [4] (Fig. 5-left) is an extensive form game with imperfect information involving three agents with two actions each ($A_i = \{l_i, r_i\}, i = 1, 2, 3$). While both agents 1 and 2 have perfect information about the state of the game, agent 3 cannot distinguish the state in which it plays (dotted line in the figure), that is, she is characterized by a single information set containing the two decision nodes where she plays. According to Definition 4, the game has a unique sequential equilibrium strategy (r_1, r_2, r_3) (we omit the derivation for lack of space). On the other hand, as one can easily verify, in the equivalent normal

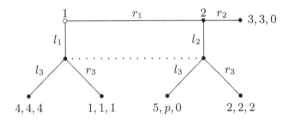

	l_1	l_2	r_2
	l_3	4,4,4	**4,4,4**
	r_3	1,1,1	1,1,1

	r_1	l_2	r_2
	l_3	5,p,0	3,3,0
	r_3	2,2,2	**3,3,0**

Fig. 5. Selten's Horse game and payoff tables of the equivalent normal form game. Parameter p is set to 5 in the original configuration of the game.

form game (Fig. 5) there are two Nash equilibria (r_1, r_2, r_3) and (l_1, r_2, l_3) (in bold in payoff tables), while there are no mixed equilibria. The joint strategy for this game is the vector $\mathbf{x} = (\mathbf{x}_1, \mathbf{x}_2, \mathbf{x}_3)$, where $\mathbf{x}_i = (x_{i1}, x_{i2})$ (being $x_{i2} = 1 - x_{i1}$) is the strategy of agent i. Strategy $\mathbf{x}_i = (1, 0)$ corresponds to action l_i, while $\mathbf{x}_i = (0, 1)$ is action r_i.

In the following, we analyze the dynamics of the strategies when all the agents learn through Q-learning. As discussed in Section 3, for the study of the learning process, we derive the dynamical system defined by the replicator dynamics for x_{11}, x_{21} and x_{31} as defined in Eq. 7, where

$$P_1 = \begin{bmatrix} 4 & 1 & 4 & 1 \\ 5 & 2 & 3 & 3 \end{bmatrix} \quad P_2 = \begin{bmatrix} 4 & 1 & p & 2 \\ 4 & 1 & 3 & 3 \end{bmatrix} \quad P_3 = \begin{bmatrix} 4 & 4 & 0 & 0 \\ 1 & 1 & 2 & 0 \end{bmatrix}$$

are the payoff matrices, where p is equal to 5 in the original setting.

The replicator dynamics is bounded in the open 3-dimensional cube of the state space (x_{11}, x_{21}, x_{31}) (the other three variables can be eliminated as $x_{i2} = 1 - x_{i1}$). The faces of the cube cannot be reached due to the exploration logarithmic terms in Eq. 7. The sequential equilibrium (r_1, r_2, r_3) corresponds to point $(0, 0, 0)$ in the state space, while the other Nash equilibrium is $(1, 0, 1)$.

Let us first consider the dynamics of the system in its original settings (panel 5 in Fig. 7). Although the equivalent normal form game has two Nash equilibria, the learning process converges to a point close to the sequential equilibrium. Starting from any initial joint strategy, the trajectories of the system reach a globally stable equilibrium close to the joint strategy (r_1, r_2, r_3). This would be the expected solution from a game theoretical perspective, since (r_1, r_2, r_3) is the unique sequential equilibrium in the game. At the opposite, the learning dynamics continues and, because of the residual exploration of the agents converges to a different equilibrium point. By exploring action l_2, agent 2 allows agent 3 to play r_3 and obtain a payoff greater than 0 (the payoff of agent 3 at the sequential equilibrium). Then, agent 3 takes advantage by mixing her strategy toward l_3, since this tempts agent 2 to play l_2 more frequently. In fact, the payoff of agent 2 for action l_2 is a weighted average between 5 and 2 depending on the agent 3 mixed strategy (Fig. 5), and the result can be greater than 3 (the equilibrium payoff). This is possible because of the payoff for agent 2 in (r_1, l_2, l_3) is sufficiently high, while this scenario is likely to change for lower values of the

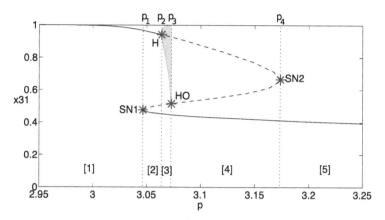

Fig. 6. Bifurcation diagram of the learning system. The curve identifies the number of equilibria and the value of their x_{31} component for each value of p in the considered range. The shaded area represents the x_{31} excursion along a family of stable limit cycles present in interval 3. Vertical dotted lines indicate bifurcation points (SN1,SN2: saddle-node, HO: homoclinic; H: Hopf). Dashed and solid parts of equilibrium curve distinguish unstable and stable equilibria (e.g., one stable and two unstable equilibria characterized by increasing value of x_{31} are present in interval 4). Parameter values: $\alpha = 0.3, \tau = 0.6$. Diagram obtained through the software package Matcont [3].

payoff. This means that, from this preliminary analysis, the system is expected to preserve structural stability only for a limited range of values of the payoff (in the following parameter p) and to possibly show complex dynamics otherwise. This is the reason for the following bifurcation analysis with respect to p.

5.2   Bifurcation Analysis

The bifurcation analysis of the learning system is reported in Fig. 6 (for variable x_{31}) and Tab. 1 and identifies five qualitatively different learning dynamics corresponding to five intervals of p (the learning dynamics are shown in Fig. 7). As discussed in Section 4, the identification of the bifurcations cannot be done by simulating the system for different values of p. A complete bifurcation analysis needs the *continuation* of equilibria and cycles in parameter space and the identification of the parameter values in which the system looses its structural stability.

The analysis starts with $p = 5$, the value in the original game setting, at which, as already discussed in Sec. 5.1, the system is characterized by a globally stable equilibrium close to $(0,0,0)$. The numerical continuation of this equilibrium with respect to p allows to track its position for different parameter values and produces the curve in Fig. 6. By decreasing p from its original value, the equilibrium moves away from $(0,0,0)$. In fact, in order to tempt agent 2 to play l_2, agent 3 is forced to mix her strategy more and more toward l_3, but so doing she vanishes her own return. Similar considerations can be made for x_{11} and x_{21}. Further

Table 1. Bifurcation analysis of the replicator dynamics with respect to parameter p

Parameter	Bifurcation	Interval		Equilibria	Limit Cycles
$p_1 = 3.04651$	SN1	[1]	$p < p_1$	1 globally stable	-
$p_2 = 3.06392$	H	[2]	$p_1 \leq p < p_2$	2 stable, 1 saddle	-
$p_3 = 3.07235$	HO	[3]	$p_2 \leq p < p_3$	1 stable, 2 saddles	1 stable
$p_4 = 3.17361$	SN2	[4]	$p_3 \leq p < p_4$	1 globally stable, 2 saddles	-
		[5]	$p \geq p_4$	1 globally stable	-

reductions of p are less easy to interpret on an intuitive ground, also because a different mix of Nash/sequential pure/mixed equilibria might arise, and this is indicative of impending dynamical complexity. In fact, the first bifurcation is encountered at $p=p_1$ (SN1), a saddle-node bifurcation at which the equilibrium collides with a saddle and they both disappear for $p < p_1$. Notice, however, that the equilibrium is not globally stable in intervals 2 and 3, since three more bifurcations occur for $p_1 < p < 5$, but involve other equilibria of the system and are therefore initially unnoticed by the local continuation of the equilibrium. The continuation direction reverts at a saddle-node bifurcation, so that we now continue the saddle for increasing values of p. The first encountered bifurcation is another saddle-node (SN2) at $p=p_4$, approaching which one of the two stable eigenvalues of the saddle vanishes, as well as one of the two unstable eigenvalues of another saddle, characterized by only one stable eigenvalue. The two saddles collide at the bifurcation and do not exist for $p > p_4$, while the continuation proceeds by tracking the new saddle for decreasing values of p. The two unstable eigenvalues are real close to p_4, but become complex (saddle-focus) somewhere before the Hopf bifurcation (H) detected at $p=p_2$. The Hopf is supercritical, so that a family of stable limit cycles can be continued for increasing values of p starting from $p=p_2$ (shaded area in Fig. 6). The saddle-focus becomes stable by crossing the bifurcation and its continuation to lower values of p does not point out new losses of structural stability. Moreover, the equilibrium becomes globally stable for $p < p_1$ and x_{31} approaches 1 as p is further reduced. At the same time, x_{11} and x_{21} approach 1 and 0, respectively, so that the equilibrium approaches $(1,0,1)$, i.e., the other Nash equilibrium of the original game. In particular, it is easy to verify that $(1,0,1)$ is Nash for all p and can be shown to be the only sequential equilibrium for p sufficiently small. Finally, increasing p from $p=p_2$, the family of limit cycles is interrupted by an homoclinic bifurcation (HO) at $p=p_3$, where the cycle gets in contact with the saddle originated at (SN1).

All together, the bifurcation analysis shows that the learning dynamics are dominated by two sequential equilibria, $(0,0,0)$ for large values of p and $(1,0,1)$ for small values of p, in the sense that close to them there is an equilibrium of the learning dynamics (the lower [upper] equilibrium in Fig. 6 for large [small] p) which attracts all initial conditions (see intervals 1 and 5 and in particular interval 4 where, though the presence of two saddles, all trajectories, except those composing the saddle stable manifolds, converge to the stable equilibrium). The switch from one equilibria to the other as p is varied involves two *catastrophes*: the homoclinic bifurcation for increasing values of p (HO) and the saddle-node

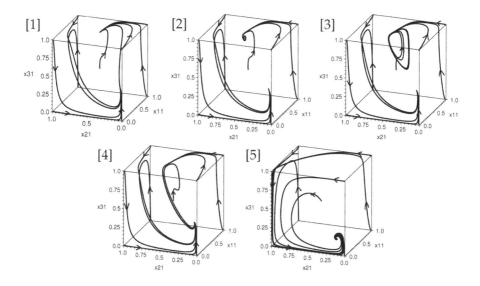

Fig. 7. Learning dynamics for five different values of p $(3.0, 3.05, 3.07, 3.1, 5)$

(SN1) for decreasing values of p. In particular, in the first case, the learning dynamics follow the family of limit cycles. The period of the cycle diverges as the bifurcation is approached and the joint strategy remains for most of the time very close to the saddle, at the point that finite-time simulations can erroneously reveal convergence to a stable equilibrium. Crossing the bifurcation, the cycle suddenly disappears and the dynamics converge to the lower equilibrium.

Finally notice that in intervals 2 and 3 the system has two alternative attractors, two equilibria in 2 and an equilibrium and a cycle in 3. The attractor which is reached by the learning process depends on the initial joint strategy and the saddle (actually its stable manifold) delimits the two attraction basins.

6   Conclusions and Future Works

In this paper we applied bifurcation analysis to the study of Q-learning multiagent dynamics in the continuous-time limit provided by the replicator dynamics of evolutionary game theory. A preliminary one-parameter analysis of the Selten's Horse game is presented as a case study. The first result of the analysis is that in extensive form games with imperfect information Q-learning may exhibit complex learning dynamics, including multiple stable equilibria and periodic non-convergent attractors. Furthermore, the analysis pointed out that Q-learning is not robust to payoff perturbations and that the corresponding dynamical system looses stability in four different bifurcation points. In particular, at the two catastrophic bifurcations, small variations of the payoff correspond to radically different asymptotic regimes, thus leading the three agents to significantly change their strategies. In general, we showed that bifurcation analysis can be an effective way to study the structural stability of learning systems and that it could also be used to compare the robustness of different learning algorithms.

Although the bifurcation analysis presented in the paper focused on a structural parameter (i.e., a payoff), the same analysis can be carried out when learning parameters are varied, and this could lead to useful suggestions about parameter settings. A preliminary joint analysis with respect to the payoff p and the exploitation factor τ showed that for low values of τ (high exploration) the bifurcation points disappear and the system is globally structurally stable, while for high values of τ (low exploration) the system becomes more robust to payoff perturbations as the regions of structural stability become larger.

In general, we believe that this novel, though preliminary, analysis opens interesting scenarios for a more complete investigation of the dynamics of multiagent learning systems. Future efforts will be devoted to: *(i)* the development of a replicator dynamics model more compliant to learning algorithms (e.g., decreasing learning rates and exploration factors), *(ii)* two parameters bifurcation analysis (e.g., a joint analysis with respect to learning and structural parameters), *(iii)* study of more complex games (e.g., signaling game, bilateral negotiations, auctions).

References

1. Börgers, T., Sarin, R.: Learning through reinforcement and replicator dynamics. Journal of Economic Theory 77(1), 1–14 (1997)
2. Dercole, F., Rinaldi, S.: Analysis of Evolutionary Processes: The Adaptive Dynamics Approach and its Applications. Princeton University Press, Princeton, NJ, (forthcoming)
3. Dhooge, A., Govaerts, W., Kuznetsov, Y.A.: MATCONT: A MATLAB package for numerical bifurcation analysis of ODEs. ACM Trans. Math. Software 29, 141–164 (2002)
4. Gintis, H.: Game Theory Evolving. Princeton University Press, Princeton, NJ (2000)
5. Kreps, D.M., Wilson, R.: Sequential equilibria. Econometrica 50(4), 863–894 (1982)
6. Kunigami, M., Terano, T.: Connected replicator dynamics and their control in a learning multi-agent system. In: IDEAL, pp. 18–26 (2003)
7. Kuznetsov, Y.A.: Elements of Applied Bifurcation Theory. 3rd edition (2004)
8. Littman, M.L.: Markov games as a framework for multi-agent reinforcement learning. In: ICML, pp. 157–163. New Brunswick, NJ, Morgan Kaufmann, San Francisco (1994)
9. Myerson, R.B.: Game Theory: Analysis of Conflict. Harvard University Press, Cambridge (1991)
10. Sato, Y., Crutchfield, J.P.: Coupled replicator equations for the dynamics of learning in multiagent systems. Phys. Rev. E 67(1), 15206 (2003)
11. Sutton, R.S., Barto, A.G.: Reinforcement Learning: An Introduction. MIT Press, Cambridge (1998)
12. Tuyls, K., Hoen, P.J., Vanschoenwinkel, B.: An evolutionary dynamical analysis of multi-agent learning in iterated games. JAAMAS 12(1), 115–153 (2006)
13. Watkins, C.J., Dayan, P.: Q-learning. Machine Learning 8, 279–292 (1992)

Bee Behaviour in Multi-agent Systems

(A Bee Foraging Algorithm)

Nyree Lemmens[1], Steven de Jong[2], Karl Tuyls[2], and Ann Nowé[1]

[1] CoMo, Vrije Universiteit Brussel, Belgium
[2] MICC-IKAT, Universiteit Maastricht, Netherlands
{nlemmens,anowe}@vub.ac.be,
{steven.dejong,k.tuyls}@MICC.unimaas.nl

Abstract. In this paper we present a new, non-pheromone-based algorithm inspired by the behaviour of bees. The algorithm combines both recruitment and navigation strategies. We investigate whether this new algorithm outperforms pheromone-based algorithms, inspired by the behaviour of ants, in the task of foraging. From our experiments, we conclude that (i) the bee-inspired algorithm is significantly more efficient when finding and collecting food, i.e., it uses fewer iterations to complete the task; (ii) the bee-inspired algorithm is more scalable, i.e., it requires less computation time to complete the task, even though in small worlds, the ant-inspired algorithm is faster on a time-per-iteration measure; and finally, (iii) our current bee-inspired algorithm is less adaptive than ant-inspired algorithms.

1 Introduction

In this paper we introduce a new, non-pheromone-based, algorithm inspired by the social behaviour of honeybees. The algorithm consists of two strategies. First, a recruitment strategy which is used to distribute knowledge to other members of the colony. More precisely, by 'dancing' inside the hive agents are able to directly communicate distance and direction towards a destination, in analogy to bees 'dancing' inside the hive [1]. Second, a navigation strategy which is used to efficiently navigate in an unknown world. For navigation, agents use a strategy named Path Integration (PI). This strategy is based on PI in bees with which they are able to compute their present location from their past trajectory continuously and, as a consequence, can return to their starting point by choosing the direct route rather than retracing their outbound trajectory [2,3].

Pheromone-based algorithms are inspired by the behaviour of ants. For an overview, we refer to [4]. In summary, ants deposit pheromone on the path they take during travel. Using this trail, they are able to navigate towards their nest or food. Ants employ an indirect recruitment strategy by accumulating pheromone trails. When a trail is strong enough, other ants are attracted to it and will follow this trail towards a destination. More precisely, the more ants follow a trail, the more that trail becomes attractive for being followed. This is known as an autocatalitic process. Short paths will eventually be preferred but it takes a certain amount of time before such pheromone trails emerge.

K. Tuyls et al. (Eds.): Adaptive Agents and MAS III, LNAI 4865, pp. 145–156, 2008.

Although ant and bee foraging strategies differ considerably, both species solve the foraging problem efficiently. In the field of Computer Science, researchers have become inspired by the behaviour of social insects, since the problems these insects cope with are similar to optimization problems humans wish to solve efficiently, for instance, the Shortest Path Problem. Ant-inspired algorithms are already used to address such problems successfully [4]. Bee-inspired algorithms are less extensively studied and research into them only started recently. For instance, [5,6,7,8] all present bee-inspired algorithms which pose solutions to different types of problems by employing bee recruitment behaviour. In [2] the navigation behaviour of bees is investigated and applied in a robot. However, these algorithms use only one aspect of bee behaviour, i.e., the recruitment behaviour or navigation behaviour respectively. As such, there are still two important open issues. First, recruitment and navigation algorithms are currently only studied separately; a combined algorithm is undiscovered land. Second, since a combined bee-inspired algorithm currently does not exist, comparative studies have not yet been performed. We want to investigate whether our bee-inspired algorithm poses a better solution to the foraging problem than a ant-inspired algorithm. More precisely, we want to investigate whether paths emerge faster with our bee-inspired algorithm. Such a comparative study would need to focus on the efficiency, scalability, and adaptability of the algorithms.

Our research addresses both issues. First, a new bee-inspired algorithm, which implements both bee recruitment and bee navigational strategies, is presented. Second, we have developed a simulation environment, named BEEHAVE, in which foraging algorithms can be compared directly. Using BEEHAVE, we are able to compare the bee-inspired algorithm with an ant-inspired algorithm (with features of Ant Colony System and MAX-MIN Ant System [4]). Extensive experiments have been performed with respect to efficiency and scalability. Moreover, we are able to give an indication of the adaptability of the new bee-inspired algorithm. In this paper, we present an overview of our research [9].

The remainder of this paper is structured as follows. In Section 2, we describe the biological background of bee behaviour. Section 3 describes how to model bee behaviour. Section 4 describes the simulation environment and the experiments. Finally, in Section 5, we present the conclusion and two options for future research.

2   Biological Background

Foraging honeybees display two types of behaviour, i.e., recruitment and navigation behaviour. In order to recruit other colony members for food sources, honeybees inform their nest mates of the distance and direction of these food sources by means of a waggling dance performed on the vertical combs in the hive [1]. This dance (i.e., the bee language) consists of a series of alternating left-hand and right-hand loops, interspersed by a segment in which the bee waggles her abdomen from side to side. The duration of the waggle phase is a measure of the distance to the food. The angle between the sun and the axis of a bee's waggle segment on the vertical comb, represents the azimuthal angle between the sun and a target location, i.e., the direction in which a recruit should fly [1,10,11] (see Figure 1). The 'advertisement' for a food source can

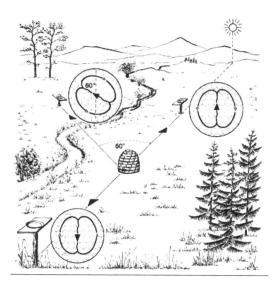

Fig. 1. Distance and direction by waggling dance. Waggling straight up on the vertical comb indicates a food source which is located at an azimuthal angle of 0° while waggling straight down indicates a food source located at an azimuthal angle of 180°. Figure is taken from [13].

be adopted by other members of the colony. The decision mechanism for adopting an 'advertised' food-source location by a potential recruit, is not completely understood. It is considered that the recruitment amongst bees is a function of the quality of the food source [12].

Different species of social insects, such as honeybees and desert ants, make use of non-pheromone-based navigation. Non-pheromone-based navigation mainly consists of Path Integration (PI) which is the continuous update of a vector by integrating all angles steered and all distances covered [2]. A PI vector represents the insects knowledge of direction and distance towards its destination. To construct a PI vector, the insect does not use a mathematical vector summation as a human does, but employs a computationally simple approximation [3]. Using this approximation, the insect is able to return to its destination directly. More precisely, when the path is unobstructed, the insect solves the problem optimally. However, when the path is obstructed, the insect has to fall back on other strategies such as exploration or landmark navigation [14,15] to solve the problem. Obviously, bees are able to fly, i.e., when they encounter an obstacle, they can mostly choose to fly over it. However, even if the path is unobstructed, bees tend to navigate over the entire path using landmarks. The landmarks divide the entire path in segments and each landmark has a PI vector associated with it. This behaviour decreases navigation errors and ensures robustness. In the remainder of this paper, we refer to a home-pointing PI vector as a Home Vector (HV). PI is used in both exploration and exploitation. During exploration insects constantly update their HV. It is however, not used as an exploration strategy. During exploitation, the insects update both their HV and the PI vector indicating the food source, and use these vectors as a guidance to a destination.

3   Modelling Bee Behaviour

In contrast to existing algorithms [5,6,7,8], our new algorithm combines both biological behaviours previously mentioned. First, recruitment behaviour is implemented in analogy with biological bees' dance behavior. Agents share information on previous search experience (i.e., the direction and distance toward a certain food source) only when they are in the hive. Agents in the hive can then decide whether to exploit previous search experience obtained from other agents in the hive, or to exploit their own search experience, if available. As mentioned earlier, bees use a (still) unknown decision mechanism to decide whether to exploit another bee's experience. In our bee-inspired algorithm, the decision is based on distance assessment. More precisely, an agent will exploit another agent's experience if this experience indicates food sources at a shorter distance from the hive than the food source currently known by the agent. Second, the navigation behaviour used in the bee-inspired algorithm either exploits previous search experience (of the agent itself or of another agent in the hive) or lets the agent explore the world using an exploration strategy similar to a Lévy flight [16]. Exploiting previous search experience is guided by the PI vector that agents either have constructed themselves or have adopted from another agent in the hive.

The general structure of our bee-inspired algorithm is quite similar to that of algorithms in Ant Colony Optimization [4]. It implements both recruitment and navigation behaviour and consists of three functions.[1]

First, $ManageBeesActivity()$ handles agents' activity based on their internal state. Each agent is in one of six internal states. In each state a specific behaviour is performed. State changes are outlined in Algorithm 1. Agent state 'AtHome' indicates that the agent is located at the hive. While in this state, the agent determines to which new state it will go. Agent state 'StayAtHome' also indicates that the agent is located at the hive. However, while in this state it will remain there unless there is previous search experience available to exploit. Previous search experience is represented by a PI vector indicating a food source. If such experience is available, the agent will leave the hive to exploit the previous search experience. Agent state 'Exploitation' indicates that the agent is exploiting previous search experience. An agent either exploits its own search experience or acquires a PI vector from other agents inside the hive. The agent determines which cell to move to in order to match the PI vector indicating the food source. Agent state 'Exploration' indicates that the agent is exploring its environment in search for food. Agent state 'HeadHome' indicates that the agent is heading home without carrying any food. The agent reaches home by following its Homing Vector (HV). The HV is a PI vector indicating the hive. From the moment an agent starts its foraging trip, this HV is continuously calculated for each agent. Agent state 'CarryingFood' indicates that the agent has found food and that it is carrying the food back toward the hive. The agent's return path depends on the same HV as with agent state 'HeadHome'.

---

[1] The last function, $DaemonActions()$, can be used to implement centralized actions which cannot be performed by single agents, such as collection of global information which can be used to decide whether it is useful to let an agent dance. In this paper, $DaemonActions()$ is not used.

Algorithm 1. Agent internal-state changes

```
 1: if State is StayAtHome then
 2:     if Vector exists then
 3:         Exploitation
 4:     end if
 5: else if Agent not AtHome then
 6:     if Agent has food then
 7:         CarryingFood
 8:     else if Depending on chance then
 9:         HeadHome, Exploration or Exploitation
10:     end if
11: else if Exploit preference AND state is AtHome then
12:     if Vector exists then
13:         Exploitation
14:     else
15:         Exploration
16:     end if
17: else if StayAtHome preference AND state is AtHome then
18:     if Vector exists then
19:         Exploitation
20:     else
21:         StayAtHome
22:     end if
23: else
24:     Exploration
25: end if
```

Second, $CalculateVectors()$ is used to compute the PI vectors for each agent, i.e., the HV and possibly the PI vector indicating the food source. A PI vector essentially consists of two values, one indicating the direction and the other indicating the distance. Our algorithm uses an exact PI vector calculation which rules out the directional and distance errors that biological PI is prone to make [3,15]. It does, however, work in a similar way. A new PI vector is always calculated with respect to the previous one. In order to calculate the new homing distance, we use the cosine rule and rewrite it as:

$$b = \sqrt{a^2 + c^2 - 2ac \times cos\beta} \tag{1}$$

Using Equation 1, a represents the distance traveled since the last turn was made, c the old homing distance, and b the new homing distance. β is the angle turned with respect to the old homing angle. Using Equation 1 we can now calculate α (the angle used for adjusting the old homing angle), once again by using the cosine rule.

$$\alpha = \arccos\left(\frac{a^2 - b^2 - c^2}{-2bc}\right) \tag{2}$$

Values obtained by Equation 1 and Equation 2 are used to construct the new PI vector.

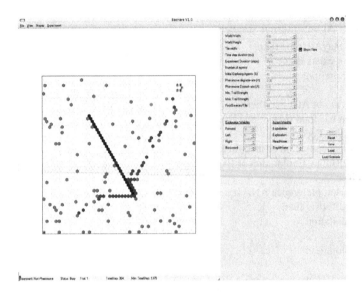

Fig. 2. The BEEHAVE tool

Bee behaviour's main feature is that it naturally constructs a direct, optimal path between a starting point (i.e., the hive) and a destination (i.e., the food source). One could argue that bee behaviour is a natural way of constructing options in a Markov Decision Process (MDP). Options are courses of action within a MDP whose results are state transitions of extended and variable duration [17]. Such courses of action have proven very useful in speeding up learning and planning, ensuring robustness and allowing the integration of prior knowledge into AI systems [18]. An option is specified by a set of states in which the option can be initiated, an internal policy and a termination condition. If the initiation set and the termination condition are specified, traditional reinforcement learning methods can be used to learn the internal policy of the option. In bee behaviour, the basic actions consist out of moving in different directions over the nodes in a MDP (i.e., the foraging world). The option's policy is represented by the (artificial) bee's PI vector, where the starting state is the hive and the termination state is the food source location.

4   Simulation Environment and Experiments

To conduct comparative experiments with the bee-inspired algorithm and the ant-inspired algorithm, we created a simulation environment. This environment is called BEEHAVE and is illustrated in Figure 2.

To obtain our data, three experiments have been performed. The experiments were conducted in (i) a small-sized world (i.e., Experiment 1; 110 cells), (ii) a medium-sized world (i.e., Experiment 2; 440 cells), and (iii) a large-sized world (i.e., Experiment 3; 2800 cells). Experiment 1 and 2 each contain five different problem cases (i.e., unobstructed, obstructed, food-source displacement, obstructed with food-source

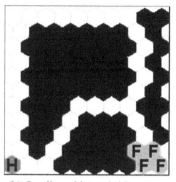

(a) Medium world, basic case   (b) Small world, two bridges case

Fig. 3. Simulation worlds

displacement, and multiple foodsources). Experiment 3 only consists of one problem case, i.e., the unobstructed problem case. Each experiment is executed with both the ant-inspired algorithm and the bee-inspired algorithm (i.e., our new algorithm). Experiment 1 is executed with 50 and 100 agents, while Experiment 2 is executed with 100 and 250 agents. Chosing higher numbers of agents in either of the two experiments leads to agents flooding in the world, preventing any path from arising. The results of Experiment 1 and 2 are used to obtain our main conclusions. Experiment 3 is used to determine how scalable the algorithms are. The algorithms' scalability is measured with respect to the world size and the number of agents used. In Experiment 3 the number of agents is set to 500.

The comparison is based on efficiency, scalability and adaptability. In Figure 3(a), an example of a medium-sized world is presented. Figure 4 and 5 present the corresponding result figures. The former shows a histogram of the total iterations needed for completing the foraging task at hand. The latter shows a histogram of the average computation time needed per iteration.

Considering efficiency, in Figure 4, we can observe that the bee-inspired algorithm is more efficient, since it uses significantly fewer iterations to complete the task at hand. With an increasing number of agents, the (relative and absolute) efficiency of the algorithm rises. These are typical results found in this research, i.e., they occur in every experiment performed.

In Figure 5(a), we present a histogram of the average computation time needed per iteration in a medium-sized experiment with 100 agents. We observe that the algorithms on average will settle around a computation time of 108ms and 106ms per iteration, respectively. In Figure 5(b) we observe that with 250 agents, the bee-inspired algorithm has a mean of 353ms while the ant-inspired algorithm's mean is 341ms and has a wide spread. Even though a statistical test reveals that in both cases, the difference is significant in favour of the ant-inspired algorithm, the total computation time required to complete the task is still much lower for the bee-inspired algorithm. Once again, these are typical results; they occur in every small- and medium-sized experiment performed.

Considering scalability, we take into account (i) increasing the number of agents and (ii) increasing the size of the world. With respect to agent scalability, in Table 1,

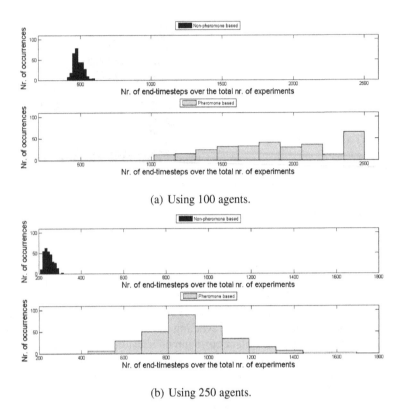

(a) Using 100 agents.

(b) Using 250 agents.

Fig. 4. Histogram of the number of iterations needed in medium-sized, basic-case experiments, with a number of agents as indicated. Black indicates the occurrences for the bee-inspired algorithm. Grey indicates the occurrences for the ant-inspired algorithm. Results are obtained after 300 experimental runs.

Table 1. Performance ratios between the ant-inspired algorithm (Pb) and the bee-inspired algorithm (NPb). I.e., $\frac{Pb}{NPb}$ ratio. Ratios marked with a (*) are influenced by the maximum number of timesteps available. Due to the fact that experiments are terminated after 2500 timesteps, the ant-inspired algorithm was not always able to complete the task set while the bee-inspired algorithm always did. The marked ratios values therefore could actually be even higher if we allowed for more timesteps.

World size (number of agents)	Time/Timestep	# Timestep	Total used time
200 × 200 (50 agents)	1.18	3.09	3.35
200 × 200 (100 agents)	0.94	3.24	3.04
300 × 300 (100 agents)	0.98	(*)3.90	(*)3.81
300 × 300 (250 agents)	0.97	3.69	(3.56
600 × 600 (500 agents)	0.99	(*)3.31	(*)3.27

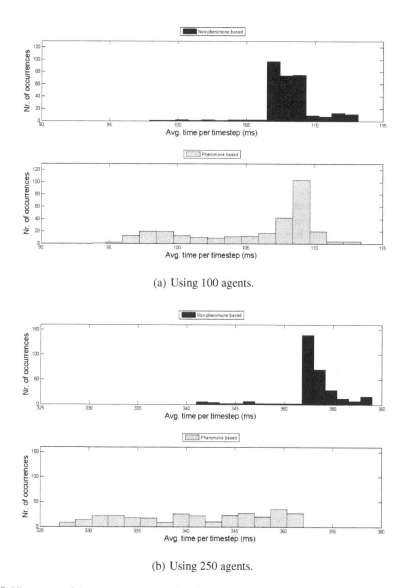

(a) Using 100 agents.

(b) Using 250 agents.

Fig. 5. Histogram of the average computation time needed per iteration in medium-sized, basic-case experiments, with a number of agents as indicated. Black indicates the occurrences for the bee-inspired algorithm. Grey indicates the occurrences for the ant-inspired algorithm. Results are obtained after 300 experimental runs.

we can observe that when we increase the number of agents and keep the world size constant, ratios decrease (i.e., the ant-inspired algorithm is more scalable with respect to the number of agents). With respect to world scalability, in Table 1, we can observe that when we increase the world size and keep the number of agents constant, ratios increase (i.e., the bee-inspired algorithm is more scalable with respect to the size of

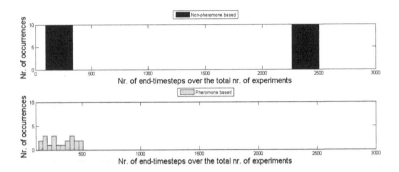

Fig. 6. Histogram of the number of iterations needed in small-sized, two bridges case experiment. Black indicates the occurrences for the bee-inspired algorithm. Grey indicates the occurrences for the ant-inspired algorithm. Results are obtained after 20 experiments with 50 agents.

the world). Overall, the bee-inspired algorithm is more scalable than the ant-inspired algorithm since it finishes its tasks much faster.

Considering adaptability, we performed an experiment in which the task set was the Deneubourg Bridge [19]. Figure 3(b) shows the world in which the experiment is performed. In this two-bridges world, the short path is blocked after a certain number of timesteps. The ant-inspired algorithm performs better than the bee-inspired algorithm in such a world, see Figure 6. This is because of the fact that by using pheromone trails, the ant-inspired algorithm has more information about the world than the bee-inspired algorithm. The latter will try to exploit its most direct path even when this most direct path is blocked. The ant-inspired algorithm however, will eventually move towards the unblocked path due to the accumulated pheromone on this path. To enable the bee-inspired algorithm to obtain this environmental information, some extra features have to be added, such as landmark navigation. The results indicate that the ant-inspired algorithm is more adaptive than the current bee-inspired algorithm.

5   Conclusion

Taking into account the results of the experiments in this research, we may conclude that our bee-inspired algorithm is significantly more efficient than the ant-inspired algorithm when finding and collecting food.

Concerning scalability, we may conclude that the ant-inspired algorithm is most scalable with respect to the number of agents used, while the bee-inspired algorithm is most scalable with respect to the size of the world used. The latter might be a desirable feature; multi-agent systems are mostly applied in large worlds. Furthermore, we may conclude that even in smaller worlds, our bee-inspired algorithm requires less total computation time than an ant-inspired algorithm, even if in some cases, the latter requires less computation time per iteration. Besides these benefits, we have to note that our bee-inspired algorithm is less adaptive than the ant-inspired algorithm.

Currently, we are extending the recruitment behaviour of our artificial bees. More precisely, we are adding quality assessment for the artificial bee's decision on dance following. Furthermore, we are extending the simulation environment to make it able to construct worlds that are even more dynamic (i.e., moving obstacles and food sources varying in quality). In order to make the algorithm more adaptive, we are investigating whether it is possible to navigate on landmarks. Such landmarks could possibly be created (and decided on) through cooperation between agents or eventually created centrally by the *Deamonactions*() function (as known in ACO). We are also evaluating to which problems the algorithm could be applied and whether graph-based problems could also make use of path approximation via PI vectors.

We give two more options for future research. First, it might be interesting to construct a hybrid algorithm. By extending the bee-inspired algorithm with, for example, pheromone direction markers, we could improve the algorithm's adaptability possibly without decreasing its efficiency or scalability. Second, by combining PI strategies with potential field searching [20], we could improve local search.

References

1. von Frisch, K.: The dance language and orientation of bees. Harvard University Press, Cambridge, Massachusetts (1967)
2. Lambrinos, D., Möller, R., Labhart, T., Pfeifer, R., Wehner, R.: A mobile robot employing insect strategies for navigation. Robotics and Autonomous Systems 30(1-2), 39–64 (2000)
3. Müller, M., Wehner, R.: Path integration in desert ants, *Cataglyphis Fortis*. Proceedings of the National Academy of Sciences 85(14), 5287–5290 (1988)
4. Dorigo, M., Stützle, T.: The ant colony optimization metaheuristic: algorithms, applications, and advances. Technical report, Université of Libre de Bruxelles (2000)
5. Lucic, P., Tedorovic, D.: Computing with bees: attacking complex transportation engineering problems. International Journal on Artificial Intelligence Tools 12, 375–394 (2003)
6. Nakrani, S., Tovey, C.: On honey bees and dynamic server allocation in internet hosting centers. Adaptive Behaviour 12, 223–240 (2004)
7. Chong, C., Low, M.H., Sivakumar, A., Gay, K.: A bee colony optimization algorithm to job shop scheduling. In: Proceedings of the 2006 Winter Simulation Conference, Monterey, CA USA, pp. 1954–1961 (2006)
8. Teodorovic, D., Dell' Orco, M.: Bee colony optimization: A cooperative learning approach to complex transportation problems. In: Proceedings of the 16th Mini - EURO Conference and 10th Meeting of EWGT (2006)
9. Lemmens, N.: To bee or not to bee: A comparative study in swarm intelligence. Master's thesis, Maastricht University, The Netherlands (2006)
10. Michelsen, A., Andersen, B., Storm, J., Kirchner, W., Lindauer, M.: How honeybees perceive communication dances, studied by means of a mechanical model. Behavioral Ecology and Sociobiology 30(3-4), 143–150 (1992)
11. Dyer, F.: When it pays to waggle. Nature 419, 885–886 (2002)
12. Camazine, S., Sneyd, J.: A model of collective nectar source by honey bees: selforganization through simple rules. Journal of Theoretical Biology 149, 547–571 (1991)
13. Barth, F.: Insects and flowers: The biology of a partnership. Princeton University Press, Princeton, New Jersey (1982)
14. Collett, T.S., Graham, P., Durier, V.: Route learning by insects. Current Opinion in Neurobiology 13(6), 718–725 (2003)
15. Collett, T., Collett, M.: How do insects represent familiar terrain. Journal of Physiology 98, 259–264 (2004)

16. Viswanathan, G.M., Afanasyevc, V., Buldyrev, S.V., Havlin, S., da Luze, M.G.E., Raposof, E.P., Stanley, H.E.: Lévy flights in random searches. Physica A: Statistical Mechanics and its Applications 282, 1–12 (2000)
17. Sutton, R.S., Precup, S., Singh, S.: Between mdps and semi-mdps: A framework for temporal abstraction in reinforcement learning. Artificial Intelligence 112, 181–211 (1999)
18. Iba, G.A.: A heuristic approach to the discovery of macro-operators. Machine Learning 3, 285–317 (1989)
19. Deneubourg, J., Aron, S., Goss, S., Pasteels, J.: The self-organizing exploratory pattern of the argentine ant. Journal of Insect Behaviour 3, 159–168 (1990)
20. de Jong, S., Tuyls, K., Sprinkhuizen-Kuyper, I.: Robust and scalable coordination of potential-field driven agents. In: Proceedings of IAWTIC/CIMCA, Sydney (2006)

Stable Cooperation in the N-Player Prisoner's Dilemma: The Importance of Community Structure

Colm O'Riordan[1] and Humphrey Sorensen[2]

[1] Dept. of Information Technology, NUI, Galway, Ireland
colm.oriordan@nuigalway.ie
[2] Dept. of Computer Science, University College Cork, Ireland
h.sorensen@cs.ucc.ie

Abstract. N-player prisoner dilemma games have been adopted and studied as a representation of many social dilemmas. They capture a larger class of social dilemmas than the traditional two-player prisoner's dilemma. In N-player games, defection is the individually rational strategy and normally emerges as the dominant strategy in evolutionary simulations of agents playing the game.

In this paper, we discuss the effect of a specific type of spatial constraint on a population of learning agents by placing agents on a graph structure which exhibits a *community structure*. We show that, by organising agents on a graph with a community structure, cooperation can exist despite the presence of defectors. Furthermore, we show that, by allowing agents learn from agents in neighbouring communities, cooperation can actually spread and become the dominant robust strategy.

Moreover, we show that the spread of cooperation is robust to the introduction of noise into the system.

Keywords: Cooperation, N-Player Prisoner's dilemma, Community structure.

1 Introduction

The placing of constraints on agent interactions and the subsequent analysis of the resulting effect of these constraints on the society has been studied in a range of subdomains in multi-agent and artificial life societies. These include spatial constraints[8][6][13], tagging mechanisms[16] and trust and reputation systems[15]. Recently, there has been much interest in studying the emergent behaviour of agents playing in social dilemma games constrained by spatial constraints defined by some form of graph structure; these include small world graphs[24][22] and scale free graphs[23][19]. In these graphs constraints may exist on the clustering coefficient, the distribution of the node degree values and the average shortest path between two nodes.

A further interesting property of many real-world social networks is that of community structure. Given the existence of a community structure in many

K. Tuyls et al. (Eds.): Adaptive Agents and MAS III, LNAI 4865, pp. 157–168, 2008.

real-world social networks[11], questions arise regarding the effect of community structure on societies of agents playing in social dilemmas. Does the existence of community structure promote the emergence of cooperation?

This paper examines N-player social dilemmas. In the recent work on analysing the effect of various graph structures on agent interactions, the focus has been on the more widely studied two-player dilemma. In this work, we focus on the more general case, the N-player prisoner's dilemma. It has been argued that the N-player extension has greater generality and applicability to real-life situations [3].

In particular, we consider the effect of enforcing a community structure on a society of agents participating in N-player social dilemmas. We show that, by having a high degree of community structure, we can ensure that cooperative agents can insulate themselves from neighbouring non-cooperating strategies. By further adopting an update mechanism, whereby members of neighbouring communities can update their strategy to imitate that of a more successful strategy, we show that cooperation can actually spread throughout the society. We also show that, despite introducing considerable levels of noise to the learning process, cooperation can remain as the outcome.

Our simulations show that a high degree of community structure coupled with simple learning mechanisms can lead to the spread of cooperative behaviours, resulting in a robust stable cooperative society. In this paper we are interested in exploring the effect community structure has on the emergence of cooperation. It is plausible to propose that there is two-way relationship between these two features and that the emergence of cooperation and trust relationships can lead to the emergence of community structure. However, in this paper, we restrict our focus to one side of this relationship i.e. on the effect community structure can have on the emergence of cooperation.

2   Related Work

2.1   N-Player Social Dilemmas

An oft-studied game to model agent interaction is the N-player iterated prisoner's dilemma. N-player dilemmas are characterised by having many participants, each of whom may choose to cooperate or defect. These choices are made autonomously without any communication between participants. Any benefit or payoff is received by all participants; any cost is borne by the cooperators only. A well-known example is the *Tragedy of the Commons*[5]. In this dilemma, land (the commons) is freely available for farmers to use for grazing cattle. For any individual farmer, it is advantageous to use this resource rather than their own land. However, if all farmers adopt the same reasoning, the commons will be over-used and soon will be of no use to any of the participants, resulting in an outcome that is sub-optimal for all farmers.

In the N-player dilemma game there are N participants. Each player is confronted with a choice: to either cooperate (C) or defect(D). We will represent the payoff obtained by a strategy which defects given i cooperators as $D(i)$ and the payoff obtained by a cooperative strategy given i cooperators as $C(i)$.

Defection represents a dominant strategy, i.e. for any individual, moving from cooperation to defection is beneficial for that player (they still receive a benefit without the cost):

$$D(i) > D(i-1) \quad 0 < i \leq N - 1 \tag{1}$$

$$C(i) > C(i-1) \quad 0 < i \leq N - 1 \tag{2}$$

$$D(i) > C(i) \quad 0 < i \leq N - 1 \tag{3}$$

However, if all participants adopt this dominant strategy, the resulting scenario is sub-optimal and, from a group point of view, an irrational outcome ensues:

$$C(N) > D(0) \tag{4}$$

If any player changes from defection to cooperation, the performance of the society improves, i.e. a society with $i + 1$ cooperators attains a greater payoff than a society with i cooperators:

$$(i+1)C(i+1) + (N-i-1)D(i+1) > (i)C(i) + (N-i)D(i) \tag{5}$$

If we consider payoffs for this game, we can see that D dominates C and that total cooperation is better for participants than total defection.

The N-person game has greater generality and applicability to real life situations. In addition to the problems of energy conservation, ecology and over population, many other real-life problems can be represented by the N-player dilemma paradigm.

Several evolutionary simulations exist which study the performance of different strategy types playing the N-player game. This work has shown that, without placing specific constraints on the interactions, the number of participants or the strategies involved, the resulting outcome is that of defection[17][25].

2.2 Community Structure

In studying the two-player game, many researchers have explored the effect of placing spatial constraints on the population of interacting agents. These include, among others, experimentation with grid size and topology [12], graph structure in a choice/refusal framework [20], different learning mechanisms and topologies[10], small world[22], scale-free graphs[19] and graphs where the actual graph topology emerges over time [18].

In more recent work analysing small world and scale-free networks, researchers are often interested in key properties of these graphs. In this paper, we are interested in one key property of a graph: that of *community structure*. This property has also been explored in recent work[9]. A graph is said to have a community structure if collections of nodes are joined together in tightly knit groups between which there are only looser connections. This property has been shown to exist in many real-world social networks[11].

Our work differs from previous research exploring the emergence of cooperation in populations of agents organised according to a given graph topology in two ways. Firstly, we deal with the N-player dilemma where direct reciprocity towards, or punishment against, an agent is not possible (which is required in work that allows agents modify their connections towards other agents[18]) and secondly we utilise two update rules.

Many algorithms have been proposed to measure the degree of community structure in graphs. One such approach is that of hierarchical clustering. An alternative approach is that proposed by Girvan and Newman[11]. The *betweeness* of an edge is defined as the number of minimum paths connecting pairs of nodes that go through that edge. The algorithm repeatedly removes these edges. Donetti and Munoz[4] present another algorithm which involves extracting the eigenvectors of a laplacian matrix representing the graph. In this paper, we define graphs that have a predefined level of community structure. We systematically tune parameters to control the level of community structure present in the graph. Hence we do not need to utilise algorithms to measure the level of community structure as is necessitated when dealing with real-world data.

3   Model

3.1   Graph Structure

In the simulations described in this paper, agents are located on nodes of a graph. The graph is an undirected weighted graph. The weight associated with any edge between nodes represents the strength of the connection between the two agents located at the nodes. This determines the likelihood of these agents participating together in games.

The graph is static throughout the simulation: no nodes are added or removed and the edge weights remain constant.

We use a regular graph: all nodes have the same degree. In this paper, nodes have four neighbours. We use two different edge weight values in each graph: one (a higher value) associated with the edges within a community and another (a lower value) associated with the edges joining agents in adjacent communities. All weights used in the this work are in range [0,1].

The graph is depicted in Fig. 1, where the thicker lines represent intra-community links (larger value as edge weight) and the thinner lines indicate inter-community links between neighbouring communities. Each rectangle with thick lines represents a community of agents; the corners of these rectangles represent and agent.

3.2   Agents Interactions and Learning

Interaction Model. Agents in this model can have a strategy of either cooperation (C) or defection (D). Agents interact with their neighbours in a N-player prisoner's dilemma. The payoffs received by the agents are calculated according to the formula proposed by Boyd and Richerson [2], i.e. cooperators receive $(Bi/N) - c$ and defectors receive Bi/N, where B is a constant (in this paper, B is set to 5), i is the number of cooperators involved in the game, N is the

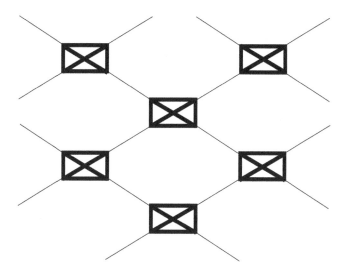

Fig. 1. Graph structure

number of participants and c is another constant (in this paper, c is set to 3). The values of B and c are chosen because they fulfill the requirements needed to ensure a dilemma.

Each agent may participate in several games. The algorithm proceeds as follows: for each agent a in the population, agents are selected from the immediate neighbourhood of agent a to participate in the game. Neighbouring agents are chosen to participate with a probability equal to the edge of the weight between the nodes. This means that, for a society with a high community structure, most games involve members of an agent's local community. This allows a high degree of insulation from agents in neighbouring communities. An agent's fitness is calculated as the average payoff received in the interactions during a generation.

3.3 Learning

Agents may change their behaviours by comparing their payoff to that of neighbouring agents. We adopt a simple update rule whereby an agent may update their strategy to that used by more successful strategies. Following each round of games, agents are allowed to learn from their neighbours. Again these neighbours are chosen stochastically; the neighbours are chosen according to the weight of the edge between agent and neighbour.

We incorporate a second update mechanism. The motivation for its inclusion is as follows: following several iterations of learning from local neighbours, each community is likely to be in a state of equilibrium—either total cooperation or total defection. Agents within these groups are receiving the same reward as their immediate neighbours. However, neighbouring communities may be receiving different payoffs. An agent that is equally fit as its immediate neighbours may look further afield to identify more successful strategies.

In the first update rule, agents consider other agents who are immediate neighbours. Let $s\_adj(x)$ denote the immediate neighbours of agents x chosen stochastically according to edge weight. The probability of an agent x updating their strategy to be that of a neighbouring agent y is given by:

$$\frac{w(x,y).f(y)}{\Sigma_{z \in s\_adj(x)} w(x,z).f(z)} \tag{6}$$

where $f(y)$ is the fitness of an agent y and $w(x,y)$ is the weight of the edge between x and y.

The second update rule allows agents to look further afield from their own location and consider the strategies and payoffs received by agents in this larger set, i.e. agents update to a strategy y according to:

$$\frac{w(x,y).f(y)}{\Sigma_{z \in adj(adj(x))} w(x,z).f(z)} \tag{7}$$

where again $f(y)$ is the fitness of agent y and now $w(x,z)$ refers to the weight of the path between x and z. We use the product of the edge weights as the path weight. Note that in the second rule, we don't choose the agents in proportion to their edge weight values; we instead consider the complete set of potential agents in the extended neighbourhood. In this way all agents in a community can be influenced by a neighbouring cooperative community.

Using the first update rule, agents can learn from their immediate neighbours and adopt a strategy of a more successful agent. Using the second rule, agents can look at their immediate neighbours and their neighbours' neighbours; this effectively gives them a larger set from which to learn. This is necessary in cases where a particular community has converged on some behaviour which is less successful than that adopted by a neighbouring community.

In our experiments we use a population of 800 agents; we allow simulations to run for 300 generations. In each generation, agents interact with their selected neighbours, update their scores based on these interactions and then learn from their immediate neighbours using the local update rule. Every four generations, agents also look to a larger community and learn from an agent in a larger set of agents. The motivation behind this is based on the notion that agents will learn from a wider set if their own neighbourhood has settled into an equilibrium state—which will be true following a set of local interactions. In our experiments, four generations is usually sufficient to allow a local community reach an equilibrium point.

4   Results and Discussion

In this section, we present the results of a number of simulations illustrating the effect of varying levels of community structure on cooperation in a population of agents playing an N-player prisoner's dilemma.

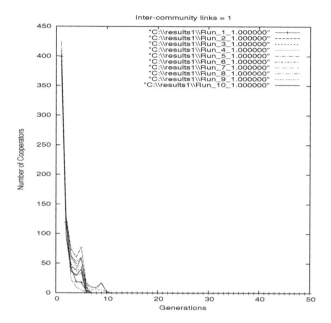

Fig. 2. Defection spreading in a regular graph

By setting the intra-community links to be high (1.0) and then varying the inter-community link weights from 0 to 1, we can model different levels of community structure. If we set the inter-community link weights to be 1, we have no community structure; we merely have a regular graph. If we set the inter-community links to zero then we have a population of separate isolated communities.

In any given N-player prisoner's dilemma game, a defector will score better than a cooperator. If we allow poorly performing strategies to imitate the behaviour of more successful strategies we see that there are two possible resultant equilibrium states—total defection and total cooperation. If any of the initial strategies are defectors, others will imitate that strategy and defection will emerge. If the initial state contains all cooperators, then cooperation will exist as an equilibrium state. Given n players, the probability of having a state of total cooperation is $1/2^n$; the probability of a non-cooperative equilibrium state is $1 - (1/2^n)$. As n increases our chances of a cooperative equilibrium state decreases rapidly.

If we consider the scenario with no community structure, agents will have 5 players in every game. If any defector exists in the original population, defection will spread throughout. This is illustrated in Fig. 2, which depicts ten separate runs of the simulator resulting in a similar outcome—that of total defection.

By introducing a community structure, clusters of cooperators in a community can survive by participating in mutually beneficial cooperative games. By having inter-community links of weight zero, the local update rule will ensure that all groups will reach an equilibrium state and the population will then remain

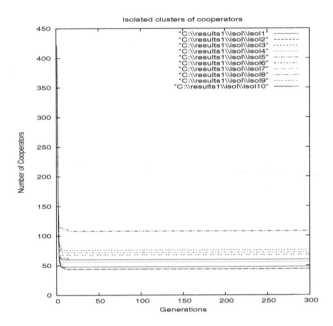

Fig. 3. Robust clusters of cooperators with local update rule and isolated communities

static with a minority of cooperative clusters existing in a large population of defectors. This allows robust groups of cooperators to exist in the environment but cooperation cannot spread throughout the population. We illustrate this for ten separate runs in Fig. 3.; in this simulation agents learn according to the local update rule only.

By allowing some interaction between neighbouring communities—i.e. having weights greater than zero with the update rules as described—we can have cooperation spreading through the population. If the relative difference between inter- and intra- community becomes too small, the community structure collapses, as does cooperation. The following graph (Fig. 4) shows a series of runs for differing values of inter-community links; these are the average of 20 runs.

As can be seen, for high levels of community structure (i.e. when the inter-community links are 0.1, 0.2), cooperation quickly emerges as a societal norm. As the community structure is decreased we see societies with both cooperation and defection co-existing. As the inter-community link weights reach higher values (0.7, 0.8, 0.9), we see defection spreading as the dominant behaviour.

We see sizable fluctuations among the runs with intermediate levels of community structure. These can be explained as follows: some members of communities of defectors neighbouring a cooperative community are likely to change their behaviour to cooperation following the second update rule. This occurs every four generations for all of the runs. Following this increase, we have a series of local updates, which leads to these cooperators being exploited and then adopting defection by updating their strategy according to the first update rule. This

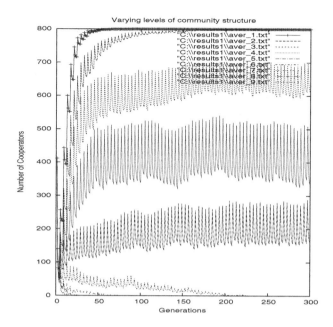

Fig. 4. Graph of number of cooperators over time for varying levels of community structure

leads to a subsequent dip in the cooperation; this occurs periodically throughout the simulation.

5   Robustness to Noise

The majority of work in multi-agent systems assumes a clean, noise-free environment i.e., moves are perfectly transmitted and received and agents learning a new strategy do so perfectly. There have been several efforts to model the effect of noise and to define strategies to deal with such effects [21],[7][14][1].

In much of the previous work, the emphasis has been placed on the effect of noise on reactive strategies. Previous research has promoted higher degrees of tolerance towards strategies whose moves may be mis-interpreted or mis-implemented[21]. Hence, strategies do not react as immediately or with the same degree of punishment.

In this work, agents with simple strategies participate in a one-shot N-player game; hence agents are not able to retaliate. Given this constraint, we implement noise in a different manner. Instead of allowing perfect imitation of more successful strategies, we introduce a probability of mis-imitation. The greater the level of noise, the more likely an agent is to fail to imitate a more successful strategy.

The effect of such noise on agents playing in these simulations is as follows: as strategies in a cluster of defectors attempt to imitate neighbouring cooperative

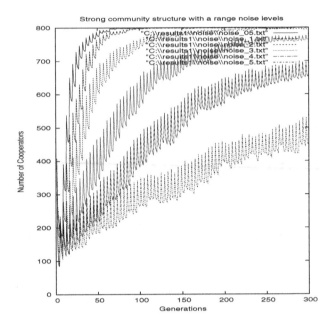

Fig. 5. Cooperation levels with noise

agents, there is an increased probability of not all agents successfully imitating their neighbours. The will lead to a cluster with mixed strategies which will quickly lead to an equilibrium of defection being reached. This slows down the spread of cooperation.

We run a number of simulations with the noise set to be the following the values (5%, 10%, 20%, 30%, 40% and 50%). For larger values, cooperation does not spread.

As can be seen in Fig. 5, cooperation can still emerge in the population as the dominant strategy despite the presence of noise in the agents' learning of strategies.

6   Conclusions and Future Work

Most investigations into the N-player social dilemma to date have shown the dominance of defection. In evolutionary simulations, defection often emerges. In our experiments, motivated by the recent work in identifying community structure in many real world social networks, we include different levels of community structure. We build graphs where we can tune the level of community structure.

In our experiments, we show that the presence of community structure can allow cooperation to be robust in the presence of defectors when using a simple learning rule whereby agents imitate nearby fitter agents. Furthermore, when allowing agents to periodically imitate from a larger set of nearby agents, we show that cooperation can emerge given the presence of a sufficiently strong community structure in the graph. We also show that cooperation will still spread even there is a relatively large level of noise in the learning of strategies by agents.

In this work, we examined how spatial constraints involving community structure can induce cooperation in a population of agents. Future work will also examine the role cooperation and cooperative relationships play in the emergence of community structure in societies of agents.

Future work will involve further exploration of several of the experimental parameters e.g. in this work we set the degree to be four for all nodes; it would be interesting to explore the effect of varying this value and also the effect of having variation in the degree throughout the graph. We will also involve further investigation into the effects resulting from community structure by considering the introduction of other types of noise, larger strategy sets and also on a wider range of graphs incorporating more features of real world social networks.

References

1. Bendor, J.: Uncertainty and the Evolution of Cooperation. Journal of Conflict Resolution 37(4), 709–734 (1993)
2. Boyd, R., Richerson, P.J.: The Evolution of Reciprocity in Sizable Groups. Journal of Theoretical Biology 132, 337–356 (1988)
3. Davis, J.H., Laughlin, P.R., Komorita, S.S.: The social psychology of small groups: Cooperative and Mixed-Motive Interaction. Annual review of Psychology 27, 501–541 (1976)
4. Doneeti, L., Munoz, M.A.: Detecting network communities: a new systematic and powerful algorithm. Journal of Statistical Mechanics, P10012 (October 2004)
5. Hardin, G.: The tragedy of the commons. Science 162(3859), 1243–1248 (1968)
6. Hauert, C.: Spatial Effects in Social Dilemmas. Journal of Theoretical Biology 240(4), 627–636 (2006)
7. Kraines, D., Kraines, V.: Learning to Cooperate with Pavlov: An adaptive strategy for the Iterated Prisoner's Dilemma with Noise. Theory and Decision 35, 107–150 (1993)
8. Lindgren, K., Nordahl, M.G.: Evolutionary Dynamics of Spatial Games. Physica D 75(1-3), 292–309 (1994)
9. Lozano, S., Arenas, A., Sanchez, A.: Mesoscopic structure conditions the emergence of cooperation on social networks. arXiv:physics/0612124v1 (2006)
10. Moran, M., O'Riordan, C.: Emergence of Cooperative Societies in Structured Multi-agent systems.In: AICS 2005. Proceedings of the 16th Irish Conference on Artificial Intelligence and Cognitive Science (September 2005)
11. Newman, M.E.J., Girvan, M.: Finding and evaluating community structure in networks. Physics Review E 69 (2004)
12. Nowak, M.A., May, R.M., Bonhoffer, S.: More Spatial Games. International Journal of Bifurcation and Chaos 4(1), 33–56 (1994)
13. Nowak, M.A., Sigmund, K.: Games on Grids. In: Dieckmann, U., Law, R., Metz, J.A.J. (eds.) The Geometry of Ecological Interaction, pp. 135–150. Cambridge University Press, Cambridge (2000)
14. O'Riordan, C.: Evolving Strategies for Agents in the Iterated Prisoner's Dilemma in Noisy Environments. AISB: Cognition in Machines and Animals (April 2003)

15. Ramchurn, S., Huynh, D., Jennings, N.R.: Trust in multiagent systems. The Knowledge Engineering Review 19(1), 1–25 (2004)
16. Riolo, R.L.: The Effects of Tag-Mediated Selection of Partners in Evolving Populations Playing the Iterated Prisoner's Dilemma. Technical report, Santa Fe Institute Working Paper 97-02-016 (1997)
17. O'Riordan, C., Griffith, J., Newell, J., Sorensen, H.: Co-evolution of strategies for an N-player dilemma. In: Proceedings of the Congress on Evolutionary Computation (June 19–23, 2004)
18. Santos, F.C, Pacheco, J.M., Lenaerts, T.: Cooperation Prevails when Individuals Adjust Their Social Ties. PLOS Compuational Biology 2(10) (October 2006)
19. Santos, F.C, Pacheo, J.M.: Scale-free Networks Provide a Unifying Framework for the Emergence of Cooperation. Physical Review Letters 95(9) (August 2005)
20. Smucker, M.D., Stanley, E.A., Ashlock, D.: Analyzing Social Network Structures in the Iterated Prisoner's Dilemma with Choice and Refusal. Technical report, University of Wisconsin, Technical Report CS-TR-94-1259 (December 1994)
21. Wu, J., Axelrod, R.: How to Cope with Noise in the Iterated Prisoner's Dilemma. Journal of Conflict Resolution 39(1), 183–189 (1995)
22. Wu, Z., Xu, X., Chen, Y., Wang, Y.: Spatial prisoner's dilemma game with volunteering in newman-watts small-world networks. Physical Review E 71, 37103 (2005)
23. Wu, Z., Xu, X., Wang, Y.: Does the scale-free topology favor the emergence of cooperation? eprint arXiv physics/0508220 (2005)
24. Wu, Z., Xu, X., Wang, Y.: Prisoner's dilemma game with heterogenuous influence effect on regular small world networks. Chinese Physics Letters (2005)
25. Yao, X., Darwen, P.J.: An experimental study of N-person iterated prisoner's dilemma games. Informatica 18, 435–450 (1994)

Solving Multi-stage Games with Hierarchical Learning Automata That Bootstrap

Maarten Peeters[1,*], Katja Verbeeck[2,**], and Ann Nowé[1]

[1] Vrije Universiteit Brussel
Computational Modeling Lab
Pleinlaan 2
1050 Brussel, Belgium
[2] Maastricht University
MICC-IKAT
P.O. Box 616
6200 MD Maastricht, The Netherlands

Abstract. Hierarchical learning automata are shown to be an excellent tool for solving multi-stage games. However, most updating schemes used by hierarchical automata expect the multi-stage game to reach an absorbing state at which point the automata are updated in a Monte Carlo way. As such, the approach is infeasible for large multi-stage games (and even for problems with an infinite horizon) and the convergence process is slow. In this paper we propose an algorithm where the rewards don't have to travel all the way up to the top of the hierarchy and in which there is no need for explicit end-stages.

1 Introduction

Over the past decade, a substantial amount of research was focused on comprehending [1] and solving single-stage games (e.g. joint-action learners [2]; ESRL [3,4] or Commitment Sequences [5]). Only recently the focus has shifted to providing algorithms and techniques for solving the more challenging multi-stage games instead of single-stage games.

The research on the learning behaviors of automata started with the work of Tsetlin [6] in the 1960's. In their research Tsetslin and co-workers introduced finite action deterministic automata in stationary random environments. It was shown that under certain conditions the automata behaved asymptotically optimal. Further research [7,8,9] looked at more challenging problems such as non-deterministic environments and variable-structure, continuous action learning automata. Learning automata (LA) research led to many practical applications in field the engineering.

---

* Research funded by a Ph.D grant of the Institute for the Promotion of Innovation through Science and Technology in Flanders (IWT- Vlaanderen).
** The author is sponsored by a grant of the Interactive Collaborative Information Systems (ICIS) project, supported by the Dutch Ministry of Economic Affairs, nr: BSIK03024 (The Netherlands).

K. Tuyls et al. (Eds.): Adaptive Agents and MAS III, LNAI 4865, pp. 169–187, 2008.

Recently, learning automata also became popular in the field of multi-agent reinforcement learning [10]. Early on, researchers looked at how multiple automata in a single environment could be interconnected and still find stable solutions [11]. One of the advantages of using learning automata in this field is that they are independent learners that without the use of communication. Furthermore, they operate without information concerning the number of other participants, their strategies or their pay-off which are constraints of some multi-agent reinforcement learning techniques (such as joint-action learners [2]). Another reason for using learning automata as the underlying framework for building a multi-agent system are the theoretical characteristics. The model of a learning automaton has a well funded mathematical basis. Both for the single automaton as in the multi-automata case convergence theorems exist [8]. A final motivation for using for using learning automata is that they have proved their usefulness in many applications. In [12], results on learning automata games formed the basis for a new multi-agent reinforcement learning approach to learning single stage, repeated normal form games. Many real-world problems, however, are naturally translated into multi-stage problems [13]. Therefore in this paper we are concerned with learning in sequential games where the agents have to take a sequence of actions [14].

Thathachar and Ramakrishnan [15,16] introduced the concept of a hierarchical LA (HLA) in which the actions are distributed over a tree-structured hierarchy of LA. In such a hierarchy different actions have to be taken before an explicit end-stage is reached. Games between hierarchical learning automata agents can be represented by multi-stage games or multi-agent Markov decision problems [14]. The authors proved that hierarchical learning automata converge to a single path in any common interest multi-stage tree using a Monte Carlo reward. Furthermore they proved that HLA converge faster and more accurately than the equivalent single automaton (which can be constructed by taking the union of all the actions of all the automata at the lowest level of the hierarchy). In [17] it was shown that hierarchical learning automata agents can solve tree-structured multi-stage games with episodic tasks by using a Monte Carlo way of updating, collecting rewards obtained along the path of the multi-stage game. However, until now only episodic tasks could be considered.

Standard single agent reinforcement learning techniques, such as Q-learning [18], which are by nature designed to solve sequential decision problems, use the mechanism of bootstrapping to handle non-episodic tasks. Bootstrapping means that values or estimates are learned on the basis of other estimates [11]. The use of next state estimates allows reinforcement learning to be applied to non-episodic tasks.

Multi-agent learning approaches that bootstrap exist; an overview of approaches based on Q-learning and through it on the Bellman equations is given in [19]. However in these approaches, agents are not independent learners since they need to know the actions taken by other agents and their associated rewards, in order to learn Q-values of joint-actions. Besides this, only weak convergence assurances are given.

Our work focuses on common interest games. In previous research we reported on a technique for solving coordination problems in simple tree-structured multi-stage games. This Hierarchical Exploring Selfish Reinforcement Learners (HESRL) [3] technique was based on the convergence theorems of hierarchical learning automata. In this setting the hierarchy is only informed about its probability of success when reaching an end-stage. This implies that the updating mechanism cannot be used in games without an explicit end-stage (i.e. infinite horizon problems). One way to solve this problem is to introduce bootstrapping [20] into the setup. If agents get informed immediately of the quality of an action we can use them in infinite horizon problems. In this paper, we introduce bootstrapping for independent HLA agents in multi-stage games. First, instead of computing a single combined reward each time an end-stage is reached and handing this reward back to each level of the agents, we will now compute a reward tailored for each level of the agent. We call this algorithm Intermediate Rewards. Second, the learning automata in the hierarchy will be updated on the basis of estimates, and these estimates will be propagated from child to parent in the LA hierarchy. Just as in single agent learning, we can develop updates going from the 1-step back-up mechanism to the complete Monte Carlo update mechanism. Empirical results show that HLA agents based on Intermediate Rewards and 1-step backups are capable of solving multi-stage games in a more efficient way. The results also show a higher percentage of convergence to the optimal path in large multi-stage games and a faster convergence [21].

In the next section we repeat the concept of bootstrapping in classical single agent reinforcement learning. We continue in Section 3 with multi-stage games, the LA model and its properties. In Section 4 we explain how we can add bootstrapping to our learning automata model. In Section 5 we discuss the effect of bootstrapping on several large random generated multi-stage games. In the last section we conclude and propose future work.

2   Bootstrapping in a Single-Agent Environment

Reinforcement learning is the problem faced by an agent that learns behavior through trial-and-error interactions with a dynamic environment [11]. To optimize the reward received from the environment it is operating in, the agent should exploit actions that it has found to be good. However discovering better actions is only possible by trying out new ones, meaning the agent should explore. This trade-off is fundamental and in the stationary, Markovian case convergence to the optimal policy[1] can be guaranteed.

Single agent control problems in stationary environments can be successfully modeled as Markov decision processes (MDPs). An MDP is defined by a set of states $\mathbb{S}$, a set of actions A, a transition function[2] $T : \mathbb{S} \times A \rightarrow P(\mathbb{S})$ that outputs

---

[1] A policy is a mapping from states to actions. An optimal policy is a mapping which maximizes some long-run measure of reinforcement.

[2] This function models the probability of ending up in a next state when an agent takes an action in a certain state.

a probability distribution over $\mathbb{S}$ and a reward function $R : \mathbb{S} \times A \rightarrow P(\mathbb{R})$ which implicitly specifies the agent's task.

Without prior knowledge of the transition probabilities or rewards, an MDP can be solved online by the theory of reinforcement learning [11].

Common reinforcement learning methods, which can be found in [22,11] are structured around estimating value functions. A value of a state or state-action pair, is the total amount of reward an agent can expect to receive in the future, starting from that state. One way to approximate the optimal policy is to find the optimal value function.

For instance the Q-learning algorithm, which is a value iteration method (see [11,23]) bootstraps its estimate for the state-action value $Q_{t+1}(s, a)$ at time $t+1$ upon the estimate for $Q_t(s', a')$ with s' the state where the learner arrives after taking action a in state s:

$$Q_{t+1}(s, a) \leftarrow (1 - \alpha)Q_t(s, a) + \alpha(r_t + \gamma \max_{a'} Q_t(s', a')) \tag{1}$$

with α the usual step size parameter, $\gamma \in [0, 1]$ a discount factor and r_t the immediate reinforcement received at time step t.

Non-bootstrapping evaluation methods such as Monte Carlo methods update their estimates based on actual returns. For instance the *every-visit Monte Carlo* method updates a state-action value $Q(s, a)$ at time $t + n$ (with n the time for one episode to finish) based on the actual return R_t and the previous value:

$$Q_{t+n}(s, a) \leftarrow (1 - \alpha)Q_t(s, a) + \alpha R_t$$

with

$$R_t = r_{t+1} + \gamma r_{t+2} + \gamma^2 r_{t+3} + \ldots + \gamma^{n-1} r_{n+1}$$

and t is the time at which (s, a) occurred.

Methods that learn their estimates, to some extend, on the basis of other estimates (i.e. they bootstrap) are called Temporal Difference learning methods. The Q-learning algorithm (equation 1) can be classified as a TD(0) algorithm. The back-up for each state is based on the next reward, an estimation of the remaining rewards is given by the value of the state one step later. One says that Q-learning is therefore a 1-step TD method. It is possible to consider backups based on a weighted combination as follows:

$$R_t^{(n)} = r_{t+1} + \gamma r_{t+2} + \ldots + \gamma^{n-1} r_{t+n} + \gamma^n V_t(s_{t+n}) \tag{2}$$

In the limit, all real rewards up-until-termination are used. This means that there is no bootstrapping, this is the Monte Carlo method. Thus there is a spectrum ranging from using simple 1-step returns to using full-backup returns.

The whole spectrum of backup schemes is denoted as TD(λ) methods, where parameter λ weights the contributions of the n-step returns $R_t^{(n)}$.

$$R_t^{\lambda} = (1 - \lambda) \sum_{n=1}^{\infty} \lambda^{n-1} R_t^{(n)}$$

In a sense, TD(λ) methods form a bridge from simple 1-step TD(0) methods to Monte Carlo methods. What was presented here is the so-called theoretical or forward view of TD(λ) methods. An equivalent backward view exists, which allows for an on-line implementation.

Advantages of TD methods over Monte Carlo methods include the fact that TD methods can be naturally implemented in an on-line, fully incremental fashion. With Monte Carlo methods, only off-line updating is possible, since only at the end of an episode the actual full return is known. This makes the latter method unsuited for contuining tasks. Moreover, TD methods learn from each transition, which can sometimes speed-up learning time.

3   Multi-agent Learning in Multi-stage Games

3.1   Multi-stage Game

A multi-stage game is a game where the participating agents have to take a sequence of actions. An MDP can be extended to the multi-agent case, referred to as a Multi-agent Markov decision process (MMDP). Formally an MMDP is a quintuple $\langle \mathbb{S}, \mathbb{A}, A_{i \in \mathbb{A}}, T, R \rangle$ where $\mathbb{S}$ is the set of states, $\mathbb{A}$ the set of agents, A_i is the finite set of actions available to agent i, $T : \mathbb{S} \times A_1 \times A_2 \times \ldots \times A_n \rightarrow P(\mathbb{S})$ the transition function and $R : \mathbb{S} \times A_1 \times A_2 \times \ldots \times A_n \rightarrow P(\mathbb{R})$ the reward function.

An MMDP can be viewed as a standard MDP in which the actions are implemented over multiple agents and the transitions depend on the joint-actions. Similar to an MDP, a credit assignment problem is present in an MMDP and because actions are distributed, coordination problems might occur. This makes the decision problem more complex and harder to solve.

In the remainder of this paper we limited ourselves to tree-structured multi-stage games. This means that there are no loops between the game stages and once branches are separated their paths will never be joined again.

An example of such a tree-structured multi-stage game can be seen in Figure 1. In this particular example, the MMDP consists of 6 states. The game starts in state s_1. Here, both agents have to take an action resulting in the joint-action (a_i, b_k). Based on this joint-action the game continues to either state s_2 or s_3 (both states give a numerical feedback of 0). In this second stage, again both agents must choose an action a_{ij} and b_{kl}. If the agents are in state s_3 no matter how the joint-action (a_{ij}, b_{kl}) looks like, the agents will always end up in state s_6 resulting in an average payoff of 0.75 (i.e. the probability of receiving a reward of 1 is 0.75) for both agents. If the agents ended up in state s_2 after the first stage then the agents have to deal with a coordination problem. If the agents can coordinate on either joint-actions (a_{11}, b_{11}), (a_{12}, b_{12}), (a_{21}, b_{21}) or (a_{22}, b_{22}) they both receive a pay-off of 1.0 (the probability of receiving a reward of 1 is 1). Miscoordination on the other hand will be penalized heavily with a penalty of 0.0 (the probability of receiving a reward of 1 is 0). When the agents end up in state s_4, s_5 or s_6 the game ends. Based on the rewards r_m obtained in process of reaching an end state a weighted reward can be formed: $r_{total} = \theta_1 r_1 + \ldots + \theta_s r_s$.

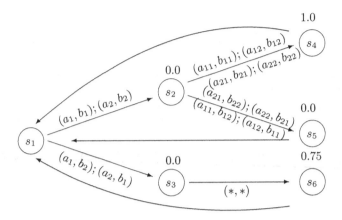

Fig. 1. An example of a simple MMPD, the Opt-In Opt-Out game [14]

The weights can be adjusted to completely in- or exclude a reward at a certain stage.

We can view a multi-stage game as a sequence of single state games. The reward matrices for the 2 stages of the game of Figure 1 are given in Figure 2. Note that in this multi-stage decision problem, we have a coordination problem

$$M^1 = \begin{pmatrix} 0.0 & 0.0 \\ 0.0 & 0.0 \end{pmatrix} \quad M^2 = \begin{pmatrix} 1.0 & 0.0 & 0.75 & 0.75 \\ 0.0 & 1.0 & 0.75 & 0.75 \\ \hline 0.75 & 0.75 & 1.0 & 0.0 \\ 0.75 & 0.75 & 0.0 & 1.0 \end{pmatrix}$$

Fig. 2. Reward matrices of the Opt-In Opt-Out multi-stage decision problem from Figure 1. Typically this game will be played with a weight $\theta_1 = 0$ for matrix M^1 since this matrix doesn't contribute to the game since all rewards are 0.0.

at the second stage. Also note that the second matrix is divided into 4 separate sub-matrices. We do this to depict that when the agents reach the second stage, they don't play the complete game, only a part of it. Which part is decided by the actions in the first stage. For instance if at the first stage, both agents select their first actions, in the second stage the sub-matrix in the upper-left corner is played. If the agents in the first stage both play their second action, the sub-matrix in the lower-right corner is activated in the second stage and so on.

3.2   Learning Automata Model

A learning automaton is an independent entity that is situated in a random environment and is capable of taking actions autonomously. The stochastic environment is responsible for generating a scalar value indicating the quality of the action taken by the learning automaton. This scalar value, which we call reward, is then fed back into the learning automaton.

Let us first describe the environment formally. An environment is a triple $\langle A, \mathbf{c}, \mathbf{R} \rangle$ with A the possible sets of inputs into the environment, $\mathbf{c} = [c(1) \dots c(n)]$ the penalty vector storing a chance of success $(= c(i))$ for each action i, and $\mathbf{R}$ the set of possible scalar rewards the environment can generate (based on $a_t \in A$: the action taken at time step t and $c(a_t)$: the probability of success for that action). The experimental setting in this paper sets: $\mathbf{R} = \{0, 1\}$, where 0 denotes failure and 1 denotes success.

A learning automaton can be expressed as a quadruple $\langle A, \mathbf{R}, \mathbf{p}, U \rangle$. $A = \{a(1), \dots, a(n)\}$ denotes the set of actions the learning automaton can take. $R_t(a_t(i)) \in \mathbf{R}$ is the input that is given to the LA to indicate the quality of the chosen action. Note that we deliberately reused the symbols A and $\mathbf{R}$ because the output from the environment is the input into the LA and vice versa.

The probabilities of the automaton for selecting action $a_t(i)$ are stored in the vector $\mathbf{p_t} = [p_t(1), \dots, p_t(n)]$. The restrictions on $p_t(i)$ are the following: $\sum_{i=1}^{n} p_t(i) = 1$ and $0 \leq p_t(i) \leq 1$. Thus all the probabilities sum up to 1 and each probability lays within the interval $[0, 1]$. Note that at the beginning of the game all action probabilities are chosen equal: $p_0(1) = p_0(2) = \dots = p_0(n) = \frac{1}{n}$. Each iteration the action probabilities are updated based on the reinforcement obtained from the environment. For the experiments in this paper, we used the Linear Reward-Inaction (L_{R-I}) [8] scheme. Let $a_t = a(i)$ be the action chosen at time step t. Then the action probability vector $\mathbf{p}$ is updated according to

$$\mathbf{p_{t+1}} = \mathbf{p_t} + \alpha r_t (\mathbf{e_{a_t}} - \mathbf{p_t}) \tag{3}$$

with α the step size parameter and $\mathbf{e_{a_t}}$ a unit vector with unity at position a_t. The L_{R-I} has been studied widely and has several nice properties such as ϵ-optimality and absolute expediency. For more details we refer to [8,7,9].

3.3 Pursuit Automaton

The automata model discussed above is the most basic update scheme of learning automata and is used in the Monte Carlo and Intermediate Rewards algorithms. In the literature many variants have been described, each with their own set of characteristics and theoretical properties.

The learning automata using the n-step algorithm are modeled as pursuit automata. A pursuit learning automaton keeps, in addition to its probability vector, two extra vectors $\mathbf{Z}$ and $\mathbf{V}$. Vector $\mathbf{Z}$ keeps the total reward obtained in response to each action and vector $\mathbf{V}$ records the number of times each action has been visited. The action probabilities are indirectly updated using these vectors. The update goes as follows: let $a_t = a(i)$ be the action chosen at time step t. Then $\mathbf{Z}$ and $\mathbf{V}$ are updated according to:

$$Z_{t+1}(i) = Z_t(i) + r_t \tag{4}$$
$$Z_{t+1}(j) = Z_t(j), \forall j \neq i \tag{5}$$
$$V_{t+1}(i) = V_t(i) + 1 \tag{6}$$
$$V_{t+1}(j) = V_t(j), \forall j \neq i \tag{7}$$

The average reinforcement obtained for each action $a_t(i)$ can be calculated as: $d_t(i) = \frac{Z_t(i)}{V_t(i)}$. Note that we need $V_t(i) > 0$ for $d_t(i)$ to be defined. The action probabilities are now updated as

$$\mathbf{p_{t+1}} = \mathbf{p_t} + \alpha(\mathbf{e_{M_t}} - \mathbf{p_t}) \tag{8}$$

with $\mathbf{e_{M_t}}$ a unit vector where the index $M_t = \arg\max_i d_t(i)$.

One interesting feature of the pursuit algorithm is that the updating of the action probabilities is not directly related to the received reward. This means that the reward doesn't need to remain in the interval $[0, 1]$ which is very usefull in application domains.

3.4   Hierarchies of Learning Automata

While learning automata make for convenient agents, one of their interesting properties is that they can be combined into more complex structures such as hierarchies.

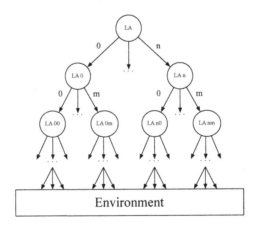

Fig. 3. An agent constructed in with a hierarchy of learning automata

A hierarchical LA works as follows. The first automaton that is active is the root at the top of the hierarchy: LA. This automaton selects one of its n actions. If, for example, the automaton selects action 2, the learning automaton that will become active is learning automaton LA 2. Then this active learning automaton is eligible for selecting an action. Based on this action, another learning automaton on the next level will become active. This process repeats itself until one of the learning automata at the bottom of the hierarchy is reached.

3.5 The Interaction Between Learning Automata Hierarchies

The interaction of the two hierarchical agents in Figure 4 goes as follows. At the top level (or in the first stage) Agent 1 and Agent 2 meet each other in a game with stochastic rewards. They both take an action using their top level learning automata LA A and LA B. Performing actions a_i by LA A and b_k by LA B is equivalent to choosing automata LA A_i and LA B_k to take actions at the next level. The response of environment E_1: $r_t \in \{0, 1\}$, is a success or failure, where the probability of success is given by c_{ik}^1. At the second level the learning automata LA A_i and LA B_k choose their actions a_{ij} and b_{kl} respectively and these will elicit a response from environment of which the probability of getting a positive reward is given by $c_{ij,kl}^2$. At the end of the episode all the automata that were involved in one of the games, update their action selection probabilities based on the actions performed and the responses of the environments.

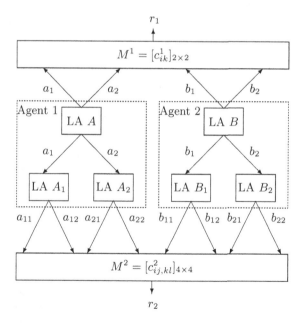

Fig. 4. An interaction of two agents constructed by learning automata hierarchies. The top-level automata play a single stage game and produce a reward r_1. Then one learning automata of each hierarchy at the second level play another single stage game, resulting in reward r_2.

4   Introducing Bootstrapping in the Learning Automata Approach

4.1   Monte Carlo

In the Monte Carlo method, the updating of the probabilities is based on averaged sample returns. This averaged return is usually generated at the end of an episode. Monte Carlo methods thus work best in episodic tasks where eventually each strategy leads to a clear end state. Each time such a clear end state is reached, an averaged return is generated by calculating a weighted sum of all the returns obtained. This sum is then given to all learning automata that were active during the last episode in order to update their action probabilities. Thus when we reach an end stage at time step t we generate the following sum: $R = \theta_1 r_1 + \theta_2 r_2 + \ldots + \theta_t r_t$ where r_i is the reward generated at time step i. Note that the following restrictions apply on the weights $\sum_{i=1}^{t} \theta_i = 1$ and $0 \le \theta_i \le 1$.

In [24] the authors proved that if all the automata of the hierarchical learning automata update their action probabilities at each stage using the L_{R-I} update scheme and if the composite reward is constructed as a Monte Carlo reward (as described above) and at each level the step sizes of the automata are chosen sufficiently small then the expected payoff of the overall system is non-decreasing. This result means that the hierarchical learning automata using a L_{R-I} update scheme will always converge to a pure equilibrium path in an identical pay-off multi-stage game. To which path the automata will converge to is not known. Neither is known how (sub-)optimal this path is. This largely depends on the initial settings of the action probability distribution and on the step size used. Under the assumption that the learning rate is set sufficiently small, the agents will converge to a Nash path in the game (i.e. a Nash equilibrium of the corresponding single stage game).

4.2   Intermediate Rewards

In [25,26] we introduced an update mechanism based on Intermediate Rewards. With this technique the learning automata at level l only get informed about the immediate reward and the rewards on the remainder of the path. It doesn't get informed about the rewards that are given to automata on the levels above because the learning automaton at this level has no direct influence over them and they would clutter up its combined reward. In [27] a theoretical proof that hierarchical learning automata using only the rewards of the remainder of the path will converge to an equilibrium path in an identical pay-off multi-stage game (under the same conditions we described above for the traditional Monte Carlo technique) is given.

The complete algorithm can be found in Algorithm 1. Because the learning automata get updated at the end of an episode, the intermediate rewards technique is still an off-line algorithm.

Algorithm 1. Intermediate Rewards Algorithm

1: All the learning automata: initialise action probabilities: $\forall a \in A : p_0(a) = \frac{1}{|A|}$
2: **for** each trial **do**
3:    Activate the top LA of the hierarchies
4:    **for** each level l in hierarchy h **do**
5:        The active learning automata take action $a_t^l(h)$
6:            $\Rightarrow$ joint-action $\mathbf{a} = [a_t^l(1), \ldots, a_t^l(h), \ldots]$
7:        Store immediate reward r_t (team reward based on $\mathbf{a}$)
8:    **end for**
9:    **for** each level l in hierarchy h **do**
10:        Compute combined reward: $R^l(h) = \theta_t r_t + \theta_{t+1} r_{t+1} + \ldots + \theta_T r_T$
11:        Update the automaton that was active at level l in hierarchy h with reward $R^l(h)$
12:    **end for**
13: **end for**

4.3 1-Step Estimates

In the 1-Step Estimates technique, which we introduced in [21], the updating of the learning automata will no longer take place at an explicit end-stage. The automata get informed immediately about the local reward they receive for their actions. In addition each automaton has estimates about the long term reward for each of its actions. These estimates are updated by combing the immediate rewards with an estimate of possible rewards that this action might give on the remainder of the path (see Line 10 and 11 in Algorithm 2). The behavior of the algorithm is controlled by three parameters: α, γ and ρ. α is the step size parameter from Equation 1, γ is the discount factor as used in Equation 2, and ρ controls the influence of the difference between the combined reward and the old-estimate on the new-estimate.

4.4 n-Step Rewards

The 1-step algorithm described above can easily be extended to the general n-step case. This creates a whole range of updating algorithms for multi-stage games, similar to the range of algorithms that exist for the single agent case. Algorithms 4–6 shows the general n-step updating algorithm for pursuit learning automata. The parameters α, γ and ρ are equivalent to those of the 1-step algorithm.

The algorithm is a natural extension of the 1-step algorithm and works as follows (we make a reference to the lines of the algorithm). The interaction between the hierarchies remains the same as for the Monte Carlo case (and the 1-step case). The learning automata at the top of the hierarchies start by selecting an action. Based on this joint-action the environment generates a reward and this reward is handed to the automata. Since this is the immediate reward, the

---

Algorithm 2. 1-Step Estimates for Pursuit Automata

1: All the learning automata: Initialise action probabilities: $\forall a \in A : p_0(a) = \frac{1}{|A|}$

2: Initialise my-estimates: $\forall a \in A : myest(a) = 0$ (estimates for all the actions, meaning: what is the long term reward associated with this action)

3: Initialise children-estimates: $\forall a \in A : est_0(a) = 0$ (estimates for all the children, meaning: what is the average of the long term rewards for the learning automaton associated with this action)

4: **for** each trial **do**

5:     Activate the top LA of the hierachies

6:     **for** each level l in hierarchy h **do**

7:         Take action $a_t^l(h)$

8:             $\Rightarrow$ joint-action $\mathbf{a} = [a_t^l(1), \ldots, a_t^l(h), \ldots]$

9:         Observe immediate reward r_t (reward based on $\mathbf{a}$)

10:        Compute $R_t = r_t + \gamma est(a_t^l(h))$

11:        Update my-estimates: $myest(a_t^l(h)) = myest(a_t^l(h)) + \rho[R_t - myest(a_t^l(h))]$

12:        Update action probability $\mathbf{p}$ using $myest(a_t^l(h))$ as the reward for the L_{R-I} scheme

13:        Propagate R_t up to parent $\Rightarrow$ see Algorithm 3: Updating estimates

14:     **end for**

15: **end for**

Algorithm 3. Updating Estimates

1: κ is the estimate received from the child (the last action this automaton took was $a_t^l(h)$)

2: $est(a_t^l(h)) \leftarrow est(a_t^l(h)) + \rho(\kappa - est(a_t^l(h)))$

Algorithm 4. n-Step Estimates for Pursuit Automata

1: All the learning automata: Initialise action probabilities: $\forall a \in A : p_0(a) = \frac{1}{|A|}$

2: Initialise the estimates of all the actions: $\forall a \in A : myEstimates(a) = 0$ (estimates for all the actions, meaning: what is the long term reward associated with this action)

3: Initialise estimates for the learning automata at level n $\forall a \in A : nStepEstimates_0(a) = 0$ (for each action this learning automaton has, keep an estimate of the automata at level $n+1$ of the branch connected to the action)

4: **for** each trial **do**

5:     Activate the top LA of the hierachies

6:     **for** each level l in hierarchy h **do**

7:         Take action $a_t^l(h)$

8:             $\Rightarrow$ joint-action $\mathbf{a} = [a_t^l(1), \ldots, a_t^l(h), \ldots]$

9:         Observe immediate reward r_{t+1} (reward based on $\mathbf{a}$) and store it for later use

10:        Propagate r_{t+1} up to the parent $\Rightarrow$ see Algorithm 5: Receive reward

11:     **end for**

12: **end for**

automata cannot yet generate the n-step truncated return (if $n > 1$) instead they propagate this reward to their parents (Algorithm 4 line 10). The automata that receive this reward check whether this is the nth reward they have received (Algorithm 5 line 1). If so, they compute the n-step truncated return (Algorithm 5 line 2), update the estimates of the long term reward of their own actions (Algorithm 5 line 3), update their probabilities (Algorithm 5 line 4) and keep their n^{th}-level-grandparents up-to-date by providing them with an accurate estimate (Algorithm 5 line 5). If the parents didn't receive the nth reward yet (thus they can't compute the n-step reward), they just propagate the reward to their parents (Algorithm 5 lines 6 and 7).

In addition to propagating the immediate rewards, the automata also propagate their updated estimates. The parents receiving an estimate from their children check wether it is the estimate they need to compute the n-step truncated return (i.e. the estimate coming from level $(n + 1)^{th}$) and they adjust the estimates of their n^{th}-level-grandchildren if necessary. This process continues for each level of the hierarchies.

Algorithm 5. Receive reward r_x

1: **if** r_x is the nth reward I receive **then**
2:     Compute the n-step truncated return: $R_t^{(n)} = r_t + \gamma r_{t+1} + \ldots + \gamma^{n-1} r_{t+n} + \gamma^n \, nStepEstimates(a_t^l(h))$
3:     Update $myEstimates(a_t^l(h))$ = $myEstimates(a_t^l(h))$ + $\rho[R_t^{(n)} - myEstimates(a_t^l(h))]$
4:     Update action probability **p** using $myEstimates(a_t^l(h))$ as the reward for the L_{R-I} scheme
5:     Propagate $myEstimates(a_t^l(h))$ up to parent $\Rightarrow$ *see Algorithm 6: Updating estimates*
6: **else**
7:     if this wasn't the nth reward, this reward also needs to go to the parent: Propagate r_x up to the parent $\Rightarrow$ *see Algorithm 5: Receive reward*
8: **end if**

Algorithm 6. Receive estimate κ

1: **if** this estimate comes from the $n + 1^{th}$ level **then**
2:     $nStepEstimates(a_t^l(h))$ $\leftarrow$ $nStepEstimates(a_t^l(h))$ + $\rho(\kappa - nStepEstimates(a_t^l(h)))$
3: **else**
4:     Keep propagating est_x up in the hierarchy $\Rightarrow$ *see Algorithm 6: Receive estimate*
5: **end if**

---

5   Empirical Results

This section reports on various results obtained comparing the different learning techniques on hierarchical learning automata playing multi-stage games. For the Monte Carlo updating and the Intermediate Rewards method, there are theoretical proofs guaranteeing that the HLA converge to an equilibrium path in any common interest multi-stage game. For each experiment, we report on the accuracy of the techniques in function of the learning rate used.

5.1 Repeated Experiment on One Randomly Generated Game

All the algorithms discussed above are tested with this first type of game. Figures 5(a)–5(d) give the average rewards for Monte Carlo updating, Intermediate Rewards, 1-step updating and 3-step updating respectively for a range of learning rates for a multi-stage game of 7 stages. The layout of the game is the following: at the first stage, there is only one state. In this state the game starts and because the automata have 2 actions, there are 4 joint-actions. Each of these joint-actions leads to a different state. Thus at the second stage we have 4 different states. Using the same reasoning, in each of these 4 states, there are 4 joint-actions leading to a different state. At the last level there are $(2^7)^2 = 16.384$ different states and since each path to one of these states is different, there are 16.384 possible solutions to this game.

Each state keeps 4 reward values (one for each joint-action). In the first set of experiments, we generated the rewards randomly. Meaning that the reward probabilities of all the reward matrices entries are sampled from a uniform distribution in $[0, 1]$. The optimal path of this game is unique and was found to give a average reward of 0.853117 (this was the largest reward we found by summing up all the rewards along one path and dividing this value by the number of stages). For every run, this game is repeatedly played by the hierarchies of learning automata until they are converged to one path in the game. Learning automata theory guarantees that the hierarchies converge to an equilibrium path in every run of the game. The theory does not guarantee that the agents will converge to the optimal path in the game. For each learning rate, the results are averaged over 1000 runs and the reward matrices remain the same in every experiment.

The results show that by using the Intermediate Reward technique, the average reward increases from 0.7 (using Monte Carlo) to almost 0.8 (using Intermediate Rewards). The variance of the rewards to which the hierarchies converge, remains the same. The results of the 1-step and 3-step algorithm show that the average convergence can remain at the same high level (compared to Monte Carlo updating) while the variance of the solution-paths is much lower. This means that if the hierarchies converge to a sub-optimal solution, they are more likely to converge to a sub-optimal solution with an average reward that is almost as good as the optimal.

We also did experiments with a game of 8 and 9 stages. The results we obtained are in line with the ones presented above. Thus the Intermediate Rewards algorithm outperforms the Monte Carlo technique, however the variance of the rewards obtained remains large. The 1-step and n-step algorithms converged to the same high average reward while also lowering the variance of the rewards obtained.

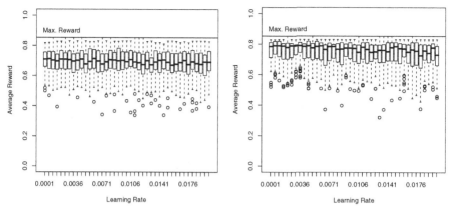

(a) The average reward using Monte Carlo rewards for various learning rates. The rewards are averaged over 1000 runs.

(b) The average reward using intermediate rewards for various learning rates. The rewards are averaged over 1000 runs.

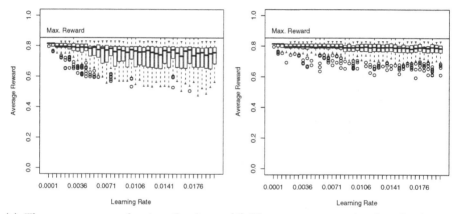

(c) The average reward using the 1-step reward for various learning rates. The rewards are averaged over 1000 runs.

(d) The average reward using the 3-step reward for various learning rates. The rewards are averaged over 1000 runs.

Fig. 5.

5.2   Experiments of a Series of 1000 Random Games

While the results presented above support the hypothesis that an n-step update outperforms the Monte Carlo and Intermediate Reward algorithms, this conclusion is based on experimental results for one single randomly generated game. To make a more thorough comparison, we ran the same tests, but this time, for each value of the learning rate we averaged the obtained reward over 1000 different randomly generated games. Thus after each of the 1000 runs, we reset the values of the reward matrices to a random number in $[0, 1]$.

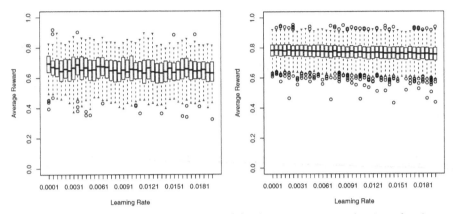

(a) The average reward using Monte Carlo rewards for various learning rates. The rewards are averaged over 1000 runs.

(b) The average reward using the 4-step reward for various learning rates. The rewards are averaged over 1000 runs.

Fig. 6.

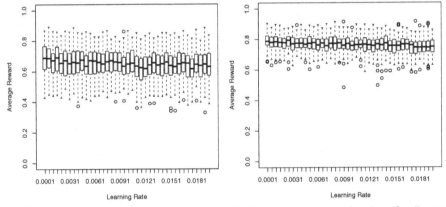

(a) The average reward using intermediate rewards for various learning rates. The rewards are averaged over 100 runs.

(b) The average reward using the 5-step reward for various learning rates. The rewards are averaged over 100 runs.

Fig. 7.

In the experiment we used 2 hierarchies of 8 levels, with 2 actions per automaton. This gives a total of $(2^8)^2 = 65.563$ solution paths. Figures 6(a)–6(b) shows the results for the Monte Carlo algorithm and the 4-step reward.

The results confirm our hypotheses. The average reward when using the Monte Carlo algorithm is systematically lower compared to the average reward of any of the n-step algorithms (the plot shown is for the 4-step algorithm, but this is true for the range 1-step to 8-step, although the performance differs).

As for a last test, we repeated the previous experiment with a game of 10 levels. The total number of possible solution paths becomes $(2^{10})^2 = 1.048.576$. Figures 7(a)–7(b) show the results for the intermediate rewards algorithm and a 5-step algorithm. The results for these experiments are averaged over 100 runs. Again, the same conclusions can be drawn. Notice that we increased the value of the n-step reward according to the number of stages in the game (= number of levels in the hierarchies). Our findings suggest that the best results are given when the value of the n-step is set to half the number of stages in the game.

All of our results demonstrate that the performance increases when the hierarchical learning automata use an n-step updating algorithm. Because our second set of experiments is carried out over 1000 different randomly generated games, our observations cannot be related to some particularity of the game.

6   Conclusion

The work in this paper shows that hierarchical learning automata are excellent tools for building a learning multi-agent systems that can solve a broad range of sequential decision problems. Learning automata can model independent learners that operate without information about the other players or their actions. Furthermore, they don't use any communication. The research started from the Monte Carlo update technique in which the automata are informed about all the rewards gathered along the path when the game reaches an end-stage. This imposes two problems. The learning automata receive information about the complete path, while they can only control the rewards which depend on the decision at their level in the hierarchy. Thus a part of the information they receive is irrelevant to them, however, they cannot choose to ignore this information because it is incorporated in the overall reward signal they receive. The solution we proposed, called Intermediate Rewards, solves this problem by using a reward signal which incorporates only the rewards that are collected on the remainder of the path, and as such are different per level of the hierarchy. By using this update mechanism, the empirical results show that the average convergences are to a path that leads to a higher reward. The Intermediate Rewards algorithm still needs an explicit end-stage in the multi-stage decision process. This problem can be solved by using only local information combined with estimates of the rest of the rewards (i.e. they bootstrap). The range of n-step algorithms are precisely created for this objective. The automata use only immediate rewards from the first n levels combined with an estimate of the rewards after n steps to update their probabilities. Empirical results show that the convergence is more accurate and faster compared to Monte Carlo updating and Intermediate Rewards algorithm.

The algorithms presented in this paper provide tools for searching for good to optimal solutions in a large solution space by a team of independent, learning agents. The use of learning automata as building blocks for a learning multi-agent system provides for a well funded theoretical basis for multi-agent reinforcement learning. This theory was used for creating a proof of convergence for some of our algorithms.

In future research, the introduction of eligibility traces in hierarchical learning automata will be investigated. By using eligibility traces, the learning automata can be updated on-line incorporating the complete spectrum of 1-step to n-step rewards. The empirical evidence shows that our algorithms always converge to a pure path. This needs to be investigated theoretically. Other research will focus on applying the algorithms in more general multi-stage games in which the flow of information is no longer confined in the tree structure.

References

1. Tuyls, K.: Learning in Multi-Agent Systems: An Evolutionary Game Theoretic Approach. PhD thesis, Vrije Universiteit Brussel (2004)
2. Claus, C., Boutilier, C.: The dynamics of reinforcement learning in cooperative multiagent systems. In: AAAI-1998. Proceedings of the Fifteenth National Conference of Artificial Intelligence, Madison, WI, pp. 746–752 (1998)
3. Verbeeck, K., Nowé, A., Peeters, M., Tuyls, K.: Multi-agent reinforcement learning in stochastic single and multi-stage games. In: Kudenko, D., Kazakov, D., Alonso, E. (eds.) Adaptive Agents and Multi-Agent Systems II, pp. 275–294. Springer, Heidelberg (2005)
4. Verbeeck, K.: Coordinated Exploration in Multi-Agent Reinforcement Learning. PhD thesis, Vrije Universiteit Brussel (2004)
5. Kapetanakis, S., Kudenko, D., Strens, M.J.A.: Learning to coordinate using commitment sequences in cooperative multi-agent systems. In: Kudenko, D., Kazakov, D., Alonso, E. (eds.) Adaptive Agents and Multi-Agent Systems II, pp. 275–294. Springer, Heidelberg (2005)
6. Tsetlin, M.L.: On the behavior of finite automata in random media. Avtomatika i Telemekhanika 22(10), 1345–1354 (1961)
7. Narendra, K.S., Thathachar, M.A.L.: Learning automata - a survey. IEEE Transactions on Systems, Man, and Cybernetics SMC-4(4) 323–334 (1974)
8. Narendra, K.S., Thathachar, M.A.L.: Learning Automata: An Introduction. Prentice-Hall, Englewood Cliffs (1989)
9. Thathachar, M.A.L., Sastry, P.S.: Networks of Learning Automata: Techniques for Online Stochastic Optimization. Kluwer Academic Publishers, Dordrecht (2004)
10. Nowé, A., Verbeeck, K., Peeters, M.: Learning automata as a basis for multi-agent reinforcement learning. In: Tuyls, K., t Hoen, P.J., Verbeeck, K., Sen, S. (eds.) LAMAS 2005. LNCS (LNAI), vol. 3898, pp. 71–85. Springer, Heidelberg (2006)
11. Sutton, R.S., Barto, A.G.: Reinforcement Learning: An Introduction. MIT Press, Cambridge, MA (1998)
12. Verbeeck, K., Nowé, A., Parent, J., Tuyls, K.: Exploring selfish reinforcement learning in repeated games with stochastic rewards. Journal of Autonomous Agents and Multi-agent Systems (to appear)
13. Panait, L., Luke, S.: Cooperative multi-agent learning: The state of the art. Autonomous Agents and Multi-Agent Systems 3(11), 383–434 (2005)
14. Boutilier, C.: Sequential optimality and coordination in multiagent systems. In: Proceedings of the Sixteenth International Joint Conference on Artificial Intelligence, pp. 478–485 (1996)
15. Thathachar, M.A.L., Ramakrishnan, K.R.: A hierarchical system of learning automata. IEEE Transactions on Systems, Man, and Cybernetics SMC-11(3), 236–241 (1981)

16. Ramakrishnan, K.R.: Hierarchical systems and cooperative games of learning automata. PhD thesis, Indian Institute of Science, Bangalore, India (1982)
17. Verbeeck, K., Nowé, A., Tuyls, K., Peeters, M.: Multi-agent reinforcement learning in stochastic single and multi-stage games. In: Kudenko, D., Kazakov, D., Alonso, E. (eds.) Adaptive Agents and Multi-Agent Systems II. LNCS (LNAI), vol. 3394, pp. 275–294. Springer, Heidelberg (2005)
18. Watkins, C., Dayan, P.: Q-learning. Machine Learning 8(3), 279–292 (1992)
19. Shoham, Y., Powers, R., Grenager, T.: Multi-agent reinforcement learning: a critical survey. Technical report, Stanford University (2003)
20. Sutton, R.S., Barto, A.G.: Reinforcement Learning An Introduction. MIT Press, Cambridge (1998)
21. Peeters, M., Verbeeck, K., Nowé, A.: The effect of bootstrapping in multi-automata reinforcement learning. In: IEEE Symposium Series on Computational Intelligence, International Symposium on Approximate Dynamic Programming and Reinforcement Learning (2007)
22. Kaelbling, L.P., Littman, M.L., Moore, A.P.: Reinforcement learning: A survey. Journal of Artificial Intelligence Research 4, 237–285 (1996)
23. Tsitsiklis, J.: Asynchronous stochastic approximation and q-learning. Machine Learning 16, 185–202 (1994)
24. Narendra, K.S., Parthasarathy, K.: Learning automata approach to hierarchical multiobjective analysis. IEEE Transactions on Systems, Man, and Cybernetics 21(2), 263–273 (1991)
25. Peeters, M., Nowé, A., Verbeeck, K.: Bootstrapping versus monte carlo in a learning automata hierarchy. Adaptive Learning Agents and Multi-Agent Systems, 61–71 (2006)
26. Peeters, M., Nowé, A., Verbeeck, K.: Toward bootstrapping in a hierarchy of learning automata. In: Proceedings of the Seventh European Workshop on Reinforcement Learning, pp. 31–32 (2005)
27. Van de Wege, L.: Learning automata as a framework for multi-agent reinforcement learning: Convergence issues in tree-structured multi-stage games. Master's thesis, Vrije Universiteit Brussel (2006)

Auctions, Evolution, and Multi-agent Learning

Steve Phelps[1], Kai Cai[2], Peter McBurney[1], Jinzhong Niu[2], Simon Parsons[1,2,3], and Elizabeth Sklar[2,3]

[1] Department of Computer Science, University of Liverpool,
Ashton Building, Ashton Street, Liverpool L69, 3BX
phelps.sg@googlemail.com, mcburney@liverpool.ac.uk
[2] Department of Computer Science, Graduate Center, City University of New York,
365 5th Avenue, New York, NY 10016, USA
{kcai, jniu}@gc.cuny.edu
[3] Department of Computer and Information Science, Brooklyn College,
City University of New York, 2900 Bedford Avenue, Brooklyn, NY 11210, USA
{parsons, sklar}@sci.brooklyn.cuny.edu

Abstract. For a number of years we have been working towards the goal of automatically creating auction mechanisms, using a range of techniques from evolutionary and multi-agent learning. This paper gives an overview of this work. The paper presents results from several experiments that we have carried out, and tries to place these in the context of the overall task that we are engaged in.

1 Introduction

The allocation of resources between a set of agents is a challenging problem, and one that has been much studied in artificial intelligence. Resource allocation problems are especially difficult to solve efficiently in an open system if the values that agents place on resources, or the values of their human principals, are private and unobservable. In such a situation, the difficulty facing somebody wishing to allocate the resources to those who value them most highly, is that participating agents cannot necessarily be relied upon to report those values truthfully — there is nothing to prevent "greedy" agents from exaggerating their resource requirements.

To overcome this problem, it has been suggested that resource allocation be solved using market mechanisms [4,32,59] in which agents support their value-claims with hard cash. This has two advantages. First it punishes greedy agents by making them pay for the resources that they have oversubscribed to. (Alternatively one can think of this as preventing agents from oversubscribing by forcing them to pay a higher price than they would otherwise have to pay for the resources they actually need.) Second, it allocates resources to the agents who pay the most, which should be the agents who value the resources most highly. Auctions are a subclass of market mechanisms that have received particular attention. This is due to the fact that, when well designed, auctions can achieve desired economic outcomes like high allocative efficiency.

Designing mechanisms to achieve specific economic requirements, such high efficiency or maximal social welfare, against self-interested intelligent traders, is no trivial matter, as can be seen from accounts of the auction design process for the recent radio spectrum auctions in Europe [25] and the US [11,30]. The economic theory of

K. Tuyls et al. (Eds.): Adaptive Agents and MAS III, LNAI 4865, pp. 188–210, 2008.
© Springer-Verlag Berlin Heidelberg 2008

mechanism design [20] approaches the task of designing efficient resource allocation mechanisms by studying the formal, analytical properties of alternative mechanisms. Mechanism design views auctions as form of game, and applies traditional analytic methods from game theory to some kinds of auctions [28], for example the second-price sealed-bid auctions or Vickrey auctions [55].

The high complexity of the dynamics of some other auction types, especially *double-sided auctions* [14] or DAs, however makes it difficult to go further in this direction [27,49,58]. As a result, researchers turned to experimental approaches. Smith pioneered the experimental approach [51], conducting auctions involving human traders that revealed many of the properties of double auctions. For example, his work showed that in *continuous double auctions* or CDAs, even a handful of traders can lead to high overall efficiency, and transaction prices can quickly converge to the theoretical equilibrium. More recently has come the suggestion that economists should take an "engineering approach" [44,46] to problems in microeconomics in general, building models of auctions, testing them experimentally, and refining them to create robust markets. We see our work as being part of this engineering approach to market design.

One approach to the computational design of markets is to use techniques from machine learning to explore the space of possible ways in which agents might act in particular markets. For example, reinforcement learning has been used to explore bidding patterns in auctions [34,44] and establish the ways in which price-setting behavior can affect consumer markets [54]. Our work is in this line. However, we differ from much of the existing work on machine learning in computational market design by using machine learning to design the auction rules themselves, rather than just in the service of exploring their behavior. We refer to this line of work as *automated mechanism design*, and the idea behind this paper is to summarize the work that we have been doing over the past few years on automated mechanism design. It does not provide any new results, but instead sketches the relationship between the series of experiments that we have carried out, describes the results that we have obtained, and tries to explain how all we have done fits into the overall scope of our work.

We should stress that we are not trying to evolve entire auction mechanisms. The computational complexity of doing so places this out of our reach at the moment. Instead we concentrate on parts of an existing mechanism, the continuous double auction, and look to automatically tune them for specific situations. Our work is experimental, and so comes with no formal guarantees. It thus stands in stark contrast to the work of Conitzer and Sandholm [9,10], which looks to create entire mechanisms subject to absolute guarantees on their performance. However, our work, like that of Cliff and Byde [5,57], addresses much more complex mechanisms, and we ourselves as addressing the same problem as Conitzer and Sandholm, but from the perspective of Wellman's *empirical game theory* [23,56].

2   Background

2.1   Auctions, Briefly

To frame our work, we borrow from Friedman's [14] attempt to standardize terminology in which *exchange* is the free reallocation of goods and money between a set of traders.

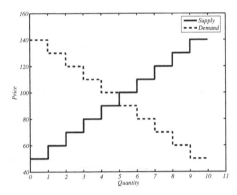

Fig. 1. Supply and demand curves

A market institution lays down the rules under which this exchange takes place, and an *auction* is a specific kind of market institution. A given institution defines what information traders can exchange, and how the reallocation of goods and money will occur, a process known as *clearing* the market. In an auction, the only information that traders can exchange are offers to buy at a given price, called *bids*, and offers to sell at a given price, called *asks*, and an auction gives priority to higher bids and lower asks. An auction can allow only buyers or only sellers to make offers, in which case it is *one-sided*, or it can allow both, in which case it is *two-sided*. A double auction is a two-sided auction, and from here on we will only deal with double auctions. In a double auction, the aim of the mechanism is to pair buyers and sellers, matching pairs such that the buyer is prepared to pay a higher price than the seller wants. We are most interested in two kinds of double auction. The *clearing house* (CH) auction matches traders by collecting offers over a period and, at the end of that period, identifying the matching pairs. The *continuous double auction* (CDA), in contrast, constantly looks for matches, identifying one as soon as it has some bid that is greater than some ask. Once matches have been found, a *transaction price* is set, somewhere in the interval between bid and ask.

In common with most work on double auctions, we only deal with the auction of a single kind of good, and we assume that every trader has a *private value* for the good — the price that the good is really worth to the agent. A rational buyer will not bid above its private value, and a rational seller will not ask below that value. If we know the private values of a set of traders, we can construct supply and demand curves for the market they are involved with, as in Figure 1. Here the heavy line, the supply curve, indicates that one seller has a private value of 50 — below that value no goods will be sold, and once the price rises to 50 exactly one good will be sold. The second trader has a private value of 60 and at a price of 60, exactly two goods will be sold. Similarly, there is one buyer who is willing to pay 140, and at that price one good will be bought, but as soon as the price falls to 130, two goods will be bought.

The intersection of the supply and demand curve indicates the point at which supply and demand are in balance — here any price between 90 and 100 will see exactly five goods bought and sold. Economic theory predicts that this *equilibrium* situation is what will hold if 20 traders with the indicated private values get together to trade. However the theory offers no clues as to how the traders will figure out which of them should trade, and at what price, and it is clear that it is not in the traders' interest to make offers that are truthful and indicate their private value — a trade which shades their offer, stating a lower price than their private value if they are a buyer, will make a profit if that offer is accepted.

If we know the private values of the traders, then, as described above, we can compute the equilibrium. Combining information about the equilibrium with information about what actually happens in the market, we can compute metrics that summarize the performance of the market. The *actual overall profit, pr^a*, of an auction is the sum of the actual profits of buyers and sellers:

$$pr^a = pr^a_b + pr^a_s$$

and these are computed as:

$$pr^a_b = \sum_i v_i - p_i$$

$$pr^a_s = \sum_j p_j - v_j$$

where p_i is the price of a trade made by *buyer i* and v_i is the private value of buyer i for all buyers who trade and p_j is the price of a trade made by *seller j* and v_j is the private value of buyer j for all sellers who trade. The *theoretical* or *equilibrium profit, pr_e*, is:

$$pr^e = pr^e_b + pr^e_s \tag{1}$$

the sum of the *equilibrium profits* of buyers and sellers, the profit that they would make if all trades took place at the *equilibrium price p_0*, the price predicted by theory. These can be computed as:

$$pr^e_b = \sum_i v_i - p_0$$

$$pr^e_s = \sum_j p_0 - v_j$$

The *allocative efficiency* of an auction is then:

$$e_a = \frac{pr^a}{pr^e} \tag{2}$$

which is often expressed as a percentage. Of course, this is the same as:

$$e_a = \frac{pr^a_b + pr^a_s}{pr^e_b + pr^e_s}$$

The allocative efficiency measures how close the market is to the equilibrium that theory predicts in terms of profit for traders. All other things being equal, economists prefer markets with high efficiency since this indicates that the market is transferring goods to the buyers that value them most from the sellers that value them least. This maximizes *social welfare*, making the traders as happy as possible. Allocative efficiency is maximal if just the traders to the left of the intersection between supply and demand curves in Figure 1 end up trading. While measuring allocative efficiency is useful, it says nothing about price. An auction that trades at equilibrium will be efficient, but high efficiency does not indicate that the market is trading near the equilibrium price [16]. The convergence coefficient, α, was introduced by Smith [51] to measure how far an active auction is away from the equilibrium point. It measures the RMS deviation of transaction prices from the equilibrium price:

$$\alpha = \frac{100}{p_0} \sqrt{\frac{1}{n} \sum_{i=1}^{n} (p_i - p_0)^2} \tag{3}$$

These are the measures that we will make most use of in this paper.

Our experimental work follows the usual pattern for work on automated trading agents. We run each auction for a number of trading *days*, with each day being broken up into a series of *rounds*. A round is an opportunity for agents to make offers, and we distinguish different days because at the end of a day, agents have their inventories replenished. As a result, every buyer can buy goods every day, and every seller can sell every day. Days are not identical because agents are aware of what happened the previous day. Thus it is possible for traders to learn, over the course of several days, the optimal way to trade. Following [34], we use a *k-double-auction* transaction pricing rule [49], in which the transaction price for each matched bid-ask pair is set according to the following function:

$$p_t = k p_a + (1 - k) p_b \tag{4}$$

where p_t is the transaction price, p_a is the ask price, p_b is the bid price and k is a parameter that can be adjusted by the auction designer. This is a *discriminatory* pricing rule since the price may be different for each transaction. In contrast, a *uniform* pricing rule ensures all transactions take place at the same price. In [34] and in much of our work, k is taken to be 0.5. To run most of the simulations described here we used JASA [21][1], which supports a wide range of auction types and trading strategies, and which matches bids and asks using the 4-heap algorithm [60].

2.2   Related Work

Much of the computational work on analyzing markets has been concerned with algorithms that can be used to decide what price to trade at. From the economics side, this work has often been motivated by the lack of an adequate theory of price formation — a theory that says how individuals decide what offers to make (though as Smith [51] demonstrated, this doesn't stop individuals being good at making these decisions) — and the desire to understand what makes markets work. From the computer science

---

[1] More accurately, JASA was developed as a result of the need to write software to run the simulations. The initial version of JASA was designed and written by Steve Phelps, and more recently has been contributed to by Jinzhong Niu and Kai Cai.

side, the motivation has usually been to find algorithms that can trade profitably and which can achieve high efficiency.

Gode and Sunder [16,17] were among the first to address this question, claiming that no intelligence is necessary for the goal of achieving high efficiency — so the outcome is due to the auction mechanism itself. They introduced two trading strategies: *zero intelligence without constraint* (ZI-U) and *zero intelligence with constraint* (ZI-C), and showed that ZI-U, the more naïve version, which shouts an offer at a random price without considering whether it is losing money or not, performs poorly. In contrast, ZI-C, which lacks the motivation of maximizing profit just like ZI-U but guarantees no loss, generates high efficiency solutions [16]. These results were however questioned by Cliff and Bruten [4,7], who thought Gode and Sunder's conclusion was not convincing because the scenarios considered were not as comprehensive as in Smith's experiments, and showed that in different scenarios the ZI-C agents performed poorly, especially in terms of convergence to the theoretical equilibrium.

Cliff and Bruten further [4,6] designed a simple adaptive trading strategy called *zero intelligence plus* or ZIP, and showed ZIP worked better than ZI-C, generating high efficiency outcomes and converging to the equilibrium price. This led Cliff and Bruten to suggest that ZIP embodied the minimum intelligence required by traders. Subsequent work has led to the development of many further trading strategies, the best known of which include Roth and Erev's [12,45] reinforcement learning strategy, which we call RE, Gjerstad and Dickhaut's [15] approach, commonly referred to as GD, which uses the past history of accepted bids and asks to compute the expected value of every offer a trader might make, and the simplification of ZIP introduced by Preist and van Tol [43].

This work on trading strategies is only one facet of the research on auctions. Gode and Sunder's results suggest that auction mechanisms play an important role in determining the outcome of an auction, and this is further borne out by the work of Tesauro and Das [53] and Walsh *et al.* [58][2] For example, if an auction is *strategy-proof*, the best strategy for a traders is not to bother to conceal their private values, but to reveal them, and in such auctions complex trading agents are not required. While typical double auctions are not strategy-proof, McAfee [29] has derived a form of double auction that is strategy-proof (though this strategy-proofness comes at the cost of lower efficiency).

3   Evolving the Whole System

Our initial approach to automated mechanism design was to use techniques from evolutionary computing. Inspired by the biological metaphor of evolution, genetic algorithms (GAs) [19] code aspects of a solution to a problem in an artificial "chromosome" (typically a binary string) and then breed a population of chromosomes using techniques like crossover (combining bits of the strings from different individuals) and mutation (flipping individual bits). Genetic programming (GP) [26] extends this approach by evolving not a bit-string-encoded solution to a problem, but an actual program to solve the problem itself. Programs are encoded as s-expressions and modeled as trees (nodes are

---

[2] This work also points out that results hinge on both auction design and the mix of trading strategies used, a point we will return to later.

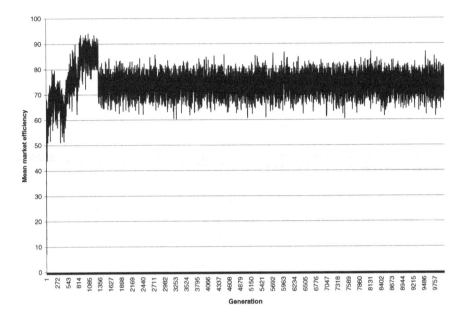

Fig. 2. Evolving traders: efficiency by generation

function names and branches arguments of those functions); and these trees are subject to crossover (swapping subtrees from different programs) and mutation (replacing
subtrees with random subtrees). Whichever approach is used, the best individuals, evaluated using a *fitness* function, are kept and "bred"; and bad individuals are rejected.
However, deciding which individuals are the best is a hard problem.

Both genetic algorithms and genetic programming perform a search through the
space of possible solutions with the theoretical advantage that random jumps around
the search space — created by crossover and mutation — can prevent the system from
getting stuck in local optima, unlike other machine learning techniques. Unfortunately,
in practice this is not always the case, at least partly because what constitutes the best
fitness measure can change over time. To overcome this problem, some researchers have
turned to *co-evolution*, for example [1,18,33].

In co-evolution, simultaneously evolving populations of agents interact, providing
each other with a fitness measure that changes as the agents evolve. In successful applications, an "arms race" spiral develops where each population spurs the other to
advance and the result is continuous learning for all populations. However, this has
been notoriously difficult to achieve. Often populations settle into a *mediocre stable
state*, reaching a local optimum and being unable to move beyond it. Consequently,
there is a growing body of work examining the dynamics of co-evolutionary learning
environments in an attempt to identify phenomena that contribute to success [2,8,13].
In the context of auction design, it is possible to look at a number of different forms
of co-evolution. First, different traders co-evolve against one another, with different

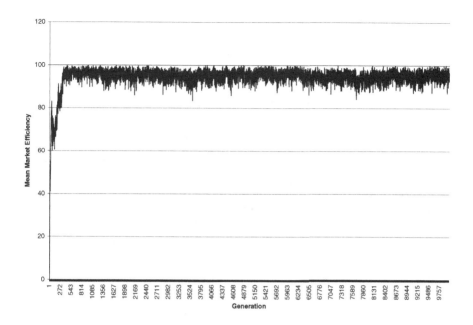

Fig. 3. Evolving traders and auctioneer: efficiency by generation

offer-making strategies being the co-evolving populations, each attempting to gain an advantage over the others. Since all traders are looking to maximize their profits, they are to some extent in competition, although it is possible for a number of successful traders to coexist. Second, traders co-evolve against the auction mechanism itself — the auctioneer if you will — as the co-evolving populations. The traders' aim is to achieve high profits while the auction(eer)'s aim is to provide an efficient market. While these aims need not be mutually exclusive, they may also be in conflict.

In [38], we explored a simple approach to co-evolving mechanisms, attempting to evolve the rules by which traders decided how to make offers, and the rules by which the auctioneer decides to set trade prices based upon those offers. When evolving rules for the traders alone, setting prices using a standard rule, we obtained the results in Figure 2. When we simultaneously evolved rules for traders and rules for the auctioneer, we obtained the results in Figure 3. While the efficiency of the whole system is not particularly high when we only evolve traders[3], when we evolve both traders and auctioneer, we obtain quite respectable efficiencies of around 95%.

There is a problem with these results, however. The problem is that it appears that the systems that we managed to evolve were systems that had fallen into the trap of a mediocre stable state. If we look at the kinds of rule that the traders were learning to use in these experiments, they are of the form:

---

[3] An average efficiency of around 75% compares poorly with the results reported in the literature for automated trading strategies, and with our own work [3].

```
if(not(QuoteBidPrice < (PrivateValue * 0.081675285))
  {
     PrivateValue
  }
else
  {
     PrivateValue * 0.081675285
  }
```

where `QuoteBidPrice` is the highest unmatched bid (this is a rule for a buyer). In other words, the traders were learning to make a constant markup, but nothing more sophisticated than that. While such a strategy can be quite successful when competing against traders doing the same — as discussed by [61] — we know that it does not compete well with more sophisticated strategies [3,47][4]. Even more worrying, the auctioneer was clearly not learning meaningful strategies — a typical evolved pricing rule was:

```
BidPrice - constant
```

which, once again, is not a terribly sophisticated strategy, and one that it is possible to imagine traders, more sophisticated than the ones we were able to co-evolve, learning to exploit.

4 Evolving Traders

One of the problems we identified with our attempt to evolve both traders and auctioneer from scratch was that this approach makes it too hard to learn sophisticated strategies for making offers. Starting, as is standard in genetic programming, from random strategies[5] means that the traders have to make huge strides to reach even the same level of sophistication as, for example, ZIP. Since traders can achieve reasonable levels of profit with the fixed margin rules we were discovering, there is little evolutionary pressure for them to continue to evolve, and lots of competitive strategies to drown out any mutations that aren't immediately successful. These observations led us to try to learn new trading strategies by starting from existing strategies.

As described in [37], we adopted the *heuristic strategy analysis* of Walsh *et al.* [58]. In its original form, the aim of this approach was to be able to compute plausible equilibria of the double auction. While performing a game theoretic analysis of the auction is infeasible (as discussed above) because of the number of players and the large number of possible actions at each of the many stages, it is possible to analyze double auctions at higher level of abstraction. The idea is to reduce the game to that of picking the best trading strategy from the literature. Thus, if you are interested in auctions with 10 participants, you pick a range of strategies for those participants, run a number of iterations of the auction, and that allows you to establish certain properties of the auction.

---

[4] The fixed margin strategy "Gamer" was not competitive in the Santa Fe tournament [47], and the fixed-markup strategy PS is one of the weakest strategies of those analyzed in [3].

[5] That is strategies composed of randomly selected functions, not strategies that bid at random — the latter perform surprisingly well [16].

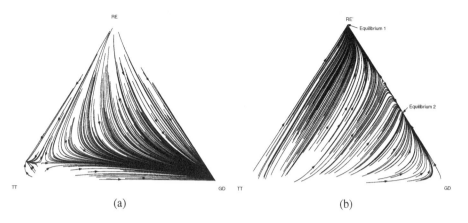

Fig. 4. The replicator dynamics direction field for a 12-agent clearing-house with trading strategies RE, TT and GD, (a) with the payoffs obtained in experiments and (b) with +5% payoffs to RE

Now, it is clear that such a static analysis will not tell us much about the auction. Why should the participants in the auction pick the strategies that you choose, particularly if those strategies aren't very successful? To deal with this problem, Walsh *et al.* used *evolutionary game theory* [52] to compute Nash equilibrium. The idea can be glossed as follows — rather than always selecting one strategy, traders are more likely to gradually adjust their strategy over time in response to to repeated observations of their own and others' payoffs. The adjustment can be modeled using the following *replicator dynamics* equation to specify the frequency with which different trading strategies should be used depending on our opponent's strategy:

$$\dot{m}_j = [u(e_j, \boldsymbol{m}) - u(\boldsymbol{m}, \boldsymbol{m})]\, m_j \tag{5}$$

where $\boldsymbol{m}$ is a mixed-strategy vector, $u(\boldsymbol{m}, \boldsymbol{m})$ is the mean payoff when all players play $\boldsymbol{m}$, and $u(e_j, \boldsymbol{m})$ is the average payoff to pure strategy j when all players play $\boldsymbol{m}$, and $\dot{m}_j$ is the first derivative of m_j with respect to time. Strategies that gain above-average payoff become more likely to be played, and this equation models a simple *co-evolutionary* process of mimicry learning, in which agents switch to strategies that appear to be more successful.

Now, for any initial mixed-strategy we can find the eventual outcome of this co-evolutionary process by solving $\dot{m}_j = 0$ for all j. This tells us the points at which the mixed strategy no longer changes — the stationary points of the replicator dynamics — and allows us to discover the final mixed-strategy that corresponds to the mixed strategy we started with. Repeating this for a range of initial mixed strategies allows us to discover all the stationary points that might develop. This model has the attractive properties that:

1. all Nash equilibria of the game are stationary points under the replicator dynamics; and

2. all focal points of the replicator dynamics are Nash equilibria of the evolutionary game.

Thus the Nash equilibrium solutions are embedded in the stationary points of the direction field of the dynamics specified by equation 5, and the replicator dynamics allows us to identify the Nash equilibria. Although not all stationary points are Nash equilibria, by overlaying a dynamic model of learning on the equilibria we can see which solutions are more likely to be discovered by *boundedly-rational* agents. Those Nash equilibria that are stationary points at which a larger range of initial states will end up, are equilibria that are more likely to be reached (assuming an initial distribution that is uniform).

Figure 4 (a) gives the direction field for a 12-agent clearing-house with traders allowed to pick between the RE, TT and GD strategies. This is a standard 2-simplex where the coordinates of any point represent a mixture of trading strategies. Each vertex denotes a situation in which all traders use a single trading strategy. Any point on an edge of the simplex denotes a situation in which all traders use one of the two strategies denoted by the vertices joined by the side. Thus every point on the bottom of the simplex in Figure 4 (a) denotes a mixture of strategies such that some traders use TT and some use GD.

We can see that in Figure 4 (a) GD is a best-response to itself, and hence is a pure-strategy equilibrium. We also see it has a very large *basin of attraction* — for any randomly-sampled initial configuration of the population, most of the flows end up in the bottom-right-hand-corner. Additionally, there is a second mixed-strategy equilibria at the coordinates $(0.88, 0.12, 0)$ in the field, corresponding to an 88% mix of TT and a 12% mix of RE, however the attractor for this equilibrium is much smaller than the pure-strategy GD equilibrium; only 6% of random starts terminate here as against 94% for pure GD. Hence, according to this analysis, we would expect most of the population of traders to adopt the GD strategy.

From the point of view of evolving new trading strategies, the interesting thing is that GD is not as dominant as it might appear from Figure 4 (a). If we perform a sensitivity analysis to assess the robustness of GD's performance, by removing 2.5% of its payoffs and assigning them to RE, along with 2.5% of the payoffs from TT, then we get the direction field in Figure 4 (b). This second direction field gives us a qualitatively different set of equilibria — the RE strategy becomes a best-response to itself with a large basin of attraction (61%) — and allows us to conclude that a slightly improved version of RE can compete well against GD.

To test this conclusion, as described in [37], we used a genetic algorithm to search for such an improved version of RE, searching through parameter settings for a combination of four strategies — the original version of RE, a variation on RE introduced in [34], stateless Q-learning, and a strategy that randomly selects offers — evaluating the evolved strategies by the size of the basin of attraction they attain under the replicator dynamics. The GA converged on a version of stateless Q-learning, and Figure 5 shows how this optimized strategy OS performs against TT, GD, and the original version of RE. Our conclusion is that it is possible to evolve trading strategies to compete with the best hand-coded strategies provided that one has the hand-coded strategies to evolve against.

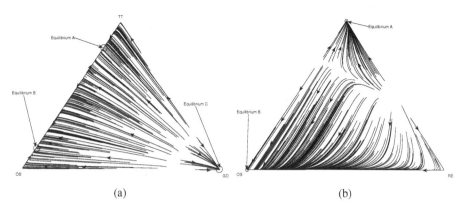

(a)   (b)

Fig. 5. Replicator dynamics direction field for a 12-agent clearing-house auction showing interaction between the GA optimized strategy OS and (a) TT and GD, and (b) TT and RE

5   Evolving Mechanisms

One lesson to draw from Sections 3 and 4 is that one can evolve better traders if that evolution takes place in a more structured way. Rather than evolving the OS strategy from scratch, we structured it as a search through the parameters of a set of existing trading strategies, and rather than evolving the auction pricing rule at the same time, we fixed the pricing rule to one that is commonly adopted. This section describes two experiments that we carried out to explore if it possible to do the reverse — evolve aspects of the auction mechanism given traders using a known trading strategy.

5.1   Evolving a Pricing Rule

The first experiment that we carried out in evolving parts of an auction mechanism separately from the traders is described in detail in [39], and considered the evolution of the rule for setting trade prices given the prices bid by buyers p_b and asked by sellers p_s. This work used a continuous double auction with 30 buyers and 30 sellers, all of them using the RE strategy to pick offers. To evaluate the rules we evolved, we used the measure F:

$$F = \frac{e_a}{2} + \frac{\widehat{mp_b} + \widehat{mp_s}}{4} \qquad (6)$$

where e_a is as defined in (2), and mp_b and mp_s measure the market power of the buyers and sellers respectively, that is the extent to which the profits made by those groups differ from what they would be at theoretical equilibrium:

$$mp_b = \frac{pr_b - pr_b^e}{pr_b^e}$$

$$mp_s = \frac{pr_s - pr_s^e}{pr_s^e}$$

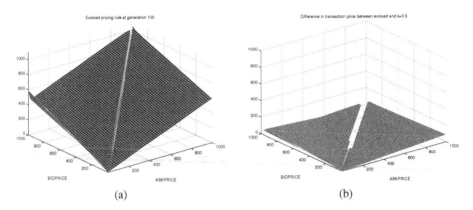

Fig. 6. The results of evolving a pricing rule, (a) the rule itself, (b) the difference between the rule and the $k = 0.5$ rule

and $\widehat{mp_b}$ and $\widehat{mp_s}$ are normalized versions of these measures:

$$\widehat{mp_b} = \frac{1}{1 + mp_b}$$

$$\widehat{mp_s} = \frac{1}{1 + mp_s}$$

We used genetic programming to evolve the rules. The functions that could be used in the genetic program consisted of the terminals $ASKPRICE$ and $BIDPRICE$, representing p_a and p_b respectively, together with the standard set of arithmetic functions $\{+, -, \times, \div\}$, and a function representing a random constant in the range $[0, 1]$. Thus all we assumed about the pricing function is that it was an arithmetic function of the bid and ask prices.

As mentioned above, pricing rules were evaluated using the measure F from (6) — we used each rule to run a series of auctions, and used the value that F reported for the auctions as the fitness of the rule. The following:

```
((0.6250385(0.93977016(ASKPRICE+0.76238054)))
 + (((((-0.19079465)/(ASKPRICE-(((BIDPRICE +BIDPRICE)/
 (((((ASKPRICE-1)+1.6088724)/(((1-ASKPRICE) -(ASKPRICE/
 ASKPRICE))+(2.5486426+(BIDPRICE + 0.000012302072)))))
 +((BIDPRICE/ASKPRICE)+((BIDPRICE+BIDPRICE)+(1.430315)/
 (BIDPRICE . ASKPRICE)))))))ASKPRICE)) ...
```

are the first few terms of a pricing rule that was evolved after 90 generations. It has been algebraically simplified, but as can be seen it is still far from straightforward, something that is not surprising given the way that standard genetic programming approaches handle the evolution of a program. Plotting the surface of the transaction price as a function of p_b and p_a, given in Figure 6 (a), and comparing it with the surface for:

$$0.5p_a + 0.5p_b$$

shows — the difference between the two rules is given in Figure 6 (b) — that these two functions are approximately equal apart from a slight variation when the ask price is very small or when the ask price is equal to the bid price. Thus the experiment effectively evolved a pricing rule for a discriminatory-price k double auction with $k = 0.5$ from the space of all arithmetic functions of ask and bid price. Our main conclusion from this is that our approach is able to evolve an eminently sensible rule, since the rule it came up with is virtually indistinguishable from one that has been widely used in practice[6].

5.2 Minimizing Price Fluctuation

The work described in the previous section looked at optimizing one very specific part of the continuous double auction, the rule for setting trade prices, with respect to one specific measure, that in (6). We can apply the same kind of optimization to different aspects of the auction mechanism, and with different measures in mind. [35] describes some experiments with some alternatives.

In particular, [35] is concerned with minimizing Smith's measure α (3), and thus fluctuations in the transaction price of the auction. The choice to minimize α was partly in order to see if it was possible to minimize this metric while keeping the efficiency of the auction high — testing the extent to which performance of the auction could be optimized — but one can imagine that this is also an attractive feature of an auction. If the auction has a low α, then transactions are, by definition, close to the theoretical equilibrium point. If this can be achieved for a range of trading strategies, then there is some guarantee that, no matter how a trader bids, the price that trader pays will be in some sense fair, saving the trader the burden of needing to bid cleverly.

To minimize α, we looked at learning a new pricing rule, a rule between that often used in a continuous double auction — where the price is the average of the bid and the ask — and the usual rule for a clearing house auction — where the price is the price that clears the market[7]. In essence, this new rule looks at the n most recent matching bid/ask pairs, and averages over them to obtain the transaction price. Figure 7 (a) compares the value of α for a continuous double auction with 10 buyers and 10 sellers all of which trade using the ZI-C strategy and the $k = 0.5$ pricing rule with that of the value of α for the same auction that sets prices using the average of the last 4 matched sets of bid and ask[8]. We only considered auctions involving ZI-C traders in order to make the problem of minimizing price fluctuation as hard as possible — ZI-C, making offers randomly, typically gives high values of α compared with other trading strategies.

Clearly the moving average rule is effective in reducing α, but the value it attains is still high compared with the levels attained using different trading strategies. Auctions

---

[6] It is also possible to argue in the other direction — that since we came up with the $k = 0.5$ rule, the rule makes sense for scenarios like the one that we were investigating.

[7] The price that would be the theoretical equilibrium if the bids and asks were truthful.

[8] Note that the rule uses *at most* four sets of matched bids and asks. Since the auction is continuous, the price of the trade between the first matched pair of offers is exactly that of the $k = 0.5$ rule since there is only one matched bid and ask pair to use, the price of the second trade is the average of the first two matched bids and the first two matched asks and the price of the third trade is the average of the first three matched sets.

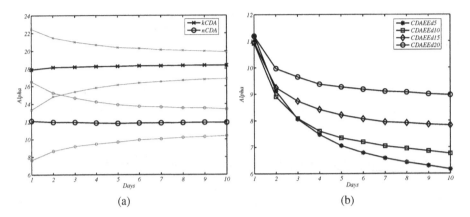

Fig. 7. The value of α for a double auctions with ZI-C traders (a) comparing the standard continuous double auction price rule with the sliding-window pricing rule, and (b) comparing α for different versions of the shout improvement rule. The gray lines denote one standard deviation above and below the average value over 400 iterations.

with traders that only use GD attain α values of around 4. To try to reduce fluctuation even more, we examined another aspect of the auction, the rule the auctioneer uses for accepting shouts as being valid. The idea is to generalize the "New York Stock Exchange (NYSE) rule", the rule used in that market, among others, which insists that successive bids and asks for the same good improve on each other. In other words, successive bids must increase, and successive asks must decrease. The generalization we adopted makes a running estimate of the equilibrium price for the market, and the shout acceptance rule (which we call the "shout improvement" rule) requires that bids are above this estimate and asks are below it. Note that our rule, unlike the NYSE rule, continues to apply after an individual good has been traded — indeed, as Figure 7 (b) shows, the effect of the rule on α improves over time.

In fact, it turns out that there is one last tweak to the shout improvement rule that it behooves us to add. If the rule is applied strictly as described, the estimate of the equilibrium price can get badly thrown off by errant offers at the start of the auction (and errant offers are common with ZI-C traders). To ameliorate this situation, we introduce a parameter δ, an increment that is applied to the estimated equilibrium price to relax the improvement rule — bids above the estimate minus δ and asks below the estimate plus δ are considered valid. Figure 7 (b) shows the effect of different values of δ.

Overall, the combination of these measures can reduce α for all-ZI-C markets to a value around 6 with little or no loss of efficiency. Indeed, for some values of δ, the efficiency of the all ZI-C market is greater than that of an all ZI-C market under the usual CDA mechanism. In addition, it seems that these new market rules do not hurt the performance of markets consisting of more sophisticated traders. We tested the same market rules when the traders all used GD, and found that, if anything, the new rules reduced α and increased efficiency.

6   Evaluating Mechanisms

The work on mechanisms that we have described so far has looked to optimize one specific aspect of an auction, and has shown that this is achievable. However, the kind of evaluation of auctions that we have used in this work, focusing on a single measure when agents are all of the same type — in the sense of which bidding strategy they used — seems a bit narrow, and so we have experimented with alternative forms of evaluating of mechanisms.

6.1   Comparing Markets

In [40] we experimented with using heuristic strategy analysis to compute metrics for different types of auction. The motivation for doing this is as follows. Most of the properties that we might use to rate auctions, whether efficiency, Smith's α, or metrics like price dispersion [16], differ for the same auction as the traders use different trading strategies. They are not properties of the traders, since the same traders generate different efficiencies, αs and price dispersions in different auctions, but they are not entirely properties of the auctions either. Thus it is difficult to say with authority that a given auction has a given property. What we can do, however, is to use a heuristic strategy analysis to establish what mixtures of trading strategies will hold at equilibrium, and use this to compute an estimate of the properties that we are interested in.

Figure 8 shows the results of a heuristic strategy analysis for the continuous double auction and the clearing house auction with different numbers of traders. For all of these analyses we used three trading strategies, truth telling TT, the Roth-Erev strategy RE that we used in the first pricing rule experiment, and the modification of ZIP proposed by Preist and van Tol (PVT) [43]. Our choice of strategies was intended to examine the relative performance of the human-like RE strategy[9] and the simple "program trader" provided by PVT, with the performance of TT measuring how far the markets are from being strategy-proof (in a strategy-proof market there is no advantage to not telling the truth about one's valuation for a good).

There are a number of conclusions that one can draw from the plots in Figure 8[10]. First, there is a significant difference between the direction fields of the continuous double auction and the clearing house auction for any number of traders. While each strategy is a pure strategy equilibrium, the basins of attraction are rather different as are the locations, along the edges and in the middle of the direction field, of the mixed equilibria. Second, the difference becomes more marked the larger the number of agents — the basin of attraction of TT shrinks as the CDA includes more traders, and grows as the CH includes more traders. The latter is in accordance with theoretical results [48] which predict that the disadvantages of truth-telling decline as the number of traders grows. Third, truth telling is not dominant in any of the markets, so none of them are strategy proof.

---

[9] Roth and Erev originally introduced their approach as a way of replicating human behavior in games [45].

[10] Note that we have not indicated the direction of the field on the plots in the interests of readability — the direction of flow is from the middle of the simplex towards the edges.

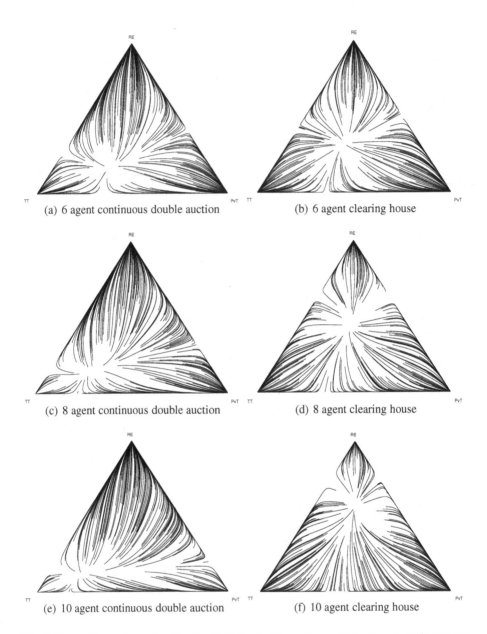

Fig. 8. The replicator dynamics direction field for double auctions with trading strategies TT, RE and PVT

It is also possible to draw more quantitative conclusions. Taking 1000 random starting points within the direction fields for each of the 10 agent clearing house and continuous double auctions, we established which of the pure strategy equilibria these starting points led to. Assuming that the starting points, each of which represents a mix

Table 1. Probabilities of equilibria for 10 agent markets

Equilibrium	CH probability	payoff	CDA probability	payoff
TT	0.38	1.00	0.05	0.86
RE	0.11	0.99	0.70	0.97
PvT	0.51	0.99	0.25	0.94

of trading strategies, are equally likely, we could then compute the relative frequency of occurrence of the pure strategies — these are given in Table 1. Now, since we can easily establish whatever metrics we want for the equilibrium points (again these are given in Table 1), we can use the probabilities of reaching these equilibria to determine the expected value of the metrics. For example for the 10 trader CDA we can compute the expected efficiency as:

$$0.05 \times 0.86 + 0.70 \times 0.97 + 0.25 \times 0.94 = 0.96$$

compared with

$$0.38 \times 1.00 + 0.11 \times 0.99 + 0.51 \times 0.99 = 0.99$$

for the 10 trader CH.

Note that the assumption of equally likely start points is not the only assumption involved in this computation. Since the probability of arriving at a particular equilibrium is a function of the replicator dynamics, we are also assuming that the replicator dynamics is an accurate description of trader behavior. One can argue this either way — the only guarantee that the replicator dynamics give is that the stationary points in the field are Nash equilibria.

6.2 Direct Competition Between Markets

The comparison between markets described above is useful, but indirect. It compares markets while still thinking of the markets as operating in isolation — it tells us nothing about how the markets would fare if they were in running in parallel, as markets often do in the real world[11]. In [36], we looked at the relative performance of markets when they are in competition with one another for traders.

To this end, we ran a series of experiments[12] where traders were offered a choice of markets at the start of every trading day, making this choice using simple reinforcement learning based on the profit that they made in the markets (learning which markets were profitable over time). The profit that a given trader makes in a market is the profit from trade — the difference between the trade price and the private value of the

---

[11] For example, Shah and Thomas [50] describe the competition between India's National Stock Exchange and the established Bombay Stock Exchange for trade in the stock of Indian companies when the National Stock Exchange opened.

[12] These experiments were run using JCAT [22], an extension of JASA [21] that allows multiple markets and provides both a mechanism for markets to charge traders, and for traders to decide which market provides them with the best profit.

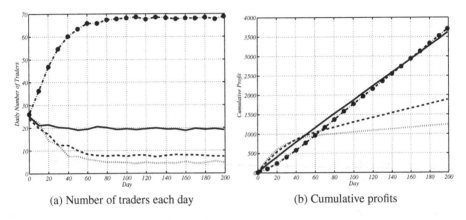

(a) Number of traders each day   (b) Cumulative profits

Fig. 9. Four markets that compete for traders

trader — minus any charges imposed by the markets. We allowed markets to charge because this is a feature of real markets, and because the profit made by markets is a natural basis of comparison.

Figure 9 shows some typical results from [36]. Figure 9 (a), which gives the number of traders in each market at the start of every trading day, shows how, as the agents learn, the markets stratify by charges. As one might expect, the lowest charging market attracts the largest number of traders and the highest charging market attracts the smallest number of traders. Note that even the highest charging market continues to attract some traders — those that make a good profit even with the charges. Figure 9 (b), which gives the cumulative profit of each market on each day, shows how the lowest charging market catches the higher charging markets over time. These results are for markets with a simple, fixed, policy for charging. [36] also considers adaptive charging policies — one that undercuts all other markets, one that cuts prices until it has a large market share and then increases prices, and one that works like ZIP — showing that the relationship between such policies has some of the complexity of the relationship between trading strategies.

7   Conclusion

Auctions are a powerful mechanism for resource allocation in multi-agent systems and elsewhere, and there are many situations in which one might make use of them. However, it is not advisable to employ auctions "off-the-peg" — as some expensive failures have demonstrated [31] — instead, it is necessary to carefully tailor auction mechanisms for the particular niche that they are required to fill. Our work is intended to automate this tailoring process. Using a combination of evolutionary computation, reinforcement learning, and evolutionary game theory, we have successfully tailored variants of the double auction for different purposes, and traders to operate in these auctions, and our future work aims to extend the scope of this automated generation. In particular, we can easily imagine combining the techniques we have described here into a high-level process for co-evolving markets and traders. For a fixed mechanism we could evolve traders, as in Section 4, and then fix the equilibrium set of traders and evolve parts of the mechanism as in Section 5, evaluating evolved mechanisms just as we did in Section 6.1. Repeating this process will then allow us to create traders that can operate in the new mechanism. Demonstrating this co-evolutionary spiral is the focus of our current work.

We should note that while this high-level co-evolution is the long term goal of our work on applying machine learning to mechanism design, there are plenty of other areas in which we can profitably use machine learning in the design of auction mechanisms. Two areas, in particular, intrigue us greatly. One is the idea, introduced by Posada [41,42], that it is possible for traders to employ a "meta-strategy" in which their task is to learn which of the standard trading strategies is best adopted, and to do this learning during the course of an auction. While this approach is similar to the evolutionary game theoretic analysis we discussed in Section 4, it differs in that traders switch strategies during the course of an auction rather than between auctions. We are interested to examine the equilibria that emerge from this kind of behavior. Another interesting idea, also related to the analysis in Section 4, is that of [24], in which heuristic search is employed to find equilibrium points. Adopting such an approach should significantly reduce the computation required to find equilibria when compared with out current, exhaustive, search.

Acknowledgments

This work was supported by the National Science Foundation under grant IIS-0329037, *Tools and Techniques for Automated Mechanism Design*, by the UK EPSRC project, *Market Based Control of Complex Computational Systems* (GR/T10657/01), who sponsored the development of JCAT and the running of the TAC Market Design (CAT) Tournament in 2007, and by the European Union under grant IST-1999-10948, *Sustainable LifeCycles for Information Ecosystems*. We are grateful to Marek Marcinkiewicz, Jarrett Chaiken and Ravi Cohen for their work on JASA, Jamari Robinson and Victoria Au for their work on JCAT, and to Jeff Mackie-Mason and Michael Wellman for helpful comments.

References

1. Angeline, P.J., Pollack, J.B.: Competitive environments evolve better solutions for complex tasks. In: Forrest, S. (ed.) Proceedings of the Fifth International Conference on Genetic Algorithms, pp. 264–270 (1993)
2. Blair, A.D., Sklar, E., Funes, P.: Co-evolution, determinism and robustness. In: Proceedings of the Second Asia-Pacific Conference on Simulated Evolution and Learning, pp. 389–396. Springer-Verlag, Heidelberg (1999)
3. Cai, K., Niu, J., Parsons, S.: An empirical game-theoretic analysis of trading strategies in a continuous double auction market. In: Tuylus, K., Nowe, A., guerssoum, Z., Kudenko, D. (eds.) Proceedings of the Symposium on Adaptive Learning Agents and Multiagent Systems. LNCS, vol. 4865, pp. 44–59. Springer, Heidelberg (2007)

4. Cliff, D.: Minimal-intelligence agents for bargaining behaviours in market-based environments. Technical Report HP-97-91, Hewlett-Packard Research Laboratories, Bristol, England (1997)
5. Cliff, D.: Evolution of market mechanism through a continuous space of auction-types. In: Proceedings of Computational Intelligence for Financial Engineering, Hawai'i (May 2002)
6. Cliff, D., Bruten, J.: Less than human: Simple adaptive trading agents for CDA markets. Technical Report HP-97-155, Hewlett-Packard Research Laboratories, Bristol, England (1997)
7. Cliff, D., Bruten, J.: Zero is not enough: On the lower limit of agent intelligence for continuous double auction markets. Technical Report HP-97-155, Hewlett-Packard Research Laboratories, Bristol, England (1997)
8. Cliff, D., Miller., G.F.: Tracking the red queen: Measurements of adaptive progress in co-evolutionary simulations. In: European Conference on Artificial Life, pp. 200–218 (1995)
9. Conitzer, V., Sandholm, T.: Automated mechanism design: Complexity results stemming from the single-agent setting. In: Proceedings of the International Conference on Electronic Commerce, Pittsburgh, pp. 17–24 (September 2003)
10. Conitzer, V., Sandholm, T.: An algorithm for automatically designing deterministic mechanisms without payments. In: Proceedings of the International Joint Conference on Autonomous Agents and Multiagent Systems, New York, pp. 128–135 (July 2004)
11. Cramton, P., Schwartz, J.: Collusive bidding: Lessons from the FCC spectrum auctions. Journal of Regulatory Economics 17(3), 229–252 (2000)
12. Erev, I., Roth, A.E.: Predicting how people play games with unique, mixed-strategy eqilibria. American Economic Review 88, 848–881 (1998)
13. Ficici, S.G., Pollack, J.B.: Challenges in coevolutionary learning: Arms-race dynamics, open-endedness, and mediocre stable states. In: Proceedings of the 6th International Conference on Artificial Life, pp. 238–247 (1998)
14. Friedman, D.: The double auction institution: A survey. In: Friedman, D., Rust, J. (eds.) The Double Auction Market: Institutions, Theories and Evidence, pp. 3–25. Perseus Publishing, Cambridge, MA (1993)
15. Gjerstad, S., Dickhaut, J.: Price formation in double auctions. Games and Economic Behaviour 22, 1–29 (1998)
16. Gode, D.K., Sunder, S.: Allocative efficiency of markets with zero-intelligence traders: Market as a partial sustitute for individual rationality. The Journal of Political Economy 101(1), 119–137 (1993)
17. Gode, D.K., Sunder, S.: Lower bounds for efficiency of surplus extraction in double auctions. In: Friedman, D., Rust, J. (eds.) The Double Auction Market: Institutions, Theories and Evidence, pp. 199–219. Perseus Publishing, Cambridge, MA (1993)
18. Hillis, W.D.: Co-evolving parasites improve simulated evolution as an optimization procedure. In: Proceedings of the Second International Conference on Artificial Life, pp. 313–324 (1992)
19. Holland, J.: Adaptation in natural and artificial systems. University of Michigan Press, Ann Arbor, MI (1975)
20. Jackson, M.O.: Mechanism theory. In: Devigs, U. (ed.) Optimization and Operations Research, The Encyclopedia of Life Support Science, EOLSS Publishers, Oxford, UK (2003) (The working paper version of this article includes a more comprehensive bibliography and some bibliographic notes)
21. http://sourceforge.net/projects/jasa/
22. http://jcat.sourceforge.net/
23. Jordan, P.R., Kiekintveld, C., Wellman, M.P.: Empirical game-theoretic analysis of the TAC supply chain game. In: Proceedings of the 6th International Conference on Autonomous Agents and Multi-Agent Systems, Honolulu, Hawai'i (2007)

24. Jordan, P.R., Wellman, M.P.: Best-first search for approximate equilibria in empirical games. In: Proceedings of the Workshop on Trading Agent Design and Analysis, Vancouver, BC (2007)
25. Klemperer, P.: How (not) to run auctions: The European 3G telecom auctions. European Economic Review 46, 829–845 (2002)
26. Koza, J.R.: Genetic programming: On the programming of computers by means of natural selection. MIT Press, Cambridge, MA (1992)
27. Madhavan, A.: Trading mechanisms in securities markets. The Journal of Finance 47(2), 607–641 (1992)
28. Maskin, E.S., Riley, J.G.: Auction theory with private values. American Economic Review 75, 150–155 (1985)
29. McAfee, R.P.: A dominant strategy double auction. Journal of Economic Theory 56, 343–450 (1992)
30. McAfee, R.P., McMillan, J.: Analyzing the airwaves auction. Journal of Economic Perspectives 10, 159–176 (1996)
31. McMillan, J.: Selling spectrum rights. Journal of Economic Perspectives 8, 191–199 (1994)
32. McMillan, J.: Reinventing the Bazaar: A Natural History of Markets. In: W. W. Norton & Company (2003)
33. Miller, G.F., Cliff, D.: Protean behavior in dynamic games: Arguments for the co-evolution of pursuit-evasion tactics. In: Proceedings of the Third International Conference on Simulation of Adaptive Behavior, pp. 411–420 (1994)
34. Nicolaisen, J., Petrov, V., Tesfatsion, L.: Market power and efficiency in a computational electricity market with discriminatory double-auction pricing. IEEE Transactions on Evolutionary Computation 5(5), 504–523 (2001)
35. Niu, J., Cai, K., Parsons, S., Sklar, E.: Reducing price fluctuation in continuous double auctions through pricing policy and shout improvement. In: Proceedings of the 5th International Conference on Autonomous Agents and Multi-Agent Systems, Hakodate, Japan (2006)
36. Niu, J., Cai, K., Parsons, S., Sklar, E.: Some preliminary results on competition between markets for automated traders. In: Proceedings of the Workshop on Trading Agent Design and Analysis, Vancouver, BC (2007)
37. Phelps, S., Marcinkiewicz, M., Parsons, S., McBurney, P.: A novel method for automated strategy acquisition in n-player non-zero-sum games. In: Proceedings of the 5th International Conference on Autonomous Agents and Multi-Agent Systems, Hakodate, Japan (2006)
38. Phelps, S., McBurney, P., Parsons, S., Sklar, E.: Co-evolutionary mechanism design: A preliminary report. In: Padget, J., Shehory, O., Parkes, D., Sadeh, N., Walsh, W.E. (eds.) Agent-Mediated Electronic Commerce IV. Designing Mechanisms and Systems. LNCS (LNAI), vol. 2531, pp. 123–142. Springer, Heidelberg (2002)
39. Phelps, S., McBurney, P., Sklar, E., Parsons, S.: Using genetic programming to optimise pricing rules for a double auction market. In: Proceedings of the Workshop on Agents and Electronic Commerce, Pittsburgh, PA (2003)
40. Phelps, S., Parsons, S., McBurney, P.: An evolutionary game-theoretic comparison of two double auction markets. In: Faratin, P., Rodríguez-Aguilar, J.A. (eds.) AMEC 2004. LNCS (LNAI), vol. 3435, pp. 101–114. Springer, Heidelberg (2006)
41. Posada, M.: Strategic software agents in a continuous double auction under dynamic environments. In: Corchado, E., Yin, H., Botti, V., Fyfe, C. (eds.) IDEAL 2006. LNCS, vol. 4224, pp. 1223–1233. Springer, Heidelberg (2006)
42. Posada, M., Hernández, C., López-Paredes, A.: Strategic behaviour in continuous double auction. In: Bruun, C. (ed.) Advances in Artificial Economies: The Economy as a Complex Dynamic System. Lecture Notes in Economics and Mathematical Systems, Berlin, vol. 584, pp. 31–43. Springer, Heidelberg (2006)

43. Preist, C., van Tol, M.: Adaptative agents in a persistent shout double auction. In: Proceedings of the 1st International Conference on the Internet, Computing and Economics, pp. 11–18. ACM Press, New York (1998)
44. Roth, A.E.: The economist as engineer: Game theory, experimentation, and computation as tools for design economics. Econometrica 70, 1341–1378 (2002)
45. Roth, A.E., Erev, I.: Learning in extensive-form games: Experimental data and simple dynamic models in the intermediate term. Games and Economic Behavior 8, 164–212 (1995)
46. Rust, J., Miller, J.H., Palmer, R.: Behaviour of trading automata in a computerized double auction market. In: Friedman, D., Rust, J. (eds.) The Double Auction Market: Institutions, Theories and Evidence, pp. 155–199. Perseus Publishing, Cambridge, MA (1993)
47. Rust, J., Miller, J.H., Palmer, R.: Characterizing effective trading strategies. Journal of Economic Dynamics and Control 18, 61–96 (1994)
48. Rustichini, A., Satterthwaite, M.A., Williams, S.R.: Convergence to efficiency in a simple market with incomplete information. Econometrica 62(5), 1041–1063 (1994)
49. Satterthwaite, M.A., Williams, S.R.: The Bayesian theory of the k-double auction. In: Friedman, D., Rust, J. (eds.) The Double Auction Market: Institutions, Theories and Evidence, pp. 99–123. Perseus Publishing, Cambridge, MA (1993)
50. Shah, A., Thomas, S.: David and Goliath: Displacing a primary market. Global Financial Markets 1(1), 14–21 (2000)
51. Smith, V.L.: An experimental study of competitive market behaviour. The Journal of Political Economy 70(2), 111–137 (1962)
52. Smith, V.L.: Microeconomics as a experimental science. The American Economic Review 72(5), 923–955 (1982)
53. Tesauro, G., Das, R.: High-performance bidding agents for the continuous double auction. In: Proceedings of the 3rd ACM Conference on Electronic Commerce (2001)
54. Tesauro, G., Kephart, J.O.: Pricing in agent economies using multi-agent Q-learning. Autonomous Agents and Multi-Agent Systems 5(3), 289–304 (2002)
55. Vickrey, W.: Counterspeculation, auctions, and competitive sealed bids. Journal of Finance 16(1), 8–37 (1961)
56. Vorobeychik, Y., Kiekintveld, C., Wellman, M.P.: Empirical mechanism design: Methods, with application to a supply chain scenario. In: Proceedings of the ACM Conference on Electronic Commerce (2006)
57. Walia, V., Byde, A., Cliff, D.: Evolving auction design in zero-intelligence trader markets. In: Proceedings of the International Conference on Electronic Commerce, IEEE Press, Los Alamitos (2003)
58. Walsh, W.E., Das, R., Tesauro, G., Kephart, J.O.: Analyzing complex strategic interactions in multi-agent systems. In: Gymtrasiwicz, P., Parsons, S. (eds.) Proceedings of the 4th Workshop on Game Theoretic and Decision Theoretic Agents (2001)
59. Wellman, M.P.: A market-oriented programming environment and its application to distributed multicommodity flow problems. Journal of Artificial Intelligence Research 1, 1–23 (1993)
60. Wurman, P.R., Walsh, W.E., Wellman, M.P.: Flexible double auctions for electronic commerce: Theory and applications. Decision Support Systems 24, 17–27 (1998)
61. Zhan, W., Friedman, D.: Markups in double auction markets. Technical report, LEEPS, Department of Economics, University of Santa Cruz (2005)

Multi-agent Reinforcement Learning for Intrusion Detection

Arturo Servin and Daniel Kudenko

Department of Computer Science, University of York
Heslington, York. YO10 5DD, United Kingdom
{aservin,kudenko}@cs.york.ac.uk

Abstract. Intrusion Detection Systems (IDS) have been investigated for many years and the field has matured. Nevertheless, there are still important challenges, e.g., how an IDS can detect new and complex distributed attacks. To tackle these problems, we propose a distributed Reinforcement Learning (RL) approach in a hierarchical architecture of network sensor agents. Each network sensor agent learns to interpret local state observations, and communicates them to a central agent higher up in the agent hierarchy. These central agents, in turn, learn to send signals up the hierarchy, based on the signals that they receive. Finally, the agent at the top of the hierarchy learns when to signal an intrusion alarm. We evaluate our approach in an abstract network domain.

1 Introduction

As computer networks and information systems become more critical and complex, researchers are looking for new techniques to protect these assets. In this paper we present our work on the application of distributed reinforcement learning to allow cooperative network devices to identify and categorize faults, attacks and in general, any abnormal state in the network. The use of heterogeneous agents to detect distributed denial of service without central processing or management is an area with very little previous work. The number of studies that use machine learning techniques to scale up the solution to inter-domain networks or to adapt it to changes in traffic and attack behavior is scarce as well.

From a machine learning perspective, network intrusion and fault detection provides challenging scenarios to test and develop new multi-agent reinforcement learning techniques. To achieve reliable intrusion detection, RL will need to deal with noisy inputs and large discrete or continuous state-action spaces. We have chosen a hierarchical architecture of agents to provide a coordination scheme and learning mechanisms using data from distributed sources. The paper is structured as follows. In Section 2 we present a brief overview of the problem of detecting and categorizing Distributed Denial of Service Attacks, a review of IDS and point out some of the challenges these systems are still facing. The last part of this section is an overview of Multi-Agent Reinforcment Learning (MARL) and the problems that it faces as the number of agents and input information grows. In Section 3 we explain our proposed technique and the assumptions

K. Tuyls et al. (Eds.): Adaptive Agents and MAS III, LNAI 4865, pp. 211–223, 2008.

that we made when designing it. In Section 4 we show some results obtained from testing different architectures varying the number of agents, the number of states per sensor agent, the exploration/exploitation strategy, the distribution of attacks as input information and the agent architecture. Finally in Section 5 we point out our conclusions and an outlook to future work.

2   Background

In this section we introduce some concepts and terminology that provide the background to our approach.

2.1   Denial of Service Attacks

Denial of Service (DoS) attacks are very common in today's internet infrastructure. In a DoS, the attacker tries to exhaust key resources of the target to refuse a service to the legitimate users. DoS can be performed directly to attack a target or they can be an effect of other security problems such as the spreading of self replicating code or worms. A more worrisome type of this threats is the Distributed Denial of Service Attack (DDoS). DDoS are launched from several sources attacking one target. The effect would depend on the number of sources, the available bandwidth for each of them and the vulnerability that they are exploiting.

Defenses against DoS and DDoS are complex to design due to several factors. DoS are always accompanied by a heavy use of some kind of resource. If this resource is not heavily used, it is easy to identify the threat comparing normal to abnormal activity. DDoS use a distributed control with thousands of attackers spreading all over the Internet. To accurately identify and stop them it is necessary to coordinate several entities along the path of the DoS attack [10,20]. Under this assumption Mirkovic and Reiher [9] in their Taxonomy of DoS attacks and defenses state: *"the need for a distributed response at many points on the Internet"*.

2.2   Intrusion Detection Systems

Intrusion Detection Systems are just one part of the whole collection of technologies and processes needed to protect computer networks and information systems from intruders and attacks. In combination with firewalls, IDSs are the first line of defense in many computer networks. An IDS monitors hosts or networks searching for abnormal or non-authorized activity. When they find attack activity, they record the event and they may perform defensive actions. There are two basic types of IDS: anomaly intrusion detection and misuse/signature intrusion detection. Anomaly IDS uses different methods to detect abnormal activity; they vary from simple statistical methods to more complex AI techniques. Misuse or signature intrusion detection system use rule matching to detect intrusions. These IDSs compare system activity with specific intrusion rules that are generally hard coded. When the observed activity matches the intrusion pattern an intrusion is detected.

Because Anomaly IDSs compare current activity with a model of normal behavior they can detect unknown attacks when the network state is deviating from normal activity. However, non-malicious activity that does not match normal behavior can also trigger the intrusion mechanism. This results in a high rate of false positives or false alarms in anomaly IDSs. On the other hand, misuse-signature IDS are very reliable and they have low rates of false positives. Nevertheless, they lack the ability to detect new types of attacks. Other dimensions along which IDSs can be categorized are the type of response to detected intrusions (passive or active), the type of data-processing and the data-collection (centralized or distributed), and the source of the audit data (host or network).

As computer networks become more complex systems and threats on them are reaching global magnitudes researchers are looking for novel approaches to adapt IDS to these new needs. Some authors [2,3,11,16,19] point out that the use of a rich diversity of sensor information may achieve the development of more reliable IDS. The rationale behind this is that sensor variety is needed because each sensor perceives different information depending on its capabilities, its function and where it is deployed in the network. The amount of information required to infer malicious activity using distributed heterogeneous sensor architectures would overwhelm any human network manager and automatic processing becomes necessary.

2.3   Reinforcement Learning

Our approach to intrusion and fault detection is based on RL, where each network node is learning to send signals to other nodes in a network hierarchy. Before describing the details of this approach, we briefly introduce the main RL concepts.

In RL, agents or programs sense their environment in discrete time steps and they map those inputs to local state information. RL agents execute actions and observe the feedback from the environment or a trainer in the form of positive or negative rewards. After performing an action and receiving a reward, the agent observes any change in the environment and it updates its policy in order to optimize the reward received for future actions [18]. There are different approaches to calculate the optimal policy and to maximize the obtained reward over the time. One of the most widely used techniques is Q-learning. In Q-learning as in other Temporal-Difference-Learning methods the agent iteratively tries to estimate the value function. To estimate the value function, Q-learning constructs a table (Q-table) whose rows are states and columns are actions. The agent in each state s chooses an action a, observes the reward r and the next state s'. Then it updates the estimated Q-value denoted by $\hat{Q}$ in Equation (1). In this equation α is the learning rate with a value $0 < \alpha < 1$ and γ is a constant with value $0 < \gamma < 1$ that represents the relative value of delayed versus immediate rewards.

$$\hat{Q}(s,a) \leftarrow (1-\alpha)\hat{Q}(s,a) + \alpha(r + \gamma\ max_a\ \hat{Q}(s',a')) \tag{1}$$

The exploration/exploitation problem is a specific challenge that is present in reinforcement learning algorithms. To obtain the best reward, the agent tends to prefer actions that have been proved to provide high rewards. In order to discover these actions the agent needs to try actions that have not been tested. We say that the agent *exploits* actions that lead to better expected rewards but also it needs to *explore* other actions that may lead it to better rewards in the future [18]. In order to converge to the optimal policy, the agent needs to explore and to exploit actions. One simple solution is to use a *random* strategy. While in theory this strategy guarantees convergence; in practice it is very slow. A more subtle alternative is to let the agent explore actions in the beginning of the learning and progressively start choosing those actions that prove to lead to better expected rewards. ϵ-*greedy* and *Boltzmann* use this alternative. ϵ-greedy is a semi-uniform random exploration strategy; it uses a small value as a base probability to choose an action. The downside of e-greedy is that it chooses among all the actions with the same probability. To address this problem Boltzmann strategy, also called *softmax action selection rules*, weights each action with a probability according to their expected value using the given equation Equation.2:

$$P\left(a\right) = \frac{e^{Q(s,a_n)/T}}{\sum_0^i e^{Q(s,a_i)/T}} \qquad (2)$$

T is a positive number called *temperature*. Under high values of temperature the action selection tends to choose equally between all actions. Low values of temperature favor actions with high expected values. In practice to speed up convergence, the value of the temperature is decreased exponentially.

Reinforcement Learning has been adopted to solve problems where on-line learning is needed and where the construction of a model is difficult or not possible. For more complex problems involving the interaction of several agents, RL becomes an appealing yet challenging alternative due to several factors. The *curse of dimensionality* that affects standalone RL and other machine techniques has an even bigger effect in MARL, as the number of agents and states increase and it becomes difficult to scale these systems to a large number of agents. Different approaches from function approximation techniques [8,17] to hierarchical reinforcement learning [1,5] have been proposed to scale MARL to large number of agents.

Some of the main issues surrounding MARL are:

1. In single agent RL, agents need to adapt their behavior in accordance with their own actions and how they change the environment. In addition to this, MARL agents also need to adapt to other agents' learning and actions.
2. MARL agents do not always have a full view of the environment and even if they have, they normally cannot predict the actions of other agents and the changes in the environment [6].
3. The *credit assignment problem* [15] describes the difficulty of deciding which agent is responsible for successes or failures of the multi-agent system. Related to this, the question arises on how to split the reward signal among the

agents. The reward can be the same for all agents *(global reward)* or it can be assigned based on the individual contribution of the agent *(local reward)*.

3   Agent Architecture and Operation

The security of computer networks is provided by devices such as IDS. As previously mentioned IDS monitor the network and detect abnormal or non authorized activity. When it detects suspicious activity, it records the event and in some cases performs defensive actions. The use of a rich diversity of sensor information may achieve more reliable detection of abnormal events in the network. Different network devices can provide diverse information based on their capabilities, their local network state observations, and their location in the network.

To process the information of distributed heterogeneous sensors to infer malicious activity there are multiple choices ranging from central control and management to peer to peer agent interaction; and from flat topologies to hierarchical central management and clustering. Since it is infeasible to assume that agents are able to communicate their complete local state observations (due to bandwidth restrictions), we have chosen an approach that is somewhere between central management and distributed control.

We propose a hierarchical architecture of Distributed Intrusion Detection Systems (DIDS) integrated by remote sensor agent diversity and reinforcement learning to detect and categorize DDoS Attacks. In this approach distributed sensors process the local state information and pass on short signals up a hierarchy of RL-IDS agents. With these signals the RL-IDS agents learn to distinguish abnormal activity from a diversity of sources. The lower the hierarchical level of the agent is; the more local information it is processing. The result is that high-level hierarchical agents have a better overview of the current state of the whole network. Under this consideration the agent on top of the hierarchy learns whether or not to trigger an overall alarm to the network operator.

Our base topology or Basic Cell is shown in Figure 1. It is composed of one central agent and n sensor agents. Sensor agents are in the form of network devices and they vary in capabilities and information that they can process. Each sensor agent receives only partial information about the global state of the network and they map local state information to communication signals which they send to the central agent (RL-IDS) of the cell (the signal constitutes the action of the sensor agent). The RL-IDS agent tries to model the state of the monitored network through these signals and decides in turn on a signal action. If the signal is in accordance with the real state of the monitored network, all the agents receive a positive reward. If the action is inaccurate, all the agents receive a negative reward. The goal is that after a certain number of iterations of the algorithm, every agent would know for each state the action that they need to execute to obtain positive rewards.

To expand the sensor architecture to analogous computer network architectures we created a hierarchical architecture with 2 levels as shown in Figure 2.

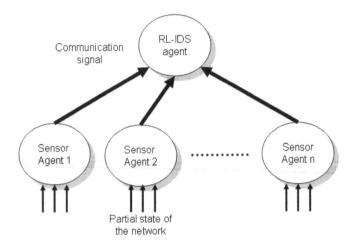

Fig. 1. Basic Cell of Agents. Each Sensor Agent sends communication signals to the RL-IDS agent.

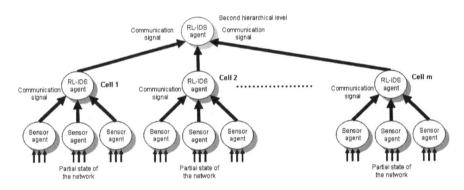

Fig. 2. Hierarchical Architecture: Each RL-IDS agent inside cells communicates with a higher level RL-IDS

This architecture is build from m cells with n agents per cell. In this topology each cell's RL-IDS agents receive local information from sensor agents and learn what signal to trigger to the next RL-IDS higher up in the hierarchy. Then, via the signals from the lower-level RL-IDS agents and the reward function, the high-level hierarchical RL-IDS agent in the topology learns which signal to trigger to the network operator or to the next hierarchical level RL-IDS. If we considered h as the number of hierarchical levels and n as the number of sensor agents per cell and the number of cells that one single RL-IDS can handle, the number of agents in a topology is denoted by Equation (3).

$$TotalNumberOfAgents = \sum_{i=0}^{h} n^{h-1} \tag{3}$$

We have opted to use a hierarchical architecture of agents instead of a flat one because we consider that the former adapts better to the topologies of real computer networks. These systems are constructed by several hierarchical layers where the lower layers perform data access to users and high layers perform high speed packet switching. Our hierarchical architecture is also easily adapted to process intrusion detection between different networks domains similarly as it occurs in real Internet interconnections.

4   Experiments and Results

We applied our algorithm to different agent architectures varying the number of agents, the exploration/exploitation strategy, the number of states per sensor agent, the distribution of attacks as input information and the agent architecture. In these initial experiments, we fell back on an idealized model of a network that nevertheless poses the principal learning and coordination challenges of the real-world case.

Each agent uses a modified version of Q-learning (see Equation (4) below) to learn which action to execute in a specific state. The value of this function is the maximum discounted cumulative reward or the value of executing action a in the state s plus the value of following the optimal policy afterward. The action selection strategy during learning is provided by Boltzmann exploration. Boltzmann exploration uses a decreasing factor (T) known as temperature to slowly decrease exploration over time. To measure the learning performance we used accuracy, precision, recall and specificity (Table 1). These four variables give us more information about the relation between False Positives (FP) and False Negatives (FN) and between FN-FP and the correct categorized events (True Negatives and True Positives).

$$\hat{Q}(s,a) \leftarrow \hat{Q}(s,a) + \alpha(r - \hat{Q}(s,a)) \tag{4}$$

Table 1. Performance Metrics

Measure	Formula	Meaning
Accuracy	(TP + TN) / (TP + TN + FP + FN)	The percentage of positive predictions that is correct
Precision	TP / (TP + FP)	The percentage of positive labeled instances that was predicted as positive. Also defined as *Intrusion Detection Rate*
Recall	TP / (TP + FN)	The percentage of negative labeled instances that was predicted as negative
Specificity	TN / (TN + FP)	The percentage of predictions that is correct

In the simplest experiment, we created a cell with two sensor agents and one RL-IDS agent. We set up the sensor agents to have 2 states (0 and 1). Note that each sensor agent cannot observe the states of other sensor agents and that the combination of all states of the sensor agents represents the global state of the network. In this simple scenario we have 4 states ([0,0],[0,1],[1,0],[1,1]) where state [1,1] represents an abnormal network state that would require an alarm signal from the RL-IDS. The sensor agents have to learn to produce the right signal action to the RL-IDS agent, while this agent needs to learn to interpret these signals. In our basic scenario there are only two sensor signals A and B. The RL-IDS must learn which signals from the sensor agents represent a normal state of the network or a warning state. As it can be observed in Figure 3, the agents in this test are able to detect and categorize the normal and abnormal states of the network.

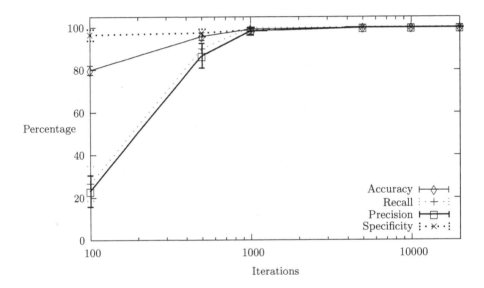

Fig. 3. Two Sensor Agents: After less than 1,000 iterations the RL-IDS agent learns how to identify abnormal activity through the signals from sensor agents

In general the global state of the network is simulated by randomly choosing between normal and abnormal states. Following a uniform distribution of possible states in tests with more than two agents creates a very small number of abnormal states compared with the number of normal states. This distribution of training data biased the agents to learn that the safer action was not to generate any alarm action at all. The result is a low performance in the intrusion detection rate and recall variables as shown in the second row of Table 2 and in Fig.5 To solve this problem we provide a minimum of 25% of abnormal states in the training data. With this new set up, the agents were able to learn to act correctly with higher levels of accuracy. Still the intrusion detection rate was low. In other words, the agents generated high rates of false positives.

We found that the agents had little time to explore all the no-attack states and to *fix* the Q-values that were miscalculated as result of the credit assignment problem and the partial observation of the environment. To tackle this problem we extended the exploitation phase of the exploration/exploitation strategy to allow the agents to exploit actions and to modify the values of their Q-tables. To carry out this task we divided the exploration/exploitation strategy in two parts. The first part was the initial Boltzmann strategy where agents slowly decrease exploration over time accordingly to a decreasing factor (T). The second part was a total exploitive strategy where agents do not explore actions any more. We denoted this as a *pure exploitive strategy*. The level of *pure exploitation* is given by Equation 5. The results presented in Table 2 and marked as *with pure exploitive strategy* uses a level value of 0.5. In other words the agents explore/exploit 50% of the time accordingly to a Boltzmann strategy and exploit actions the rest of the time. In Figure 4 there is a graphical comparsion between tests with four agents. One of the test was performed with 25% of abnormal activity and Boltzmann strategy (exploitive Level = 1). The other test was performed with 25% of abnormal activity and an exploitive level equal to 0.5. As shown, the use of new strategy (Boltzmann + total exploitive) provided higher values of accuracy (See Table 2 for comparsion between three agents) as well as high values of intrusion detection rates compared with test with only Boltzmann exploration/exploitation.

$$ExploitiveLevel = \frac{Number\ of\ pure\ exploitive\ iterations}{total\ of\ iterations} \tag{5}$$

The next step in our testing was to increase the number of states and review the maximum numbers of agents per cell with acceptable levels of performance. As shown in Figure 5; when we increased the number of agents the levels of precision went down due to high rates of false negatives. Under this assumption we considered that the maximum number of agents per cell is less than 6. As it can be observed in Table 2 the remaining variables had very little effect as the number of agents increased. This is the effect of the previously mentioned problems often found in MARL such as credit assignment, partial observation, curse of dimensionality and mis-coordination penalized with high negative rewards. It is important to note that the number of iterations presented in the graphs of Figure 5 and Figure 6 are per hierarchical level; for a test with 9 agents in 2 hierarchical levels the test needs 10,000 iterations per level (as shown in the figures) or 20,000 iterations in total to reach the performance levels listed.

In order to adapt our architecture to detect abnormal activity on inter-domain networks or in intra-domain networks with geographical zones we develop a hierarchical architecture of agents (See Figure 2). In this new architecture sensor agents and RL-IDS inside a cell learn how to identify local normal and abnormal activity. Once they have learned this, the RL-IDS agents inside the cells send communication signals to the next RL-IDS in the hierarchy which is learning

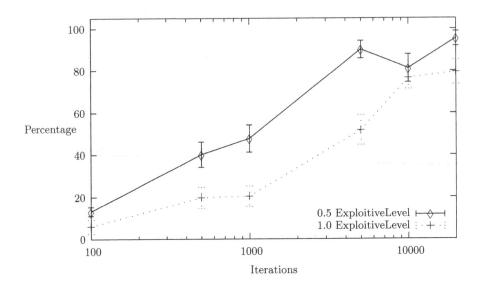

Fig. 4. Intrusion Detection Rate Four Agents with different Exploitive levels of Exploration/Exploitation and 25% abnormal activity

Table 2. Performace (Percentages)

Test	Accu.	Error	Prec.	Error	Recall	Error	Spec.	Error
Two sensor agents (3)	98.9	1.1	90.0	10.0	90.0	10.0	100.0	0.0
Three sensor agents	96.1	0.8	10.0	10.0	10.0	10.0	100.0	0.0
Three sensor agents (1)(2)	99.9	0.0	92.0	5.0	90.0	7.5	100.0	0.0
Six sensor agents (1)(2)	99.5	0.2	37.9	11.3	100.0	0.0	99.5	0.2
Six sensor agents Hierarchical (9 total) (1)(2)	99.9	0.0	90.0	10.0	90.0	10.0	100.0	0.0
9 sensor agents Hierarchical (13 total) (1)(2)	99.9	0.0	85.0	7.5	100.0	0.0	100.0	0.0
27 sensor agents Hierarchical (40 total) (1)(2)(3)	99.9	0.0	83.0	8.0	100.0	0.0	100.0	0.0

(1) 25 abnormal training, (2) Pure exploitive strategy, (3) 2 states per sensor agent 10,000 iterations in all tests.

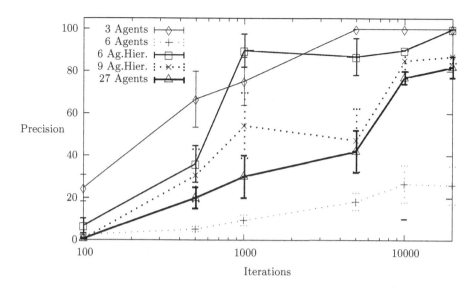

Fig. 5. Comparison of Precision (Intrusion Detection Rate) by number of agents

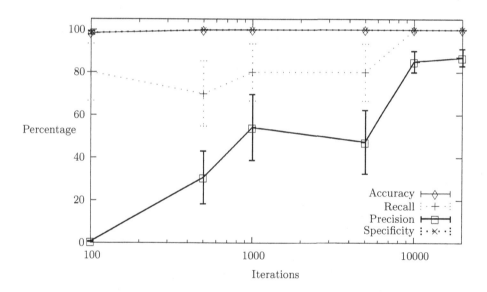

Fig. 6. Performance Metrics with Nine Agents

to signal in turn. This procedure is repeated iteratively until it reaches the last RL-IDS in the topology, i.e. the agent responsible for determining the state of the whole system. We compared the performance of 6 agents using this hierarchical design with 2 levels against the flat approach of 6 agents in one cell. We found that this architecture presents high levels of performance on all of our metrics than the flat approach.

Additionally, this approach permits the use of more than 6 agents arranged in various hierarchical levels. We expanded the architecture up to 9 sensor agents and 4 RL-IDS agents (13 agents in total) in 2 hierarchical levels and up to 27 sensor agents and 13 RL-IDS agents (40 agents in total) in three hierarchical levels. These tests shown (Figure 6) very acceptable levels of performance on all of our metrics.

5   Conclusion and Further Work

This paper presented RL experiments in an abstract network model where distributed network sensor agents learn to send signals up a hierarchy of agents. Higher agents in the hierarchy learn how to interpret local collected information from these signals and signal an overall abnormal state to the network operator when it is necessary. We presented solutions that enable the agents to learn an accurate signal policy and we have shown that the approach scales up to a large number of agents. In future work we plan to port the abstract network model to a realistic network simulation.

In our work, we used a fairly straightforward Q-update function and simple exploration/exploitation strategy. We intended to use this simple approach and to focus on the hierarchical mechanism to expand our proposal to several connected cells resembling real computer network environments. We do believe that a more complex approach to exploration/exploitation strategy or to calculating the value function may yield similar results but with fewer iterations, more input features and more agents per cell. We also plan to apply some techniques from single-state games [7], hierarchical reinforcement learning [1,5] function approximation [8,13,17] techniques and others [4,14].

References

1. Barto, A.G., Mahadevan, S.: Recent Advances in Hierarchical Reinforcement Learning. Discrete Event Dynamic Systems 13(4), 341–379 (2003)
2. Barford, P., Jha, S., Yegneswaran, V.: Fusion and Filtering in Distributed Intrusion Detection Systems. In: Proceedings of the 42nd Annual Allerton Conference on Communication, Control and Computing (September 2004)
3. Bass, T.: Intrusion Detection Systems and Multisensor Data Fusion. Communications of the ACM 43(4), 99–105 (2000)
4. Chang, T.H., Kaelbling, L.: All learning is local: Multi-agent learning in global reward games. In: Advances in NIPS, vol. 14 (2004)
5. Elfwing, S., Uchibe, E., Doya, K., Christensen, H.I.: Multi-agent reinforcement learning: using macro actions to learn a mating task. In: IROS 2004. Intelligent Robots and Systems (2004)
6. Jennings, N., Sycara, K., Wooldridge, M.: A roadmap of agents research and development. Autonomous Agents and Multi-Agent Systems 1, 7–38 (1998) In: [12]

7. Kapetanakis, S., Kudenko, D., Strens, M.: Learning to coordinate using commitment sequences in cooperative multi-agent systems. In: AISB 2003. Proceedings of the Third Symposium on Adaptive Agents and Multi-agent Systems, Society for the study of Artificial Intelligence and Simulation of Behaviour (2003)
8. Kostiadis, K., Hu, H.: KaBaGe-RL: Kanerva-based generalisation and reinforcement learning for possession football. In: IROS 2001. Proceedings of the IEEE/RSJ International Conference on Intelligent Robots and Systems (2001)
9. Mirkovic, J., Reiher, P.: A taxonomy of DDoS attack and DDoS defense mechanisms. ACM SIGCOMM Computer Communication Review 34(2) (April 2004)
10. Moore, D., Shannon, C., Voelker, G.M., Savage, S.: Internet Quarantine: Requirements for Containing Self-Propagating Code. In: INFOCOM 2003. 22th Joint Conference of the IEEE Computer and Communications Societies, March 30- April 3, 2003, vol. 3, pp. 1901–1910 (2003)
11. Neumann, P.G., Porras, P.A.: Experience with EMERALD to DATE. In: 1st USENIX Workshop on Intrusion Detection and Network Monitoring, Santa Clara, California (April 11-12, 1999)
12. Panait, L., Luke, S.: Cooperative Multi-Agent Learning: The State of the Art. Autonomous Agents and Multi-Agent Systems 11(3), 387–434 (2005)
13. Porta, J., Celaya, E.: Reinforcement Learning for Agents with Many Sensors and Actuators Acting in Categorizable Environments. Journal of Artificial Intelligence Research 23, 79–122 (2005)
14. Powers, R., Shoham, Y.: New criteria and a new algorithm for learning in multi-agent systems. In: Advances in Neural Information Processing Systems (forthcoming), Rubinstein, A.: Modeling Bounded Rationality. MIT Press, Washington (1998)
15. Sen, S., Weiss, G.: Learning in Multiagent Systems. In: Weiss, G. (ed.) Multiagent Systems, A Modern Approach to Distributed Artificial Intelligence, pp. 259–298. MIT Press, Cambridge (1999)
16. Siaterlis, C., Maglaris, B.: Towards multisensor data fusion for DoS detection. In: Proceedings of the 2004 ACM Symposium on Applied Computing, pp. 439–446 (2004)
17. Stone, P., Sutton, R.S., Singh, S.: Reinforcement Learning for 3 vs. 2 Keepaway. In: Stone, P., Balch, T., Kreatzschmarr, G. (eds.) RoboCup-2000: Robot Soccer World Cup IV, Springer, Berlin (2001)
18. Sutton, R., Barto, A.: Reinforcement Learning, An Introduction. MIT Press, Cambridge (1998)
19. Wasniowski, R.A.: Multisensor Agent Based Intrusion Detection. Transactions on Engineering, Computing and Technology 5, 110–113 (2005)
20. Yegneswaran, V., Barford, P., Jha, S.: Global Intrusion Detection in the DOMINO Overlay System. In: Proceedings of the Network and Distributed System Security Symposium (2004)

Networks of Learning Automata and Limiting Games

Peter Vrancx[1,*], Katja Verbeeck[2], and Ann Nowé[1]

[1] Computational Modeling Lab, Vrije Universiteit Brussel
{pvrancx,ann.nowe}@vub.ac.be
[2] MICC-IKAT Maastricht University
k.verbeeck@micc.unimaas.nl

Abstract. Learning Automata (LA) were recently shown to be valuable tools for designing Multi-Agent Reinforcement Learning algorithms. One of the principal contributions of LA theory is that a set of decentralized, independent learning automata is able to control a finite Markov Chain with unknown transition probabilities and rewards. This result was recently extended to Markov Games and analyzed with the use of limiting games. In this paper we continue this analysis but we assume here that our agents are fully ignorant about the other agents in the environment, i.e. they can only observe themselves; they do not know how many other agents are present in the environment, the actions these other agents took, the rewards they received for this, or the location they occupy in the state space. We prove that in Markov Games, where agents have this limited type of observability, a network of independent LA is still able to converge to an equilibrium point of the underlying limiting game, provided a common ergodic assumption and provided the agents do not interfere each other's transition probabilities.

1   Introduction

Learning automata (LA) are independent, adaptive decision making devices that were previously shown to be very useful tools for building new multi-agent reinforcement learning algorithms in general [1]. The main reason for this is that even in multi-automata settings, LA still exhibit nice theoretical properties. One of the principal contributions of LA theory is that a set of decentralized learning automata is able to control a finite Markov Chain with unknown transition probabilities and rewards. Recently this result has been extended to the framework of Markov Games, which is a straightforward extension of single-agent markov decision problems (MDPs) to distributed multi-agent decision problems [2].

In a Markov Game, actions are the result of the joint action selection of all agents and rewards and state transitions depend on these joint actions. Moreover, each agent has its own private reward function. When only one state is

---

* Funded by a Ph.D grant of the Institute for the Promotion of Innovation through Science and Technology in Flanders (IWT Vlaanderen).

K. Tuyls et al. (Eds.): Adaptive Agents and MAS III, LNAI 4865, pp. 224–238, 2008.

assumed, the Markov game is actually a repeated normal form game well known in game theory, [3]. When only one agent is assumed, the Markov game reduces to an MDP. Due to the individual reward functions for each agent, it usually is impossible to find policies which maximise the summed discounted rewards for all agents at the same time. The latter is possible in the so-called team games or multi-agent MDPs (MMDPs). In this case, the Markov game is purely coopera- tive and all agents share the same reward function. In MMDPs the agents should learn how to find and agree on the same optimal policy. In a general Markov game, an equilibrium policy is sought; i.e. a situation in which no agent alone can change its policy to improve its reward when all other agents keep their policy fixed. It was shown that in the set-up of [4] a network of independent learning automata is able to reach equilibrium strategies in Markov Games [4] provided some common ergodic assumptions are fulfilled.

In the case of single state multi-agent problems, the equilibrium strategies coin- cides with the Nash equilibria of the corresponding normal form game. In the case of multi stage problems, limiting games can be used as analysis tool. The limiting game of a corresponding multi-agent multi-state problem can be defined as follows: each joint agent policy is viewed as a single play between players using the agent's policies as their individual actions. The payoff given to each player is the expected reward for the corresponding agent under the resulting joint policy. Analyzing the multi state problem now boils down to explaining the behaviour of the multi-agent learning technique in terms of Nash equilibria in this limiting game.

In this paper we continue the analysis of networks of LA but we assume here that our agents are fully ignorant about the other agents in the environment, i.e. they can only observe themselves; they do not know how many other agents are present in the environment, the locations they occupy, the actions they took, or the rewards they received for this. We prove that in Markov Games, where agents have this limited type of observability, a network of independent LA is still able to find an equilibrium point of the underlying limiting game, provided a common ergodic assumption is satisfied and provided the agents do not interfere with each other's transition probabilities.

This paper is organized as follows. In the next section the definitions of MDPs, MMDPs and Markov games are given. We then give an example of a simple 2- agent grid game with limited observability and its corresponding limiting game. In Section 4 learning automata theory is summarised; the LA network mod- els used for controlling respectively MDPs and Markov games with full state observability are discussed. Next, in section 5 the LA update mechanism for agents with limited observability is given. This model is analyzed in section 6. Some illustrations are added in section 7. Finally we conclude in the last section.

2   Markov Games

2.1   Definition of an MDP

The problem of controlling a finite Markov Chain for which transition probabili- ties and rewards are unknown, called a Markov Decision Problem (MDP), can be formalised as follows. Let $S = \{s_1, \ldots, s_N\}$ be the state space of a finite Markov chain $\{x_l\}_{l \geq 0}$ and $A^i = \{a_1^i, \ldots, a_{r_i}^i\}$ the action set available in state s_i. Each starting state s_i, action choice $a^i \in A^i$ and ending state s_j has an associated transition probability $T^{ij}(a^i)$ and reward $R^{ij}(a^i)$. The overall goal is to learn a policy α, or a set of actions, $\alpha = (a^1, \ldots, a^N)$ with $a^j \in A^j$ so that the expected average reward $J(\alpha)$ is maximized:

$$J(\alpha) \equiv lim_{l \to \infty} \frac{1}{l} E \left[\sum_{t=0}^{l-1} R^{x(t)x(t+1)}(\alpha) \right] \tag{1}$$

The policies we consider are limited to stationary, nonrandomized policies. Under the assumption that the Markov chain corresponding to each policy α is ergodic, it can be shown that there exists an optimal pure strategy in any state, independent of the time at which the state is occupied [5]. A Markov chain $\{x_n\}_{n \geq 0}$ is said to be ergodic when the distribution of the chain converges to a limiting distribution $\pi(\alpha) = (\pi_1(\alpha), \ldots, \pi_N(\alpha))$ with $\forall i, \pi_i(\alpha) > 0$ as $n \to \infty$. Thus, there are no transient states and the limiting distribution $\pi(\alpha)$ can be used to rewrite Equation 1 as:

$$J(\alpha) = \sum_{i=1}^{N} \pi_i(\alpha) \sum_{j=1}^{N} T^{ij}(\alpha) R^{ij}(\alpha) \tag{2}$$

2.2 Definition of a Markov Game

An extension of single agent Markov decision problems (MDPs) to the multi-agent case can be defined by Markov Games [2]. In a Markov Game, actions are the joint result of multiple agents choosing an action separately. Note that $A_k^i = \{a_{k1}^i, \ldots, a_{kir}^i\}$ is now the action set available in state s_i for agent k, with $k : 1 \ldots n$, n being the total number of agents present in the system. Transition probabilities $T^{ij}(a^i)$ and rewards $R_k^{ij}(a)$ now depend on a starting state s_i, ending state s_j and a joint action from state s_i, i.e. $a^i = (a_1^i, \ldots a_n^i)$ with $a_k^i \in A_k^i$. The reward function $R_k^{ij}(a)$ is now individual to each agent k. Different agents can receive different rewards for the same state transition. Since each agent k has its own individual reward function, defining a solution concept becomes difficult. Again we will only treat non-randomized policies and we will assume that the Markov Game is ergodic in the sense that there are no transient states presents and a limiting distribution on the joint policies exists. We can now use Equation 2 to define the expected reward for agent k, for a given joint policy α.

$$J_k(\alpha) = \sum_{i=1}^{N} \pi_i(\alpha) \sum_{j=1}^{N} T^{ij}(\alpha) R_k^{ij}(\alpha) \tag{3}$$

Due to the individual reward functions of the agents, it is in general impossible to find an optimal policy for all agents. Instead, equilibrium points are sought. In an equilibrium, no agent can improve its reward by changing its policy if all other agents keep their policy fixed. In a special case of the general Markov game framework, the so-called team games or multi-agent MDPs (MMDPs) [6] optimal policies exist. In this case, the Markov game is purely cooperative and all agents share the same reward function. This specialization allows us to define the optimal policy as the joint agent policy, which maximizes the payoff of all agents. An MMDP can therefore also be seen as an extension of the single agent MDP to the multi-agent case.

3   The Limiting Game of a Simple Grid Problem; Limited State Observability

As an example we describe a 2-agent coordination problem depicted in Figure 1. The game consists of only two grid locations $L1$ and $L2$. Two agents A and B try to coordinate their behavior in order to receive the maximum reward. Each time step both agents can take one of 2 possible actions. If an agent chooses action 0 it stays in the same location, if it chooses action 1 it moves to the other grid location. The transitions in the grid are stochastic, with a action 1 having a probability of 0.9 to change location and a probability of 0.1 to stay in the same location and visa versa for action 0. Each agent chooses an action based only on its present location. The agents cannot observe the location or action of the other agent. The agents receive a reward that is determined by their joint location after moving. Table 1 gives reward functions $R1$ and $R2$ for 2 different learning problems in the grid of Figure 1. Column 1 gives the joint location of the agent, while columns 2 and 3 give the reward for both agents under reward functions $R1$ and $R2$ respectively. This problem can be transformed into a Markov game by considering the product space of the locations and actions. A state in the Markov game

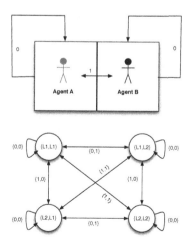

Fig. 1. (Top)The grid-world game with 2 grid locations and 2 non-mobile LA in every location.(Bottom) Markov game representation of the same game.

Table 1. Reward functions for 2 different Markov Games. Each function gives a reward (r_1, r_2) for agent 1 and 2 respectively. Rewards are based on the joint locations of both agents after moving. Function $R1$ results in a Team Game with identical payoffs for both agents, while R2 specifies a conflicting interest Markov game.

state	$R1$	$R2$
{L1,L1}	(0.01,0.01)	(0.5,0.5)
{L1,L2}	(1.0,1.0)	(0.0,1.0)
{L2,L1}	(0.5,0.5)	(1.0,0.0)
{L2,L2}	(0.01,0.01)	(0.1,0.1)

consists of the locations of both agents, e.g. $S1 = \{L1, L1\}$ when both agents are in grid cell 1. The actions that can be taken to move between the states are the joint actions resulting from the individual actions selected by both agents. The limiting game corresponding to each reward function can be determined by calculating the expected reward for each policy in the grid game, provided that the corresponding markov chain is ergodic. This is the case here, so we can calculate transition probabilities for the given grid world problem. For instance in location $\{L1, L1\}$ with joint action $\{0, 0\}$ chosen, the probability to stay in state $\{L1, L1\}$ is 0.81. The probabilities corresponding to moves to states $\{L1, L2\}, \{L2, L1\}$ and $\{L2, L2\}$ are $0.09, 0.09$ and 0.01 respectively. The transition probabilities for all states and joint action pairs can be caluclated this way. With the transition probabilities and the rewards known, we can use Equation 3 to calculate the expected reward.

The complete limiting games corresponding to both reward functions are shown in Table 2. Reward function $R1$ results in a common interest game with a suboptimal equilibrium giving a payoff of 0.4168 and the optimal equilibrium

Table 2. Limiting games for the reward functions given in Table 1 (Top)Common interest game with both an optimal and a suboptimal equilibrium (Bottom) Conflicting interest game with a dominated equilibrium. Equilibria are indicated in bold.

		agent 1		
policy	{0,0}	{0,1}	{1,0}	{1,1}
agent 2 {0,0}	0.38	0.48	0.28	0.38
{0,1}	0.28	0.1432	**0.4168**	0.28
{1,0}	0.48	**0.8168**	0.1432	0.48
{1,1}	0.38	0.48	0.28	0.38

		agent 1		
policy	{0,0}	{0,1}	{1,0}	{1,1}
agent 2 {0,0}	(0.4,0.4)	(0.28,0.68)	(0.52,0.12)	(0.4,0.4)
{0,1}	(0.68,0.28)	(0.496,0.496)	(0.864,0.064)	(0.68,0.28)
{1,0}	(0.12,0.52)	(0.064,0.864)	**(0.176,0.176)**	(0.12,0.52)
{1,1}	(0.4,0.4)	(0.28,0.68)	(0.52,0.12)	(0.4,0.4)

resulting in a payoff of 0.8168. Reward function $R2$ results in a conflicting interest limiting game with a single equilibrium giving a reward of 0.176 to both players. In this game several plays exist that give both players a higher payoff than the equilibrium play. Note that the underlying limiting game in case of full observability would be different. In this case, an agent policy can be described based on joint state-information rather than single agent locations. In this case an agents' policy is described by a 4-tuple, i.e. for each state of the corresponding Markov game an action is given. This would result in an underlying limiting game of size $2^4 \times 2^4$.

4   Learning Automata

Learning Automata are simple reinforcement learners originally introduced to study human behavior. The objective of an automaton is to learn an optimal action, based on past actions and environmental feedback. Formally, the automaton is described by a quadruple $\{A, \beta, p, U\}$ where $A = \{a_1, \ldots, a_r\}$ is the set of possible actions the automaton can perform, p is the probability distribution over these actions, β is a random variable between 0 and 1 representing the evironmental response, and U is a learning scheme used to update p.

4.1   A Simple LA

A single automaton is connected in a feedback loop with its environment. Actions chosen by the automaton are given as input to the environment and the environmental response to this action serves as input to the automaton. Several automaton update schemes with different properties have been studied. Important examples of linear update schemes are linear reward-penalty, linear reward-inaction and linear reward-ϵ-penalty. The philosophy of these schemes is essentially to increase the probability of an action when it results in a success and to decrease it when the response is a failure. The general algorithm is given by:

$$p_m(t+1) = p_m(t) + \alpha_r(1 - \beta(t))(1 - p_m(t)) - \alpha_p\beta(t)p_m(t) \qquad (4)$$
$$\text{if } a_m \text{ is the action taken at time } t$$
$$p_j(t+1) = p_j(t) - \alpha_r(1 - \beta(t))p_j(t) + \alpha_p\beta(t)[(r-1)^{-1} - p_j(t)] \qquad (5)$$
$$\text{if } a_j \neq a_m$$

The constants α_r en α_p are the reward and penalty parameters respectively. When $\alpha_r = \alpha_p$ the algorithm is referred to as linear reward-penalty (L_{R-P}), when $\alpha_p = 0$ it is referred to as linear reward-inaction (L_{R-I}) and when α_p is small compared to α_r it is called linear reward-ϵ-penalty ($L_{R-\epsilon P}$).

4.2   Parameterized Learning Automata

Parameterized Learning Automata (PLA) keep a real number, internal state vector $\mathbf{u}$, which is not necessarily a probability vector. The probabilities of various actions are generated based on this vector $\mathbf{u}$ and a probability generating function $g : \Re^M \times A \to [0,1]$. The probability of action a_i at time t is then given by $p_{a_i}(t) = g(\mathbf{u}(t), a_i)$ with $g(\mathbf{u}, a_i) \geq 0$ and $\sum_{a_i} g(\mathbf{u}, a_i) = 1$, $i = 1 \ldots |A|$, $\forall \mathbf{u}$.[1]

This system allows for a richer update mechanism by adding a random perturbation term to the update scheme, using ideas similar to Simulated Annealing. It can be shown that owing to these perturbations, PLA are able to escape local optima. When the automaton receives a feedback $r(t)$, it updates the parameter vector $\mathbf{u}$ instead of directly modifying the probabilities. In this paper we use following update rule proposed by Thathachar and Phansalkar [7]:

$$u_i(t+1) = u_i(t) + b\beta(t)\frac{\delta \ln g}{\delta u_i}(\mathbf{u}(t), \alpha(t)) + bh'(u_i(t)) + \sqrt{b}s_i(t) \qquad (6)$$

with:

$$h(x) = \begin{cases} -K(x-L)^{2n} & x \geq L \\ 0 & |x| \leq L \\ -K(x+L)^{2n} & x \leq -L \end{cases} \qquad (7)$$

where $h'(x)$ is the derivative of $h(x)$, $\{s_i(t) : k \geq 0\}$ is a set of i.i.d. variables with zero mean and variance σ^2, b is the learning parameter, σ and K are positive constants and n is a positive integer. In this update rule, the second term is a gradient following term, the third term is used to keep the solutions bounded with $|u_i| \leq L$ and the final term is a random noise term that allows the algorithm to escape local optima that are not globally optimal. In [7] the authors show that the algorithm converges weakly to the solution of the Langevin equation, which globally maximizes the appropriate function.

4.3   Automata Games

Automata games, [8,9] were introduced to see if learning automata could be interconnected so as to exhibit group behavior that is attractive for either modeling or controlling complex systems. A play $a(t) = (a_1(t) \ldots a_n(t))$ of n automata is a set of strategies chosen by the automata at stage t. Correspondingly, the outcome is now a vector $\beta(t) = (\beta_1(t) \ldots \beta_n(t))$. At every instance, all automata update their probability distributions based on the responses of the environment. Each automaton participating in the game operates without information concerning the number of participants, their strategies, their payoffs or actions. In general non zero sum games [9] it is shown that when the automata use a L_{R-I} scheme and the game is such that a unique pure equilibrium point exists, convergence is guaranteed. In cases where the game matrix has more than one pure equilibrium, which equilibrium is found depends on the initial conditions. Summarized we have the following [10]

Theorem 1. [10] *When the automata game is repeatedly played with each player making use of the L_{R-I} scheme with a sufficiently small step size, then local convergence is established towards pure Nash equilibria.*

---

[1] An example probability generating function is given in the experiments section.

For team games, in which all players receive the same pay-off for each play, Thathachar and Phansalkar [7] show that a group of PLA using update scheme 6 will converge to the global optimum, even when suboptimal equilibria exist.

4.4 A Network of LA Solving an MDP

The (single agent) problem of controlling a Markov chain can be formulated as a network of automata in which control passes from one automaton to another. In this set-up every action state[2] in the Markov chain has a LA that tries to learn the optimal action probabilities in that state with learning scheme given in Equations (4,5). Only one LA is active at each time step and transition to the next state triggers the LA from that state to become active and take some action. LA^i active in state s_i is not informed of the one-step reward $R^{ij}(a^i)$ resulting from choosing action $a^i \in A^i$ in s_i and leading to state s_j. When state s_i is visited again, LA^i receives two pieces of data: the cumulative reward generated by the process up to the current time step and the current global time. From these, LA^i computes the incremental reward generated since this last visit and the corresponding elapsed global time. The environment response or the input to LA^i is then taken to be:

$$\beta^i(t_i + 1) = \frac{\rho^i(t_i + 1)}{\eta^i(t_i + 1)} \tag{8}$$

where $\rho^i(t_i + 1)$ is the cumulative total reward generated for action a^i in state s_i and $\eta^i(t_i + 1)$ the cumulative total time elapsed. The authors in [5] denote updating scheme as given in Equations (4,5) with environment response as in (8) as learning scheme T1. The following results were proved:

Lemma 1 (Wheeler and Narendra, 1986). *The (N state) Markov chain control problem can be asymptotically approximated by an identical payoff game of N automata.*

Theorem 2 (Wheeler and Narendra, 1986). *Associate with each action state s_i of an N state Markov chain, an automaton LA^i using learning scheme T1 and having r_i actions. Assume that the Markov Chain, corresponding to each policy α is ergodic. Then the decentralized adaptation of the LA is globally ϵ-optimal[3] with respect to the long-term expected reward per time step, i.e. $J(\alpha)$.*

4.5 A Network of LA Solving a Markov Game; Full State Observability

In a Markov Game the action chosen at any state is the joint result of individual action components performed by the agents present in the system. The LA

---

[2] A system state is called an action state, when the agent can select more than one action.

[3] A LA is said to behave ϵ-optimal when it approaches the optimal action probability vector arbitrarily close.

network of the previous section can be extended to the framework of Markov Games just by putting a simple learning automaton for every agent in each state [4].

Instead of putting a single learning automaton in each action state of the system, we propose to put an automaton LA_k^i in each action state s_i with i : $1 \ldots N$ and for each agent k, $k : 1 \ldots n$. At each time step only the automata of a single state are active; a joint action triggers the LA from that state to become active and take some joint action.

As before, LA LA_k^i active for agent k in state s_i is not informed of the one-step reward $R^{ij}(a^i)$ resulting from choosing joint action $a^i = (a_1^i, \ldots, a_n^i)$ with $a_k^i \in A_k^i$ in s_i and leading to state s_j. When state s_i is visited again, all automata LA_k^i receive two pieces of data: the cumulative reward collected by agent k to which the automaton belongs up to the current time step and the current global time. From these, all LA_k^i compute the incremental reward generated since this last visit and the corresponding elapsed global time. The environment response or the input to LA_k^i is exactly the same as in Equation 8.

The following result was proven in [4]:

Theorem 3. *The Learning Automata model proposed for ergodic Markov games with full state observability converges to an equilibrium point in pure strategies for the underlying limited game.*

5   A Network of LA Solving a Markov Game; Limited State Observability

The main difference with the previous setup for learning Markov games [4] is that in this paper we do not assume that agents can observe the complete system state. Instead, each agent learns directly in its own observation space, by associating a learning automaton with each distinct state it can observe. Since an agent does not necessarily observe all state variables, it is possible that it associates the same LA with multiple states, as it cannot distinguish between them. For example, in the 2-location grid world problem of section 3, an agent associates a LA with each location it can occupy, while the full system state consists of the joint locations of all agents. As a consequence, it is not possible for the agents to learn all policies. For instance in the 2-location problem, the automaton associated by agent A with location $L1$ is used in state $S1 = \{L1, L1\}$ as well as state $S2 = \{L1, L2\}$. Therefore it is not possible for agent A to learn a different action in state $S1$ and $S2$. This corresponds to the agent associating actions with locations, without modeling the other agents.

The definition of the update mechanism here is exactly the same as in the previous model, the difference is that here agents only update their observable states which we will call locations to differentiate with the global system state of the corresponding Markov game. This will give the following: LA_k^i, active for agent k in location l_i is not informed of the one-step reward $R_j^i(a^i)$ resulting from choosing joint action $a^i = (a_1^i, \ldots, a_n^i)$ with $a_k^i \in A_k^i$ in s_i and leading to location l_j. Instead, when location l_i is visited again, automaton LA_k^i receive two pieces of data: the cumulative reward for the agent k up to the current time step and the current global time. From these, automaton LA_k^i computes the incremental reward generated since this last visit and the corresponding elapsed global time. The environment response or the input to LA_k^i is then taken to be: $\beta^i(t_i+1) = \frac{\rho^i(t_i+1)}{\eta^i(t_i+1)}$ where $\rho^i(t_i+1)$ is the cumulative total reward generated for action a^i in location l_i and $\eta^i(t_i+1)$ the cumulative total time elapsed. We still assume that the Markov chain of system states generated under each joint agent policy α is ergodic. In the following, we will show that even when the agents have only knowledge of their own location, in some situations it is still possible to find an equilibrium point of the underlying limiting game.

6   Illustration on the Simple Grid Problem

Figure 2 (Left) and (Right) show the results obtained with the L_{R-I} update scheme in the Markov games using reward function $R1$ and $R2$ respectively. Since we are interested in the value that the agents converge to, we show a single typical run, rather than an average over multiple runs. To show convergence to the different equilibria we restart the agents every 2 million time steps, with action probabilities initialized randomly.

We can observe that with in the game with reward function $R1$ agents move to either the optimal or the suboptimal equilibrium of the underlying limiting game given in Table 2(Top), depending on their initialization. Using $R2$ the agents always converge to same, single equilibrium of the limiting game of

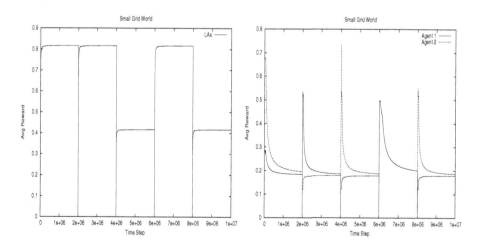

Fig. 2. Results for the grid world problem of Figure 1 (Left)Average reward over time for agent 1, using identical rewards of $R1$ (Right) Average reward over time for both agents, using reward function $R2$. Settings were $\alpha_p = 0, \alpha_r = 0.05$.

Table 3. Results of L_{R-I} and PLAs on the small grid world problem with reward function $R1$. Table shows the average convergence to each equilibrium, total convergence over all trials and average time steps needed for convergence. Standard deviations are given between parentheses. PLA settings were $b = 0.1, \sigma = 0.2, K = L = n = 1$.

	Eq.	Exp. Reward	Average (/20)	Total (/12500)	Avg Time
L_{R-I}	((1,0),(0,1))	0.41	1.73(3.39)	1082	1218.78(469.53)
$\alpha_r = 0.1$	((0,1),(1,0))	0.82	15.62(4.62)	9762	
L_{R-I}	((1,0),(0,1))	0.41	0.82(3.30)	515	11858.85(5376.29)
$\alpha_r = 0.01$	((0,1),(1,0))	0.82	19.14(3.34)	11961	
PLA	((1,0),(0,1))	0.41	0.08(0.33)	50	21155.24(8431.28)
	((0,1),(1,0))	0.82	19.81(0.59)	12380	

Table 2(Bottom). Even when the agents start out using policies that give a higher payoff, over time they move to the equilibrium.

Figure 2 (Left) shows that even when all automata receive the same reward convergence to the global optimum is not guaranteed using the L_{R-I} scheme. To obtain improved convergence to the optimum we apply the algorithm with PLA in each location. Each PLA has a parametervector $\mathbf{u} = (u_0, u_1)$ with parameters corresponding to actions 0 and 1. The action probabilities are calculated using following probability generating function:

$$g(\mathbf{u}(t), a_i) = \frac{e^{u_i(t)}}{\sum_j e^{u_j(t)}} \tag{9}$$

Table 3 shows a comparison of PLA with L_{R-I} on the grid world problem with reward function $R1$. For these experiments, each automaton was initialized to play action 0 with a probability of $0.18, 0.35, 0.5, 0.65$, or 0.82. This gives a total of 625 initial configurations for the 4 automata in the grid world problem. For each configuration, 20 runs were performed, resulting in a total of 12500 runs for each algorithm. Table 3 gives the average number of times the algorithms converged to each of the equilibria, the total equilibrium convergence over all runs and the average amount of time steps needed for all LA to converge. A learning automaton was considered to have converged if it played a single action with a probability of 0.98 or more. Each trial was given a maximum of 250000 time steps to let the automata converge. It is immediately clear from Table 3 that the PLA converge to the optimal equilibrium far more often, but on average take more time to converge.

Figure 3 shows results on an initial configuration for which the L_{R-I} automata always converge to the suboptimal equilibrium. The PLA, however, are able to escape the local optimum and converge to the globally optimal equilibrium point. Due to the random noise added to the update scheme, the PLA do receive a slightly lower pay-off than is predicted in Table 2(a).

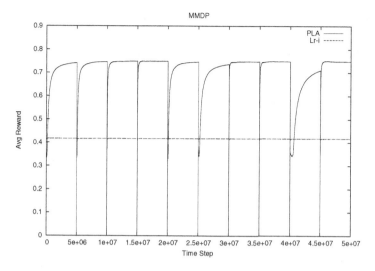

Fig. 3. Comparison of PLA with L_{R-I} on the grid world problem of Figure 1, using reward function $R1$. The automata were initialized to play their suboptimal equilibrium action with probability 0.82. Settings were $\alpha_r = 0.01$ for L_{R-I} and $b = 0.1, \sigma = 0.2, K = L = n = 1$ for the PLA.

7   Theoretical Analysis

The above illustration shows the convergence of the proposed LA-model to one of the equilibrium points of the underlying limiting game. In case of the 2-state example given above, we can observe that with reward function $R1$ agents move to either the optimal or the suboptimal equilibrium, depending on their initialization. Using $R2$ the agents always converge to same, single equilibrium. Even when the agents start out using policies that give a higher payoff, over time they move to the equilibrium. We can justify these results with a proof of convergence.

Theorem 4. *The network of LA that was proposed here for myopic agents in Markov Games, converges to a pure equilibrium point of the limiting game provided that the Markov chain of system states generated under each joint agent policy is ergodic and agents' transition probabilities[4] do not depend on other agents' activities.*

Proof Outline. This result will follow from the fact that a game of reward-inaction LA will always converge to a pure equilibrium point of the game, see Theorem 1.

---

[4] We refer here to transitions of the local agent state e.g. an agent's movement in the grid. Transitions between system states in the global Markov game generally depend on the actions of all agents present in the system, as can been seen in the example of Figure 1.

Consider all LA present in the system. The interaction between these LA can be formulated as a game with each LA as a player. Rewards in this game are triggered by the joint LA actions as follows: the joint action of all LA in the game corresponds to a joint agent policy. This policy has an expected average reward J_i for each agent i. All LA that are associated with agent i (but which reside in different locations of the system) will get exactly this reward in the LA game. In [5] it is shown that under the ergodicity requirement stated above, this game approximates the LA interaction, even though the LA in the system update in an asynchronous manner.

The idea is to prove that this LA game has the same equilibrium points as the limiting game the agents are playing. If this is the case the result follows from Theorem 1. It is easy to see that an equilibrium in the limiting game is also an equilibrium of the LA-game, since in any situation where it is impossible for a single agent to improve its reward, it is also impossible for a single automaton to improve its reward.

Now assume that we can find an equilibrium policy α in the LA-game that is not an equilibrium point of the limiting game. In this case an agent a and a new policy β can be found that produces more reward for agent a than policy α and differs from α in the actions of at least 2 LA, belonging to the same agent a.

A single agent Markov problem can then be formulated for agent a as follows: the state space is exactly the set of locations for agent a, the action set consist of the action set of agent a (and these can be mapped to joint actions by assuming that the other agents are playing their part of policy α), the transitions are given by agent a's transitions (they were assumed to be independent from other agents activities) and finally the rewards for a given action of agent a is given by the rewards for the corresponding joint actions were the other agents play their policy part of α. For this Markov chain the result of [5] applies (see theorem 2): the problem can be approximated by a limiting game τ with only optimal equilibria. However it cannot be the case that agent a's part of policy α is an optimal equilibrium in τ, since the part of policy β gives a better reward.

In [5] it is shown that a better policy can be constructed by changing the action in only one state of the MDP. So this means that a single automaton of agent a can change its action to receive a higher reward than agent a's part of policy α. However, this contradicts the original assumption of α being an equilibrium point of the LA game. Therefore, the assumption made was wrong, an equilibrium point from the LA game should also be an equilibrium point in the limiting game.

8   Related Work

Few approaches toward analyzing multi-stage MAS settings can be found in literature. In [11] the Nash Q-values of the equilibrium point of the limiting game are considered. Nash Q-values are Q-functions over joint actions. These are updated based on the Nash equilibrium behavior over the current Nash Q-values. The idea is to let these Q-values learn to reach the Nash Q-values of the equilibrium of the limiting game through repeated play. However only in very restrictive cases, this actually happens. Besides, the approach assumes that the agents have full knowledge of the system: the agents know their current joint state, the joint action played and the reinforcement signals all agents receive. In [12] team Markov Games are also approximated as a sequence of intermediate games. In team Markov Games, all agents get the same reward function and the agents should learn to select the same optimal equilibrium strategy. The authors present optimal adaptive learning and prove convergence to a Nash equilibrium of the limiting game, however agents know the joint actions played, they all receive the same reward and thus are able to build the game structure. In [13] the agents are not assumed to have a full view of the world. All agents contribute to a collective global reward function, but since domain knowledge is missing, independent agents use filtering methods in order to try to recover the underlying true reward signal from the noisy one that is observed. This approach seems to work well in the example domains shown.

9   Discussion

In this paper the behavior of individual agents learning in a shared environment is analyzed by considering the single stage limiting game, obtained by considering agent policies as single actions. We show that when agents are fully ignorant about the other agents in the environment and only know their own current location, a network of learning automata can still find an equilibrium point of the underlying single stage game, provided that the Markov game is ergodic and that the agents do not interfere each others transition probabilities.

We have shown that local optimum points of the underlying limiting games are found using the L_{R-I} update scheme. The parameterized learning automata scheme enables us to find global optimum points in case of team Markov Games [7]. In more general Markov games coordinated exploration techniques could be considered to let the agents reach more fair solutions [14].

References

1. Nowé, A., Verbeeck, K., Peeters, M.: Learning automata as a basis for multi-agent reinforcement learning. In: Tuyls, K., 't Hoen, P.J., Verbeeck, K., Sen, S. (eds.) LAMAS 2005. LNCS (LNAI), vol. 3898, pp. 71–85. Springer, Heidelberg (2006)
2. Littman, M.: Markov games as a framework for multi-agent reinforcement learning. In: Proceedings of the 11th International Conference on Machine Learning, pp. 322–328 (1994)
3. Osborne, J., Rubinstein, A.: A Course in Game Theory. MIT Press, Cambridge (1994)
4. Vrancx, P., Verbeeck, K., Nowé, A.: Decentralized learning of markov games. Technical Report COMO/12/2006, Computational Modeling Lab, Vrije Universiteit Brussel, Brussels, Belgium (2006)
5. Wheeler, R., Narendra, K.: Decentralized learning in finite markov chains. IEEE Transactions on Automatic Control AC-31, 519–526 (1986)

6. Boutilier, C.: Planning, learning and coordination in multiagent decision processes. In: Proceedings of the 6th Conference on Theoretical Aspects of Rationality and Knowledge, Renesse, Holland, pp. 195–210 (1996)
7. Thathachar, M., Phansalkar, V.: Learning the global maximum with parameterized learning automata. IEEE Transactions on Neural Networks 6(2), 398–406 (1995)
8. Narendra, K., Thathachar, M.: Learning Automata: An Introduction. Prentice-Hall International, Inc, Englewood Cliffs (1989)
9. Thathachar, M., Sastry, P.: Networks of Learning Automata: Techniques for Online Stochastic Optimization. Kluwer Academic Publishers, Dordrecht (2004)
10. Sastry, P., Phansalkar, V., Thathachar, M.: Decentralized learning of nash equilibria in multi-person stochastic games with incomplete information. IEEE Transactions on Systems, Man, and Cybernetics 24(5), 769–777 (1994)
11. Hu, J., Wellman, M.: Nash q-learning for general-sum stochastic games. Journal of Machine Learning Research 4, 1039–1069 (2003)
12. Wang, X., Sandholm, T.: Reinforcement learning to play an optimal nash equilibrium in team markov games. In: Proceedings of the Neural Information Processing Systems: Natural and Synthetic (NIPS) conference (2002)
13. Chang, Y.H., Ho, T., Kaelbling, L.P.: All learning is local: Multi-agent learning in global reward games. In: Thrun, S., Saul, L., Schölkopf, B. (eds.) Advances in Neural Information Processing Systems 16, MIT Press, Cambridge (2004)
14. Verbeeck, K., Nowé, A., Parent, J., Tuyls, K.: Exploring selfish reinforcement learning in repeated games with stochastic rewards. Technical report, Accepted at Journal of Autonomous Agents and Multi-Agent Systems (to appear 2007)

Multi-agent Learning by
Distributed Feature Extraction

Michael Wurst

University of Dortmund, AI Unit
michael.wurst@uni-dortmund.de

Abstract. Finding the right data representation is essential for virtually every machine learning task. We discuss an extension of this representation problem. In the collaborative representation problem, the aim is to find for each learning agent in a multi-agent system an optimal data representation, such that the overall performance of the system is optimized, while not assuming that all agents learn the same underlying concept. Also, we analyze the problem of keeping the common terminology in which agents express their hypothesis as compact and comprehensible as possible by forcing them to use the same features, where this is possible. We analyze the complexity of this problem and show under which conditions an optimal solution can be found. We then propose a simple heuristic algorithm and show that this algorithm can efficiently be implemented in a multi-agent system. The approach is exemplified on the problem of collaborative media organization and evaluated on a several synthetic and real world datasets.

1 Introduction

Finding an adequate data representation is a key to successful machine learning. Such a representation is often expressed in terms of a feature space, the space in which items in the universe of discourse are described. The problem of finding an optimal feature space can be denoted as *representation problem*. Methods that solve this problem are referred to as *feature extraction* or *feature construction* methods [1]. This term covers such diverse approaches as feature extraction from raw data, feature selection, feature space transformation, dimensionality reduction, meta data extraction, etc.

Feature extraction is a very general approach. By constructing appropriate features, simple data mining algorithms can be extended to handle complex concepts, as e.g. trigonometric relationships, without modifying them [2]. Kernel methods, that have found increasing attention in the recent years, can be regarded as feature transformation methods as well [3]. They do however not create the target feature space explicitly but through an implicit mapping. The same holds for dimensionality reduction methods such as Principal Component Analysis (PCA) or Singular Value Decomposition (SVD) (see e.g. [4]).

A family of methods that are particularly powerful for feature extraction are so called *wrapper approaches* [5]. The idea of wrapper approaches is to invoke

K. Tuyls et al. (Eds.): Adaptive Agents and MAS III, LNAI 4865, pp. 239–254, 2008.
© Springer-Verlag Berlin Heidelberg 2008

the target (machine learning) method subsequently with different feature sets and to apply an objective function to measure how well suited a feature set is for solving the problem. Optimization algorithms can then be used to select an optimal feature set. A downside of this generality is, however, that the optimization process can be computationally very demanding. This can be especially a problem in agent system that work with restricted resources. e.g. autonomous robots. If we face only a single learning task, there is not much, that we can do about this.

In many current scenarios, not a single, separated task is learned, but rather several, partially related ones. Work in multi-agent learning, for instance, focuses primarily on the question of how agents can share their experience to improve the overall performance of a system. Usually it is assumed that the agents learn the same or similar concepts. They can profit from the experience other agents made or evolve a common behavior by sharing training examples or by asking other agents for advice ([6,7,8]). This principle has been applied for supervised as well as for reinforcement learning.

A related topic that recently regained a lot of attention is *multi-task learning* [9,10]. The idea is, that solving learning several tasks, that are related to each other, at once, may be easier than solving them individually. This assumption is based on the observation, that some learning tasks resemble each other to some extent and that parameters to solve these tasks resemble each other as well. First approaches to multi-task learning used for instance a common set of inner neurons in a neural net, which they shared among several tasks [9]. These common neurons encode common parameters among different tasks. More current methods for multi-task learning make use of SVM, kernel methods [11,12] and Gaussian processes [13] to achieve a corresponding effect. The idea in all cases is to have a class of models (for instance SVM) and several learning tasks. Then a distribution among the parameters of the models is assumed, that allows to group tasks into clusters of tasks with similar parameters. [14] discussed the problem of outlier tasks and how to robustify existing approaches to multi-task learning. Finally, [15] proposes an interesting variant to the problem by allowing to calculate a small number of artificial features, that are common to all tasks.

Almost all approaches to multi-task and to multi-agent learning make very restrictive assumptions. For instance, they assume that all learners use the same underlying model class and the same set of features. Multi-task learning does furthermore assume that all learning tasks are solved at once in parallel.

In this work, a more general viewpoint is taken. Based on the paradigm of wrapper approaches, the problem of selecting appropriate features is analyzed as a *combinatorial optimization problem*. We assume a possibly very large set of features $\mathcal{X}$. The task is to find for each agent and each task a subset $\mathbf{X} \subseteq \mathcal{X}$ such that the estimated accuracy, by the task is solved, is optimized.

Furthermore, we want the union set of all local feature sets to be as small as possible. Features are the building blocks with which the agents express their hypothesis about the concept they aim to capture. It is desirable that the agents use a common vocabulary (and thus features) to express hypothesis. First, this allows agents not only to share examples but also hypothesis or other information in subsequent steps. Second, agent systems are rarely closed systems. Often these systems communicate with other systems or with human users. This communication is simplified a lot, if all agents use the same or a similar terminology. Imagine, for instance, agents that inform users about the relation between different environmental factors and water pollution at different places. From a point of view of accuracy, it could be for instance equally well for a given agent to express the degree of water pollution in relation to water temperature or in relation to the amount of bacteria in the water. If, however, all agents expressed their hypothesis in terms of water temperature so far, it will be confusing for the user to hear about the number of bacteria in a new case. Even worse, this will make it very hard for her, to compare the hypothesis given by different agents. If all agents express their hypothesis in terms of water temperature, comparing hypothesis is on the other hand a very simple task. Therefore, it can even pay to force agents to use the same features, if this means that the overall accuracy is slightly decreased.

We will analyze how concepts as feature relevance or redundancy and minimality, well known from single-task learning, can be generalized to the case of multi-agent learning. This will lead to the *collaborative representation problem,* thus the problem of finding an optimal local feature set for each agent and each task in a set of tasks. It will be shown that constraints on the order in which tasks are solved have an influence on whether we can guarantee to find an optimal solution. Based on this analysis, a simple, heuristic algorithm, called prioritized forward selection, is proposed. This algorithm solves two problems. First, it forces the agents to use the same features and thus the same vocabulary to express their hypothesis. Second, it helps agents to achieve a faster increase in accuracy while performing feature selection compared to traditional forward selection by helping them to focus on relevant features only. If resources are limited, good results can be achieved, even if only few cycles of feature selection are performed.

2   Feature Extraction and Feature Relevance

Almost all research on feature extraction has focused on classification and regression tasks. In the following we assume, that a feature X is a vector, assigning a continuous value to each observation in a given domain. Sets of features will be denoted as $\mathbf{X}$. The set of all possible features is denoted as $\mathcal{X}$.

Classification is defined as follows.

Definition 1. *The aim of* classification *as a learning task is to find a function* $h : \mathbf{X} \to C$ *that approximates a true concept* $f : \mathbf{X} \to C$ *given some observations.* [4]

Classification plays an important role in may applications, such as pattern recognition, decision support, information retrieval, etc. Given a classification task, we can separate the features in $\mathbf{X}$ into relevant features and irrelevant features according to this task.

In [16] a systematic analysis of feature relevance is given. The authors argue, that concerning a (classification) task, features can not only be relevant or irrelevant, but relevant features must be further divided into weakly and strongly relevant features. The following formalization follows the presentation in [17].

Definition 2. *A feature $X \in \mathbf{X}$ is strongly relevant for classification with respect to features $\mathbf{X}$, iff*

$$P(C|\mathbf{X}) \neq P(C|\mathbf{X}\backslash\{X\})$$

Thus omitting feature X changes in the conditional probability distribution concerning the class value.

Definition 3. *A feature $X \in \mathbf{X}$ is weakly relevant for classification with respect to features $\mathbf{X}$, iff*

$$P(C|\mathbf{X}) = P(C|\mathbf{X}\backslash\{X\})$$

and

$$\exists \mathbf{X}' \subseteq (\mathbf{X}\backslash\{X\}) : P(C|\mathbf{X}', X) \neq P(C|\mathbf{X}')$$

For features that are weakly relevant, omitting them may lead to a change in the conditional probability, depending on which other features are selected.

Definition 4. *A feature $X \in \mathbf{X}$ is irrelevant for classification with respect to features $\mathbf{X}$, iff*

$$\forall \mathbf{X}' \subseteq (\mathbf{X}\backslash\{X\}) : P(C|\mathbf{X}', X) = P(C|\mathbf{X}')$$

If a feature can be omitted without affecting the conditional distribution not regarding which other features are selected, it is irrelevant for the classification task, as it can be omitted under all circumstances.

Feature extraction solves the combinatorial problem of finding a subset $\mathbf{X} \subseteq \mathcal{X}$ that contains no irrelevant and as few weakly relevant features as possible. Existing approaches to feature selection can be roughly classified in wrappers, filters and embedded methods [1]. Filters select features without invoking the actual learning process. They mostly produce a ranking of the features, according to their relevance. While these methods are very efficient, they usually cannot capture feature interaction appropriately, as features are regarded only individually and not in combination with each other. Embedded method are feature selection methods that are part of an existing data mining algorithm. An example are decision tree learners.

3   Generalized Feature Relevance and Minimal Subsets

Almost all existing work on feature relevance and redundancy has been focusing on classification tasks. While classification plays an important role for agent learning, there are many other relevant tasks, such as clustering, that should be regarded as well.

Following the paradigm of wrapper approaches, we give a very general definition of an agent learning task. The idea is, that a data mining task is a black box, the gets a feature set as input and delivers a quality measure as output. We will denote this quality as *accuracy* in the following.

Definition 5. *An* agent learning task *is any task for which we can define a accuracy measure that depends on the subset of features* $\mathbf{X}' \subseteq \mathcal{X}$ *that the agent uses to solve the task*

$$q : 2^{\mathcal{X}} \to \mathbb{R}$$

For the special case of classification, the quality is estimated as the expected classification error on new observations [4]. Other quality functions can be defined, for instance, for clustering tasks [18].

Given a set of features $\mathbf{X} \subseteq \mathcal{X}$ we define the following.

Definition 6. *A feature* $X \in \mathbf{X}$ *is* strongly relevant *with respect to features* $\mathbf{X}$, *iff*

$$\forall \mathbf{X}' \subseteq \mathbf{X} \backslash \{X\} : q(\mathbf{X}') < q(\mathbf{X}' \cup \{X\})$$

Thus omitting the feature X leads always to a performance that is inferior than the one achieved if X is part of the feature space.

Definition 7. *A feature* $X \in \mathbf{X}$ *is* weakly relevant *with respect to features* $\mathbf{X}$, *iff it is not strongly relevant and*

$$\exists \mathbf{X}' \subseteq \mathbf{X} : q(\mathbf{X}' \backslash \{X\}) < q(\mathbf{X}')$$

For features that are weakly relevant, omitting them may lead to a decrease in performance dependent on the which other features are used for data mining. Many learners can for instance easily deal with linear transformations of features (e.g. SVM). If a feature and a linear transformation of the feature are contained in the features space, both features are not strongly relevant, as either one can be omitted, as long as the other one is used.

Definition 8. *A feature* $X \in \mathbf{X}$ *is* irrelevant *with respect to features* $\mathbf{X}$, *iff*

$$\neg \exists \mathbf{X}' \subseteq \mathbf{X} : q(\mathbf{X}' \backslash \{\mathbf{X}\}) < q(\mathbf{X}')$$

If a feature can be omitted without affecting the accuracy not regarding which other features are used, it is irrelevant for the task, as it can be omitted under all circumstances.

Now we can give a formal definition for combinatorial feature extraction problem.

Definition 9. *An* optimal, minimal feature set *is such a set of features* $\mathbf{X} \subseteq \mathcal{X}$ *that* $q(\mathbf{X})$ *is maximized and there is no* $\mathbf{X'} \subseteq \mathcal{X}$, *such that* $q(\mathbf{X}) = q(\mathbf{X'})$ *and* $|\mathbf{X'}| < |\mathbf{X}|$.

This is also sometimes referred to as *minimal sufficient feature subset* for the case of classification (see e.g. [1], page 20). It is not necessary to state that a minimal feature set should not contain any redundant or irrelevant features, as this is entailed by the minimality condition.

Finding an optimal feature set is a non-trivial problem. As we cannot make any assumption concerning the nature of q, optimizing this objective function involves in the worst case evaluating each subset of $\mathcal{X}$ which is exponential in the size of this set.

Several search heuristics have been proposed (see e.g. [1]). Probably best known are forward selection and backward elimination. The forward selection algorithms starts with an empty set of features $\mathbf{X} = \emptyset$. In each round, each feature not yet in the $\mathbf{X}$ is added to the current feature set and the quality of the resulting feature set is assessed. In each round, a single feature that increases the objective function maximally is added to the current set of features. If no such feature exists the algorithm terminates.

Backward elimination starts with a given feature set $\mathbf{X} = \mathcal{X}$ and removes in each round the feature for which the resulting feature set leads to an optimal accuracy. If no such feature exists or if all features were deselected, the algorithm terminates.

4   The Collaborative Representation Problem

A set of learning tasks will be denoted as T. We assume that each agent solves exactly one agent learning task, such that there is a one-to-one relation between tasks and agents.

Each task $t_i \in T$ is connected to an objective function q_i, as described above.

Definition 10. *The overall accuracy of a several data mining tasks* T *is the sum over all individual qualities*

$$q_T^*(\mathbf{X_1}, .., \mathbf{X_i}, ., \mathbf{X_{|T|}}) = \sum_{i=1}^{|T|} q_i(\mathbf{X_i})$$

where $\mathbf{X_i} \subseteq \mathcal{X}$ *denotes the feature set used to solve task* t_i.

Given more than one learning agent, we can generalize the notion of feature relevance and feature set optimality. To do so, we regard the accumulated feature set that contains exactly the features that are used for at least one task in T.

Definition 11. *The* accumulated set of features *is the union of all locally selected features*

$$\mathbf{X_T} = \bigcup_{i=1}^{|T|} \mathbf{X_i}$$

Example 1. Assume an application in which personal agents learn the preferences of their users concerning music. Also assume, that we can extract three features from each music clip that represent, for instance, loudness X_l, rhythm X_r and color X_c of the music, thus $\mathcal{X} = \{X_l, X_r, X_c\}$. Each user defines a learning task for her personal agent by tagging music clips with a positive or a negative label, according whether she likes them or not. This results in one agent learning task per user, for which we assume a true but unknown concept f_i. For each of the users, another subset of $\mathcal{X}$ maybe relevant. For the first user, preferences may only depend on the loudness, which should be high, e.g. $f_1 \equiv X > 2.3$. For a second user, preference may depend on the loudness and the rhythm, e.g. $f_2 \equiv X_l + X_r > 3$. For a third user, the preferences could depend on the loudness again, which should however be small in this case, e.g. $f_3 \equiv X_l < 1$. The task for each agent is to find a subset of features and a predictive model, that captures the preferences of the corresponding user in a way that allows predictions with a high accuracy. If the true concepts were known, optimal feature subsets $\mathbf{X_1} = \{X_l\}$, $\mathbf{X_2} = \{X_l, X_r\}$ and $\mathbf{X_3} = \{X_l\}$ could be selected easily. The accumulated set of features is then $\mathbf{X_T} = \{X_l, X_r\}$. In a real application, we can only approximate the real concepts f_i by hypothesis, as described above.

We can now generalize the notions of strongly and weakly relevant features.

Definition 12. *A feature $X \in \mathbf{X_T}$ is* globally strongly relevant *with respect to features $\mathbf{X_T}$, iff it is strongly relevant for at least one task $t \in T$.*

If X is deleted from $\mathbf{X_T}$ the overall accuracy decreases, as it must by definition decrease for at least one task.

Definition 13. *A feature $X \in \mathbf{X_T}$ is* globally weakly relevant *with respect to features $\mathbf{X_T}$, iff it is not globally strongly relevant and is weakly relevant at least for one task $t \in T$.*

Globally weakly relevant features can be omitted, as long as there are alternative features left that replace them in a way that does not affect the global accuracy.

Definition 14. *A feature $X \in \mathbf{X_T}$ is* globally irrelevant *with respect to features $\mathbf{X_T}$, iff it is irrelevant for every task.*

Globally irrelevant features can be omitted from $\mathbf{X_T}$ in any case without affecting the accuracy at all, as by definition, they do not affect the accuracy of any individual agent learning task.

Definition 15. *An optimal set of feature sets selects for each task $t_i \in T$ a set of features $\mathbf{X_i} \subseteq \mathcal{X}$ in a way that $q^*(\mathbf{X_1}, ..., \mathbf{X_{|T|}})$ is maximized and that there does not exist another set of features $\mathbf{X'_1}...\mathbf{X'_{|T|}}$ for each task, such that*

$$q^*(\mathbf{X_1}, ..., \mathbf{X_{|T|}}) = q^*(\mathbf{X'_1}, ..., \mathbf{X'_{|T|}}) \text{ and } |\mathbf{X_T}'| < |\mathbf{X_T}|, \text{ where } \mathbf{X'_T} = \bigcup_{i=1}^{|T|} \mathbf{X'_i}.$$

An optimal, minimal set of feature sets $\mathbf{X_1}...\mathbf{X_{|T|}}$ does not contain any globally irrelevant features or features that are redundant with respect to $\mathbf{X_T}$.

Why does it matter, whether the set of accumulated features is minimal? Assume the following example.

Example 2. A first agent tries to learn the concept $f_1(X_a, X_b, X_c, X_d) \equiv X_a + X_b > 4$ from data, a second agents tries to learn $f_2(X_a, X_b, X_c, X_d) = X_b + X_d < 2$. We assume, that $X_b = X_c$. In this case, it would be perfectly reasonable from a accuracy point of view, to select $\mathbf{X_1} = \{X_a, X_b\}$ and $\mathbf{X_2} = \{X_c, X_d\}$. Both feature sets are locally optimal and do not contain redundant features. The accumulated feature set $\mathbf{X_T} = \{X_a, X_b, X_c, X_d\}$ does however contain redundancy. This is not desirable for several reasons. First, if the feature sets are inspected by a human user, it is hard for her to see the relationship between the tasks. Assume an analyst, that tries to discover patterns in several branches of a large company. It is much easier to recognize patterns or influence factors known from another case than being faced with completely new features. Second, features can be seen as atomic parts of a representation language to express a hypothesis. To allow for optimal cooperation, agents should share the same representation language, as far as this is possible. Thus it would be much better, if both agents chose X_b (or X_c) leading to an accumulated feature set $\mathbf{X'_T} = \{X_a, X_b, X_d\}$ or $\mathbf{X''_T} = \{X_a, X_c, X_d\}$ respectively, both of which do not contain any redundant features.

5 Distributed Feature Extraction

The problem of distributed feature extraction, is the task of finding a set of optimal (and minimal) feature sets $\mathbf{X_i} \subseteq \mathcal{X}$ for each task $t \in T$.

This problem inherits its NP-completeness from the single-task optimization problem as we can neither make any assumption on the nature of the objective functions q_i nor on how they are related. As for the single-task case, we can still apply heuristic search schemes.

A very obvious way to do distributed feature extraction would be to apply heuristic optimization in each agent individually. There are two reasons, why not to do so:

1. It would not necessarily yield an accumulated feature set that is optimal *and* minimal. This is however a desirable property, as was shown above.
2. Solving several learning tasks can be computationally less expensive, than solving them independently, if it is possible to share information among these learning tasks. In the remainder of this chapter we will show different methods of how to do so.

In this section we present a simple generalized forward selection algorithm that will be the point of departure for further optimizations. First, we must further specify the scenario, we are talking about, in terms of the temporal order in which tasks are solved. While for stating the distributed representation problem, the order in which the tasks are solved did not have any significance, this order plays an important role for solving it.

In the following we assume an order relation on tasks, that denotes that the agent have to solve a task before another one is solved.

Definition 16. *The* temporal order relation *for tasks* $\prec \subseteq T^2$ *represents constraints on the order, in which the tasks have to be solved, i.e.* $t_i \prec t_j$, *denotes that task* t_i *must be solved by the agents before* t_j *is solved, which as a consequence means, that the feature set* $\mathbf{X_i}$ *must be chosen, before* $\mathbf{X_j}$ *is chosen.* $\prec$ *is assumed to be transitive and anti-symmetric.*

If there are no restrictions on the order in which the learning tasks must be solved by the agents, a simple approach to find a minimal subset of accumulated features is to solve all tasks at once. Let us assume an agent, that enumerates all possible subsets $\mathbf{X} \subseteq \mathcal{X}$. For each subset $\mathbf{X}$, optimal feature selection is applied for each task separately and the accumulated accuracy and the size of the accumulated feature set is measured. Similar to optimal feature selection for a single task, this would also lead to an optimal and minimal feature set for several tasks (although it would be computationally extremely expensive).

However, in many applications we cannot assume that all tasks are solved at once. Mostly, tasks are solved in some kind of a temporal order. In real world scenarios, agents face new tasks continuously. Still, the system has to output some result for the first task it faces.

Given constraints on the order in which task are solved, can we still find an optimal and minimal feature set? Surprisingly, the answer is no, in general. In fact, it is not possible to formulate any algorithm that guarantees to find such a set in general, given at least two tasks $t_i, t_j \in T$ that are in temporal relation to each other.

Theorem 1. *There is no algorithm that can guarantee to find an optimal, minimal set of feature sets, given that* $\exists t_i, t_j \in T : t_i \prec t_j$.

Proof. As a proof, we construct a counter example. Assume that the feature selection algorithm would first face t_i, for which the concept $f_i(X_a, X_b) \equiv (X_a < 4)$ should be induced. Assume, that $X_a = X_b$, for $X_b < 4$ and $X_a = 4$ else. For this task, either $\{X_a\}$ or $\{X_b\}$ can be chosen to optimize it. Let us assume that $\{X_a\}$ is chosen. The second task t_j the concept $f_j(X_a, X_b) \equiv X_b > 10$ is faced. In this case, $\{X_b\}$ must be chosen. This leads to a non-minimal overall feature set $\mathbf{X_T} = \{X_a, X_b\}$. If for t_i, $\{X_b\}$ would have been chosen, the we could construct a similar example leading to the a non-minimal subset $\mathbf{X_T} = \{X_a, X_b\}$. Thus any choice for the first task, can turn out to be suboptimal in the second task. Therefore, no algorithm that solves t_i and t_j in sequential order can guarantee to yield a minimal and optimal set of features $\mathbf{X_T}$.

While this is somewhat discouraging, it still allows us to look for heuristic approaches that lead at least to approximately minimal sets of feature sets.

6   Prioritized Forward Selection

In the following, an extension to forward selection is proposed, that is denoted as *prioritized forward selection*. The basic idea is, that if we solve a task t, we first take a look at all tasks T', that already are solved. This leads to the accumulated feature set $\mathbf{X_{T'}} = \bigcup_{t_i \in T'} \mathbf{X_i}$ containing all feature used in at least one task, already solved or currently solved. Then we perform forward selection twice. First, we perform forward selection using only the features in $\mathbf{X_{T'}}$. Thus an agent first tries to optimize the local feature set using only such features already used by other agents and thus already part of the common vocabulary. This is done just as in the case of traditional forward selection by subsequently adding features until no further improvement can be achieved. Then the agent performs a second forward selection using all remaining features in $\mathcal{X}$. This can be combined with a threshold ε, such that new features are only added, if this increases the performance above a certain level.

Prioritized forward selection serves two purposes. First, it helps to at least heuristically find small accumulated feature sets, which is an important property when facing feature extraction for several tasks. A second purpose, at least equally important, is that efficiency and even accuracy can be increased.

The idea is the following. We assume that in most application areas, some of the tasks in T resemble each other to some extend and require similar feature sets to be solved optimally. If good solutions for some tasks were already identified, applying these "know-to-work-well" features on new tasks seems quite promising, as if the new task is similar to an existing one, the set $\mathbf{X_{T'}}$ will already contain all relevant features. Selecting features from $\mathbf{X_{T'}}$ is always more efficient than selecting from $\mathcal{X}$, as $\mathbf{X_{T'}} \subseteq \mathcal{X}$. Especially, if we consider feature construction, where $\mathcal{X}$ might contain millions of possible features, this can make the problem for subsequent tasks much easier to solve.

Furthermore, it may even lead to better solutions. Agents often work with bounded resources. As a consequence, they must terminate the feature extraction process after a given amount of time, or after the performance is "good enough", thus a given accuracy threshold is exceeded. Finding relevant features as early as possible is therefore crucial, as it can speed up the process of finding a good solution. Given a maximum effort an agent allows for optimization, it can even improve the solutions. If good solutions are evaluated late in the feature extraction process, they might not be found at all, if the process is terminated early on.

The approach proposed above can easily be implemented in a multi-agent system. The idea is, that each agent facing a learning task queries the other agents for features. Each agent that already solved its task responds with the features used in an optimal and minimal solution. In this way, the set $\mathbf{X_{T'}} \subseteq \mathcal{X}$ is assembled in a fully distributed way.

We propose a model for feature sharing that is based on the contract net protocol. Agents send a queries for features to other agents and receive bids, possibly containing a score of how well the feature performed. Then they actually request the features.

We propose an optional scoring framework especially tailored to the collaborative media organization application presented in section 7 or similar applications. Agents query other agents with a message that contains a set of observation example ids. In the case of collaborative media organization, this could be an identifier that uniquely identifies media items. These observation ids may additionally contain label or feedback information. We denote the last case as supervised feature query, while an unsupervised feature query denotes the case in which no such information is available.

An agent i that receives an unsupervised query measures the information content of all features in $\mathbf{X_i}$ on the requested observations. This is the amount of information contained in the feature, in the sense of information theory. Obviously, if this value is small (for instance all observations have the same value for a feature), the feature is not likely to be relevant to the requesting agent. Image, for instance, a first user that tries to separate her rock and pop music. A second user provides features for some of these music items that consist of manual annotations of these items by tags. Unfortunately, this user tagged all of the requested items only with the tag "rock". In this case, the feature would have the same value for all items and would not be helpful for learning a hypothesis that separates them. In our practical applications, these threshold were set to zero, thus only definitely useless features were omitted.

On a request, agent i returns the label of the best features together with their score as bid to the requesting agent. This agent consecutively requests feature value for the feature with the best bids, incorporates them and applies prioritized forward selection. This process terminates as there are no more bids or as the requesting agent does not have resources for further optimization. If the requesting agent receives a bid on a feature it already uses, it can simply ignore it.

Supervised feature queries works very similar as their unsupervised variant. In this case features are evaluated according to the information gain, given the class values. This approach can only be applied to classification problems, while unsupervised queries could be applied to any problem. The discussion of this problem is beyond the scope of this work.

7   Application to Distributed Multimedia Organization

Our reference application is the distributed media organization framework Nemoz[1]. Nemoz is a multi-agent system that support users to organize their music collections by applying distributed machine learning algorithms. Each user may create arbitrary classification schemes to organize her locally stored music items. Such schemes may be highly personal, e.g. based on mood, time of day,

---

[1] http://nemoz.sf.net

personal genres etc. One important task of the agents is to assign new items to these classes automatically. This requires agents to create classifiers for each user-created tag structure using diverse features ranging from meta-data to audio features. To improve the efficiency of the system, prioritized forward selection is used.

Nemoz is an ideal test case for our approach and multi-agent learning in general. First, the management of multi media data is a very hard task, requiring cost intensive preprocessing. Second, media collections are usually inherently distributed. Third, music is stored and managed on a large variety of different devices with very different capabilities concerning network connection and computational power. This demands for adaptive methods to distribute the work load dynamically. As shown above, agents can decide autonomously, how much effort they put in feature extraction and transformation. Agents with low capabilities can therefore profit from the presence of agents with high computational capabilities.

8 Evaluation

The advantage of using prioritized forward selection in multi-agent learning was argued to be two-fold. First, the size of the accumulated feature set can be reduced. This effectively reduces the vocabulary in which the agents describe their hypothesis about the underlying relationship they are trying to represent and makes the learned models and their differences much easier to comprehend. Second, by focusing on promising features only, agents are able to find good feature set quicker. This is essential in time-critical applications, were agents work with bounded resources.

Correspondingly we would like to clarify the following two questions:

(Q1)   Is PFS able to reduce the size of the accumulated feature set compared to traditional forward selection? How does this affect the averaged accuracy?

(Q2)   Does PFS achieve a faster accuracy increase in the feature selection process compared to traditional forward selection?

To analyze these questions we use six datasets, four synthetic ones and two real-world datasets.

The first real world data set is taken from the Nemoz application described in section 7. This dataset contains the 39 tag structures on 1886 audio files. Each tag structure is a hierarchical taxonomy in which each inner node or leaf node may contain references to a subset of the underlying audio files. These tag structures reflect the ways in which the students organized their files. The task is to assign new audio files to these personal tag structures automatically. This reduces the effort for the users to tag new audio files while still enabling them to use personal categories instead of predefined ones. Each audio file is described by a set of 49 features. These features were extracted from the raw wave data using the method described in [2] and were shown to work well in a wide variety

Table 1. Overview of the datasets: the number of examples for each task (examples), the number of different classes for the tasks (classes), the number of features (feat..), the number of relevant features (rel. feat.), the number of underlying generic functions (funct.) and a reference of the datasets (ref.). The number of relevant features and the number of generative functions are only known for the synthetic datasets.

	tasks	examples	classes	feat.	rel. feat.	funct.	ref.
synth1	5	93 - 108	2	7	4	1	
synth2	5	90 - 111	2	20	4	1	
synth3	10	86 - 112	2	15	10	3	
synth4	10	87 - 116	2	30	10	3	
garageband	39	16 - 674	2-9	49	?	?	[19]
register	9	92 - 777	2	26	?	?	[20]

of applications. For the given experiments, only the top level of each taxonomy was used. This leads to 39 datasets. The number of classes varies between 2 and 9. The dataset is publicly available. Details can be found in [19].

The second dataset is taken from an application of automatically classifying musical instruments which is essential for decentralized sound optimization. This dataset contains 9 different tasks. Each tasks corresponds to a single musical instrument and contains examples for notes played in alto and bass. The aim is to separate high and low notes for each instrument. All notes are stored as wave forms. From these waveforms 26 features were extracted. The dataset is described in detail in [20] and can be obtained from the corresponding authors.

The first synthetic dataset was created in the following way. First, an arbitrary, multidimensional, polynomial function was chosen. This function was applied to 200 examples with six attributes assigned random values based on a Gaussian-distribution with zero mean and standard deviation one. Of the six attributes, four are relevant to the function, two are irrelevant. Using a threshold, a binary label for each example was inferred. This threshold was chosen such, that the amount of positive and negative examples was about equal. Then each individual data set (each task) was created by first selecting a random subset of examples. The probability of selecting an example was set to 0.5. For each task, a noise term was applied to the label attribute by flipping a label value with probability 0.05. Five tasks were generated in this way. The remaining three datasets were created accordingly, varying the number of generative functions and the number of irrelevant features. These datasets and the generator can be obtained on request from the author. The most important properties of the individual datasets are described in table 1.

Each of the datasets constitutes a scenario that is evaluated independently from the other scenarios. In each scenario, we assume that each agent is assigned exactly one task. Thus solving the garageband dataset, for instance, involves 39 agents. These agents solve their corresponding tasks in an arbitrary total sequential order. Each agent performs feature selection to its assigned task. In a first experiment traditional forward selection was used, in a second one prioritized forward selection was used. Also, a third experiment was performed not

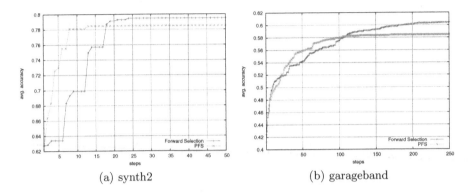

(a) synth2   (b) garageband

Fig. 1. The development of the accuracy in the course of feature selection. The accuracy increases faster for PFS. If the agents can only afford to perform some few cycles, the resulting accuracy is higher. In general, the accuracy achieved by traditional forward selection can be slightly higher, as the minimality criterion is not optimized. For the other datasets, similar observations can be made.

using feature selection at all. Each feature set is evaluated on a task by applying 10-fold stratified cross-validation to the corresponding examples. As learning algorithm, Nearest Neighbor is used.

Traditional and prioritized forward selection are compared in terms of the average estimated accuracy over all tasks, the size of the accumulated feature set and the speed with which the accuracy increases in the feature selection process. The latter property is captured as graph, with the number of steps (feature set evaluations) on the x-axis and the current best accuracy on the y-axis. This graph is created by first creating a graph for each task in a set of tasks. Then these graphs are averaged. All experiments were performed with Rapid Miner[2] and the distributed data mining simulator[3] both of which can be obtained as open source software.

Table 2 and table 3 show the results for average accuracy and total number of features. Figure 1 shows the averaged accuracy for all six datasets depending on the number of evaluations performed.

We can see the following. Traditional forward selection produces the larger or equally large sets of aggregated features over all six datasets. PFS selects on five of six datasets less features than traditional forward selection. Concerning accuracy, PFS mostly performs equally well or only slightly worse. This supports that PFS can actually reduce the size of the aggregated feature set without sacrificing too much accuracy. In figure 1 we see, that the increase in accuracy is much faster for PFS than for traditional forward selection. This answers questions two. Later tasks can exploit the work done on preceding tasks by directly focusing on promising features. This works even if the tasks are heterogeneous.

---

[2] http://www.rapid-i.de
[3] http://www-ai.cs.uni-dortmund.de/SOFTWARE/ddm_simulator

Table 2. The average accuracy for traditional and prioritized forward selection and for learning without feature selection. As can be seen, feature selection can improve the accuracy. PFS produces mostly equal or only slightly inferior average accuracy over all tasks.

	synth1	synth2	synth3	synth4	garageband	register
no selection	0.72	0.74	0.61	0.58	0.45	0.96
FS	0.79	0.79	0.76	0.79	0.61	0.96
PFS	0.79	0.79	0.74	0.79	0.59	0.96

Table 3. The size of the accumulated feature set for traditional and prioritized forward selection and for learning without feature selection. As can be seen, the number of features used by the agents is smaller for PFS in almost all cases.

	synth1	synth2	synth3	synth4	garageband	register
no selection	7	20	15	30	49	26
FS	5	6	15	24	43	16
PFS	5	4	9	20	27	11

With an increasing number of alternative and irrelevant features, the difference between PFS and traditional forward selection may become even stronger, as can be seen on the dataset synth2.

9   Conclusion

Selecting an adequate set of features is a key to successful machine learning in many domains. In this work, the problem of selecting optimal sets of features for several learning agents was discussed. We formalized this problem as combinatorial optimization problem. It was shown that a particularly interesting task is to find feature sets, that fulfill two conditions. First, each agent should use a feature set that allows to solve the learning task it faces optimally. Second, the union of features should be as small a possible. This reduces the terminology used by the agents to represent their hypothesis and thus leads to more coherent and interpretable results.

It was shown that if we assume temporal constraints on the order in which the agents have to accomplish the learning tasks, there is no algorithm that is guaranteed to produce an optimal and minimal solution. We therefore propose a heuristic approach, called prioritized forward selection. Using this approach, each agent aims to use features already used by other agents to solve a task. Only if this does not lead to any further improvement, novel features are added.

Sharing features, and thus representation, among agents is a very general approach. We exemplified this approach on the task of classification. The methods proposed here would be, however, applicable to many other agent learning problems as well, including clustering and reinforcement learning.

References

1. Guyon, I., Gunn, S., Nikravesh, M., Zadeh, L.A.: Feature Extraction: Foundations and Applications (Studies in Fuzziness and Soft Computing). Springer-Verlag, New York (2006)
2. Mierswa, I., Morik, K.: Automatic feature extraction for classifying audio data. Machine Learning Journal 58, 127–149 (2005)
3. Schlkopf, B., Smola, A.J.: Learning with Kernels — Support Vector Machines, Regularization, Optimization, and Beyond. MIT Press, Cambridge (2001)
4. Hastie, T., Tibshirani, R., Friedman, J.: The Elements of Statistical Learning: Data Mining, Inference, and Prediction. Springer series in statistics. Springer, Heidelberg (2001)
5. Kohavi, R., John, G.H.: Wrappers for feature subset selection. Artificial Intelligence 97, 273–324 (1997)
6. Nunes, L., Oliveira, E.: Learning from multiple sources. In: Proc. of the International Joint Conference on Autonomous Agents and Multiagent Systems, pp. 1106–1113 (2004)
7. Kapetanakis, S., Kudenko, D.: Reinforcement learning of coordination in heterogeneous cooperative multi-agent systems. In: Adaptive Agents and Multi-Agent Systems, pp. 119–131 (2005)
8. Ontañón, S., Plaza, E.: A bartering approach to improve multiagent learning. In: Proc. of the International Joint Conference on Autonomous Agents and Multiagent Systems, pp. 386–393 (2002)
9. Caruana, R.: Multitask learning: A knowledge-based source of inductive bias. In: International Conference on Machine Learning, pp. 41–48 (1993)
10. Caruana, R.: Multitask learning. Machine Learning 28, 41–75 (1997)
11. Evgeniou, T., Micchelli, C.A., Pontil, M.: Learning multiple tasks with kernel methods. Journal of Machine Learning Research 6, 615–637 (2005)
12. Jebara, T.: Multi-task feature and kernel selection for svms. In: Proceedings of the International Conference on Machine Learning (2004)
13. Yu, K., Tresp, V., Schwaighofer, A.: Learning gaussian processes from multiple tasks. In: Proceedings of the International Conference on Machine Learning (2005)
14. Yu, S., Tresp, V., Yu, K.: Robust multi-task learning with t-processes. In: Proceedings of the International Conference on Machine Learning (2007)
15. Argyriou, A., Evgeniou, T., Pontil, M.: Multi-task feature learning. In: Advances in Neural Information Processing Systems (2007)
16. John, G., Kohavi, R., Pfleger, K.: Irrelevant Features and the Subset Selection Problem. In: Proceedings of the International Conference on Machine Learning, pp. 121–129 (1994)
17. Yu, L., Liu, H.: Efficient feature selection via analysis of relevance and redundancy. Journal of Machine Learning Research 5 (2004)
18. Mierswa, I., Wurst, M.: Information preserving multi-objective feature selection for unsupervised learning. In: Proceedings of the International Conference on Genetic and Evolutionary Computation (2006)
19. Homburg, H., Mierswa, I., Möller, B., Morik, K., Wurst, M.: A benchmark dataset for audio classification and clustering. In: Proceedings of the International Conference on Music Information Retrieval (2005)
20. Weihs, C., Szepannek, G., Ligges, U., Luebke, K., Raabe, N.: Local models in register classification by timbre. In: Data Science and Classification (2006)

Author Index

Lecture Notes in Artificial Intelligence (LNAI)

Vol. 4692: B. Apolloni, R.J. Howlett, L. Jain (Eds.), Knowledge-Based Intelligent Information and Engineering Systems, Part I. LV, 882 pages. 2007.

Vol. 4687: P. Petta, J.P. Müller, M. Klusch, M. Georgeff (Eds.), Multiagent System Technologies. X, 207 pages. 2007.

Vol. 4682: D.-S. Huang, L. Heutte, M. Loog (Eds.), Advanced Intelligent Computing Theories and Applications. XXVII, 1373 pages. 2007.

Vol. 4676: M. Klusch, K.V. Hindriks, M.P. Papazoglou, L. Sterling (Eds.), Cooperative Information Agents XI. XI, 361 pages. 2007.

Vol. 4667: J. Hertzberg, M. Beetz, R. Englert (Eds.), KI 2007: Advances in Artificial Intelligence. IX, 516 pages. 2007.

Vol. 4660: S. Džeroski, L. Todorovski (Eds.), Computational Discovery of Scientific Knowledge. X, 327 pages. 2007.

Vol. 4659: V. Mařík, V. Vyatkin, A.W. Colombo (Eds.), Holonic and Multi-Agent Systems for Manufacturing. VIII, 456 pages. 2007.

Vol. 4651: F. Azevedo, P. Barahona, F. Fages, F. Rossi (Eds.), Recent Advances in Constraints. VIII, 185 pages. 2007.

Vol. 4648: F. Almeida e Costa, L.M. Rocha, E. Costa, I. Harvey, A. Coutinho (Eds.), Advances in Artificial Life. XVIII, 1215 pages. 2007.

Vol. 4635: B. Kokinov, D.C. Richardson, T.R. Roth-Berghofer, L. Vieu (Eds.), Modeling and Using Context. XIV, 574 pages. 2007.

Vol. 4632: R. Alhajj, H. Gao, X. Li, J. Li, O.R. Zaïane (Eds.), Advanced Data Mining and Applications. XV, 634 pages. 2007.

Vol. 4629: V. Matoušek, P. Mautner (Eds.), Text, Speech and Dialogue. XVII, 663 pages. 2007.

Vol. 4626: R.O. Weber, M.M. Richter (Eds.), Case-Based Reasoning Research and Development. XIII, 534 pages. 2007.

Vol. 4617: V. Torra, Y. Narukawa, Y. Yoshida (Eds.), Modeling Decisions for Artificial Intelligence. XII, 502 pages. 2007.

Vol. 4612: I. Miguel, W. Ruml (Eds.), Abstraction, Reformulation, and Approximation. XI, 418 pages. 2007.

Vol. 4604: U. Priss, S. Polovina, R. Hill (Eds.), Conceptual Structures: Knowledge Architectures for Smart Applications. XII, 514 pages. 2007.

Vol. 4603: F. Pfenning (Ed.), Automated Deduction – CADE-21. XII, 522 pages. 2007.

Vol. 4597: P. Perner (Ed.), Advances in Data Mining. XI, 353 pages. 2007.

Vol. 4594: R. Bellazzi, A. Abu-Hanna, J. Hunter (Eds.), Artificial Intelligence in Medicine. XVI, 509 pages. 2007.

Vol. 4585: M. Kryszkiewicz, J.F. Peters, H. Rybinski, A. Skowron (Eds.), Rough Sets and Intelligent Systems Paradigms. XIX, 836 pages. 2007.

Vol. 4578: F. Masulli, S. Mitra, G. Pasi (Eds.), Applications of Fuzzy Sets Theory. XVIII, 693 pages. 2007.

Vol. 4573: M. Kauers, M. Kerber, R. Miner, W. Windsteiger (Eds.), Towards Mechanized Mathematical Assistants. XIII, 407 pages. 2007.

Vol. 4571: P. Perner (Ed.), Machine Learning and Data Mining in Pattern Recognition. XIV, 913 pages. 2007.

Vol. 4570: H.G. Okuno, M. Ali (Eds.), New Trends in Applied Artificial Intelligence. XXI, 1194 pages. 2007.

Vol. 4565: D.D. Schmorrow, L.M. Reeves (Eds.), Foundations of Augmented Cognition. XIX, 450 pages. 2007.

Vol. 4562: D. Harris (Ed.), Engineering Psychology and Cognitive Ergonomics. XXIII, 879 pages. 2007.

Vol. 4548: N. Olivetti (Ed.), Automated Reasoning with Analytic Tableaux and Related Methods. X, 245 pages. 2007.

Vol. 4539: N.H. Bshouty, C. Gentile (Eds.), Learning Theory. XII, 634 pages. 2007.

Vol. 4529: P. Melin, O. Castillo, L.T. Aguilar, J. Kacprzyk, W. Pedrycz (Eds.), Foundations of Fuzzy Logic and Soft Computing. XIX, 830 pages. 2007.

Vol. 4520: M.V. Butz, O. Sigaud, G. Pezzulo, G. Baldassarre (Eds.), Anticipatory Behavior in Adaptive Learning Systems. X, 379 pages. 2007.

Vol. 4511: C. Conati, K. McCoy, G. Paliouras (Eds.), User Modeling 2007. XVI, 487 pages. 2007.

Vol. 4509: Z. Kobti, D. Wu (Eds.), Advances in Artificial Intelligence. XII, 552 pages. 2007.

Vol. 4496: N.T. Nguyen, A. Grzech, R.J. Howlett, L.C. Jain (Eds.), Agent and Multi-Agent Systems: Technologies and Applications. XXI, 1046 pages. 2007.

Vol. 4483: C. Baral, G. Brewka, J. Schlipf (Eds.), Logic Programming and Nonmonotonic Reasoning. IX, 327 pages. 2007.

Vol. 4482: A. An, J. Stefanowski, S. Ramanna, C.J. Butz, W. Pedrycz, G. Wang (Eds.), Rough Sets, Fuzzy Sets, Data Mining and Granular Computing. XIV, 585 pages. 2007.

Vol. 4481: J. Yao, P. Lingras, W.-Z. Wu, M.S. Szczuka, N.J. Cercone, D. Ślęzak (Eds.), Rough Sets and Knowledge Technology. XIV, 576 pages. 2007.

Vol. 4476: V. Gorodetsky, C. Zhang, V.A. Skormin, L. Cao (Eds.), Autonomous Intelligent Systems: Multi-Agents and Data Mining. XIII, 323 pages. 2007.

Vol. 4460: S. Aguzzoli, A. Ciabattoni, B. Gerla, C. Manara, V. Marra (Eds.), Algebraic and Proof-theoretic Aspects of Non-classical Logics. VIII, 309 pages. 2007.

Vol. 4457: G.M.P. O'Hare, A. Ricci, M.J. O'Grady, O. Dikenelli (Eds.), Engineering Societies in the Agents World VII. XI, 401 pages. 2007.

Vol. 4456: Y. Wang, Y.-m. Cheung, H. Liu (Eds.), Computational Intelligence and Security. XXIII, 1118 pages. 2007.

Vol. 4455: S. Muggleton, R. Otero, A. Tamaddoni-Nezhad (Eds.), Inductive Logic Programming. XII, 456 pages. 2007.

Vol. 4452: M. Fasli, O. Shehory (Eds.), Agent-Mediated Electronic Commerce. VIII, 249 pages. 2007.